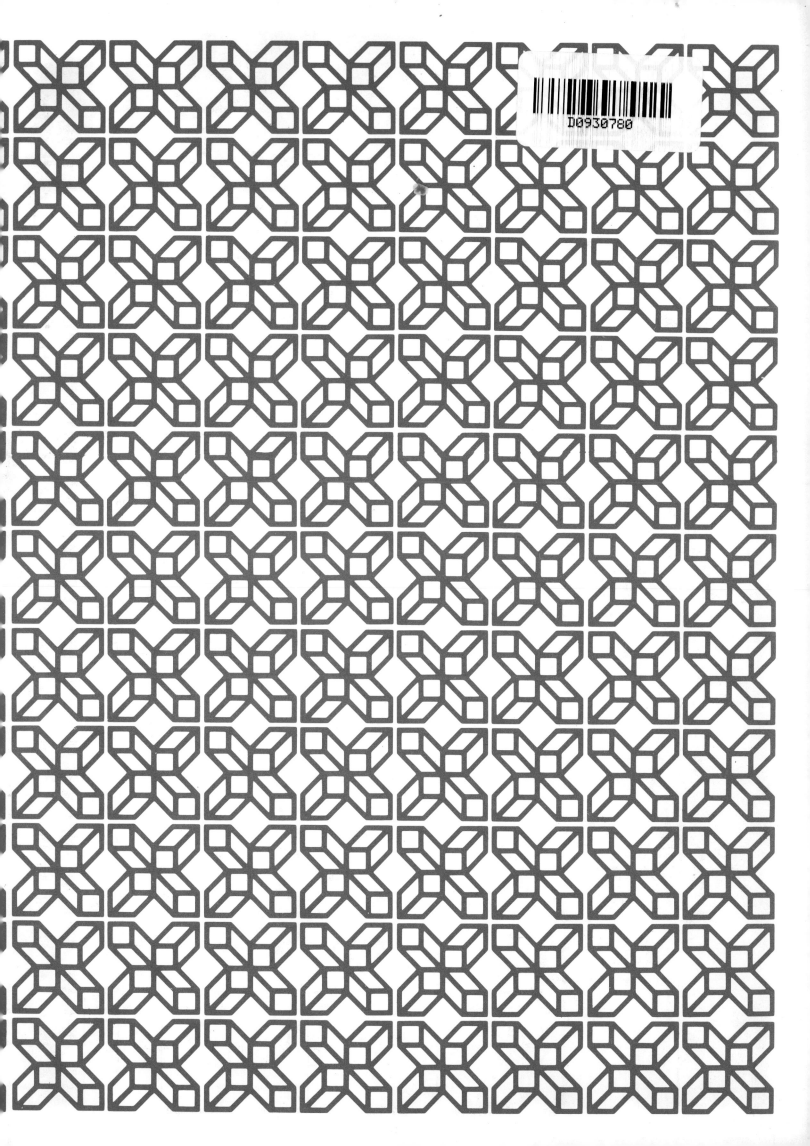

**Perspectives in
Geography 2
GEOGRAPHY
OF
THE GHETTO**
*PERCEPTIONS,
PROBLEMS,
AND
ALTERNATIVES*

NORTHERN ILLINOIS UNIVERSITY

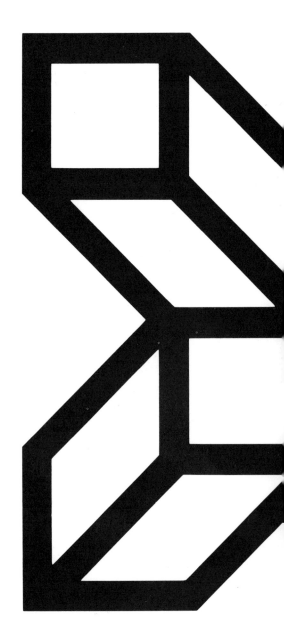

NORTHERN ILLINOIS UNIVERSITY PRESS

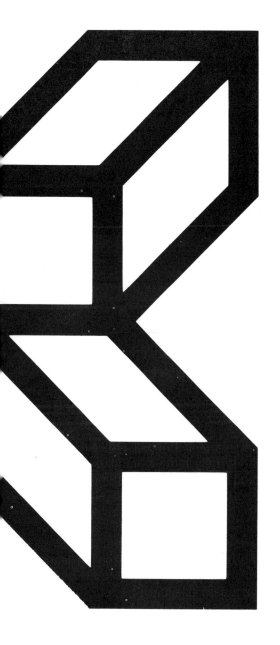

Perspectives in Geography 2
GEOGRAPHY OF THE GHETTO
PERCEPTIONS, PROBLEMS, AND ALTERNATIVES

VOLUME EDITOR

HAROLD M. ROSE

GENERAL EDITOR

HAROLD McCONNELL

Harold M. Rose is chairman of the Department of Urban Affairs at the University of Wisconsin-Milwaukee. Harold McConnell is chairman of the Department of Geography at Florida State University.

Library of Congress Cataloging in Publication Data
Main entry under title:

Geography of the ghetto.

(Perspectives in geography, 2)
Includes bibliographies.
1. Sociology, Urban—Addresses, essays, lectures.
2. Cities and towns—United States—Addresses, essays,
lectures. 3. Slums—United States—Addresses, essays,
lectures. I. Rose, Harold M., ed. II. McConnell,
Harold, ed. III. Series.
HT151.G36   301.36   72–1388
ISBN 0–87580–031–9

TABLE
OF
CONTENTS

Contents

SERIES EDITOR'S NOTE

Harold McConnell

This, the second volume of *Perspectives in Geography,* hallmarks what we intend to be a lasting departure from the ivory tower viewpoint which prevailed from the time of initial conversations about such a series with David Yaseen in 1968 through the publication of Volume I in 1971. From the standpoint of editorial accountability, the new philosophy reflects, for all practical purposes, a meeting of the minds of Frank Horton and Harold McConnell about which direction the series should take to make it responsive to the needs of the 1970s.

Thus, with the following thoughts in mind — (1) no one person can conceivably possess the expertise required to edit the possible range of topics which might be treated by the series, and (2) geographers have become aware, albeit somewhat belatedly, of the need to deal with socially relevant matters — we have instituted an editorial policy whereby each volume will dwell upon the geographic aspects of an issue of vital concern to society. Also, we will ask a geographer who is an internationally recognized authority in the area stressed by said volume to organize it.

Yaseen has left Northern Illinois University. Thus, only I remain as series editor. As before, all papers will be commissioned (at least in the immediate future). The series will continue to be a labor of love, since neither the volume editor, the series editor, nor the contributors will be remunerated for their efforts. We will continue to urge the contributors to utilize new and innovative modeling strategies, whatever the theme of the volume.

Returning for the moment to the present volume, it seems evident that geography has been a comparative laggard among the social sciences in addressing itself to the problem of social justice for poor and minority residents of America's urban areas. However, it is my considered opinion that because of our unique spatial emphasis, geographers can and should be saying something about this — one of the most crucial and vexing ills of our society. Volume 2 considers specifically a geographic inquiry into the urban ghetto. Thus, it seemed most appropriate that I ask Harold Rose to assume the editorial reins. Happily, he accepted the task, and I am proud to have been associated with his and our contributors' efforts.

INTRODUCTION

Harold M. Rose

For Volume 2 of *Perspectives in Geography* the geography of the ghetto has been selected as the topic of investigation. For a new publication without a captive readership, this represents a bold move, given the limited attention devoted to aspects of social geography at this stage in the discipline's development. The papers presented herein, however, should give further impetus to the development of an urban social geography. At this point in time, geographic analysis of minorities in United States cities largely owes its growth and development to concern with the problems confronting Black America. This interest is expressed through the research efforts of a growing contingent of socially concerned geographers.

The status of interest in the geography of the ghetto is rapidly moving away from that of the curious and unique to a systematic aspect of the urban field that cannot be overlooked in any rational attempt to understand the evolution of metropolitan American spatial systems. The contributions appearing in this issue should go far toward enhancing that understanding. It is both fortunate and unfortunate that to date most of the work on this topic has had to appear in the form of special publications or special issues of journals. It is fortunate that much of the work has appeared in this format, since this tends to focus attention on the phenomenon and also serves as the basis for further work because the social climate is such that there is no longer a tendency to ignore this area of inquiry. The unfortunate aspect of the problem is associated with the absence of historical continuity in the development of a research base upon which to support future research efforts. Some of the contributors to this issue have been active in providing the modest research base for the geography of the ghetto which already exists. Others represent newcomers to the list and thus constitute new voices and perspectives which reflect a diversity of interests and approaches to an understanding of the ghetto phenomenon, as it moves from infancy to adolescence in the research phase of its development.

The papers appearing in this issue can be conveniently grouped under the heading "Perceptions, Problems, and Alternatives." The essays by Harvey, Morrill, and Gale and Katzman represent a diverse array of perceptions, both in terms of ghetto research strategies and model designs for perception of optimal systems in which the ghetto is viewed as a conceptual building block. Harvey's highly esoteric paper in which the major focus is upon the strengths and weaknesses of alternative economic systems is used to set the stage for the variety of approaches and interests which follow. The essays by Morrill and by Gale and Katzman reflect their interest and approaches to ghetto model-building. Morrill's work represents a sophisticated improvement of his pioneer ghetto model of the middle sixties, which has probably done more to spur additional work in this area than any other single contribution from the discipline. Colenutt's work straddles the perception bias and the problem orientation of a number of the other papers. What does come through rather clearly is the perception of the ghetto and the research approach taken toward it among British and American contributors.

The other eight papers clearly focus upon the problem aspect of the ghetto and/or alternatives, either in terms of the nature of the configuration or the nature of available services. Clark (mobility), Meyer (alternative strategies), Davies (transportation), and Mercer (housing quality) devote attention to aspects of the ghetto which have received a good deal of attention by researchers in other disciplines (although they have seldom emphasized the spatial perspective). These papers are generally concerned with the quality of life. The Deskins paper falls into this general category but treats an aspect of Black behavior that has been the focus of but limited attention by any social science. The paper by Marr, which treats aspects of the delivery of social services to ghetto residents, represents a real breakthrough in the nature of geographic research as it relates to this area of interest. The final item in this collection probably fits best under the heading of perception, since it represents the combined effort of an African and a Black American geographer in an attempt at cross-cultural comparison of similar spatial phenomena in different areas of the world.

The appearance of Volume 2 of *Perspectives in Geography* represents a milestone in the development of research on the geography of the ghetto. This volume contains the largest single number of essays on the spatial aspects of the ghetto to appear anywhere under a common cover.

1

REVOLUTIONARY AND COUNTER-REVOLUTIONARY THEORY IN GEOGRAPHY AND THE PROBLEM OF GHETTO FORMATION

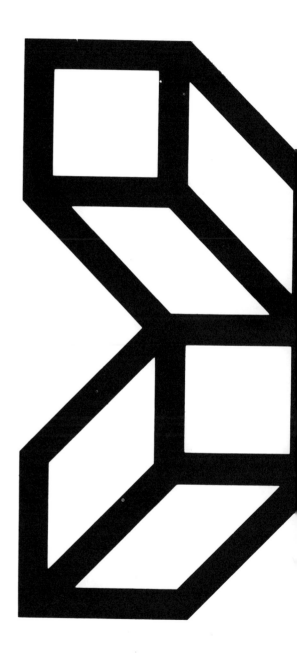

David Harvey
Johns Hopkins University

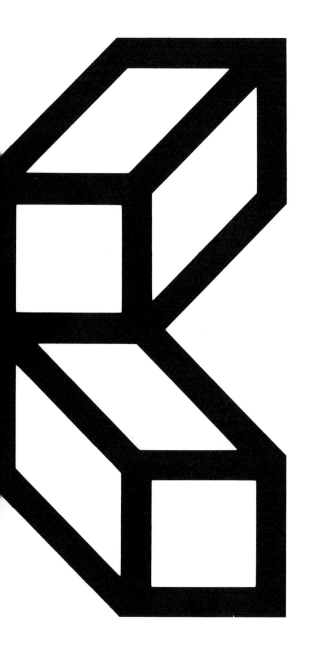

Revolutionary and Counter-revolutionary Theory in Geography and the Problem of Ghetto Formation

How and why would we bring about a revolution in geographic thought? In order to gain some insight into this question, it is worth examining how revolutions and counter-revolutions occur in all branches of scientific thought. Kuhn provides an interesting analysis of this phenomenon as it occurs in the natural sciences.[1] He suggests that most scientific activity is what he calls normal science. This amounts to the investigation of all facets of a particular paradigm (a paradigm being a set of concepts, categories, relationships, and methods which are generally accepted throughout a community at a given point in time). In the practice of normal science, certain anomalies arise — observations or paradoxes which cannot be resolved within an existing paradigm. These anomalies become the focus of increasing attention until science is plunged into a period of crisis in which speculative attempts are made to solve the problems posed by the anomalies. Out of these attempts there eventually arises a new set of concepts, categories, relationships, and methods which successfully resolves the existing dilemmas as well as successfully incorporates the worthwhile aspects of the old paradigm. Thus, a new paradigm is born and is followed once more by the onset of normal scientific activity.

Kuhn's schema is open to criticism on a number of grounds. I shall discuss two problems very briefly. First, there is no explanation as to how anomalies arise and how, once they have arisen, they generate crises. This criticism could be met by distinguishing between significant and insignificant anomalies. For example, it was known for many years that the orbit of Mercury did not fit Newton's calculations, yet this anomaly was insignificant because it had no relevance to the use of the Newtonian system in an everyday context. If, for example, certain anomalies had arisen in bridge construction, then they would obviously have been deemed highly significant. Therefore, the Newtonian paradigm remained satisfactory and unchallenged until something of practical importance and relevance could *not* be accomplished using the Newtonian system. Secondly, there is the question, never satisfactorily answered by Kuhn, concerning the way in which a new paradigm becomes accepted. Kuhn admits that acceptance is not a matter of logic. He suggests rather that it involves a leap of faith. The question is, however, what this leap of faith should be based on. Underlying Kuhn's analysis is a guiding force which is never explicitly examined. This guiding force amounts to a fundamental belief in the virtues of control and manipulation of the natural environment. The leap of faith, apparently, is based on the belief that the new system will allow an extension of manipulation and control over some aspect of nature. Which aspect of nature? Presumably it will once again be an aspect of nature which is important in terms of

1. T. S. Kuhn, *The Structure of Scientific Revolutions* (Chicago: University of Chicago Press, 1962).

everyday activity and everyday life as it exists at a particular point in history.

The central criticism of Kuhn, which these two cases point out, is his abstraction of scientific knowledge from its materialistic base. Kuhn provides an *idealist's* interpretation of scientific advancement, while it is clear that scientific thought is fundamentally geared to material activities. The materialistic basis for the advancement of scientific knowledge has been explored by Bernal.[2] Material activity involves the manipulation of nature in the interests of man, and scientific understanding cannot be interpreted independently of that general thrust. However, at this juncture, we are forced to add a further perspective because "the interest of man" is subject to a variety of interpretations, depending upon which group of men we are thinking of. Bernal points out that the sciences in the West have, until very recently, been the preserve of a middle-class group, and even recently with the rise of what is often called the "meritocracy," the scientist is often drawn into middle-class ways of life during the course of his career. We may thus expect the natural sciences to tacitly reflect a drive for manipulation and control over those aspects of nature which are relevant to the middle class. Far more important, however, is the harnessing of scientific activity by a process of patronage and funded research to the special interests of those who are in control of the means of production. The coalition of industry and government heavily directs scientific activity. Consequently, manipulation and control means manipulation and control in the interests of a particular group in society rather than in the interests of society as a whole.[3] With these perspectives we are better able to understand the general thrust of scientific advancement hidden within the recurrent scientific revolutions which Kuhn has so perceptively described.

It has frequently been questioned whether Kuhn's analysis could be extended to the social sciences. Kuhn appears to view the social sciences as "pre-scientific" in the sense that no one social science has really established that corpus of generally accepted concepts, categories, relationships, and methods which form a paradigm. This view of the social sciences as pre-scientific is, in fact, quite general among philosophers of science.[4] However, a quick survey of the history of thought in the social sciences shows that revolutions do indeed occur within the disciplines and that they are marked by many of the same features which Kuhn identified in the natural sciences. There is no question that Adam Smith provided a paradigmatic formulation for economic thought which was subsequently built upon by Ricardo. In modern times Keynes succeeded in doing something essentially similar to Smith's formulation. Johnson, in a recent article, explores such revolutions

2. J. D. Bernal, *Science in History* (Cambridge, Mass.: MIT Press, 1970).

3. Bernal, *Science in History,* p. 2; H. Rose and S. Rose, *Science and Society* (Harmondsworth, U. K.: Penguin Books, 1969).

4. Kuhn, *The Structure of Scientific Revolutions,* p. 37; E. Nagel, *The Structure of Science* (New York: Free Press, 1961).

in thought in economics. His analysis parallels in many respects that of Kuhn's, adding, however, several extra twists.[5] At the heart of the Keynesian revolution, Johnson asserts, was a crisis generated by the failure of pre-Keynesian economics to deal with the most pressing and significant problem of the 1930s—unemployment. Thus, unemployment provided the significant anomaly. Johnson suggests that:

"By far the most helpful circumstance for the rapid propogation of a new and revolutionary theory is the existence of an established orthodoxy which is clearly inconsistent with the most salient facts of reality, and yet is sufficiently confident of its intellectual power to attempt to explain those facts, and in its efforts to do so exposes its incompetence in a ludicrous fashion."

Thus the objective social realities of the time overtook the conventional wisdom and served to expose its failings.

"In this situation of general confusion and obvious irrelevance of orthodox economics to real problems, the way was open for a new theory that offered a convincing explanation of the nature of the problem and a set of policy prescriptions based on that explanation."

So far, the similarity to Kuhn is quite remarkable. But Johnson then adds new considerations, some of which really stem from the sociology of science itself. He asserts that, to be accepted, a theory needs to possess five main characteristics.

"First, it had to attack the central proposition of conservative orthodoxy . . . with a new but academically acceptable analysis that reversed the proposition. . . . Second, the theory had to appear to be new, yet absorb as much as possible of the valid or at least not readily disputable components of existing orthodox theory. In this process, it helps greatly to give old concepts new and confusing names, and to emphasize as crucial analytical steps that have previously been taken as platitudinous. . . . Third, the new theory had to have the appropriate degree of difficulty to understand . . . so that senior academic colleagues would find it neither easy nor worthwhile to study, so that they would waste their efforts on peripheral theoretical issues, and so offer themselves as easy marks for criticism and dismissal by their younger and hungrier colleagues. At the same time the new theory had to appear both difficult enough to challenge the intellectual interest of younger colleagues and students, but actually easy enough for them to master adequately with sufficient investment of intellectual endeavour. . . . Fourth, the new theory had to offer to the more gifted and less opportunistic scholars a new

5. H. G. Johnson, "The Keynesian Revolution and the Monetarist Counter-revolution," *American Economic Review* 61:2 (1971): 1–14. I would like to thank Gene Mumy for drawing my attention to this reference.

methodology more appealing than those currently available. . . . Finally, [it had to offer] an important empirical relationship . . . to measure."[6]

The history of geographic thought in the last ten years is exactly mirrored in this analysis. The central proposition of the old geography was the qualitative and the unique. This clearly could not resist the drive in the social sciences as a whole toward tools of social manipulation and control which require an understanding of the quantitative and the general. Nor can there be any doubt that during the transition process old concepts were given new and confusing names and that fairly platitudinous assumptions were subject to rigorous analytical investigation. Moreover, it cannot be denied that the so-called quantitative revolution allowed the opportunity to pillory the elder statesmen in the discipline, particularly whenever they ventured into issues related to the newly emerging orthodoxy. Certainly, the quantitative movement provided a challenge of appropriate difficulty and opened up the prospect for new methodologies—many of which were to be quite rewarding in terms of the analytic insights they generated. Lastly, new things to measure were in abundance; and in the distance-decay function, the threshold, the range of a good, and the measurement of spatial patterns, we found four apparently crucial new empirical topics which we could spend an inordinate amount of time investigating. The quantitative movement can thus be interpreted partly in terms of a challenging new set of ideas to be answered, partly as a rather shabby struggle for power and status within a disciplinary framework, and partly as a response to outside pressures to discover the means for manipulation and control in what may broadly be defined as "the planning field." In case anyone misinterprets the author's remarks as pointing a finger at any one particular group, let me say that all of us were involved in this process and that there was and is no way in which we could or can escape such involvement.

Johnson also introduces the term "counter-revolution" into his analysis. In this regard his thought is not very enlightening, since he clearly has an axe to grind in criticizing the monetarists whom he designates as counter-revolutionaries, even though a significant anomaly (the combination of inflation and unemployment) exists as a pressing challenge to the Keynesian orthodoxy. But, there is something very important in this term which requires analysis. It seems intuitively plausible to think of the movement of ideas in the social sciences as a movement based on revolution and counter-revolution, in contrast to the natural sciences to which such a notion does not appear to be so immediately applicable.

6. Johnson, "The Keynesian Revolution."

We can analyze the phenomena of counter-revolution by using our insight into paradigm formation in the natural sciences. Paradigm formation in the natural sciences is based on the extension of man's ability to manipulate and control naturally occurring phenomena. Similarly, we can anticipate that the driving force behind paradigm formation in the social sciences is the desire to manipulate and control human activity and social phenomena in the interest of man. Immediately the question arises as to who is going to control whom, in whose interest is the controlling going to be exercised, and if control is exercised in the interest of all, who is going to take it upon himself to define that public interest? We are thus forced to confront directly in the social sciences what arises only indirectly in the natural sciences, namely, the social bases and implications of control and manipulation. We would be extraordinarily foolish to presuppose that these bases are equitably distributed throughout society. Our history until the present time shows that usually these bases are highly concentrated within a few key groupings in society. These groups may be benevolent or exploitive with respect to other groups. This, however, is not the issue. The point is that social science formulates concepts, categories, relationships, and methods which are not independent of the existing social relationships in society. As such, the concepts used are the product of the very phenomena they are designed to describe. A revolutionary theory upon which a new paradigm is based will gain general acceptance only if the nature of the social relationships embodied in the theory are actualized in the real world. A counter-revolutionary theory is one which is deliberately proposed to deal with a revolutionary theory in such a manner that the threatened social changes which general acceptance of the revolutionary theory would generate are, either by co-optation or subversion, prevented from being realized.

This process of revolution and counter-revolution in social science can most explicitly be examined by studying the relationship between the political economic theories of Adam Smith and Ricardo and those of Karl Marx. For this comparison, Engels, in his "Preface" to Volume II of *Capital,* provides some quite extraordinary insights. At issue was the charge that Marx had plagiarized the theory of surplus value. Marx, however, clearly acknowledged that both Adam Smith and Ricardo had discussed and partially understood the nature of surplus value. Engels sets out to explain what was new in Marx's utterances on surplus value and how it was that Marx's theory of surplus value "struck home like a thunderbolt out of a clear sky."[7] To explain this, Engels resorted to an analogy of an incident in the history of chemistry which, quite coincidentally, turns out to be one of the inspirations for Kuhn's thesis regarding the structure of

7. Karl Marx, *Capital,* vol. 2, preface by F. Engels (New York: International Publishers, 1967). This whole incident is discussed in depth by L. Althusser and E. Balibar, *Reading "Capital"* (London: NLB, 1970).

7

revolutions in the natural sciences.[8] The incident concerns the relationship between Lavoisier and Priestley in the discovery of oxygen. Both conducted similar experiments and produced similar results. However, there was an essential difference between them. Priestley insisted for the rest of his life on interpreting his results in terms of the old phlogiston theory and therefore called his discovery "dephlogisticated air." Lavoisier, however, recognized that his discovery could not be reconciled with the existing phlogiston theory and, as a consequence, was able to re-construct the theoretical framework of chemistry on a completely new basis. Thus Engels, and Kuhn after him, states that Lavoisier was the "real discoverer of oxygen vis-à-vis the others who had only produced it without knowing what they had produced." Engels continues:

"Marx stands in the same relation to his predecessors in the theory of surplus value as Lavoisier stood to Priestley. . . . The existence of that part of the value of products which we now call surplus-value had been ascertained long before Marx. It had also been stated with more or less precision what it consisted of. . . . But one did not get any further. . . . [All economists] remained prisoners of the economic categories as they had come down to them. Now Marx appeared upon the scene. And he took a view directly opposite to that of all his predecessors. What they had regarded as a *solution,* he considered but a *problem.* He saw that he had to deal neither with dephlogisticated air nor with fireair, but with oxygen—that here it was not simply a matter of stating an economic fact or of pointing out the conflict between this fact and eternal justice and morality, but of explaining a fact which was destined to revolutionise all economics, and which offered to him who knew how to use it the key to an understanding of all capitalist production. With this fact as his starting point he examined all the economic categories which he found at hand, just as Lavoisier proceeding from oxygen had examined the categories of phlogistic chemistry."[9]

The Marxist theory was clearly dangerous in that it appeared to provide the key to understanding capitalist production from the position of those *not* in control of the means of production. Consequently, the categories, concepts, relationships, and methods which had the potential to form a new paradigm were an enormous threat to the power structure of the capitalist world. The subsequent emergence of the marginal theory of value did away with many of the basics of Smith's and Ricardo's analysis (in particular the labor theory of value) and also, incidentally, served to turn back the Marxist challenge in economics. The counter-revolutionary co-optation of Marxist theory in Russia after Lenin's death and a similar counter-revolutionary co-optation of much of

8. Kuhn, *The Structure of Scientific Revolutions,* pp. 52–56.

9. Marx, *Capital,* vol. 2, pp. 11–18.

the Marxist language into Western sociology (so much so that some sociologists suggest that we are all Marxists now) without conveying the essence of Marxist thinking has effectively prevented the true flowering of Marxist thought and, concomitantly, the emergence of that humanistic society which Marx envisaged. Both the concepts and the projected social relationships embodied in the concepts were frustrated.

Revolution and counter-revolution in thought are therefore characteristic of the social sciences in a manner apparently not characteristic of the natural sciences. Revolutions in thought cannot ultimately be divorced from revolutions in practice. This may point to the conclusion that the social sciences are indeed in a pre-scientific state. The conclusion is ill-founded, however, since the natural sciences have never been wrested for any length of time out of the control of a restricted interest group. It is this fact, rather than anything inherent in the nature of natural science knowledge itself, that accounts for the lack of counter-revolutions in the natural sciences. In other words, those revolutions of thought which are accomplished in the natural sciences pose no threat to the existing order since they are constructed with the requirements of that existing order broadly in mind. This is not to say that there are not some uncomfortable social problems to resolve *en route,* for scientific discovery is not predictable and it can therefore be the source of social tension. What this does suggest, however, is that the natural sciences are in a pre-social state. Accordingly, questions of social action and social control, which the techniques of natural science frequently help to resolve, are not incorporated into natural science itself. In fact there is a certain fetishism about keeping social issues out of the natural sciences since incorporating them would supposedly "bias" research conducted at the behest of the existing social order. The consequent moral dilemmas for those scientists who take their social responsibility seriously are real indeed. Contrary to popular opinion, therefore, it seems appropriate to conclude that the philosophy of social science is potentially much superior to that of natural science and that the eventual fusion of the two fields of study will not come about through attempts to "scientize" social science but instead by the socialization of natural science.[10] This may mean the replacement of manipulation and control with the realization of human potential as the basic criterion for paradigm acceptance. In such an event all aspects of science would experience both revolutionary and counter-revolutionary phases of thought which would undoubtedly be associated with revolutions and counter-revolutions in social practice.

Let us return now to the initial question. How and why would we bring about a revolution in geographic thought? The quantitative revolution has run its course,

10. Marx clearly envisaged this kind of resolution of the conflict between the natural and social sciences. See Karl Marx, *The Economic and Philosophic Manuscripts of 1844* (New York: International Publishers, 1964), p. 164.

and diminishing returns seem to be setting in; yet another piece of factorial ecology, yet another attempt to measure the distance-decay effect, yet another attempt to identify the range of a good, serve to tell us less and less about anything of great relevance. In addition, there are younger geographers now, just as ambitious as the quantifiers were in the early sixties, a little hungry for recognition, and somewhat starved for interesting things to do. So there are murmurs of discontent within the social structure of the discipline as the quantifiers establish a firm grip on the production of graduate students and on the curricula of various departments. This sociological condition within the discipline is not sufficient to justify a revolution in thought (nor should it), but the condition is there. More importantly, there is a clear disparity between the sophisticated theoretical and methodological framework which we are using and our ability to say anything really meaningful about events as they unfold around us. There are too many anomalies between what we purport to explain and manipulate and what actually happens. There is an ecological problem, an urban problem, an international trade problem, and yet we seem incapable of saying anything of depth or profundity about any of them. When we do say something, it appears trite and rather ludicrous. In short, our paradigm is not coping well. It is ripe for overthrow. The objective social conditions demand that we say something sensible or coherent or else forever (through lack of credibility or, even worse, through the deterioration of the objective social conditions) remain silent. It is the emerging objective social conditions and our patent inability to cope with them which essentially explains the necessity for a revolution in geographic thought.

How should we accomplish such a revolution? There are a number of paths we could take. We could, as some suggest, abandon the positivist basis of the quantitative movement for an abstract idealism and hope that the objective social conditions will improve of their own accord or that concepts forged through idealist modes of thought will eventually achieve enough content to facilitate the creative change of objective social conditions. It is, however, a characteristic of idealism that it is forever doomed to search fruitlessly for real content. We could also reject the positivist basis of the 1960s for a phenomenological basis. This appears more attractive than the idealists' course since it at least serves to keep us in contact with the concept of man as a being in constant sensuous interaction with the social and natural realities which surround him. Yet, phenomenological approaches can lead us into idealism or back into naïve positivist empiricism just as easily as they can into a socially aware form of materialism. The so-called behavioral revolution in geography points in both of these directions. Therefore, the most fruitful strategy at this juncture is to explore that area of understanding in which certain aspects of positivism, materialism, and phenomenology overlap to provide adequate interpretations of the social reality in which we find ourselves. This overlap is most clearly explored in Marxist thought. Marx, in the *Economic and Philosophic Manuscripts of 1844* and in the German *Ideology,* gave his system of thought a powerful and appealing phenomenological basis.[11]

There are also certain things which Marxism and positivism have in common. They both have a materialist base and both resort to an analytic method. The essential difference, of course, is that positivism simply seeks to understand the world whereas Marxism seeks to change it. Put another way, positivism draws its categories and concepts from an existing reality with all of its defects while Marxist categories and concepts are formulated through the application of the dialectical method to history as it is written, here and now, through events and actions. The positivist method involves, for example, the application of traditional bi-valued Aristotelian logic to test hypotheses (the null hypothesis of statistical inference is a purely Aristotelian device). As such, hypotheses are either true or false and once categorized remain ever so. The dialectic, on the other hand, proposes a process of understanding which allows the interpenetration of opposites, incorporates contradictions and paradoxes, and points to the processes of resolution. Insofar as it is relevant to talk of truth and falsity, truth lies in the dialectical process rather than in the statements derived from the process. These statements can be designated as "true" only at a given point in time and, in any case, can be contradicted by other "true" statements. This method allows us to invert analyses if necessary, to regard solutions as problems, to regard questions as solutions.[12]

And so at last I come to the question of ghetto formation. The reader may feel that the foregoing was an elaborate introduction which has only fringe relevance to the question of understanding ghetto formation and devising solutions to the ghetto problem. In fact, the foregoing was crucial to the case, for I shall argue that we are able to say something relevant to the problem only if we self-consciously seek, in the process, to establish a revolutionary geographical theory to deal with the phenomena in question. I shall also argue that we can devise this understanding using many of the tools which are currently available to us. However, we must be prepared to interpret those tools in a new and rather different way. In short, we need to think in terms of oxygen instead of in terms of de-phlogisticated air.

The ghetto has attracted a good deal of attention as one of the major social problems of the American city. In British cities, fears of "polarization" and "ghettoiza-

11. Karl Marx and F. Engels, *The German Ideology,* second edition (New York: International Publishers, 1971); Marx, *The Economic and Philosophic Manuscripts of 1844.* Marx derived his phenomenological position from Hegel. See G. Hegel, *The Phenomenology of Mind* (New York: Harper Torch Books, 1967).

12. Marx also derived his dialectical method from Hegel. See *The Economic Manuscripts of 1844,* pp. 170–93.

tion" are rising. It is generally held that ghettos are bad things and that it would be socially desirable to eliminate them, preferably without eliminating the populations they contain. (Banfield's position with respect to the latter question appears somewhat ambiguous.) The intention here is not to attempt a detailed analysis of the literature on the ghetto nor to become embroiled in definitions of it.[13] Instead, examination shall be made of those geographical theories which appear to have some relevance for understanding ghetto formation and ghetto maintenance. The most obvious corpus of theory which calls for examination here is, of course, urban land-use theory.

One large segment of urban land-use theory in geography draws its inspiration from the Chicago school of sociologists.[14] Park and Burgess wrote voluminously on the city and elaborated an interpretation of city form in ecological terms. They noted the concentration of low-income groups and various ethnic groups within particular sections of the city. They also discovered that cities exhibited a certain regularity of spatial form. From this, Burgess elaborated what came to be known as the concentric zone theory of the city. Park and Burgess both appeared to regard the city as a sort of man-produced, ecological complex within which the processes of social adaptation, specialization of function and of life style, competition for living space, and so on acted to produce a coherent spatial structure, the whole being held together by some culturally derived form of social solidarity which Park called "the moral order."[15] The various groups and activities within the city system were essentially bound together by this moral order, and they merely jockeyed for position (both social and spatial) within the constraints imposed by the moral order. The main focus of interest was to find out who ended up where and what conditions were like when they got there. The main thrust of the Chicago school was necessarily descriptive. This tradition has had an extraordinarily powerful influence over geographic thinking and, although the techniques of description have changed somewhat (factorial ecology essentially replacing descriptive human ecology), the general direction of the work has not changed greatly. The Chicago school of urban geographers is thus firmly derivative of the Chicago school of sociologists.[16] It is curious to note, however, that Park and Burgess did not pay a great deal of attention to the kind of social solidarity generated through the workings of the economic system nor to the social and economic relationships which derive from economic considerations. They did not ignore the issue, of course, but it was of secondary importance to them. As a result, the urban land-use theory which they developed has a critical flaw when it is used to explain the ghetto. It is interesting to observe

13. A. Downs, *Urban Problems and Prospects* (Chicago: Markham Publishing Co., 1970), particularly chapter 2.

14. R. E. Park, E. W. Burgess, and R. D. McKenzie, *The City* (Chicago: University of Chicago Press, 1925).

15. R. E. Park, "The Urban Community as a Spatial Pattern and a Moral Order," in E. W. Burgess, *The Urban Community* (Chicago: University of Chicago Press, 1926).

16. B. J. L. Berry and F. Horton, *Geographic Perspectives on Urban Systems* (Englewood Cliffs, New Jersey: Prentice-Hall, 1970).

that Engels, writing some eighty years before Park and Burgess, noted the phenomenon of concentric zoning in the city, but sought to interpret it in economic class terms. The passage is worth quoting, for it has several insights into the spatial structure of cities.

"Manchester contains, at its heart, a rather extended commercial district, perhaps half a mile long and about as broad, and consisting almost wholly of offices and warehouses. Nearly the whole district is abandoned by dwellers, and is lonely and deserted at night. . . . The district is cut through by certain main thoroughfares upon which the vast traffic concentrates, and in which the ground level is lined with brilliant shops. In these streets the upper floors are occupied, here and there, and there is a good deal of life upon them until late at night. With the exception of this commercial district, all Manchester proper, all Salford and Hulme . . . are all unmixed working people's quarters, stretching like a girdle, averaging a mile and a half in breadth, around the commercial district. Outside, beyond this girdle, lives the upper and middle bourgeoisie, the middle bourgeoisie in regularly laid out streets in the vicinity of working quarters . . . the upper bourgeoisie in remoter villas with gardens . . . in free, wholesome country air, in fine, comfortable homes, passed every half or quarter hour by omnibuses going into the city. And the finest part of the arrangement is this, that the members of the money aristocracy can take the shortest road through the middle of all the labouring districts without ever seeing that they are in the midst of the grimy misery that lurks to the right and left. For the thoroughfares leading from the Exchange in all directions out of the city are lined, on both sides, with an almost unbroken series of shops, and are so kept in the hands of the middle and lower bourgeoisie . . . [that] they suffice to conceal from the eyes of the wealthy men and women of strong stomachs and weak nerves the misery and grime which form the complement of their wealth. . . . I know very well that this hypocritical plan is more or less common to all great cities; I know, too, that the retail dealers are forced by the nature of their business to take possession of the great highways; I know that there are more good buildings than bad ones upon such streets everywhere, and that the value of land is greater near them than in remote districts, but at the same time I have never seen so systematic a shutting out of the working class from the thoroughfares, so tender a concealment of everything which might affront the eye and the nerves of the bourgeoisie, as in Manchester. And yet, in other respects, Manchester is less built according to plan, after official regulations, is more an outgrowth of accident, than any other city; and when I consider in this connection the eager assurances of the middle class, that the working class is doing famously, I cannot help feeling that the liberal manufacturers, the Big Wigs of Manchester, are not so innocent after all, in the matter of this sensitive method of construction."[17]

The line of approach adopted by Engels in 1844 was and still is far more consistent with hard economic and social realities than was the essentially cultural approach of Park and Burgess. In fact with certain obvious modifications, Engels's description could easily be made to fit the contemporary American city (concentric zoning with good transport facilities for the affluent who live on the outskirts, sheltering of commuters into the city from seeing the grime and misery which is the complement of their wealth, etc.). In this regard, it seems a pity that contemporary geographers have looked to Park and Burgess rather than to Engels for their inspiration. The social solidarity which Engels noted was not generated by any superordinate "moral order." Instead, the miseries of the city were an inevitable concomitant to an evil and avaricious capitalist system. Social solidarity was enforced through the operation of the market exchange system. Engels reacted to London thus:

"These Londoners have been forced to sacrifice the best qualities of their human nature, to bring to pass all the marvels of civilization which crowd their city, a hundred powers which slumbered within them have remained inactive, have been suppressed in order that a few might be developed more fully and multiply through union with those of others. . . . The brutal indifference, the unfeeling isolation of each in his private interest becomes the more repellant and offensive, the more these individuals are crowded together within a limited space. . . . The dissolution of mankind into monads, of which each one has a separate principle, the world of atoms, is here carried out to its utmost extreme. . . . Hence it comes too, that the social war, the war of each against all, is here openly declared . . . people regard each other only as useful objects; each exploits the other, and the end of it all is, that the stronger treads the weaker under foot, and that the powerful few, the capitalists, seize everything for themselves, while to the weak many, the poor, scarcely a bare existence remains. . . . Everywhere barbarous indifference, hard egotism on one hand, and nameless misery on the other, everywhere social warfare, every man's house in a state of seige, everywhere reciprocal plundering under the protection of the law, and all so shameless, so openly avowed that one shrinks before the consequences of our social state as they manifest themselves here undisguised, and can only wonder that the whole crazy fabric still hangs together."[18]

17. F. Engels, *The Condition of the Working Class in England in 1844* (London: Allen and Unwin, 1962), pp. 46–47.

18. Engels, *The Condition of the Working Class in England in 1844*, pp. 23–25.

If we cleaned up the language a bit (by eliminating the references to capitalism, for example), we would have a description worthy of the Kerner Report.[19]

The common spatial structure of cities noted by Engels and by Park and Burgess has thus been analyzed from economic and cultural points of view. The question which Engels posed concerning the way in which such a systematic spatial structure could evolve without guidance by the "Big Wigs" and yet be to their clear advantage has been the subject of more detailed economic analysis. The possibility of using marginalist economic principles to explain this phenomenon was first indicated in the work of von Thunen in an agricultural context. This work laid the basis for an economic theory of the urban land-market in the relatively recent work of Alonso and Muth.[20] The details of von Thunen's theory need not detain us, but it is worth examining that general facet of the theory which contributes to an understanding of ghetto formation. Urban land use is determined through a process of competitive bidding for the land. The competitive bidding proceeds so that land rents are higher near the center of activity (in the theory it is usually assumed that all employment is concentrated at one central location). If we now consider the residential choice open to two groups in the population, one rich and one poor, with respect to one employment center, we can predict where each must live by examining the structure of their bid rent curves. For the poor group the bid rent curve is characteristically steep since the poor have very little money to spend on transportation; therefore, their ability to bid for the use of the land declines rapidly with distance from place of employment. The rich group, on the other hand, characteristically has a shallow bid rent function since its ability to bid is not greatly affected by the amount of money it spends for transportation. When put in competition with each other, we find the poor group forced to live in the center of the city and the rich living outside (just as Engels described it). However, this means that the poor are forced to live on high rent land. The only way they can adjust to this, of course, is to save on the quantity of space they consume and crowd into a very small area. The logic of the model indicates that poor groups will be concentrated in high-rent areas near the city center in overcrowded conditions. Now it is possible to construct a number of variants to the model since the shape of the bid rent curve of the rich is really a function of their preference for space relative to transport cost. Lave points out that the spatial structure of the city will change if these preferences change.[21] If congestion costs increase in the central city, for example, and the rich decide that the time and frustration are not worth it, they can with ease alter their bid rent function and move back into the center of the city. Thus various city

19. Kerner Commission. *Report of the National Advisory Commission on Civil Disorders* (New York: Bantam Books, 1968).

20. W. Alonso, *Location and Land Use* (Cambridge, Mass.: Harvard University Press, 1964); R. Muth, *Cities and Housing* (Chicago: University of Chicago Press, 1969).

21. L. Lave, "Congestion and Urban Location," *Papers of the Regional Science Association* 25 (1970): 133–52.

structures can be predicted, depending on the shape of the bid rent curves, and it is perfectly feasible to find the rich living in the center of the city and the poor located on the outskirts. In this case, the poor are forced to adjust, for example, by exchanging time for cost distance so that they expend large quantities of time walking to work in order to save on transport costs (a condition not unknown in Latin American cities). All this actually means is that the rich group can always enforce its preferences over a poor group because it has more resources to apply either to transport costs or to obtaining land in whatever location it chooses. This is the natural consequence derived from applying marginalist economic principles (the bid rent curve being a typical marginalist device) to a situation in which income differences are substantial. The theory rests on the achievement of what is usually called "Pareto optimality" in the housing market.[22]

It is possible to use theoretical formulations of this sort to analyze disequilibrium in a city system and to devise policies which will serve to bring conditions back into equilibrium. For example, with the rapid suburbanization of employment in the period since 1950, we would anticipate an outward shift of poor populations (given their bid rent functions) as they attempt to locate nearer their employment centers. This shift has *not* occurred because of the exclusive residential zoning in suburban areas. We may thus attribute the seriousness of the ghetto problem in modern society to a function of those institutions which prevent the achievement of equilibrium. We may, through court suits and the like, challenge the legality and constitutionality of exclusive zoning. (Interestingly enough, this effort is supported both by civil rights groups and corporations, since the former regard suburban zoning as discriminatory whereas the latter are concerned by the lack of low-income labor in suburban locations.) We may also try to modify land-use controls so that the kind of situation reported for some twenty communities in the Princeton, New Jersey, area, in which there is industrial and commercial zoning for 1.2 million jobs and residential zoning adequate for 144,000 workers, would be avoided.[23] We might also try to overcome the problem of insufficient transportation from inner city areas to outer suburbs by subsidizing transport systems or organizing special transport facilities to get ghetto residents out to suburban employment. Of necessity, this requires the ghetto resident to substitute time for cost (if service is subsidized). Most of these programs have been failures.[24] We might also try to get back into equilibrium by attracting employment back into the city center by urban renewal projects, support of Black capitalism, and the like. All of these solutions have as their basis the tacit assumption that there is disequilibrium in urban land

22. An interesting account of this coalition of interest is provided in the *Wall Street Journal,* 27 November 1970, p. 1.

23. *Wall Street Journal,* 27 November 1970.

24. The programs in Boston and New York seem to have failed miserably. The one in Baltimore is still alive, however.

use and that policy should be directed toward getting urban land use back into balance. These solutions are liberal in that they recognize inequity but seek to cure that inequity within an existing set of social mechanisms (in this case, mechanisms which are consistent with the von Thunen theory of urban land use).

How can we identify more revolutionary solutions? Let us go back to Muth's presentation of the von Thunen theory. After an analytic presentation of the theory, Muth seeks to evaluate the empirical relevance of the theory by testing it against the existing structure of residential land use in Chicago.[25] His tests indicate that the theory is broadly correct, with, however, certain deviations explicable by such things as racial discrimination in the housing market. We may thus infer that the theory is a true theory. This truth, arrived at by classical positivist means, can be used to help us identify the problem. What for Muth was a successful test of a social theory becomes for us an indicator of what the problem is. The theory predicts that poor groups must, of necessity, live where they can least afford to live.

Our objective is to eliminate ghettos. Therefore, the only valid policy with respect to this objective is to eliminate the conditions which give rise to the truth of the theory. In other words, we wish the von Thunen theory of the urban land market to become *not* true. The simplest approach here is to eliminate those mechanisms which serve to generate the theory. The mechanism in this case is very simple—competitive bidding for the use of the land. If we eliminate this mechanism, we will presumably eliminate the result. This is immediately suggestive of a policy for eliminating ghettos. This policy would presumably supplant competitive bidding with a socially controlled urban land market and socialized control of the housing sector. Under such a system, the von Thunen theory (which is a normative theory anyway) would become empirically irrelevant to our understanding of the spatial structure of residential land-use. This approach has been tried in a number of countries. In Cuba, for example, all urban flats were expropriated in 1960. Rents were paid to the government "and were considered as amortization toward ownership by the occupants, who must pay promptly and regularly and maintain the premises."[26] Change of occupancy could occur only through a state institution.

"Those living in homes built in or prior to 1940 were to cease payment in 1965 if rent had been paid punctually since 1959. And after May 1961, all new vacant units were distributed to families who had to pay rent equal to 10% of the family income. Moreover, in mid–1966, the right to live rent free for the rest of their lives was granted to all occupants of run-down tenements who

25. Muth, *Cities and Housing.*

26. N. P. Valdes, "Health and Revolution in Cuba," *Science and Society* 35 (1971): 311–35.

had made at least 60 months payment. A total of 268,089 families no longer were paying rent in 1969."[27]

Obviously, a small country, such as Cuba, in a fairly primitive stage of economic development is going to suffer chronic housing shortages, and poor housing per se cannot be eliminated through such action. However, the solutions adopted are interesting in that they will ultimately render the Alonso–Muth theory of the urban land market irrelevant to an understanding of residential spatial structure, and this, presumably, is what must happen if we are to succeed in eliminating the ghetto.[28]

This approach to the ghetto land and housing market is suggestive of a different framework for analyzing problems and devising solutions. Notice, for example, that all old housing became rent free. If we regard the total housing stock of an urban area as a social (as opposed to a private) good, then obviously the community has already paid for the old housing. By this calculus, all housing in an urban area built before, say, 1940 (and some of it built since) has been paid for. The debt on it has been amortized and retired. The only costs attached to it are maintenance and service charges. We have an enormous quantity of social capital locked up in the housing stock, but in a private market system for land and housing, the value of the housing is not always measured in terms of its use as shelter and residence, but in terms of the amount received in market exchange, which may be affected by external factors such as speculation. In many inner city areas at the present time, houses patently possess little or no exchange value. This does not mean, however, that they have no use value. As a consequence, we are throwing away use value because we cannot establish exchange values. This waste would not occur under a socialized housing market system and it is one of the costs we bear for clinging tenaciously to the notion of private property.

It has, of course, been an assumption of economic theory for some time that use value is embodied in exchange value. While the two are obviously related, the nature of the relationship depends upon who is doing the using.[29] In the inner city housing market we get quite different use values when we contrast the landlord, who uses the house as a source of income, and a tenant, who is interested in shelter. This argument with respect to the Alonso–Muth residential land-use theory is overly simplistic. Since it is frequently the case that a mechanism which is assumed for the purposes of the theory is not necessarily the same as the real mechanisms which generate results in accordance with the theory, it would be dangerous indeed to point immediately to competitive market processes as being the root cause of ghetto formation. All a successful

27. Valdes, "Health and Revolution in Cuba."

28. The impact of this kind of institutional change on the ecological structure of Prague is discussed by J. Musil, "The Development of Prague's Ecological Structure," in R. E. Pahl, ed., *Readings in Urban Sociology* (London: Pergamon, 1968).

29. The distinction between "use value" and "exchange value" was made first by Adam Smith. See *The Wealth of Nations,* Introduction by A. Skinner (Harmondsworth, U. K.: Penguin Books, 1970), pp. 131–32. It was subsequently analyzed in great detail by Karl Marx, *Capital,* vol. 1 (New York: International Publishers, 1967), pp. 35–83. One of the impacts of the marginalist theory of value was, of course, to by-pass this discussion which is reasonable if all institutions and mechanisms of allocation are working well.

test of the theory should do, therefore, is to alert us to the possibility that it is the competitive market mechanism which is at fault. We need to examine this mechanism in some detail.

A market functions under conditions of scarcity. Put another way, the allocation of scarce resources is the foundation for the market economy. In this regard it is important for us to analyze the content of the two concepts "resource" and "scarcity." Geographers have long recognized that a resource is a technical and social appraisal.[30] This means that materials and people become natural and human resources only when we possess the appropriate technology and social form to be able to make use of them. Uranium became a resource with technological advances in nuclear physics, and people become resources when they are forced to sell their labor on the market in order to survive (this is the real content of the term human resources). The concept of scarcity, likewise, does not arise naturally, but it becomes relevant only in terms of social action and social objectives.[31] Scarcity is socially defined and not naturally determined. A market system becomes possible under conditions of resource scarcity, for only under these conditions can price-fixing commodity exchange markets arise. The market system is a highly decentralized control device for the co-ordination and integration of economic action. The extension of this co-ordinative ability has historically allowed an immense increase in the production of wealth. We therefore find a paradox, namely that wealth is produced under a system which relies upon scarcity for its functioning. It follows that if scarcity is eliminated, the market economy, which is the source of productive wealth under capitalism, will collapse. Yet capitalism is forever increasing its productive capacity. To resolve this dilemma many institutions and mechanisms are formed to ensure that scarcity does not disappear. In fact many institutions are geared to the maintenance of scarcity (universities being a prime example, although this is always done in the name of "quality"). Other mechanisms ensure control over the flow of other factors of production. Meanwhile, the increasing productive power has to find an outlet and hence the process of waste (on military ventures, space programs, and the like) and the process of need creation. What this suggests, of course, is that scarcity cannot be eliminated without also eliminating the market economy. In an advanced productive society, such as the United States, the major barrier to eliminating scarcity lies in the complicated set of interlocking institutions (financial, judicial, political, educational, and so on) which support the market process. Let us examine how this situation is revealed in the inner-city housing market.

There are some curious features about ghetto hous-

30. See A. Spoehr, "Cultural Differences in the Interpretation of Natural Resources," in W. L. Thomas, ed., *Man's Role in Changing the Face of the Earth* (Chicago: University of Chicago Press, 1956).

31. H. Pearson, "The Economy Has No Surplus: A Critique of a Theory of Development," in K. Polanyi, C. M. Arensberg, and H. W. Pearson, eds., *Trade and Market in the Early Empires* (New York: Free Press, 1957).

ing. One paradox is that the areas of greatest over-crowding are also the areas with the largest number of vacant houses. There are *circa* 5,000 vacant structures in Baltimore; a good many of which are in reasonable condition, and they are all located in areas of greatest overcrowding. Other cities are experiencing something similar. The same areas are characterized by a large proportion of houses being let go in lieu of property taxes. Landlords in the inner-city housing market, contrary to popular opinion, are not making huge profits. In fact, the evidence suggests that they are making less than they would elsewhere in the housing market.[32] Some are unethical, of course, but good, rational, ethical landlord behavior provides a relatively low rate of return. Yet, the rents such landlords charge are very high relative to the quality of the accommodations, while properties, if they do change hands, do so at negligible prices. The banks, naturally, have good rational business reasons for not financing mortgages in inner city areas. There is a greater uncertainty in the inner city and the land is, in any case, frequently regarded as "ripe" for redevelopment. The fact that failure to finance mortgages makes it even riper is undoubtedly understood by the banking institutions, since there are good profits to be reaped by redevelopment under commercial uses. Given the drive to maximize profits, this decision cannot be regarded as unethical. In fact, it is a general characteristic of ghetto housing that if we accept the mores of normal, ethical, entrepreneurial behavior, there is no way in which we can blame anyone for the objective social conditions which all are willing to characterize as appalling and wasteful of potential housing resources. It is a situation in which we can find all kinds of contradictory statements "true." Consequently, it seems impossible to find an effective policy within the existing economic and institutional framework which is capable of rectifying these conditions. Thus, federal subsidies to private housing fail, rent subsidies are quickly absorbed by market adjustments, and public housing has little impact because it is too small in quantity, too localized in distribution (usually in those areas where the poor are forced to live anyway) and devised for use by the lowest classes in society only. Urban renewal merely moves the problem around and in some cases does more harm than good.

Engels, in a set of essays entitled *The Housing Question,* published in 1872, predicted that this was the impasse into which capitalist solutions to housing problems would inevitably lead. Theoretically, this prediction can be derived from criticizing von Thunen's analysis in exactly the same way as Marx criticized Ricardo's. Since the conceptualization of rent in von Thunen's model (and in the Alonso-Muth model) is essentially

32. This is suggested by G. Sternlieb, *The Tenement Landlord* (New Brunswick, New Jersey: Rutgers University Press, 1966). A detailed study of landlords' accounts in Baltimore (being undertaken in the Department of Geography at Johns Hopkins University) confirms this impression.

the same as that which Ricardo put forward (it merely arises under somewhat different circumstances), we can use Marx's arguments with respect to it directly.[33] Rent, according to Marx, was but one manifestation of surplus value under capitalist institutions (such as private property), and the nature of rent could not be understood independently of this fact. To regard rent as something "in itself," independent of other facets of the mode of production and independent of capitalist institutions is to commit a conceptual error. It is precisely this error which is committed in the Alonso—Muth formulations. Further, this "error" is manifest in the capitalist market process itself for it requires that rents (or return on capital) be maximized rather than realizing a maximum social surplus value. Since rent is merely one possible and partial manifestation of surplus value, the drive to maximize it rather than the surplus value which gives rise to it is bound to create tensions in the capitalist economy. In fact it sets in motion forces which are antagonistic to the realization of surplus value itself. Hence, the decline in production which results as potential work forces are separated from work places by land-use changes brought about by commercial interests' seeking to maximize the return on the land under their control and by communities' seeking to maximize their available tax bases. Engels, as long ago as 1872, pointed to the whole gamut of consequences which flowed from this sort of competitive market process.

"The growth of the big modern cities gives the land in certain areas, particularly in those which are centrally situated, an artificial and colossally increasing value; the buildings erected on these areas depress this value, instead of increasing it, because they no longer correspond to the changed circumstances. They are pulled down and replaced by others. This takes place above all with worker's houses which are situated centrally and whose rents, even with the greatest overcrowding, can never, or only very slowly increase above a certain maximum. They are pulled down and in their stead shops, warehouses and public buildings are erected."[34]

This process (which is clearly apparent in every contemporary city) results from the necessity to realize a rate of return on a parcel of land which is consistent with its location rent. It does not necessarily have anything to do with facilitating production. The process is also consistent with certain other pressures.

"Modern natural science has proved that so-called 'poor districts' in which the workers are crowded together are the breeding places of all those epidemics which from time to time afflict our towns. . . . Capitalist rule cannot allow itself the pleasure of creating epidemic

33. Karl Marx, *Capital*, vol. 3, part vi (New York: International Publishers, 1967); *Theories of Surplus Value*, part 2 (Moscow: Progress Publishers, 1968).

34. F. Engels, *The Housing Question* (New York: International Publishers, 1935), p. 23.

diseases among the working class with impunity; the consequences fall back on it and the angel of death rages in its ranks as ruthlessly as in the ranks of the workers. As soon as this fact had been scientifically established the philanthropic bourgeoisie began to compete with one another in noble efforts on behalf of the health of their workers. Societies were founded, books were written, proposals drawn up, laws debated and passed, in order to close the sources of the ever-recurring epidemics. The housing conditions of the workers were examined and attempts were made to remedy the most crying evils. . . . Government Commissions were appointed to inquire into the hygienic conditions of the working classes."[35]

Today it is social pathology—drugs and crime—which is important, but the problem does not seem essentially different. The solutions devised still have the same characteristics. Engels states:

"In reality the bourgeoisie has only one method of solving the housing question after *its* fashion—that is to say, of solving it in such a way that the solution continually reproduces the question anew. This method is called 'Haussmann.' . . . By 'Haussmann' I mean the practice which has now become general of making breaches in the working class quarters of our big towns, and particularly in areas which are centrally situated, quite apart from whether this is done from considerations of public health and for beautifying the town, or owing to the demand for big centrally situated business premises, or owing to traffic requirements, such as the laying down of railways, streets (which sometimes appear to have the strategic aim of making barricade fighting more difficult). . . . No matter how different the reasons may be, the result is everywhere the same; the scandalous alleys disappear to the accompaniment of lavish self-praise from the bourgeoisie on account of this tremendous success, but they appear again immediately somewhere else and often in the immediate neighborhood! . . . The breeding places of disease, the infamous holes and cellars in which the capitalist mode of production confines our workers night after night, are not abolished; they are merely *shifted elsewhere!* The same economic necessity which produced them in the first place, produces them in the next place also. As long as the capitalist mode of production continues to exist, it is folly to hope for an isolated solution of the housing question or of any other social question affecting the fate of the workers. The solution lies in the abolition of the capitalist mode of production and the appropriation of all the means of life and labour by the working class itself."[36]

35. Engels, *The Housing Question.*

36. Engels, *The Housing Question,* pp. 74–77.

The experience gained from implementing urban policies in contemporary American cities indicates some disturbing similarities to Engels's account, and it is difficult to avoid concluding that the inherent contradiction in the capitalist market mechanism contributes to it. Therefore, there is good reason to believe that our initial suspicion is correct and that the market mechanism is the culprit in a sordid drama. If we think in these terms, we can explain why almost all policies devised for the inner city have both desirable and undesirable outcomes. If we "urban renew," we merely move the poverty around; if we don't, we merely sit by and watch decay. If we prevent blockbusting, we also prevent Blacks from getting housing. The frustration consequent upon such a situation can easily lead to contradictory conclusions. The poor can be blamed for conditions (a conclusion which Banfield finds appropriate), and we can institute policies based on "benign neglect" which will at least not provoke the kinds of questions which policy failures inevitably raise. It is therefore interesting to note that urban policy at the present time appears to involve a shift in emphasis from trying to save the inner cities (where programs are doomed to failure) to trying to preserve the "gray areas" where the market system is still sufficiently vigorous to make it possible to achieve some degree of success. Whether such a policy will prevent disaffection and the spread of decay may be doubted. However, unfortunately it also entails writing off the accumulated use values in the inner cities as well as the fates and lives of those 15–25 million people who are currently condemned to live out their existence in such locations. This seems a high price to pay for merely avoiding a realistic consideration of both the conclusion which Engels reached and the theoretical basis upon which that conclusion rests. The point I am working toward is that although all serious analysts concede the seriousness of the ghetto problem, few call into question the forces which rule the very heart of our economic system. Thus we discuss everything except the basic characteristics of a capitalist market economy. We devise all manner of solutions except those which might challenge the continuance of that economy. Such discussions and solutions serve only to make us look foolish, since they eventually lead us to discover what Engels was only too aware of in 1872—that capitalist solutions provide no foundation for dealing with deteriorated social conditions. They are merely "dephlogisticated air." We can, if we will, discover oxygen and all that goes with it by subjecting the very basis of our society to a rigorous and critical examination. It is this task which a revolutionary approach to theory must first accomplish. What does this task entail?

Let me say first what it does not entail. It does not

entail yet another empirical investigation of the social conditions in the ghettos. In fact, mapping even more evidence of man's patent inhumanity to man is counter-revolutionary in the sense that it allows the bleeding-heart liberal to pretend he is contributing to a solution when in fact he is not. This kind of empiricism is irrelevant. There is already enough information in congressional reports, daily newspapers, books, articles, and so on to provide us with all the evidence we need. Our task does not lie here. Nor does it lie in what can only be termed "moral masturbation" of the sort which accompanies the masochistic assemblage of some huge dossier on the daily injustices to the populace of the ghetto, over which we beat our breasts and commiserate with each other before retiring to our fireside comforts. This, too, is counter-revolutionary for it merely serves to expiate guilt without our ever being forced to face the fundamental issues, let alone do anything about them. Nor is it a solution to indulge in that emotional tourism which attracts us to live and work with the poor "for a while" in the hope that we can really help them improve their lot. This, too, is counter-revolutionary — so what if we help a community win a playground in one summer of work to find that the school deteriorates in the fall? These are the paths we should *not* take. They merely serve to divert us from the essential task at hand.

This immediate task is nothing more nor less than the self-conscious and aware construction of a new paradigm for social geographic thought through a deep and profound critique of our existing analytical constructs. This is what we are best equipped to do. We are academics, after all, working with the tools of the academic trade. As such, our task is to mobilize our powers of thought to formulate concepts and categories, theories and arguments, which we can apply to the task of bringing about a humanizing social change. These concepts and categories cannot be formulated in abstraction. They must be forged realistically with respect to the events and actions as they unfold around us. Empirical evidence, the already assembled dossiers, and the experiences gained in the community can and must be used here. But all of those experiences and all of that information means little unless we synthesize it into powerful patterns of thought.

However, our thought cannot rest merely on existing reality. It has to embrace alternatives creatively. We cannot afford to plan for the future on the basis of positivist theory, for to do so would merely reinforce the status quo. Yet, as in the formation of any new paradigm, we must be prepared to incorporate and reassemble all that is useful and valuable within that corpus of theory. We can restructure the formulation of existing theory in the light of possible lines of future action. We can criticize existing theories as "mere apologetics" for the dominant force in our society—the capitalist market system and all its concomitant institutions. In this manner we will be able to establish the circumstances under which location theory can be used to create better futures and the circumstances in which it reinforces modes of thought conducive to the maintenance of the status quo. The problem in many cases is not the marginalist method per se nor optimizing techniques per se but that these methods are being applied in the wrong context. Pareto optimality as it enters location theory is a counter-revolutionary concept, as is any formulation which calls for the maximization of any one of the partial manifestations of surplus value (such as rent or return on capital investment). Yet programming solutions are clearly extremely relevant devices for understanding how resources can best be mobilized for the production of surplus value.[37] Formulations based on the achievement of equality in distribution are also counter-revolutionary unless they are derived from an understanding of how production is organized to create surplus value.[38] By examining questions such as these, we can at least begin to evaluate existing theory and in the process (who knows?) perhaps begin to derive the lineaments of new theory.

A revolution in scientific thought is accomplished by marshalling concepts and ideas, categories and relationships, into such a superior system of thought when judged against the realities which require explanation that we succeed in making all opposition to that system of thought look ludicrous. Since we are, for the most part, our own worst opponents in this matter, many of us will find that a first initial step on this path will be to discomfort ourselves, to make ourselves look ludicrous to ourselves. This is not easy, particularly if we are possessed of intellectual pride. Further, the emergence of a true revolution in geographic thought is bound to be tempered by commitment to revolutionary practice. Certainly the general acceptance of revolutionary theory will depend upon the strengths and accomplishments of revolutionary practice. There will be many hard personal decisions to make—decisions that require "real" as opposed to "mere liberal" commitment. Many of us will undoubtedly flinch before making such a commitment, for it is indeed very comfortable to be a mere liberal. However, if conditions are as serious as many of us believe, then we will increasingly come to recognize that nothing much can be lost by that kind of commitment and that almost everything stands to be gained should we make it and succeed.

37. The experience of Russian central planning in this regard provides some interesting lessons as Kantrovich developed programming solutions to many of the allocation distribution problems which arose in the economy. See M. Ellman, *Soviet Planning Today* (Cambridge: Cambridge University Press, 1971). This suggests that some of the programming solutions to urban location problems will probably be useful as the basis for a revolutionary urban land use theory.

38. Karl Marx, *Capital,* vol. 3, pp. 876–86. It is on this ground that I now reject my attempt in a previous paper to examine questions of distribution in a manner distinct from the problem of production. See D. Harvey, "Social Justice in Spatial Systems," in R. Peet, ed., *Geographical Perspectives on American Poverty* (Worcester, Mass.: Antipode Monographs in Social Geography, No. 1, 1972). To be reprinted in D. Harvey, *Cities and Surplus: Essays on the Space Economy of Urbanism* (London: Edward Arnold, forthcoming).

2

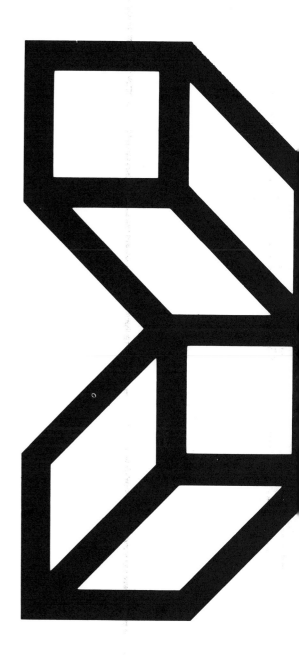

Richard L. Morrill
University of Washington

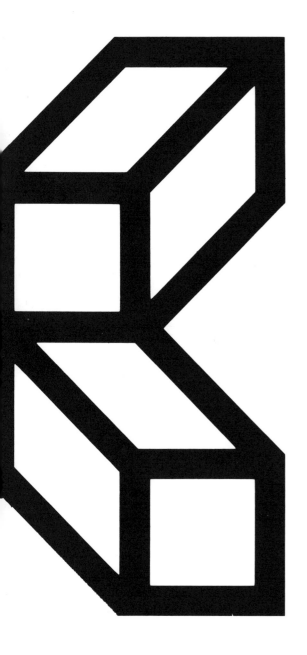

A Geographic Perspective of the Black Ghetto

ABSTRACT

In part 1, the origin and development of the Black ghetto is traced. The origin dates from before the Revolution, but concentration in urban ghettos did not become common until the great migrations from the rural South to southern and northern cities after 1910. Black occupancy of urban ghettos has proved permanent, because of the strength and persistence of discrimination on the basis of color and the sense of identity with the Black community. The civil rights movement from 1950–1960 worked toward integration, but since 1965 there has been increasing Black sentiment for making the most of ghetto solidarity.

In part 2, a temporal-spatial behavioral model of ghetto growth is developed and tested. Growth is seen as a gradual diffusion from Black core areas. The pattern of spread depends on the size and growth of the Black and White communities, relative income and educational levels, housing characteristics of the areas, location of areas with respect to the existing ghetto, reaction of Whites (whether to resist or to flee) and Blacks searching for and finding residences outside of the ghetto. The model is applied to Seattle with good results for the period 1950–1960 but only fair results for 1960–1970.

In part 3, the prospects for the disappearance of the Black ghetto are discussed. The traditional kind of assimilation is unlikely both because of White fear and racism and because of the emergence of a strong Black sense of community. Spatial integration is not likely to be acceptable until economic equality is achieved, and this is deemed unlikely in the near future.

Ghettos are the homes of some fifteen million Black Americans—spatially separate colonies developing within American cities, mainly during the last 60 years. A century ago, almost all Blacks were either share-croppers in rural areas of the South or servants. Today the Black ghettos are becoming so large that their populations are becoming the ethnic majority in several cities, North and South.

The ghettos developed as Blacks left the farm and plantation for the hope of better opportunities in the cities. Blacks were confined to separate ghetto spaces, owing to external social, economic, and political discrimination and to internal pressures of group solidarity and cultural preference. However, as a result of additional migration and natural increase, the ghetto had to grow; Blacks diffused block by block into White areas of least, but often violent, resistance.

During the early years of the recent civil rights movement (1955–1965), many Blacks and Whites worked toward residential integration and the eventual disappearance of the ghetto. However, the "Black Nationalist" movement together with White fears and resistance have prevented any significant integration, and the prospects for the disappearance of the ghetto appear dim.

1. ORIGIN AND DEVELOPMENT OF THE BLACK GHETTO

The Ghetto Before 1900

Long before the Civil War, thousands of slaves escaped from the South via the underground railroad (Still, 1871). Most headed for the nearest northern city, e.g., Philadelphia, Cincinnati, Indianapolis, or Pittsburgh. Some continued on to New York, Chicago, Rochester, Boston, Buffalo, and other cities in which there had generally been free but very small Black communities since about 1790.

Up to 1900, these Black communities, North and South, remained rather small. In 1880, the largest Black populations were in New Orleans (58,000), Baltimore (54,000), Washington, D.C. (52,000), Philadelphia (32,-000), and New York (28,000). A high proportion of Blacks worked as domestic servants in the homes of middle- and upper-class Whites. Consequently, much of the Black population lived dispersed throughout the city (Rose, 1969). Some did live from the very beginning in small colonies and in incredibly poor conditions in the growing slums close to the city center, often along the main industrial railways or near the wharves. In the South, both these patterns occurred, but since the Black proportion was sometimes half of the total population, there was often a Black "quarter"—at times within the city, at times on the outskirts as a semi-rural slum similar to the Latin American "barrios" (Wade, 1964). Many Blacks lived in alleys behind the homes of the wealthy; others lived in small shantytowns, often outside the city limits. In the old seaport towns of the South, mixed residence was fairly common; in the newer mercantile and industrial cities, such as Atlanta or Birmingham, segregation was the rule from the beginning (Meier and Radwick, 1966; Rose, 1969).

In the northern cities, especially after 1850, ethnic ghettos began to form due to the rapid pace of immigration from Europe. The newest group was looked down upon by earlier immigrants and was set apart, usually in the worst slums near the city center. This segregation occurred not only because of outside discrimination but also because of a need for ethnic solidarity and mutual protection (Bennett, 1964). However, White residence in the ghetto was of comparatively short duration, typically a generation or perhaps two. The upward mobility made possible by the pace of economic expansion brought about an almost surprising dispersal of most White ethnic groups.

Establishment of the Black Ghettos: 1900–1920

After 1900, the pace of Black northward migration quickened, partly as a result of the increasingly miserable conditions of the southern sharecropper and partly because of the frequency of lynching and other forms of violence against Blacks (Bontemps and Conroy, 1966; Hart, 1960). After 1914 and with the outbreak of war in Europe, White immigration slowed just as the demand for labor increased in northern industry. After the United States entered the war, labor requirements grew so rapidly that Blacks were able for the first time to enter low-level industrial jobs. Some companies even recruited in the South to the outrage of many White Southerners.

Between 1900 and 1920, as many as 600,000 rural Blacks moved to the cities (Farley, 1968). Flows moved rather narrowly up the eastern seaboard from the south Atlantic states to the Middle Atlantic states and up the Mississippi and Ohio Valleys from the south central states to the north central states. Later flows reflected the earlier moves of relatives and friends (Smith, 1966; Taeuber and Taeuber, 1965). Before 1915, the Middle Atlantic states had taken the most Black migrants; the main destinations were New York, Philadelphia, and Baltimore. During and after World War I, ghettos grew rapidly in the industrial cities of the north central states, Detroit, Cleveland, Gary, and Columbus, as well as in the traditional centers of Chicago, St. Louis, and Cincinnati. The East South Central states became the leading source of migrants and the East North Central states the leading destination (Hart, 1960).

31

The Black communities grew explosively. By 1920, for example, New York reached 169,000; Philadelphia, 134,000; and Chicago, 109,000. For the first time the Black population of these northern cities surpassed that in the southern cities which had grown more slowly—Washington to 110,000, Baltimore to 108,000, New Orleans to 101,000. These numbers were much too large to be accommodated in the tiny Black communities. Fear, prejudice, and poverty, however, prevented Black access to the general housing market, although the decline of immigration from Europe permitted the rapidly increasing Black population to move into some former ethnic ghettos. Naturally, the burgeoning Black communities met with resistance, both because many present residents, especially the elderly, did not want or could not afford to move, and even more because of the underlying White fear and prejudice against Blacks—economically, psychologically, and physically (Clark, 1965). After the wartime economy collapsed, unemployment rose, especially for Blacks, who were first to be fired. A series of race riots occurred in many American cities and were especially severe in Washington, Chicago, Philadelphia, Omaha, Knoxville, and East St. Louis (Bennett, 1964).

The ghetto almost always originated in the mixed residential-industrial-wholesale slums on the "wrong side of the tracks," and *economic* discrimination has markedly curtailed opportunities for upward mobility. Most of the major ghettos which exist at present had at least begun to develop by 1920. The process of ghetto expansion is investigated in greater depth in the next section. An outline of the development of the ghetto over time is presented here.

At times, growth was accommodated by yet more overcrowding and subdivision of the old houses, but the rapid growth required that the ghetto continually extend its boundaries. Sometimes the growth occurred "concentrically"—that is, into similarly low-class housing (Rose, 1969). This occurred most often when economic conditions were particularly low or when the rate of in-migration of the most poverty-stricken, least-educated Blacks was very high and was often accompanied by violence and unrest. In order to find "invadable" lower-class housing, it was often necessary to jump over very resistant areas of lower-class Whites who were unable to move to better housing, over industry, or over a wedge of middle- or upper-class housing. Mainly for this reason, many cities had more than one ghetto community (some of which may later have coalesced).

Somewhat more commonly, growth occurred "sectorially"—outwardly in wedge fashion into somewhat newer and better housing. This was possible because of the growth of a Black middle-class and because of the willingness, ability, and sometimes the desire of White residents of areas in the path of ghetto expansion to shift farther outward, often to suburban housing. In general, this process was easier in areas with Jewish ethnic communities, that were apparently less prejudiced and economically more able to move than Catholic and Orthodox eastern and southern European groups.

The Black occupancy of the ghetto has proved to be permanent; and instead of gradually disappearing as members assimilated into the wider society, the Black ghettos have grown continually larger to accommodate both natural increases and further migration out of the rural South. One reason for the continuance, and indeed strengthening, of a segregated ghetto was the sheer size and the rapid increase of the Black population in the ghettos. By far the main reason for permanence of the Black ghetto was the simple fact of blackness. A large majority of the White population has an ingrained fear and distrust of Blacks because they are physically different in such an obvious and visible way. Fear has led, in turn, to prejudice and discrimination. Whereas the White immigrant, upon learning English and accumulating some income, could move out of the ghetto into middle-class areas, the Black people were *social* prisoners of the ghetto, irrespective of whether they achieved a middle- or upper-class education and income (Myrdal, 1964). A third major reason for the permanence of the ghetto is the strong sense of community and identity which has developed because of the special status and isolation of Blacks, resulting in a distinct American subculture. Therefore, the majority of Blacks express a preference for living with other Blacks.

This Black community is thus properly called a "ghetto." While the majority of the residents of the Black ghetto may be poor, by no means should it be assumed that all ghetto residents are poor. The ghetto contains all social and economic classes of Blacks—simply because they are Black.

The Ghettos in the Twenties and Thirties

Despite riots and unabated social and economic discrimination, the urban ghettos continued to expand throughout the twenties and thirties as Blacks abandoned farms or fled their peasant share-cropping serfdom in the South. So miserable was this life that in spite of love for the countryside, thousands moved into the ghettos of southern cities and into the distant, fearful, concrete jungles of the northern metropolitan ghettos.

In the 1920s, the increasing size and economy of the ghettos resulted in some beginnings of Black political representation on city councils, in legislatures, and finally, in 1928, in Congress when Chicago elected the first Black representative since Reconstruction. Black-owned businesses, especially banks, insurance companies, and funeral homes began (Drake and Cayton, 1962). Since Whites were unwilling to let the Blacks participate equally in their world, a movement to make the best of the separate ghetto developed.

The Depression of the 1930s was, of course, very hard on Blacks, although in the long run, the New Deal measures of minimum wages, social security, unemployment compensation, and welfare (aid to dependent children) proved to be of great benefit. The agricultural programs of the New Deal were equally revolutionary because they speeded the process of mechanization of southern agriculture and resulted in the wholesale displacement, after 1940, of millions of Blacks (farmers and farm laborer families) from the rural South (Bennett, 1964). Some well-meaning people consider this aspect of agricultural mechanization cruel and inhuman, but in the final analysis, it was very fortunate because only in the cities could Blacks find the organization and strength to fight for better jobs and schools and political power.

The Ghettos Since the Forties

In the 1940s, World War II again brought better industrial job opportunities for Blacks and increased the rate of urban migration. After the war, the familiar pattern of recession, high rates of Black unemployment, and race riots ensued. Ghettos now spread even farther from traditional areas to such West Coast cities as Los Angeles, Oakland, and San Francisco and to such Midwestern Plains cities as Milwaukee and Omaha. The traditional northerly flows from the south Atlantic and south central states continued, but an additional large flow from the west central states (Texas) to the Pacific was added (Smith, 1966).

During the Korean War, the status of Blacks began to improve, slowly, following President Truman's integration of the Armed Forces. The returning veterans were not prepared to return to inferior status and jobs. By 1955, a strong wave of protest and action, a determination to win the full social and political rights of citizenship and to share in the economic wealth of the nation, had irresistibly begun. White resistance and indifference to these demands inevitably led to greater and greater militancy, culminating in the severe riots and demonstrations of the middle 1960s, which finally forced the enactment of significant civil rights legislation.

The effectiveness and strength of the civil rights movement was surely aided by the continuing growth of the ghettos and the emergence of second generation leadership (Mack, 1965). New York achieved a Black population of one million in 1950 and 1.5 million in 1960; Chicago, 600,000 in 1950 and almost one million in

1960; Philadelphia, 484,000 in 1950 and 671,000 in 1960; and Detroit, 362,000 in 1950 and 559,000 in 1960. In 1944, New York elected its first Black congressman, followed by Detroit in 1954; Philadelphia in 1962; and Los Angeles, Cleveland, and St. Louis in 1968.

During the early phases of the civil rights movement (1955–1965), the notion of residential integration and the belief that the ghetto as a segregated residential space should disappear was supported by both the Black leadership and White liberal supporters (Weaver, 1948). Attempts at residential integration met with particularly violent and emotional resistance. At the same time, the prevailing attitude of Blacks shifted toward a pride in the Black community. The Black Power movement took hold, especially among the young, as an appreciation for cultural distinctiveness and the political potentiality of spatial concentration developed. A strategy of gaining recognition as a distinct but equal kind of American has replaced the idea of assimilation. It is therefore not surprising that the ghettos have continued to grow in size and solidarity and that relatively little actual integration has occurred (see part 3, "Prospects for Disappearance of the Ghetto").

The Ghetto Today

By 1970, the Black ghettos of many metropolises had become large cities in themselves—the 1920s dream of a "Black Metropolis" is becoming true in a sense (Drake and Cayton, 1962). In 1970, the New York ghettos reached a population of approximately 2,350,000; Chicago, 1,300,000; Philadelphia, 800,000; Detroit, 750,000; Los Angeles, 750,000; Washington, 700,000; and Baltimore, 500,000. Blacks became the ethnic majority (within the city limits) in Atlanta, Gary, and Newark and, by 1980, may be the majority in Detroit, Richmond, Cleveland, St. Louis, Baltimore, and New Orleans. Gary, Indiana; Newark, New Jersey; and Cleveland have Black mayors. Blacks represent most major cities, South as well as North, on city councils and state legislatures.

The income and educational levels of Black ghetto residents have improved relative to Whites, mainly since 1965, but still remain at only two-thirds to three-fourths of the White level. Unemployment among Blacks remains double to triple that of Whites. Ghettos remain "colonies," in an economic sense. Since a high proportion of land, housing, and business is owned outside the community, a large cash outflow results (Blauner, 1969). Modern shopping centers are absent; professional services are limited. Most Black ghettos, being in central cities, lack the option of newer suburban housing, although recent expansion is typically into fairly nice middle-class housing. Cities have tried to improve housing conditions of poor Blacks (and at the same time have attempted to entice Whites back to the central city) through urban renewal, but this "gilded ghetto" approach has failed to recognize that better job and income opportunities are the real problems of Blacks. To many Blacks, the high rise, dangerous, and unfriendly slum towers are even worse than the tenements they left (Moore, 1969).

Growth of the Chicago Ghetto

The Chicago Ghetto provides perhaps the best example of twentieth-century ghetto growth—from 30,000 in 1900 to well over one million in 1970. In 1920, the Black population was situated mainly along and between the railroads, and south of the Loop (25th to 39th streets) (Drake and Cayton, 1962). During the 1920s, the population almost doubled and was contained almost entirely in a long wedge extending southward. Small outliers were added along railroads much farther south and southwest of the Loop on the Near West side. Much of this expansion displaced Irish, Italian, and Jewish ethnic groups. Little areal expansion took place in the 1930s. Areal expansion was also difficult in the 1940s, and overcrowding and housing deterioration were common. Small expansions occurred on the Near West side, over to the lake south of the Loop, in an outlier southwest of the main ghetto and in a jump across to the poor parts of the Near North side. In contrast, the areal spread in the 1950s was massive, perhaps tripling the area of dense ghetto, spreading both to the southeast and southwest. The sectorial growth was most pronounced, and the ghetto now extended well into middle-class areas, especially in the south. Since 1960, growth has continued to the west, reaching to the edge of Cicero but has extended even more southward. All this time, however, the wealthy areas along the Lakeshore north of the Loop, and the lower income Polish and Italian areas northwest and southwest of the Loop successfully resisted Black entry.

2. EXPANSION OF THE GHETTO—A MODEL OF GHETTO GROWTH

Since the population of a Black ghetto is growing both from natural increase and from outside migration, severe pressure is being placed on the housing supply. For a while, increasing population can be accommodated through over-crowding, but eventually the real estate market must accommodate the demand. In practice, the industry selects the edges along which extension will be permitted. At any one time, the most likely areas are those where the present residents have risen sufficiently in status to permit a shift to better and newer housing and where the proximity of the ghetto serves to encourage the move. Thus, areas of poor Whites who cannot escape to better housing will not be chosen. Rather areas of older middle-class housing may become available as the residents become able to afford small homes in the suburbs and flee the encroaching Blacks. Because of White fear of intimate contact with Blacks and the unwillingness of most Whites to become an ethnic minority, the transition from all-White to all-Black occurs rather quickly over a very few blocks (McEntire, 1960).

Extension of the ghetto is often accomplished by a block-by-block transition. At the proper moment, only prospective Black (but no White) buyers are shown housing on the block, and White owners are advised to sell before values fall. Panic may ensue, prices temporarily fall in a kind of "self-fulfilling" manner, and the transition from White to Black is quickly completed (Wolf, 1963). Real estate control has been markedly successful at guiding the direction of growth and minimizing social contact between races. Truly integrated areas are very rare, and probably none can be considered stable. Regardless of how people may answer in surveys, the facts of behavior show that most Whites will not remain in an area after the transition is carried through — that is, at equilibrium, most areas will be either more than 90 percent Black or less than 25 percent Black (McEntire, 1960). The few exceptions include some public housing projects and a few upper-middle-class areas of unusually well-educated professional people (Rapkin and Grigsby, 1960). It is interesting that in the time of slavery the legal social distance was so great that physical separation was not so necessary. On the other hand, with theoretical equality, Whites apparently need the psychological protection of geographic distance.

Certain geographic changes in the ghetto will now be examined in more detail: (A) intensification or reduction in the proportion of Blacks, (B) areal expansion or stagnation (or contraction) of the ghetto, (C) deterioration, no change, or upgrading in the residential quality of the ghetto, and (D) government-induced changes such as urban renewal or freeways. Combinations of these outcomes are possible in the same ghetto during the same time period, depending on the behavior of the "actors" and the nature of internal and external forces. The principal "actors" include (1) Black families, (2) Black organizations and media, (3) White families, (4) White organizations and media, (5) the real estate industry, (6) financial institutions, and (7) government. Each group contains actors with conflicting goals — Black and White individuals and organizations who favor integration or segregation or who are indifferent and governmental actions which foster integration or separation. Some more explicit goals include: (1) for Blacks, enhancement of social and educational opportunities through integration, (2) for Blacks, obtaining newer and better housing, usually through integration, (3) for many Blacks, reduction of social friction and maintenance of social relations within the Black community, (4) for Blacks, obtaining better housing while maintaining social solidarity by trying to expand the ghetto into areas of better housing, (5) for many Whites, preservation of the existing community character by resisting Black encroachment, (6) for Whites, fear of Blacks and the desire to avoid contact either by resistance or by flight, (7) for the real estate and financial institutions, a traditional goal to maintain racial segregation and to control ghetto growth so as to minimize the area of conflict, (8) for some Whites and Blacks, a belief in integration as such as a means of achieving equality and reducing racial conflict, and (9) for government, responses to these various goals depending on the relative power of their proponents; the practical aim being to appease each faction. As far as the geographic outcome is concerned, it is apparent that this is not a simple matter of Black against White, but more of Blacks and Whites who favor integration vis-à-vis Blacks and Whites who, for different reasons, favor separatism.

The extent to which these goals are realized and the likelihood of the geographic outcomes depend on a variety of other forces, such as (1) the absolute size of the Black and White communities, (2) the rate of growth of the Black and White communities by natural increase and migration, (3) the income and educational levels of the Black and White communities, (4) the volume of housing stock and the rate of its expansion, (5) the history of relations between Whites and Blacks over the years, (6) long-term bias of government in the area, for or against Blacks and integration.

Now examination may be made of the circumstances under which the various outcomes (or combinations) may be expected to occur. Intensification without expansion may result from increasing identification of Blacks with the community and/or from very strong White and institutional resistance probably with limited in-migration. If the rate of population growth and in-migration is high, intensification and areal expansion are both likely, and racial conflict is probable. Areal expansion, with consequent dilution of the proportion of Blacks, might occur when the Black community is fairly small and of high status and when the Whites tend to be integrationist in their views. Deterioration of housing quality is likely with a high rate of growth and in-migration of lower status Blacks together with low rates of home ownership and high White resistance. Upgrading and rehabilitation of the housing stock is possible when population growth is slow and the community is experiencing improved incomes. Also, where White fear is great and newer suburban housing is available, Whites may flee to the suburbs, allowing fairly peaceful ghetto expansion into better housing. Governmental public works, such as urban renewal or construction of freeways, will depend on the power of competing groups. Barriers to expansion, such as freeways, are likely if White groups have sufficient strength to seal off the ghetto or provide a high-speed tunnel through it. Renewal more often results from White attempts to hide the slums in the guise of high-rise apartments and to maintain some middle-class Whites near the city center; only recently have Blacks become strong enough to influence the nature of renewal housing.

One may well ask what kinds of behavior and geographic outcomes would be most rational in the long run. For Blacks, the answer is uncertain; for Whites, the fostering of spatial integration is clearly rational, though emotionally unlikely. Obviously, if Blacks are dispersed throughout the much larger White community, then the likelihood of unified Black action, including riots and property damage, is vastly reduced. White majority behavior, which is biased toward maintaining separation, is irrational because it increases the level of fear and distrust and the probability of racial conflict. The apparent belief "out of sight, out of mind" is not really possible. For Blacks, it may seem rational to integrate in the expectation of better education and job opportunities. On the other hand, there is a risk of total loss of power and possible permanent discrimination. Thus, in the medium time range, it may be more rational for the Black community to maintain ghetto solidarity as a means to gain the power to force economic, social, and political equality (see part 3).

Most individuals are not totally committed to an inflexible position. Rather their decisions, e.g., of whether or where to move, result from weighing the "benefits and costs." For example, a Black family may desire newer and better housing but wish to remain in the Black community. They may choose to rehabilitate existing housing or not move until there is better housing in an expansion path of the ghetto. A White family may fear Blacks' becoming too numerous in an area but at the same time be very attached to their home and neighborhood. They may not leave until most of their old acquaintances are gone. Another White family may long have considered a move to the suburbs and thus move when the edge of the ghetto is still several blocks away.

The Model

A model of spatial change in the ghetto is obviously complex. To make the model "live," however, requires knowledge of how intensively goals are held and pursued—i.e., some scaling of values or benefits and/or dysvalues and costs and the circumstances under which locational change decisions are made. For example, to a White who very much fears or dislikes Blacks, a fairly distant threat might impel a move. However, a White who only slightly fears Blacks might not move until the Black proportion around him reaches some socially critical level as perceived by the Whites, such as 50 percent. Similarly, if two White areas in the path of ghetto expansion are alike in every respect except that White resistance is strong in one but absent or weak in the other, Black families will reasonably take the path of least resistance.

In order to incorporate the behavioral complexities discussed above, a stochastic simulation model is proposed. The model is deterministic in that only one outcome is possible from a given set of initial conditions and exogenous forces, but behavior is controlled by a complex set of probabilities, which open certain paths under particular conditions. These are sufficiently diverse to permit a wide range of outcomes.

Operation of the Model

A study area is chosen, consisting of the Black ghetto and an area at least as large surrounding it, and ideally is divided into blocks or groups of blocks (such as enumeration districts).

Initial Conditions

For each area at a point in time, an estimate is needed of the numbers of homes for at least three classes— lower, middle, and upper—occupied by Whites and Blacks and of houses which are vacant. An estimate of the net number of new households formed by each class is also required.

Mobility

For *Blacks,* the approximate proportions who are integrationist, separationist, and indifferent must be estimated. For present purposes, it is sufficient to guess that one-third of the Blacks will hold each view. In effect, half will tend to prefer the ghetto, half will not. The next requirement is an approximation of the proportions of people with a motivation to move at all during a given time period. Again, for simplicity, one may guess that one-third of the residents want very much to move during a five-year period, one-third are moderately motivated, and one-third do not wish to move.

Under the above conditions, the one-ninth who are integrationist and half of the one-ninth who are indifferent make up together one-sixth of the Blacks who also want very much to move. Likewise, one-ninth who are integrationist and half of the one-ninth who are indifferent make up another one-sixth who are only weakly motivated to move. In sum, one-third of the old residents begin the house-searching process in White areas, and one-third wish to remain in the ghetto. In addition, new households are being formed because of natural increase, marriage and separation, and in-migration. The migrants may be assumed to live temporarily with friends and relatives, distributed in direct proportion to the existing Black population, and to view the housing market from the perspective of the older residents.

Availability of Housing

Beyond desire, there is the problem of the objective possibility and capability of a move. This is a matter of discovering (matching) whether there is housing available in the mover's class at a particular destination area. For any set of origins and destinations, the match is between potential movers of a given class and housing in that class. For the entire set of areas, there may well be a shortage (or surplus) of housing of a given class or type. Random selection of origin areas accomplishes a "first come, first serve" solution.

Allocation by Distance

Next is the problem of the location of potential moves. Both information about available housing and the desire to live there may be expected to decline fairly regularly with distance from the present location. Thus, within the set of appropriate housing, actual moves will in turn be biased in favor of closest opportunities. This function is not precisely known, but evidence from earlier studies suggests values approximating those in table 1.

In general, middle-class people have more information and are more willing to move farther from existing ties. Those far inside the ghetto, especially the lower-class, have less information; and even if they desire to live outside, many may remain within the ghetto. The allocation can be accomplished in the following manner. Let the lower-classes move first. The order of origin areas may be given randomly. Available housing by destination areas is known (in mixed areas, origins and destination areas may coincide). The 40 percent of movers from any particular origin area who seek housing within one-half mile of the ghetto edge may be assigned to the closest available housing. If numbers are sufficient, the movers may be allocated among destination areas in proportion to available housing

Table 1. *Probability of Having Information About and Desiring to Live in Housing in Relation to Distance Beyond the Ghetto**

Distance (Miles)	Lower Class		Middle and Upper	
	Close	Far*	Close	Far*
In ghetto		.30		.20
0–0.5	.40	.40	.30	.30
0.5–0.75	.30	.20	.25	.20
0.75–1.5	.20	.10	.20	.15
1.5–2	.10		.15	.10
> 2			.10	.05

*Ghetto edge defined as the 50 percent line; "close" means the Black is within one mile of the edge; "far" means he is more than a mile inside the ghetto.

Table 2. *Proportion of Whites Fleeing as Result of Black Search*

Distance (Miles)	Class of Area	
	Middle Class	Lower and Upper
0–0.5	.10	.05
0.5–1	.08	.04
1–1.5	.06	.03
1.5–2	.04	.02
2–3	.02	.01

Table 3. *Probability of Real Estate Rebuff*

Class of Area	Black Proportion		
	Under 10 Percent	10 to 30 Percent	Over 30 Percent
Middle	.60	.40	.20
Upper and lower	.90	.60	.30

Table 4. *Probability of Financial Rebuff*

Class of Mover	
Middle and upper	.40
Lower	.80

and distance. If insufficient housing is available within the indicated zones, the remaining potential movers wait for housing to open up (see below). This step yields a spatial distribution of potential moves by origin and destination areas.

White Reaction to Black Search

Meanwhile, the very threat of ghetto expansion and the act of searching by Blacks leads to White reaction. This may take the form of resistance through the real estate industry, banks, or in other ways but may also lead to some White flight. This initial flight is likely to be proportional to the intensity of the Black search, that is, it will reflect the foregoing distance probabilities. Thus as Blacks are searching, the number of vacancies is slightly increasing, permitting some further moves (by those who at first could not find vacancies). Undoubtedly, lower-class residents (who are less able to pay) and upper-class residents (who have more to protect) are less likely to flee than members of the middle-classes.

Real Estate Barriers

Next, the prospective mover, although he is matched to an available house (home or rental unit) must overcome institutional and private resistance. The behavior of the real estate industry reflects the views of the residents of an area. In areas with very little entry, resistance will probably be very great (in an effort to prevent change), while in areas of clear transition (over 10 and particularly over 30 percent Black), resistance will fall and indeed may reverse (Blacks encouraged, Whites discouraged). In upper- and lower-class areas, resistance is probably higher (for reasons noted above) than in middle-class areas.

The probabilities in table 3 are hypothetical, since there is a lack of precise knowledge, but they are probably reasonable. The potential Black mover with only a moderate motivation to move will probably give up at a real estate rebuff. Those with strong desires to move will certainly try again. This may happen several times, but for model purposes, it is hypothesized that those who try again will have a 50 percent chance of success in getting through the real estate barrier.

Financial Barriers

Even if shown a home, the prospective buyer must arrange finances. One may hypothesize that the resistance from financial institutions will be greater for lower-class buyers than for middle- and upper-class buyers (table 4).

The less motivated potential movers will give up at the financial rebuff; again, perhaps one-half of those greatly desiring to move will succeed in making some financial arrangements. This barrier further reduces the number of surviving movers. Those who have searched, found housing, and passed through the real estate and financial barriers are at least temporarily successful movers. The next action is generally White.

White Reaction to Black Entry:
I. Organizing Resistance

Whites within an area may react by either organizing resistance to or fleeing from Black in-migration. Lower-class people will probably be more likely to resist entry through such techniques as threats, cross-burnings, or harrassment of children than upper- or middle-class Whites. The intensity of the resistance will also depend on the proportion of Black population and will normally be highest where there is a low proportion of Blacks in the neighborhood (table 5).

A high proportion of less motivated movers will again give up upon such overt resistance. Half of the highly motivated movers will probably give up, while half will hold out. By this time, only a fraction of those with a desire to move into White areas will have succeeded. Still, this is sufficient to cause panic and fear among many Whites, as well as to extend the ghetto.

In the following example of the operation of the model, a simplified system of barriers was utilized, combining the real estate, financial, and White resistance barriers into a net probability of *not* succeeding in moving. The probabilities used in table 6, although hypothetical, are based closely on experience in Seattle and other cities.

White Reaction to Black Entry: II. Flight from the Area

The flight of Whites governs the creation of vacancies and is of fundamental importance (Rose, 1970).

Table 5. *Probability of White Resistance*

	Percentage of Blacks	
Class of Area	Under 15	Over 15 but under 50
Middle and upper	.30	.10
Lower	.60	.20

Table 6. *Probability of Not Being Able to Move, Because of Real Estate, Financial and White Resistance*

	Class of Destination Area										
	Middle Class (Percentage of Blacks)					Lower and Upper Class (Percentage of Blacks)					
Movers	5	5–15	15–25	25–35	35–50	5	5–15	15–25	25–35	35–50	50
Strongly motivated											
Lower class	.60	.50	.40	.30	.20	.75	.65	.55	.45	.35	.25
Middle class	.40	.30	.20	.10	.00	.55	.45	.35	.25	.15	.05
Weakly motivated											
Lower class	.80	.67	.55	.42	.30	1.00	.87	.75	.62	.50	.37
Middle class	.55	.42	.30	.17	.05	.75	.62	.50	.42	.25	.12

43

Table 7. *Probability of White Flight and Vacancy Creation* (*5-Year Period*)

Black (Percent)	Class of Area			
	Lower	Middle	Upper	Highly Educated
Under 5	.05	.10	.05	.00
5–15	.10	.10	.10	.00
15–30	.20	.35	.20	.10
30–50	.30	.50	.40	.20
50–100	.40	.60	.70	.40

Our knowledge of this process is again inadequate. As before, the probability that lower- and upper-classes will move is smaller than for the middle-classes; the higher educated are least likely to move. A plausible working set of probabilities is given in table 7.

During a given time period, when there is a high level of Blacks, lower-class residents are less likely to move because they are less able to do so. The identification of subareas with high levels of education is important, too, since they are the main areas likely to achieve a fairly stable integration.

Summary of Change

At the end of these steps, some areas will have had very little change, some will have remained White, and some will have integrated; whereas other areas will have increased in the proportion of Black, and some will have passed to almost totally Black. A new pattern of vacancies will be created by White flight which sets the stage for *repetition* of the entire process in the ensuing time period (in our example, about five years). The new pattern of Black population changes the areas of preference for those who would move from the ghetto and changes the probability of resistance in many areas.

Example Operation of the Model: Seattle

This model was applied to the Seattle ghetto ("Central Area") and the surrounding area of the central city for the period 1950 to 1970 (see also Morrill, 1965). For 1950–1960, the aim was to replicate as closely as possible the actual pattern of change. For 1960–1970, the aim was to predict the pattern of change, since at the time of this analysis 1970 control data were not available. The study area was divided into 40 analysis zones, generally halves of census tracts. A finer mesh would have been preferable but could not be utilized at this time. Five-year time periods, again larger than desirable, were used. All areas with sufficient Black population generated new households from natural increase and aging. A high rate of in-migration (60 percent) occurred in the period 1950–1960. New migrants were temporarily and proportionally assigned to all areas with over 10 percent Black population and were assumed to view the housing market from those locations.[1] Areas with over 40 percent Blacks were assumed to have some older residents who wanted to seek less segregated housing.

In order to illustrate the operation of the reasonably complex model, one may examine the assignment of movers from the northernmost ghetto core area, J1a, for the period 1955–1960 (figure 1). In 1955, according to results of the first stage, J1a had 422 Black house-

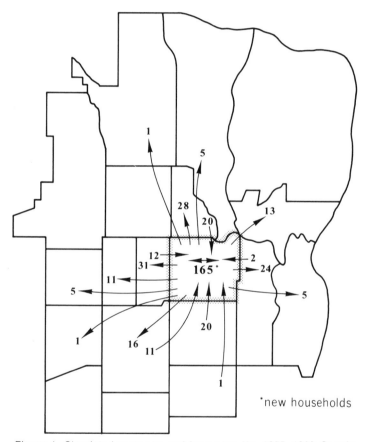

*new households

Figure 1. Simulated moves to and from area J1a, 1955–1960, Seattle central area.

1. Analysis of results suggests that this assignment caused excess dispersal; probably more of the migrants stayed temporarily in the more central parts of the ghetto (over one-third Black).

holds (64 percent of the population), 250 White households and 144 vacancies, most of which resulted from flight of Whites, given the increase in the Black population in the first stage. Thirty-three new households were formed; in-migration added 140. In addition, one-third (140) of the old families wished to move—half very strongly, half less strongly. Half the newcomers, 86 according to the model, will be expected to remain in the ghetto (J1a). From the composition of the population, the number of middle- and lower-class movers can be estimated (table 8).

Rearranged—of 100 lower-class movers, 70 strongly wish to move; 30 do not. Of 127 middle-class movers, 87 strongly wish to move; 40 do not. To allocate the movers to homes, we first arrange eligible (non-ghetto communities) by distance (table 9).

The spatial distribution of home seekers is given in table 10.

These potential movers must pass through real estate, financial, and White resistance barriers. These may be combined into a composite probability of not succeeding in moving, varying by class of mover, destination area, and motivation of the mover. From table 6, given knowledge of the areas, the barriers for the sample area may be computed (table 11).

When these probabilities were applied to the potential movers, the spatial distribution of final moves was produced (table 12).

Table 8. *Mobility in Sample Area*

86 new households wish to stay in ghetto, i.e., J1a
87 new households want to move out: 40 lower-class, 47 middle
70 old resident households strongly wish to leave: 30 lower-class, 40 middle
70 old resident households less strongly wish to leave: 30 lower-class, 40 middle

Table 9. *Probability of Moving to Non-ghetto Communities*

| Movers | | Communities |
Lower	Middle	
.40	.30	Adjacent, close: K2b, I3b, J2a
.30	.25	Adjacent, far: I2b, K2a
.20	.20	Next, close: K3, I3a
.10	.15	Next, far: I1b, J2c, K1a
	.10	Far: H2, I1a, K1b, I2a

Table 10. *Location of Potential Movers (Black Searchers)*

		K2b	I3b	J2a	I2b	K2a	K3	I3a	I1b	J2c	K1a	H2	I1a	K1b	I2a
Lower-	strong	11	11	11	8	8	6	6	3	3	3				
class	weak	5	6	6	3	3	2	2	1	1	1				
Middle-	strong	12	12	12	9	9	7	7	4	4	4	2	2	2	1
class	weak	5	6	6	4	4	3	3	2	2	2	1	1	1	

Table 11. *Probability of Not Succeeding in Moving*

		K2b	I3b	J2a	I2b	K2a	K3	I3a	I1b	J2c	K1a	H2	I1a	K1b	I2a
Lower	strong	.10	.30	.40	.50	.60	.20	.60	.60	.60	.60				
	weak	.20	.40	.55	.70	.80	.30	.80	.80	.80	.80				
Middle	strong	.00	.10	.20	.30	.40	.00	.40	.40	.40	.40	.40	.55	.40	.55
	weak	.00	.20	.30	.40	.55	.10	.55	.55	.55	.55	.55	.75	.55	.75

Table 12. *Destinations of Successful Movers*

	K2b	I3b	J2a	I2b	K2a	K3	I3a	I1b	J2c	K1a	H2	I1a	K1b	H2a
Lower	14	12	10	5	4	6	2	2	2	2				
Middle	17	16	14	8	7	10	5	3	3	3	1	1	1	

Table 13. *Growth of the Seattle Central Area 1950–1970*

Area	1950 Black Households	Percentage	1960 Black Households (Actual)	Percentage	Black Households (Simulated)	Percentage	1970 Black Households (Actual)	Percentage	Black Households (Simulated)	Percentage
H2	2		2	<1	9	<1	31	2	79	5—
I1a	0		2	<1	7	<1	45	5	87	10—
I1b	1		19	5	15	4	95	18	132	27
I2a	0		0		2	<1	20	1.5	48	4
I2b	3	1	28	11	38	13	55	15	133	35
I3a	0		3		35	5	30	4	135	20
I3b	55	14	203	49	155	40	230	55	328	80
J1a	340	48	645	89	508	72	600	92	694	93
J1b	310	44	580	81	468	65	550	88	654	89
J2a	15	3	247	52	157	31	400	80	405	80
J2b	27	5	270	58	195	38	450	82	466	83
J2c	0		14	2+	19	3	70	15	139	30
J2d	0		9	2+	29	10	80	25	150	49
J3a	127	17	470	69	378	57	500	88	574	85
J3b	108	15	435	69	420	68	600	92	658	90
K1a	2		1		21	1+	25	2	140	8
K1b	8		5		59	5	35	6	216	16
K2a	2		21	2+	72	8	130	12	158	16
K2b	136	25	284	70	268	68	350	80	353	80
K3	309	16	656	42	709	45	650	50	782	47
K4a	33	3	110	15	201	25	100	20	308	35
K4b	134	14	220	31	366	45	190	35	329	42
K5a	305	47	380	69	398	70	380	80	400	71
K5b	345	36	450	54	507	60	440	67	468	56
M1	80	2	85	6	98	7	90	12	90	6
O1	(400)	16	(350)	20	(370)	21	150	24	(350)	20
O2	(450)	15	(350)	18	(385)	20	160	20	(350)	18
O3	(50)	11	(25)	9	(40)	10	15	4	(25)	9
P1a	220	34	235	44	299	51	180	50	254	45
P1b	140	25	190	39	195	40	150	46	217	40
P2a	2		25	4—	115	13	100	12	244	30
P2b	26	4	100	15	94	14	150	22	292	41
P3			100	5			375	15	185	7
Q1a	228	20	685	55	644	63	800	75	959	82
Q1b	8		125	22	84	16	250	40	409	66
Q2a	155	12	105	12	224	18	500	40	311	28
Q2b			25	2			250	30	85	12
TOTAL	4,121		7,454				9,926		11,708	

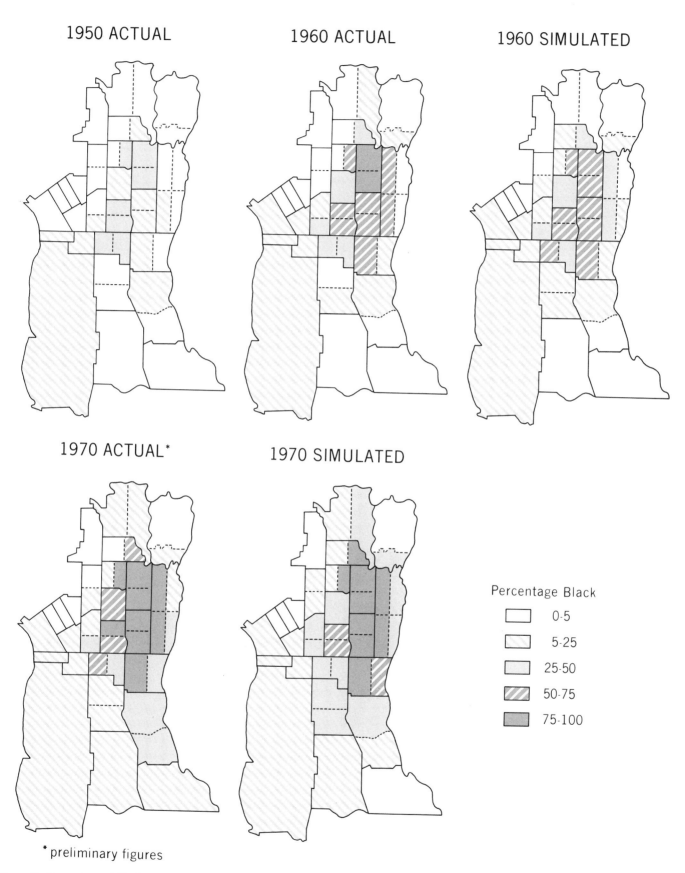

1950 ACTUAL   1960 ACTUAL   1960 SIMULATED

1970 ACTUAL*   1970 SIMULATED

Percentage Black

0-5

5-25

25-50

50-75

75-100

*preliminary figures

Figure 2. Percentage of Blacks among the population of the Seattle Central area.

When these are summed, it is found that 41 of the potential lower-class (of 100) and 38 of the middle-class movers (of 127) were not successful in moving out of the ghetto. These will remain in J1a. Of those that move, the majority move to areas with an already appreciable Black population. The pattern of moves is depicted in figure 1. Flows to J1a from other areas are included.

The results of the model for the decades 1950–1970, as summarized in table 13 and figure 2, are remarkably in accord with the actual pattern of moves. Until applied elsewhere, however, the generality of the model is untested. The pattern of errors is fairly simple. In general, the model failed to recognize the extent of upward social mobility—that is, it inflated the demand for lower-class homes and areas and underestimated the demand for middle-class housing. Thus, too many households were assigned to older, poorer parts of the ghetto (K4b, K5b) and too few to middle-class areas (J2a, J2b, J1a, J1b). At the same time, the model somewhat underestimated the rate of decline in moving with distance and also underestimated the strength of the barriers to movement by allowing a somewhat wide and large dispersion of movers.

Analysis of preliminary 1970 census results reveals that the predictive simulation could have been much better. Comparison of the actual and predicted Black households for 1970 (see table 13) indicates an almost universal overprediction which becomes especially marked in areas on the northern and western margins of the ghetto (H2, 12, 13, K1). The total number of Black households is far smaller than predicted. Perhaps half the difference is due to uncritical acceptance of high estimates of the Black population, thus exaggerating the migration pressure of the ghetto on surrounding areas. Also, the magnitude of the drop in housing stock (or demand for older housing by an upwardly social mobile group) in much of the core ghetto and adjacent poorer areas was unanticipated. This explains why such areas as J3, K3, K5, M1, O1, and P1 show a reduction in the number of Black households but an increase in the proportion of the Black population. Unfortunately, the other half of the explanation for overprediction is a failure to appreciate the radical change that took place in the direction of growth of the ghetto after 1960, namely a fairly rapid and large expansion to the South into areas not even included in the study area. This omission was critical; since in hindsight, there was plentiful evidence in 1960 that the area possessed just the appropriate set of characteristics for middle-class White flight in response to critical levels of Black entry which the model might well have been able to recognize. The model will be recalibrated, using added information, but there is no escaping the admissions that the predictive ability of the model might have been better and that its shortcomings were largely due to placing unnecessary restrictions on its free operation.

3. PROSPECTS FOR THE DISAPPEARANCE OF THE BLACK GHETTO

One credo of the liberal view of the future relations of Black and White in the United States is that integration means, among other things, the disappearance of the all-Black ghetto as a distinct segregated area. Such a prospect is far from certain, even if conditions within the ghetto and attitudes toward the Black minority were to change radically.

The "ghetto" has been described above as the geographic manifestation of a social phenomenon—the physical as well as social segregation of a group discriminated against by a more powerful one because of its real and/or perceived differences. The Afro-American and also the Puerto Rican and Mexican-American are the most recent targets of this process and are the present occupants of the ghettos (Handlin, 1959). It is popular among certain White groups to argue that since earlier occupants—the Irish, Italians, or Polish immigrants—have been rather thoroughly assimilated into the wider culture that the Black ghetto, too, is but a passing phenomenon. However, for good reasons, especially the sheer physical distinction of blackness and subsequent partially isolated cultural development, time may not erase this ghetto. In order to assess the prospects of a ghetto's disappearing, it is necessary to understand the conditions which created it. The ghetto of the American city appears to be a product of social incompatibility (a euphemism for fear and discrimination), poverty, and relative power (Mack, 1965; Myrdal, 1964). This process has been discussed in part 1.

The traditional route of escape from the ghetto has been to overcome social and economic differences gradually. Very small groups tended to quickly abandon their former customs and embrace the majority culture freely (this path is not readily available to the Blacks, of course). At the other extreme, very large groups have been able to obtain sufficient power to force the majority to accept the group as equal (Handlin, 1959). Now the Black minority is adopting this strategy, hoping, through power, to gain recognition as a distinct but equal segment of the American culture.

It is essential to realize that when the ghetto occupants became Blacks from the American South, rather than European immigrants, a whole new level of fears emerged—the obvious physical and rather great cultural differences unleashed far more basic physical and psychological fears among Whites which in turn led to much more formidable barriers to social contact and more effective means for maintaining physical segregation. The ghetto occupant, naturally, reacted to outside hostility by turning inward for protection— along the whole spectrum from physical security to ease of social interaction within the group (Clark, 1965; Weaver, 1948).

Maintenance of the Ghetto: Enforcement of Segregation

To assess the chances of the ghetto's disappearing, one must ask whether the forces that maintain segregation are likely to be overcome. As discussed in part 2, forces external to the ghetto include (1) legal barriers, (2) discriminatory real estate practices, (3) discriminatory financial practices, (4) organized resistance groups, and (5) land-use barriers (Becker, 1957; McEntire, 1960). Internal forces include (1) poverty, (2) fear of the consequences of trying to escape, and (3) preference for the group.

Prior to 1950, both recommendations and prescriptions against mixed racial occupancy were incorporated into federal, state, and local housing legislation (Million, 1963). After direct legal barriers were removed, the real estate industry, obviously in co-operation with the average seller or renter, easily maintained segregation by such methods as refusing to show the home to potential buyers, saying it had already been sold, quoting an inflated price, and other impossible conditions. The banking industry co-operated by refusing to make loans to Blacks or by demanding impossibly high down payments or security conditions (McEntire, 1960). Indeed, the ostensible reason for the real estate's or banking industry's discriminatory practices was the argument that racial integration in an area would reduce property values. Since this was known to be false, the real reason was reduced simply to White fear of physical and cultural differences (Laurenti, 1960).

The bounds of the ghetto are more easily maintained, too, if the residents of adjacent areas can create a strong community organization. These seem most effective in areas of poor Whites who are unable to escape to better housing elsewhere and who are dominantly of one ethnic and religious background (Spear, 1967). Organizations reduce the temptation to flee the proximity of the ghetto and make much more ominous the risks to possible pioneers from the ghetto. Finally, it is clear that certain kinds of land use such as cemeteries, large parks, freeways or railways, and industrial corridors can serve as effective buffers between a ghetto and the White population, and there is some evidence that freeways or parks have been purposely located to provide such limits (Weaver, 1948; Edwards, 1970).

Poverty alone prevents much of the ghetto population from seeking different housing (Becker, 1957). More importantly, the ghetto is not likely to have more than its share of "heroes"—that is, Black families who are willing to risk probable psychological and physical harassment and long-term social ostracism of themselves and their children if they choose to move into an all-White area. It takes a high level of dissatisfaction with the ghetto, a great dedication to the cause of integration, much courage, and faith in the ability of the Whites to change attitudes to become a pioneer (Clark, 1965). To a sizeable, but unknown, proportion of ghetto residents, the company of one another and qualities of the Black community and culture are more important than the discomforts and psychology of the ghetto (Detwiler, 1966).

Can the Black Ghetto Be Ended?

There is very little reason to expect the imminent disappearance of the ghetto since those conditions noted previously have not changed much nor are they likely to change sufficiently for a long time to come (Downs, 1965). Neither Blacks nor Whites are really ready for residential integration so long as the majority of Whites remain fearful, awkward, and paternalistic in the midst of Blacks and so long as the majority of Blacks remain convinced that the Whites do not really understand or accept them, and indeed so long as social and political advantages of the ghetto are perceived to more than offset its physical, economic, and psychological drawbacks. Black people now realize that "equality" and "integration" are not inherent qualities of society because the law so specifies, rather they are belated recognitions of achieved status—an acceptance usually forced upon the majority (the word "earned" is preferred by this majority).

"Black Power" and the Ghetto

To some extent, then, "Black Power" represents the following of a traditional route to acceptance. Through united action, racial instead of ethnic solidarity in this case, political power can perhaps be obtained. In turn, this may provide the leverage or pressure for access to better economic and educational opportunities and higher income. Like the earlier large White minorities, the Blacks realize that such opportunities are simply not going to be freely offered but have to be fought for (Carmichael and Hamilton, 1968).

Integration, in the sense of physical dispersion of Blacks, is looked upon by many Blacks as something that might be ultimately desirable or possible but currently useless (Clark, 1965). Many Black people fear that dispersion will only aggravate their economic and psychological weakness. As long as the White man *considers* and *treats* the Black man as "different" and "inferior," mere physical integration will only reinforce the current pattern of superiority–inferiority relations.

The logic behind Black solidarity is that only after greater power is achieved and acceptance as equals is admitted can Blacks afford to give up the social, psychological, and economic security of the ghetto. The Black man may be equal to the White on any number of objective measures, but the achievement of power through united effort is needed, not only to pry recognition from Whites, but also to create awareness of his own potentials and to generate self-confidence (Carmichael and Hamilton, 1968; Mack, 1965).

Open Housing?

To the extent that Black people believe this, then even White promotion of physical integration, which is not too likely, will not bring about the disappearance of the ghetto (Sloane, 1968). From the regularity with which they have defeated the most innocuous open-housing ordinances, the White majority evidently believes that Blacks are anxious to abandon the ghetto. The evidence is contrary. In cities or states with open-housing legislation, the Black and White ghettos are as intact as ever; only a minimal number of court cases have been generated. Evasion of open-housing laws is not difficult; and even where laws exist, Blacks do not in fact have free access. Civil rights groups in many cities do have fair-housing lists of homes outside the ghetto available for Blacks, but they have few takers, often because of cost. Quite probably, even the new federal open-housing occupancy law will have only minimal effects in the short run, contrary to White belief.

Assume (and this implies revolutionary change!) that economic, political, educational, and employment equality have been achieved and, as a consequence, at least grudging acceptance as social—man-to-man—equals. Would physical integration then come about? It is difficult to speculate because the Black man has never been afforded the choice. Perhaps very gradually, interspersal would occur, although not to a degree much greater than the concomitant rate of intermarriage which is a logical consequence of true acceptance but also highly unpredictable.[2] However, some fairly high proportion of Blacks might even then prefer to stay together for a variety of reasons. One potent reason, which the White community is loath to accept, is that the Black community may have something going for it—that is, the Black way of life has some creative

2. Of course, there has long since been much admixture, but most Whites will not admit it.

and exciting qualities that the White lacks—even though most of the culture may coincide (Carmichael and Hamilton, 1968; Hannerz, 1969).

The Black Ghetto in the Context of the Future American Metropolis

Although many central cities may have Black majorities within the next generation, the Black proportion of the SMSA (Standard Metropolitan Statistical Area) will rarely exceed one-fifth (Taueber and Taueber, 1965). The Blacks have a logical interest in legal separateness, in order to permit or maintain political power; the Whites, in order to keep the Blacks out. There is the risk, too, of gaining power just when the city has become non-viable (Friesma, 1969). There is also increasing recognition that meeting the problems and future needs of the city requires a metropolitan approach. Metropolitan government might be expected to aid in reconstruction of the central city and in the gradual breakdown of the ghetto.

Achieving Income Equality

Whether or not the Black man desires in the end to become physically integrated, what are the chances of obtaining economic equality? Will "Black Power" help achieve it? The Black man has little choice but to try it. Waiting for law and good will to effect the necessary change has obviously been frustratingly slow. Why should people wait another century for what is morally and legally theirs now? More and more Black people are willing, in pursuing "Black Power," to risk the alienation of moderate Whites as well as the backlash of the less sympathetic, since the patient approach has long been tried and found wanting (Carmichael and Hamilton, 1968).

The economic goal of "Black Power" is partly to force free entry into the labor market—all sectors at all levels—but mainly to foster Black ownership in and control of Black communities. The commissions convened to study the "Negro problem" are still far behind. They continue to hope that prejudice and discriminatory thinking and actions will melt away if society but invests enough in "social capital," i.e., in urban renewal housing, education (including Head Start and other compensatory programs), and job training. Poverty areas in general, often predominantly Black areas today, have received grossly inadequate investment in public services and social capital—schools are often old and poorly maintained and staffed, libraries are often absent, police protection is lacking, parks and playgrounds are few and poor. The costs of long-term neglect are surely enormous (Clark, 1965).

Nevertheless, as desirable and necessary as these programs are, their effects will be long range, and they cannot undo the simple fact that equivalently educated and trained Black people do *not* have equal access to jobs, do not get equal pay for the same work, and do not have the same job security. In Chicago in 1965, of 6,838 executives with decision-making power in private occupations, only 42 were Black (Baron, 1968). In the final analysis, there is but one conclusion possible: on the average, the employer discriminates because of blackness (and associated cultural attributes). There is no other explanation for the facts. A corollary conclusion is that some occupations in which Blacks are prominently represented are underpaid—no matter how hard the work, for example, personal service, the price he can command will leave a worker in poverty (Taueber and Taueber, 1965). The exponent of "Black Power" knows that these conditions will not just disappear and that united action via political power and the power of disruption through demonstrations will probably be required to bring change.

The question is often asked: why haven't the Blacks brought themselves up by the bootstraps like the other groups? Why should they get special help today? We should keep in mind three major differences between the Black American today and the earlier poor immigrants. (1) The latter were not Black, hence, there was some assurance that acceptance would follow economic improvement—this is not so for the Blacks. (2) The latter were not slaves. As free men, they fervently believed in and strove for the riches America promised, but the psychology of centuries of enforced second-class status is not easily overcome. (3) The White immigrants' labor, usually unskilled, was desperately needed in the building of the nation's rails, cities, and industries. Technical change has far upgraded the average level of skill needed by those entering the labor force today. The large immigrant groups all gradually achieved economic and political power and, therefore, acceptance into the American mainstream. If, in spite of the above difficulties, the Black man, too, achieves such power, a similar "melting out" of the ghetto *cannot* be expected to follow, because of the overpowering distinction of color.

Prospects of Black Power for Achieving Equality

If Blacks remain concentrated in central cities which continue to be separately administered, then we may expect Black majorities to achieve political control of several cities within the next decade. Certainly, control of the police force could ameliorate one of the major perceived complaints—police harassment. The resultant greater pride and self-assurance might be expected to help sustain separation. Political control could also serve to equalize the quality and quantity of public services and social capital — transportation, education, police protection, and parks. Political power, however, is not likely to raise income levels, even if control of the "war on poverty" funds resulted in direct investment in Black-owned businesses, Black home ownership, etc. (Friesma, 1969). The creation of Negro business is an understandable reaction to White administration. Unfortunately, the viability and variety of such enterprises is severely limited by generally low income levels, so that businesses initiated and operated by Black entrepreneurs are not likely to thrive until Blacks have equal access to the general industrial and service employment structure.

Are Radical Proposals Needed?

The least that will be necessary appears to be federal programs which subsidize employers in hiring and training Blacks and for the federal government to become the "employer of last resort." The latter, of course, is both recognition of and compliance with a system of discrimination. Actually, far more radical programs may be needed — including the interposition of federal representatives in the hiring and firing process itself (rather like the federal voting registrars) and imposition of much higher minimum wages (probably $2.50).[3]

The threat of interference in personnel decisions may be enough to bring radical improvement. It may be argued that raising minimum wages will be inflationary and "will take away jobs from the very people you're trying to help." But perhaps the lowest sectors are underpaid more because of their bargaining weakness than because of low productivity. The elimination of jobs which inherently enslave one to poverty is not to be regretted. Unless occupations can give decent returns to the worker, they ought not to exist.

CONCLUSION

The Black community may prefer to remain and work together in order to achieve economic and political equality. The White majority, however, may strongly resist the measures that are probably necessary to bring about radical change, so that the realistic expectation is for an era of greater unrest and bitterness.

Some White and Black leaders suggest an alternate route to equality, beginning with physical integration and eventually reaching economic equality and social acceptance. In this somewhat paternalistic approach, the Black population is purposefully dispersed. Although the families are not truly accepted, the children

3. A wage of $1.50 will yield an annual income of but $3,000. Even $2.50 is far from affluent: $5,000.

55

attend school with the more "advantaged" White children and become accepted by them, so that presumably the next generation will be naturally received into both good jobs and general social circles. This method is, indeed, chosen by some Blacks, and it works reasonably well in areas where there are rather few Blacks, probably well under 5 percent. A necessary price, however, is the abandonment of any elements of a "Black" culture, and many Blacks are not willing to take this step. Also, most of the Black population live in such large concentrations that the Whites could not or would not adopt such a policy. Nevertheless, this author remains an "unreconstructed" liberal who believes that a plural society with separate Black and White cultures is inherently unstable and violent and, in the long run, that total integration, including intermarriage, is the only solution to the "American Dilemma."

The disappearance or maintenance of the Black ghetto, then, rests ultimately on the perseverance of a discriminatory reaction to color and on the persistence of a somewhat distinct Black culture. If the Whites abandon the former and Blacks the latter, integration in all its manifestations may occur. But there is little precedence in human history to expect either.

REFERENCES CITED

Baron, Harold M. 1968. "Black Powerlessness in Chicago." *Transaction* 6:27–33.

Beauchamp, A. 1966. "Processual Indices of Segregation: Some Preliminary Comments." *Behavioral Science* 11:190–92.

Becker, G. 1957. *The Economics of Discrimination.* Chicago: University of Chicago Press.

Bennett, Lerone, Jr. 1964. *Before the Mayflower.* rev. ed. Baltimore: Penguin Books.

Blauner, Robert. 1969. "Internal Colonialism and Ghetto Revolt." *Social Problems* 16:393–408.

Blumberg, Leonard. 1964. "Segregated Housing, Marginal Location, and the Crisis of Confidence." *Phylon* 25:321–30.

Blumberg, Leonard and Lalli, Michael. 1966. "Little Ghettoes: A Study of Negroes in the Suburbs." *Phylon* 27:117–31.

Bontemps, Arna and Conroy, Jack. 1966. *Anyplace But Here.* New York: Hill and Wang.

Brandt, Lillian. 1903. "Negroes of St. Louis." *Journal of the American Statistical Association* 8:203–68.

Carmichael, Stokely and Hamilton, Charles V. 1968. *Black Power, The Politics of Liberation in America.* New York: Random House.

Clark, Kenneth. 1965. *Dark Ghetto.* New York: Harper and Row.

Conrad, Earl. 1966. *The Invention of the Negro.* New York: Paul S. Erickson.

Detwiler, Bruce. 1966. "A Time to be Black." *New Republic* 156:18–22.

De Vise, Pierre, et. al. 1969. *Slum Medicine: Chicago's Apartheid Health System.* Chicago: Community and Family Study Center, University of Chicago.

Downs, A. 1965. "The Future of American Ghettoes." *Daedalus* 97:1346–47.

Drake, St. Clair and Cayton, Horace. 1962. *Black Metropolis.* New York: Harper and Row.

Edwards, Ozzie. 1970. "Patterns of Residential Segregation within a Metropolitan Ghetto." *Demography* 7:187.

Farley, Reynolds. 1968. "The Urbanization of Negroes in the United States." *Journal of Social History* 1:241–441.

Friesma, H. Paul. 1969. "Black Control of Central Cities: The Hollow Prize." *Journal of the American Institute of Planners* 35:75–79.

Glazer, Nathan and McEntire, Davis, eds. 1960. *Studies in Housing and Minority Groups.* Berkeley: University of California Press.

Green, Constance McLaughlin. 1967. *The Secret City.* Princeton: Princeton University Press.

Handlin, Oscar. 1959. *The Newcomers.* New York: Harvard University Press.

Hannerz, Ulf. 1969. *Soulside, An Inquiry into Ghetto Culture.* New York: Columbia University Press.

Hansell, Ch. R. and Clark, W. A. V. 1970. "Expansion of the Negro Ghetto in Milwaukee." *Tijdschrift voor Economische en Sociale-geographie* 61:267–77.

Hart, John F. 1960. "The Changing Distribution of the American Negro." *Annals of the Association of American Geographers* 50: 242–66.

Jacobs, Paul. 1966. *Prelude to Riot.* New York: Random House.

Laurenti, Luigi. 1960. *Property Values and Race.* Berkeley: Commission on Race and Housing, University of California Press.

Lowi, Theodore J. 1970. "Apartheid U.S.A." *Transaction* 7:32–39.

McEntire, Davis. 1960. *Residence and Race.* Berkeley: University of California Press.

Mack, Raymond. 1965. *Race, Class and Power.* New York: American Book Company.

Marston, Wilfred. 1969. "Socioeconomic Differences within Negro Areas of American Cities." *Social Forces* 48:67–68.

Meier, August and Radwick, Elliot. 1966. *From Plantation to Ghetto.* New York: Hill and Wang.

Milio, Nancy. 1970. *9226 Kercheval.* Ann Arbor: University of Michigan Press.

Million, Elmer M. 1963. "Racial Restrictive Covenants Revisited." in Alfred Avins, ed. *Open Occupancy vs. Forced Housing Under the Fourteenth Amendment: Symposium.* New York: Bookmailer.

Moore, William, Jr. 1969. *The Vertical Ghetto.* New York: Random House.

Morrill, Richard L. 1965. "The Negro Ghetto: Problems and Alternatives," *Geographical Review* 55:339–61.

Muth, Richard. 1969. *Cities and Housing.* Chicago: University of Chicago Press.

Myrdal, Gunnar. 1964. *An American Dilemma.* New York: McGraw-Hill.

Rapkin, Chester and Grigsby, William. 1960. *The Demand for Housing in Racially Mixed Areas.* Berkeley: Commission on Race and Housing, University of California Press.

Rose, Harold M. 1969. "Social Processes in the City: Race and Urban Residential Choice." Washington, D.C.: Commission on College Geography Resource Paper No. 6.

Rose, Harold. 1969. "Origin and Pattern of Development of Urban Black Social Areas." *Journal of Geography* 7:327–32.

Rose, Harold. 1970. "Development of an Urban Sub-system: The Case of the Negro Ghetto." *Annals of the Association of American Geographers* 60:1–17.

Sloane, Martin E. 1968. "The Housing Act of 1968: Best Yet But Is It Enough?" *Civil Rights Digest* 1:1–19.

Smith, T. Lynn. 1966. "The Redistribution of the Negro Population of the United States." *Journal of Negro History* 51:155–73.

Spear, Allen H. 1967. *Black Chicago.* Chicago: University of Chicago Press.

Still, William. 1871. *The Underground Railroad.* Philadelphia: People's Publishing Co.

Taeuber, Karl and Taeuber, Alma F. 1965. "The Changing Character of Negro Migration." *American Journal of Sociology* 70:429–41.

Taeuber, Karl and Taeuber, Alma F. 1965. *Negroes in Cities*. Chicago: Aldine Publishing Co.

Taeuber, Karl. 1968. "Change and Transition of the Black Population in the United States." *Population Index* 34:124–45.

Wade, Richard C. 1964. *Slavery in the Cities: The South 1820–1860*. New York: Oxford University Press.

Weaver, Robert. 1948. *The Negro Ghetto*. New York: Harcourt, Brace.

Wolf, E. P. 1963. "The Tipping Point in Racially Changing Neighborhoods." *Journal of the American Institute of Planners* 29:217–22.

Zelder, Raymond. 1970. "Racial Segregation in Urban Housing Markets." *Journal of Regional Science* 10:96–101.

3

BLACK COMMUNITIES:
A PROGRAM FOR
INTERDISCIPLINARY RESEARCH

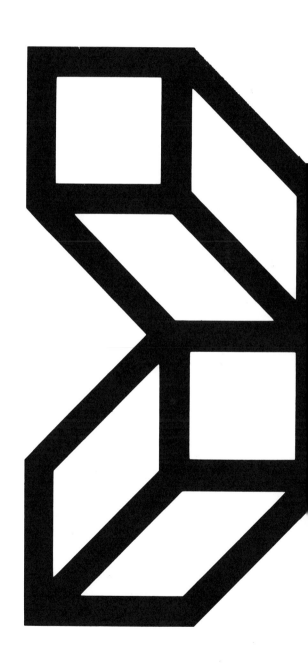

Stephen Gale*
Northwestern University

David M. Katzman
University of Kansas

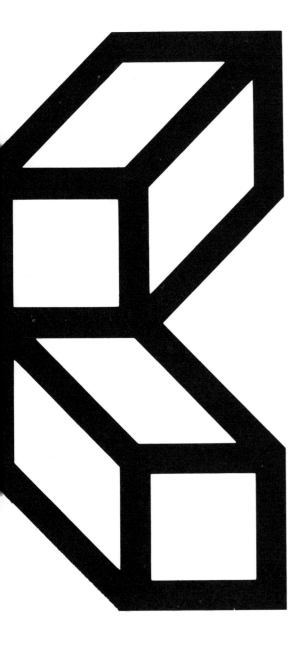

Black Communities: A Program for Interdisciplinary Research

ABSTRACT

This paper outlines a program for exploratory research into Black residential mobility and neighborhood development. The argument is presented in three parts. First, a discussion of the limitations of much of the previous research on the social history and the residential and socio-economic mobility patterns of Blacks in the United States is given. In the second section, an outline of a comprehensive methodology which avoids some of these limitations is proposed: it includes (A) the employment of disaggregated data and (B) a methodological strategy based on the use of dynamic contingency tables, and associated statistical techniques for analyzing these matrices. The final section provides an illustration of the use of this methodology on data from a recent study of Black residential mobility in a small Michigan community in the nineteenth century.

*The support of the Social Science Research Council, Research Training Fellowship, is gratefully acknowledged.

Our knowledge of Black communities is, at best, scattered and primitive. Generalizations about Black America, when they are available at all, have usually been made without either a firm empirical foundation or a comprehensive descriptive and analytical methodology. The result has been that while it is known—and here only to a limited extent—what is unique about Philadelphia Negroes in 1898, Harlem in 1900, or Black Chicago in 1910, little knowledge has been gained of how and why Black communities form or how they change over time.[1] Existing studies have, for example, treated Black communities as if they were composed of homogeneous groups of individuals or of census tracts and wards. This knowledge is important, of course, but it also tends to be short-sighted, viewing society only at the extreme micro- or macro-level. Black America, and indeed any community, must be viewed as a dynamic component of society in which men and women, their families and children, their jobs and homes, their churches and clubs, change over the course of their lives, their parents' lives, their grandparents' lives, and so forth. Furthermore, this view must not be related only to Chicago and New York, but must include Ann Arbor, Michigan; Langston, Oklahoma; Mound Bayou, Mississippi—all of those places where Black communities have developed.

In this paper, a program for the systematic examination of historical patterns of residential and social mobility in Black communities and neighborhoods will be outlined. Disaggregated individual-level information on the structure, distribution, and mechanisms of residential change will be the empirical basis of the program. The study itself will focus on the investigation of the contingent relationship of various social and economic characteristics and their effect on the propensity to change residences. The proposed program is thus viewed as providing a foundation for the investigation of the determinants of the demand aspects of intraurban residential location processes where the distribution and structure of the population at several time periods are depicted. Using methods similar to those employed in the analysis of demographic change and social mobility patterns, the mechanisms (or processes) of transformation can be identified. Since these data consist of observations of individual movements and their associated socio-economic conditions, inferences concerning the behavioral antecedents should also be possible. The intention therefore is to detail a methodology which employs a rich descriptive foundation as the basis for explanatory inferences and hypothesis formulation. This direction follows to some extent from the recent comments on the initiation of social and demographic analysis by Orcutt et al. (1961), Goodman (1964), Nordbotten (1970), and others;[2] in

1. W. E. B. DuBois, *The Philadelphia Negro* (1899; reprint ed., New York: Schocken Books, 1967); G. Osofsky, *Harlem: The Making of a Ghetto* (New York: Harper & Row, 1966); A. H. Spear, *Black Chicago: The Making of a Negro Ghetto, 1890–1920* (Chicago: University of Chicago Press, 1967).

2. G. H. Orcutt et al. *Microanalysis of Socioeconomic Systems: A Simulation Study* (New York: Harper, 1961). Their argument, stated briefly, is that there is "some reason to hope that the reliability of the predictions might be improved if they were generated by a model constructed in terms of the behavior and interaction of the fundamental units of our socioeconomic system" (p. 13). Also see, L. A. Goodman, "How to Ransack Social Mobility Tables and Other Kinds of Cross-Classification Tables," *American Journal of Sociology* 70 (July, 1969): 564–85; S. Nordbotten, "Individual Data Files and Their Utilization in Socio-Demographic Model Building in the Norwegian Central Bureau of Statistics," *Review of the International Statistical Institute* 38 (1970): 193–201; I. Blumen, M. Kogan, and P. J. McCarthy, *The Industrial Mobility of Labor as a Probability Process* (Ithaca, N.Y.: New York State School of Industrial and Labor Relations, Cornell University, 1955); C. C. Harris, *A Stochastic Model of Suburban Development* (Technical Report No. 1, Center for Real Estate and Urban Economics, Institute of Urban and Regional Development, Berkeley, 1966); and S. Gale, "Explanation Theory and Models of Migration" (Paper presented to the Third Conference on the Mathematics of Population, Chicago, Illinois, July, 1970).

effect, it may be regarded as a means for using data on individuals to describe and explain macro-level processes. The emphasis on *Black* communities in particular stems from the importance of racial and ethnic neighborhoods in American society.

In view of these very general aims, three specific areas of interest for the proposed methodology may be discerned: (A) description, (B) explanation, and (C) hypothesis formulation.

A. Description

The empirical foundation of the proposed program is the use of disaggregated historical information of individual residence locations and socio-economic status in the detailed description of migration patterns. A time-dependent contingency table or K^N model is employed as the basis of the description (see section 2). The description itself is composed of a distribution of individuals in the classificatory states of the contingency table (e.g., by residence and social class categories) and a transition matrix which expresses the (observed) probability of changing states in a given time period. Additional descriptions of those individuals who enter and leave the system can also be obtained. This part of the program is, of course, closely linked with data collection and classification.

B. Explanation

For present purposes, explanation may be defined as "discerning patterns from descriptive information."[3] Given a descriptive characterization in the form of a multi-way contingency table (as noted above), it will thus be possible to examine four classes of explanatory hypotheses: (1) temporal and spatial stationarities; (2) temporal properties of the processes of change; (3) degree of association (or correlation) among attributes; and (4) differences among tables. Methods for evaluating each of these classes of hypotheses will be outlined below (see section 2).

The explanatory value of each of these classes of hypotheses is related to an a priori theoretical conception of the residential mobility process. In particular, the methodology is directed at the following types of questions.

1a. Given a particular classification of residential neighborhoods (e.g., as designated by the percentage of residents who are Black), do the probabilities of each of the particular migration patterns (i.e., descriptions) remain invariant over time?

1b. Are these patterns spatially invariant?

2. Are the residential mobility patterns best described by first, second, or m-th ordered processes? (That

3. For a more detailed discussion of this point, see Gale, "Explanation Theory."

is, to what extent does the past history of the migration process determine its subsequent distribution? Clearly, this is closely linked with both the particular time interval over which the process is defined as well as the measure of time which is employed.)

3. To what extent does each of the social and economic variables (given in the data set) influence the pattern of residential mobility?

4a. Are the movement patterns invariant for different segments of the population?

4b. What subgroups of the population are distinctive in their pattern of movement behavior? Do these subgroup affiliations influence the formation and growth of neighborhoods?

The proposed program is therefore concerned not so much with deductions from known laws but rather with the organization and unification of observations and low-level generalizations. The methodology may be regarded more as a means of "structured induction" or "pattern recognition and specification" than a hypothetical-deductive process of theory confirmation.

C. Hypothesis Formulation

Perhaps the most important part of the proposed research program is its capacity to provide a rational basis for the formulation of general hypotheses. The questions which were noted above can be answered only in terms of information relating to the data of specific communities. Our over-all concern, however, is with residential mobility and neighborhood development in a more comprehensive sense. Thus, the extension of these questions to general hypotheses which can be tested on a wide variety of communities constitutes a major aim of the proposed methodology. It should be noted that the use of disaggregated data and an inductive view of analytical methodology is particularly important here. The data, for example, can be collected (e.g., from the available published sources) on a uniform (disaggregated) level. Classification procedures which are functionally oriented rather than locationally or temporally specific can also be clearly specified. The contingency tables and the associated non-parametric statistical tests will then provide a representational model from which additional explanatory insights may be formulated.[4]

In the short run, then, the aim of the proposed program is to present a foundation for a detailed, historical account of the demand aspects of the process of residential mobility and neighborhood development.[5] In the long run, however, by systematically testing hypotheses on a wider range of communities, it is ex-

4. For a more detailed discussion of this point, see M. Bunge, "Phenomenological Theories," in M. Bunge, ed., *The Critical Approach to Science and Philosophy* (Glencoe, Ill.: The Free Press, 1964), pp. 234–54.

5. All of the questions thus far noted pertain particularly to the consumer (or demand) aspects of residential mobility. Individual residential patterns are incorporated within a description of the general pattern for the community. Social and economic factors act as (explanatory) conditional predicates. No attempt is made, however, to include a description or explanation of the supply aspects. Previous studies have indicated that this information is almost impossible to obtain and, where it is available (say, for housing purchases), it is nevertheless incomplete.

pected that a comprehensive picture of the antecedents, processes, and consequences of residential change and neighborhood growth can also be developed.

The discussion of the program will be developed as follows: after outlining some of the background material on Black communities, and social and residential mobility (section 1), a detailed discussion of the proposed methodology will be presented (section 2). To illustrate the argument, several examples from a recent study will then be given (section 3). Section 4 summarizes the main points of the discussion and offers some tentative conclusions regarding the efficacy of the proposed research strategy.

1. BACKGROUND: BLACK SOCIAL HISTORY AND RESIDENTIAL MOBILITY

The social history of Black communities and neighborhoods has been treated on a number of occasions; but, for the most part, these studies have suffered from a distinct lack of much important information.[6] Unlike the social structure of White communities, which has drawn some degree of attention, the study of Black society has been hampered by both a dearth of strictly empirical information and a failure to employ consistent descriptive and explanatory procedures. The available studies are important, of course, but, as noted above, they tend to be short-sighted—viewing society only at the extreme micro- or macro-level.

To paraphrase Thernstrom,[7] ahistorical social science is often as narrow and superficial as primitive interdisciplinary history, and it is certainly no less common. Thernstrom used disaggregated data to test the conclusions of Warner's "Yankee City" research[8] and has demonstrated that there are errors in Warner's arguments which are linked not only to weak analytical techniques but also to "ahistorical methodological presuppositions." Historians and sociologists who sought to correct this limitation have not fared much better. Recent research, including studies such as Rogoff's *Recent Trends in Occupational Mobility* and Davidson and Anderson's earlier *Occupational Mobility in an American Community,* which deal primarily with the occupational mobility of a son vis-à-vis his father at given points in time, has generally neglected the historical setting.[9] When individual cases have been grouped into aggregated occupational categories, people are viewed independently of their temporal and spatial roots, thereby suggesting that they are uninfluenced by the world around them.

This point is also well illustrated by those historians who have pioneered in the use of disaggregated data—e.g., Handlin, *Boston's Immigrants;* Curti, *The Making*

6. The problems in this area are legion. Among the best studies, some have suffered from ahistoricism—e.g., DuBois, *Philadelphia Negro;* J. Dollard, *Caste and Class in a Southern Town* (New Haven: Yale University Press, 1937); A. Davis, B. Gardiner, and M. Gardner, *Deep South* (Chicago: University of Chicago Press, 1941); and H. Lewis, *Blackways of Kent* (Chapel Hill: University of North Carolina Press, 1955). Some have suffered from focusing on only a segment of the community—e.g., E. F. Frazier, *Black Bourgeoisie* (Glencoe, Ill.: The Free Press, 1957), and most have suffered from an unsystematic approach—e.g., Spear, *Black Chicago;* Osofsky, *Harlem;* S. M. Scheiner, *Negro Mecca* (New York: New York University Press, 1965); and R. A. Warner, *New Haven's Negroes* (New Haven: Yale University Press, 1949). The few attempting a systematic and comprehensive approach have failed to use all the data available—e.g., St. C. Drake and H. Cayton, *Black Metropolis: A Study of Negro Life in a Northern City* (New York: Harcourt Brace, 1945).

7. S. Thernstrom, *Poverty and Progress: Social Mobility in a Nineteenth Century City* (Cambridge, Mass.: Harvard University Press, 1964), p. 225.

8. W. Warner and P. Lunt, *The Social Life of a Modern Community* (New Haven: Yale University Press, 1941); Warner and Lunt, *The Status System of a Modern Community* (New Haven: Yale University Press, 1942); Warner and L. Srole, *The Social Systems of American Ethnic Groups* (New Haven: Yale University Press, 1945); Warner and J. O. Low, *The Social System of the Modern Factory* (New Haven: Yale University Press, 1947); and Warner, *The Living and The Dead: A Study of the Symbolic Life of Americans* (New Haven: Yale University Press, 1959).

9. N. Rogoff, *Recent Trends in Occupational Mobility* (Glencoe, Ill.: The Free Press, 1953); P. E. Davidson and H. D. Anderson, *Occupational Mobility in an American Community* (Stanford: Stanford University Press, 1937).

of An American Community; and even Thernstrom, *Poverty and Progress* — in that they have often failed to analyze systematically patterns of social change.[10] Methodological errors and errors of neglect have led to somewhat tenuous empirical conclusions and even more limited theoretical contributions. Furthermore, structural change such as "occupational mobility is [often] studied as an index of the relative 'openness' of a social structure."[11] This concern has led researchers to seek confirmation or denial (depending upon the investigator's outlook) of the democratic nature of the American economic order.[12] Thernstrom and Knights's recent work on urban population mobility is one of the first studies to employ extensive disaggregated data as the basis for inductive inference concerning residential change.[13] However, since their research stresses population turnover in urban areas rather than the *process* of residential mobility *within* a city, its orientation is somewhat different from that which has been proposed here.

The various studies of individual Black communities have also been as myopic as those which have gone under the broader framework of social and residential mobility. The larger number of works have dealt primarily with Black–White relations whether by design or by inadequacy of research.[14] A smaller and potentially more valuable group has dealt with the Black community itself, focusing mainly on the biographies of individuals and institutions and on aggregate residential patterns. A few of these more incisive studies — such as those dealing with Chicago by Drake and Cayton and by Spear — have examined institutional and community structure, but these also suffer from inadequate data foundations.[15] An exception to this is Katzman's *Before the Ghetto* which is perhaps the first study to use disaggregated data to focus on the formation and internal structure of a Black community.[16]

In the social sciences, the emphasis on mobility research has been more formal. Two classes of studies can be distinguished: (A) the development of formal models of social and residential mobility, and (B) the analysis of survey data to discern the causes of migration behavior.

A. Formal Models of Social and Residential Mobility

The so-called "social gravity" model was probably the first attempt to provide a formal model of migration behavior. In effect, it may be regarded as an analogue of the Newtonian gravitation formulation which describes the interactions (e.g., migrations) between places as functions of an individual's origin and destination, their respective populations, and the distance between them.[17] The explanatory connection here is

10. O. Handlin, *Boston's Immigrants: A Study in Acculturation* (rev. ed.; Cambridge: Harvard University Press, 1959); M. E. Curti, *The Making of an American Community: A Case Study of Democracy in a Frontier Community* (Stanford: Stanford University Press, 1959); Thernstrom, *Poverty and Progress.*

11. Rogoff, *Occupational Mobility*, p. 19.

12. Curti's subtitle "A Case Study of Democracy in a Frontier Community" reveals his concern in *The Making of an American Community* as does Thernstrom's title *Poverty and Progress* taken from Henry George's *Progress and Poverty.* O. Pancoast, Jr., in *Occupational Mobility: Democratic Efficiency through the Use of Human Resources* (New York: Columbia University Press, 1941) began his study with the challenge to America by the totalitarian nations of the 1930s.

13. S. Thernstrom and P. R. Knights, "Men in Motion: Some Data and Speculations about Urban Population Mobility in Nineteenth Century America," *Journal of Interdisciplinary History* 1 (1970): 7–35.

14. The traditional studies of Black communities, such as Osofsky's *Harlem* fall in this category as well as works such as Constance McGreen's *The Secret City* (Princeton: Princeton University Press, 1968).

15. Drake and Cayton, *Black Metropolis;* Spear, *Black Chicago.*

16. David M. Katzman, *Before the Ghetto: Caste and Class in Late Nineteenth Century Detroit* (Urbana: University of Illinois Press, 1972, in press).

17. For a review of the literature on gravity models, see G. Olsson, *Distance and Human Interaction* (Philadelphia: Regional Science Research Institute, 1965).

usually made in terms similar to Zipf's "Principle of Least Effort,"[18] although more recently, Isard and Wilson (among others) have (independently) attempted to provide stronger theoretical bases.[19] It has also been noted that although the model has had some success in short-run predictions, none of these efforts has succeeded in providing an explanatory foundation for inferences concerning the decision to move.[20] Since there have been few empirical studies which have employed the gravity model in the analysis of micro-level historical migration patterns of particular ethnic and racial groups within cities, it is difficult to assess the value of the formulation in contributing to an understanding of Black mobility and neighborhood development.

In light of the deficiencies of gravity-type formulations, several alternative courses of research strategy have been proposed. Moore, for example, has developed two models of intraurban migration, one based on urban population density models and the other a form of ecological model.[21] Brown and Moore have extended these formulations into a more comprehensive, decision-oriented, systems-theoretical model.[22] Brown and Longbrake[23] have also followed a similar line of reasoning in their use of Wolpert's[24] notion of "place utility" in the specification of the migration-decision function. Other formal approaches have been suggested by Tobler[25] (in his use of a diffusion-equation model of population change) and Hudson[26] (in his use of quadrat analysis methods in the study of settlement patterns) as well as several nonformal investigations via simulation methods.[27] As Gale has noted elsewhere, however, none of these approaches is sufficient as an explanatory model of migration behavior.[28] In effect, their arguments are predicated neither on micro-level behavioral investigations of individual, context–dependent, residential decisions nor on theoretical formulations requisite for higher-level generalizations.[29]

An alternative to these models has been suggested by the use of discrete-space, stochastic-process formulations in the investigation of general social mobility. Blumen, Kogan, and McCarthy's (1955) work on the intergenerational mobility of labor is one of the earliest such studies.[30] Other studies, employing similar formulations, include those by Goodman, Hallberg, McGinnis, Mayer, McFarland, Prais, and Spilerman.[31] Extensions of this type of model to the case of geographic (residential) mobility have been made by Beshers, Gale, Ginsberg, Land, Morrison, Olsson and Gale, Rogers, and Tarver and Gurley, among others.[32] However, though most of these studies have been cognizant of the importance of the context-dependent nature of explanations of migration behavior, few have been able to obtain the necessary contingent information which is requisite for such inferences. In fact, Gale's recent in-

18. G. K. Zipf, *Human Behavior and the Principle of Least Effort* (Cambridge, Mass.: Addison–Wesley, 1949).

19. W. Isard, *Methods of Regional Analysis* (New York: John Wiley, 1960), chap. 11 by D. F. Bramhall; A. G. Wilson, *Entropy in Urban and Regional Modelling* (London: Pion, 1970).

20. S. Gale, "Probability and Interaction: A Stochastic Approach to Intraregional Mobility," (Ph.D. dissertation, University of Michigan, 1969); G. Olsson, "Inference Problems in Locational Analysis," in K. R. Cox and R. G. Golledge, eds., *Behavioral Problems in Geography: A Symposium* (Evanston: Northwestern Studies in Geography, 1969), pp. 14–34; and D. L. Huff, "A Note on the Limitations of Intraurban Gravity Models," *Land Econ.* 38 (1962): 64–66.

21. E. G. Moore, "Models of Migration and the Intra-Urban Case," *Australian and New Zealand Journal of Sociology* 2 (1966): 16–37; E. G. Moore, "The Structure of Intra-Urban Movement Rates: An Ecological Model," *Urban Studies* 6 (1969): 17–33.

22. L. A. Brown and E. G. Moore, "The Intra-Urban Migration Process: A Perspective," *Geografiska Annaler* 52, ser. B. (1970): 1–13.

23. L. A. Brown and D. B. Longbrake, "Migration Flows in Intra-Urban Space: Place Utility Considerations," *Annals of the Association of American Geographers* 60 (1970): 368–84.

24. J. Wolpert, "Behavioral Aspects of the Decision to Migrate," *Papers, Regional Science Association* 15 (1965): 159–69.

25. W. R. Tobler, "A Computer Movie Simulating Urban Growth in the Detroit Region," *Economic Geography* 46 (1970): 234–40, supplement.

26. J. C. Hudson, "Theoretical Settlement Geography," (Ph.D. dissertation, University of Iowa, 1967). Also see M. F. Dacey, "Two Studies of Settlement Distributions," mimeographed (Evanston, Ill.: Department of Geography, Northwestern University, 1967).

27. See, for example, R. L. Morrill, "The Negro Ghetto: Problems and Alternatives," *Geographical Review* 55 (1965): 339–61.

28. Gale, "Probability and Interaction"; "Explanation Theory" and "Some Formal Properties of Hägerstrand's Model of Spatial Interactions," *Journal of Regional Science* (1972): forthcoming.

29. The reasoning here follows, in part, from M. G. Kendall's warnings concerning "premature generalization" in his article on "Natural Law in the Social Sciences," *Journal of the Royal Statistical Society* 124, Ser. A (1961): 5. Similar comments have also been made by A. Kaplan, *The Conduct of Inquiry* (San Francisco: Chandler, 1964), pp. 70–71; Orcutt et al., *Microanalysis of Socioeconomic Systems;* R. M. Cyert and J. G. March, *A Behavioral Theory of the Firm* (Englewood Cliffs, N.J.: Prentice-Hall, 1963); G. P. E. Clarkson, *The Theory of Consumer Demand: A Critical Appraisal* (Englewood Cliffs, N.J.: Prentice-Hall, 1963); and Gale "Probability and Interaction."

30. Blumen, Kogan, and McCarthy, *The Industrial Mobility of Labor.*

31. L. A. Goodman, "Statistical Methods for Analyzing Processes of Change," *American Journal of Sociology* 68 (1962): 57–78; M. C. Hallberg, "Projecting the Size Distribution of Agricultural Firms—An Application of a Markov Process with Non-Stationary Transition Probabilities," *American Journal of Agricultural Economics* 51 (1969): 289–302; R. McGinnis, "A Stochastic Model of Social Mobility," *American Sociological Review* 33 (1968): 712–22; T. Mayer, "Birth and Death Process Models of Social Mobility," mimeographed (Ann Arbor, Mich.: Department of Sociology University of Michigan, 1968); D. D. McFarland, "Intragenerational Social Mobility as a Markov Process: Including a Time-Stationary Model that Explains Observed Declines in Mobility Rates Over Time," *American Sociological Review* 35 (1970): 463–76; S. J. Prais, "Measuring Social Mobility," *Journal of the Royal Statistical Society* 118, ser. A (1955): 55–66; S. Spilerman, "Extensions of the Mover-Stayer Model" (Paper presented at the Third Conference on the Mathematics of Population, University of Chicago, 1970); and S. Spilerman, "The Analysis of Mobility Processes by the Introduction of Independent Variables into a Markov Chain," mimeographed, Institute for Research on Poverty, University of Wisconsin, Madison, 1970).

32. J. M. Beshers, "Computer Models of Social Process: The Case of Migration," *Demography* 4 (1967): 838–42; Gale, "Probability and Interaction"; S. Gale, "'Black-boxes' and 'Transparent-boxes': The Rhetoric of Behavioral Geography" (Paper presented at the Sixteenth Annual Meeting of the Regional Science Association, Santa Monica, 1969); Gale, "Explanation Theory;" and S. Gale and D. M. Katzman, "Black Communities: An Interdisciplinary Approach" (Paper presented at the Annual Meetings of the American Historical Association, Boston, 1970); R. B. Ginsberg, "Semi-Markov Processes and Mobility," mimeograph (Philadelphia Department of Sociology, University of Pennsylvania, 1970); R. B. Ginsberg, "On the Use and Interpretation of Probabilistic Models: Application of the Semi-Markov Model to Migration," mimeographed (Philadelphia, Department of Sociology, University of Pennsylvania, 1971); K. C. Land, "Duration of Residence and Prospective Migration: Further Evidence," *Demography* 6 (1969): 133–40; P. A. Morrison, "Duration of Residence and Prospective Migration: The Evaluation of a Stochastic Model," *Demography* 4 (1967): 553–61; G. Olsson and S. Gale, "Spatial Theory and Human Behavior," *Papers, Regional Science Association* 21 (1968): 229–42; A. Rogers, *Matrix Analysis of Interregional Population Growth and Distribution* (Berkeley: University of California Press, 1968); and J. D. Tarver and W. R. Gurley, "A Stochastic Analysis of Geographic Mobility and Population Projections of the Census Divisions in the United States," *Demography* 2 (1965): 134–39.

33. Gale, "Probability and Interaction"; Gale and Katzman, "Black Communities."

34. Olsson and Gale, "Spatial Theory"; Gale, "Probability and Interaction."

35. P. H. Rossi, *Why Families Move* (Glencoe, Ill.: The Free Press, 1955).

vestigation of nineteenth-century residential mobility is perhaps the only instance in which the parameters of the models were estimated from information on individuals which included social and economic as well as locational predicates.[33] To this end, a multi-variable extension of the ordinary simple Markov process model was employed, wherein residential change could be pictured as a conditional, N–way probability process.[34]

B. Surveys of Migration Behavior

Aside from the above-mentioned approaches, other researchers have attempted to analyze migration behavior in terms of the variations in the parameters of particular social, psychological, and economic determinants. The information employed in these studies is usually derived from cross-sectional surveys and is analyzed within a correlation and regression framework. Most commonly, these migration studies have focused on macro-scale, interregional movements, although several have attempted to deal specifically with micro-scale, intraregional (e.g., intraurban) residential changes. Rossi's seminal work on *Why Families Move,* for example, treats migration from three points of view: area mobility, household mobility, and moving decisions.[35] Simmon's recent survey of the literature on residential change in urban areas develops a similar —but distinctly more behaviorally oriented—categorization.[36] Sabagh, van Arsdol, and Butler, on the other hand, present their review of intraurban mobility determinants in terms of (1) the structural and social-psychological *dimensions* which affect the "push and pull" of migrants and (2) the influence of frictional factors.[37] Other reviews which treat intraurban migration include those by Bogue, Butler et al., Goldstein, and Kenkel.[38]

For the most part, the studies on which these reviews are based have not proven to be a sufficient foundation for either the explanation of particular processes or the advancement of reasonable, testable hypotheses concerning intraregional mobility. On the one hand, the descriptive characterizations have been based mainly on cross-sectional, macro-level data. (Goldstein's study is a notable exception, but it is nevertheless confined to only a subset of the relevant information.[39]) The explanation and generation of hypotheses, on the other hand, have proceeded from a naïve view of the nature of the data, that is, the information has been falsely viewed as conforming to the requisites of regression analysis. Finally, in almost all previous investigations the interest has ultimately been in predicting changes for specific communities rather than developing an understanding of the process of change. Data collection and analysis are almost uniformly treated as pragmatic tools, e.g., for the immediate needs of planners, rather than in terms of the need for explanation and theory formulation. Few, if any, of these previous studies have attempted to provide either mutually comparable characterizations of the migration process or to take up questions of neighborhood formation.

In brief, we can distinguish four related concerns which serve to distinguish the proposed research program from previous approaches: (A) disaggregated data on individuals are used as the information base; (B) the over-all temporal and spatial development of the community is traced and the focus of the inferences is on the explanation of the process itself, *not* prediction; (C) the pattern of relationships among individuals is expressed in a uniform manner (as the parameters of discrete space, stochastic models); and (D) any number of communities can be studied, thereby broadening the spatial scope and providing a basis for cross- and intra-societal comparisons. Our objective, then, is to examine the pattern of Black residential and social mobility in American communities and to do this by utilizing a methodological framework which views micro-behavioral information and consistent population measures as the foundation for explanatory inferences.[40]

2. DATA AND METHODS: PATTERNS OF DISCOVERY

It has been argued thus far that previous studies on the formation and growth of Black communities, by and large, have dealt almost exclusively with its functional attributes. Most of this research, for instance, has been in the nature either of surveys of the occupational structure (where internal changes in the state of the system, such as the percentage of Blacks in particular job categories, have been stressed) or of historical investigations of unique individuals and circumstances. Little consideration has been given to the general mechanisms of change or to the relationships between individuals and their society.[41] Although information on both the spatial distribution and the process of change of individuals in communities is clearly important, these issues have been consistently neglected in favor of purely functional considerations.

From our point of view, the limitation of studies of community formulation to specific functional considerations is often short-sighted and misleading. In Thernstrom's words, "The nature of class structure cannot be answered without reliable information about the nature of the class structure yesterday—and the day before yesterday, and even the century before yesterday!"[42] Since a pattern, once established, has a tendency to

36. J. W. Simmons, "Changing Residence in the City: A Review of Intra-Urban Mobility," *Geographical Review* 58 (1968): 622–51.

37. G. Sabagh, M.D. van Arsdol, and E. W. Butler, "Some Determinants of Intrametropolitan Residential Mobility: Conceptual Considerations," *Social Forces* 48 (1969): 88–98.

38. D. J. Bogue, "Internal Migration," in P. M. Hauser and O. D. Duncan (eds.), *The Study of Population* (Chicago: University of Chicago Press, 1959); Butler et al., *Moving Behavior;* N. N. Foote et al., *Housing Choices and Housing Constraints* (New York: McGraw-Hill, 1960); S. Goldstein, *The Norristown Study* (Philadelphia: University of Pennsylvania Press, 1958); and W. F. Kenkel, "The Family Moving Decision Process," *Family Mobility in our Dynamic Society* (Ames: Iowa State University Press, 1965).

39. Goldstein, *Norristown.*

40. This point should not be misconstrued as simply an argument for methodological individualism. Rather, in the initial (exploratory) stage of an investigation, it is very often the case that holistic generalizations must be preceded by analysis of more detailed information.

41. Stephan Thernstrom, for example, has pointed out that there has been a general parochialism about spatial and temporal considerations. See S. Thernstrom, "Notes on the Historical Study of Social Mobility," *Comparative Studies in Society and History* (January, 1968): 162–72. A similar point has been noted by J. Eichenbaum and S. Gale, "Form, Function, and Process: A Methodological Inquiry," *Economic Geography* 47 (1971): 525–44.

42. Thernstrom, "Notes on the Historical Study of Social Mobility," p. 162.

remain, study should be made of both the historical and the current aspects, but, most importantly, study must be made of its formative stages. And this, of course, applies to spatial as well as temporal processes. The beginning of a process (in time) clearly bears directly on its current state; similarly, the initial arrangement of people in space (e.g., in different towns and within cities) affects their current residential propensities.[43]

In order to investigate the current structure of Black communities in America, we must therefore seek to understand and describe its processes of development. Change does not take place *in vacuo* any more than behavioral processes exist independently of temporal or spatial referrants. One of the major functions of this paper, therefore, is to present a strategy for the synthesis of historical data on the behavioral patterns of individuals, together with spatial and functional information, in a single model of residential mobility and neighborhood development.

At this point, specific methodological guidelines for empirical research must be carefully considered. After a review of the background of the proposed methodology (A), three specific issues will be treated: (B) data collection and coding; (C) classification, contingency tables, and stochastic processes; and (D) parameter estimates and statistical tests.

A. Background

Methodology and the development of scientific theory are closely related. The choice of a particular methodology and of a particular means of argument depends heavily on the nature of the desired theory, whereas verification of specific hypotheses is at least indirectly contingent upon the methodological foundation employed. In classical logical empiricism, this relationship would appear to be relatively uncomplicated: a specific approach is selected with regard to the simplicity of the formulation (in some sense of the word) and its accuracy in terms of deductive prediction. No distinction is made between understanding a system or process and the prediction of events. From quite another perspective, however, deduction and prediction may be seen as only one means for examining the postulates of a theory. Alternative methodological strategies can play far more comprehensive roles with regard to generalization, theory formulation, and explanation. This problem is, of course, far from reconciled. The roles of explanation, prediction, and description in science are not altogether clear; neither is the relationship between a particular methodological position and the choice of an appropriate set of analytic techniques. The position taken here is that although these issues

43. For a discussion of this point see L. Curry, "The Random Spatial Economy: An Exploration in Settlement Theory," *Annals of the Association of American Geographers* 54 (1964): 138–46. Similar comments have been made by S. C. Dodd, "How Random Interacting Organizes a Population," *Synthese* 12 (1960): 40–70 and F. M. Fisher, "On the Analysis of History and the Interdependence of the Social Sciences," *Philosophy of Science* 27 (1960): 147–58.

have not been resolved in general, solutions nevertheless exist with respect to specific classes of empirical questions.

At least three alternative approaches to the choice of a methodology for examining questions relating to the analysis of empirical phenomena in general and to the historical analysis of residential mobility in particular may be noted—the approaches to empirical research taken by (1) model theorists,[44] (2) inductive logicians,[45] and (3) "pattern" theorists.[46] The last approach serves as the principal motivation for our argument.

In effect, the point of the patternist's theory of explanation is that the need in social research is not so much a rationalization in terms of the logical-deductive process of hypothesis verification as a structured procedure for developing hypotheses and answering specific, context-dependent questions. Although deductive arguments (employing axiomatic versions of social behavior) are undoubtedly of importance in the long-run, it is the initial (inductive) steps which are crucial to the provision of realistic explanations of those social processes for which little information is currently available (such as is the case for Black communities). The requirements of positivist and neo-positivist science preclude much of what social scientists are equipped to treat; we have no "universal laws" on which to base a deductive theory of social processes, nor do we have realistic approximations of such laws. We can, however, begin to build such theories by undertaking to examine the individual, low-level components of social structure and mobility—i.e., the patterns of decisions of the members of society.

The distinction made here becomes particularly important when we translate the philosophic arguments into operational models. More specifically, it allows us to dismiss immediately certain approaches as being inapplicable, given the types of inferences which are required. Gross statistical indicators, such as those employed by Taeuber and Taeuber in their recent study *Negroes in Cities*,[47] can be seen as generally inadequate for advancing explanations where there is no basic information concerning individual propensities and motivations. Similarly, the analysis of social interaction with such macro-level conceptualizations as gravity and potential models permits explanatory inferences only in terms of principles of least effort and the like.[48] Our position, on the other hand, maintains that the investigation of the characteristics and behavior of individuals (particularly with regard to residential choice) requires indicators of disaggregated movement patterns based on micro-level information. As has been noted in earlier studies, these requirements are reasonably satisfied by the use of a discrete space stochastic process model (or, alternatively, dynamic contingency tables).[49] This point will be discussed in greater detail in part C below.

44. See, for example, M. Przelecki, *The Logic of Empirical Theories* (London: Routledge and Kegan Paul, 1969).

45. See, for example, R. Hilpinnen, "Rules of Acceptance and Inductive Logic," *Acta Philosophica Fennica* 22 (1968).

46. This general term includes Kaplan, *Conduct of Inquiry;* N. R. Hanson, *Patterns of Discovery* (Cambridge: Cambridge University Press, 1965); M. Scriven, "Explanations, Predictions, and Laws," in H. Feigl et al., eds. *Minnesota Studies in the Philosophy of Sciences,* vol. 3 (Minneapolis: University of Minnesota Press, 1962); S. Gale, "Evolutionary Laws in the Social Sciences," (Paper presented to the Fourth International Congress of Logic, Methodology and Philosophy of Science, Bucharest, Romania, 1971); A. R. Louch, *Explanation and Human Action* (Berkeley: University of California Press, 1969); and G. H. von Wright, *Explanation and Understanding* (Ithaca: Cornell University Press, 1971).

47. K. E. Taeuber and A. F. Taeuber, *Negroes in Cities* (Chicago: Aldine Publishing Co., 1965).

48. The review by Olsson, *Distance and Human Interaction,* presents an excellent discussion of this point. Also see Olsson, "Inference Problems."

49. See Gale, "Explanation Theory," and Olsson and Gale, "Spatial Theory and Human Behavior."

B. Data Collection and Coding

The empirical basis of the proposed study is to be provided by the development of descriptions of the historical migration patterns in individual communities. It is thus important to note the sources of data for the residential and socio-economic mobility of individuals.

Data on individual residential movements and socio-economic status are available from both published and manuscript records. The federal decennial census schedules for the period from 1850 to 1880 are available to researchers. Prior to 1850 the federal census consisted only of a head count, and it is no more useful for our purposes than the composite published census volumes. The 1890 census was almost totally destroyed by fire and access to the census after 1890 is restricted by law. Thus, the manuscript censuses from 1850 to 1880 can be used to provide data on individuals (by family name) at ten-year intervals. Schedule 1 (population) and Schedules 2 through 8 (social statistics) are available on microfilm from the National Archives.

Although the questions asked in the enumerations varied from census to census, the following information is available throughout for each person: (1) name, (2) sex, (3) age, (4) race, (5) marital status, (6) relation to head-of-household, (7) occupation, (8) place of birth, (9) place of father's birth, (10) place of mother's birth. In 1880, the exact residential address of each person became part of the enumeration.

City directories, although biased in favor of the needs of the business community, are invaluable as a cross-check to the census enumerations and provide information for years between and in decennial censuses. The information in city directories includes: (1) name, (2) residential address, (3) occupation, (4) business address or employer's address. Most city directories distinguish Blacks until approximately 1925, thus making it possible to collect racially stratified historical information.

Another invaluable source of information is public records—e.g., county and city tax rolls; building permits; school, court, incorporation, voting, and land records. Tax rolls, for instance, indicate the value of personal and real property and the assessment for each individual. Newspapers, both general and Negro, can be used as supplementary evidence on social and economic status. It should also be noted that, while the quantity and quality of the data increase directly with the social level of the individual—the higher the social class, the more numerous the data—by utilizing all of these sources, a record of intraurban migrations and associated socio-economic variables can be collected for virtually all individuals within a given community.

C. Classification, Contingency Tables, and Stochastic Processes

The proposed methodology is similar to that used in the analysis of demographic and social mobility and consists of the use of the discrete observations based on individual movement patterns, structured within a framework of dynamic contingency tables (or stochastic matrices). The information on the micro-level components of the system (the individuals) can include residential, social, and economic data recorded at different points in time. A conditional probability model (implicit in the notion of stochastic matrices) is thus used to express the contingent relationships among the various components of social and residential mobility parameters over time. These conditional probabilities may themselves be conceived of either as point or vector valued processes and, following the suggestions of Balogh, Gale, Oldenburger, and others in their extension of the definition of a stochastic matrix to higher dimensional forms, these more descriptively accurate relationships can be used to express the general class of social process relationships.[50]

The formal properties of this model may be described in the following manner. Let K^N denote a general finite-dimensional cross-classification table where $N = \{n_1, \ldots, n_N\}$ is the set of properties or conditional predicates and $K = \{k_1, \ldots, k_K\}$ is the set of classifications associated with each of the properties. The total number of elements of the sets N and K are given (respectively) by N, the total number of properties, and K, the total number of classifications associated with each property. Thus in the simple 2×2 or 2^2 case, $N = \{n_1, n_2\}$, $K^{n_1} = \{k_1^{n_1}, k_2^{n_1}\}$, and $K^{n_2} = \{k_1^{n_2}, k_2^{n_2}\}$; the superscripts n_1 and n_2 indicate the specific predicates over which the partition of N is defined. Dynamic properties of cross-classification tables arise immediately from a consideration of the K^2 model. As before, $N = \{n_1, n_2\}$, but here $n_1 = n_{t-1}$ and $n_2 = n_t$ — i.e., the model represents a partition on one conditional predicate defined at two points in time, the specification of K as $K^{n_{t-1}} = \{k_1^{n_{t-1}}, \ldots, k_K^{n_{t-1}}\}$ and $K^{n_t} = \{k_1^{n_t}, \ldots, k_K^{n_t}\}$ follows directly. Where the same classification is employed over time, then K can be denoted more simply as $\{k_1, \ldots, k_K\}$. Finally, the model may also be extended to the case wherein $N = \{n_1, \ldots, n_N\}$, $N > 2$; the N conditional predicates may be defined for any interesting state space — e.g., temporal, spatial, social, etc. — and these provide the basis of multi-way extensions of simple contingency tables. Probability measures (both frequentist and Bayesian) may be obtained for each partition.

The descriptive basis of the methodological design is thus the use of a form of multi-dimensional contin-

50. T. Balogh, "Matrix Valued Stochastic Processes," *Publications Mathematiques Debrecen* 8 (1961): 368–78; Gale, "Probability and Interaction"; and R. Oldenburger, "Composition and Rank of n-way Matrices and Multilinear Forms," *Annals of Mathematics* 25 (1934): 622–57. Also see L. A. Goodman, "On Some Statistical Tests for M-th Order Markov Chains," *Annals of Mathematical Statistics* 30 (1959): 154–64 and Fisher, "On the Analysis of History and the Interdependence of the Social Sciences."

gency tables in which the state space is variously defined over time, location, and social conditions. Gale has dealt with this model in recent studies and has noted that under conditions of stationarity and first-orderedness, this dynamic contingency table framework can be regarded as equivalent to that of the Markov process model.[51] In its usual form, of course, a Markov process is defined only for changes in the states of one variable conditional on its state at one point earlier in time:

$$p_{ij}(t_r) = Pr[X(t_r) = j | X(t_{r-1}) = i] \qquad (i, j = 1, \ldots, j;$$
$$r = 1, \ldots, T) \qquad (1)$$

The $\{p_{ij}(t_r)\}$'s are, of course, subject to the usual probability conditions:

$$0 \leqslant p_{ij}(t_r) \leqslant 1 \qquad (i, j = 1, \ldots, m; r = 1, \ldots, T) \qquad (2a)$$

$$\sum_{j=1}^{m} p_{ij}(t_r) = 1 \qquad (i = 1, \ldots, m; r = 1, \ldots, T) \qquad (2b)$$

The more general, multi-dimensional case yields higher dimensional transition matrices, $P' = \{p'_{n_1}, \ldots, n_N\}$ which may be defined over any N conditional predicates. As an analogue to Eqs. (1) and (2), the functional form is thus given by

$$P' = \{p'_{n_1}, \ldots, n_N\} = \{Pr[X_{q+1} = x_{q+1} \wedge \ldots \wedge X_N = x_N$$
$$| X_1 = x_1 \wedge \ldots \wedge X_q = x_q]\}, \qquad (3)$$

where

$$0 \leqslant p_{n_1}, \ldots, p_{n_N} \leqslant 1 \qquad \forall n_j \qquad (4a)$$

and

$$\sum_{n_j \epsilon Q_2} \cdots \sum_{n_j \epsilon Q_2} p'_{n_1}, \ldots, p'_{n_N} = 1. \qquad (4b)$$

Here Q is a partition of N, with $Q_1 = \{n_1, \ldots, n_q\}$ and $Q_2 = \{n_{q+1}, \ldots, n_N\}$. Q_2 may be regarded as the set of events whose probability of occurrence is to be ascertained; Q_1 is the subset of (predetermined) conditioning variables. The sole interpretative restriction on the elements of Q_1 is that they be, a priori, some theoretically interesting (explanatory) conditional predicates. In the case of migration, for example, the set might include measures of economic and social status as well as temporal and locational parameters. In Eq. (3) the elements of N, the $\{n_j; j = 1, \ldots, q, \ldots, N\}$, are ordered such that the conditional predicates of $n_j \epsilon Q_2$ have the range $(j = q + 1, \ldots, N)$; the range of each of the x_i's is the same as the classificatory partition of each k_i. In addition, where time is one of the conditioning states—i.e., where each variable is given for ν points in time—then the total number of predicates is correspondingly reduced to N/ν.

Clearly, the use of contingency tables is a standard research procedure. Properties of individual units are identified, classifications are defined, and frequency ta-

51. Gale, "Explanation Theory."

bles computed. What is perhaps unusual in the present treatment is the inclusion of spatial and temporal predicates or the interpretation of the frequencies as conditional probabilities, but even these are conceptually simple extensions. It is, however, the manner by which particular hypotheses are tested and explanations proposed that makes them singularly important here. This issue will be treated below (see part D of this section). For the present we can summarize our argument in terms of the following four points:

(1) Descriptively accurate models, incorporating parameters defined over disaggregated data, often provide a firmer foundation both for explanatory and predictive inferences.

(2) Stochastic matrices, by expressing all relationships in terms of similarly defined conditional probabilities, permit the intercomparison of processes defined over different populations.

(3) Statistical techniques are available for the analysis of stochastic matrices — i.e., since they are effective contingency tables defined over a temporal state space.

(4) And finally, given that certain properties hold (or can be assumed to hold) for these stochastic matrices (i.e., stationarity and first-order properties), the theorems of Markov processes can be applied to deduce certain predictive consequences such as equilibrium distributions and mean time to transition (change of state).

D. Parameter Estimates and Statistical Tests

In a number of recent studies, several methods have been outlined for estimating parameters and analyzing dynamic contingency tables (or stochastic matrices). Goodman has investigated both the analysis of contingency tables and Markov processes;[52] Maxwell has presented some techniques for analyzing qualitative data in a contingency framework;[53] Cox has focused on the examination of contingency tables but with particular reference to binary data;[54] Spilerman and Hallberg have (independently) discussed methods for estimating contingent transition probabilities via the use of multiple regression procedures;[55] and Good and Lee, Judge, and Zellner have reviewed the general methods available for estimating probabilities in contingency tables.[56]

(1) The computation of the parameters of the generalized cross-classification table is straightforward. Where the classifications are defined directly in terms of some predetermined categories, the parameters are simply the total number of data points recorded for each k_i^{nj} ($i = 1, \ldots, K$; $j = 1, \ldots, N$). Frequencies may be computed in the usual manner, and when interpreted as probabilities, these methods are analogous to maxi-

52. See, for example, L. A. Goodman, "Statistical Methods for the Mover-Stayer Model," *Journal of the American Statistical Association* 56 (1961): 841–68; "Statistical Methods for Analyzing Processes of Change," *American Journal of Sociology* 68 (1962): 57–58; and "Social Mobility Tables." Also see T. W. Anderson and L. A. Goodman, "Statistical Inference about Markov Chains," *Annals of Mathematical Statistics* 20 (1957): 89–110.

53. A. E. Maxwell, *Analysing Qualitative Data* (London: Methuen, 1961).

54. D. R. Cox, *Analysis of Binary Data* (London: Methuen, 1969).

55. Spilerman, "The Analysis of Mobility Processes"; Hallberg, "Projecting the Size Distribution of Agricultural Firms."

56. I. J. Good, *The Estimation of Probabilities: An Essay on Modern Bayesian Methods* (Cambridge: MIT Press, 1965); T. C. Lee, G. G. Judge, and A. Zellner, *Estimating the Parameters of the Markov Probability Model from Aggregate Time Series Data* (Amsterdam: North-Holland, 1970).

mum likelihood estimates of the transition probabilities of stochastic matrices.[57] As noted above, Bayesian estimation procedures are also available.[58]

The maximum likelihood estimates are computed as follows. Given that detailed, disaggregated information is available on the flows between states and over time, the estimates of the $\{p_{ij}\}$'s of the K^2 model are obtained from Eq. (5):

$$\hat{p}_{ij} = \frac{q_{ij}}{q_i^*}, \tag{5}$$

where q_{ij} is the number of individuals in each cell of the contingency table and $q_i^* = \sum_{j=1}^{m} q_{ij}$. The $\hat{p}_{ij}$'s are, of course, subject to the probability restrictions given in Eq. (2). In the case where the transition probabilities are not necessarily stationary, the same general approach is employed, but the estimate is time specific. Thus, we obtain maximum likelihood estimates of the $\{p_{ij}(t_r)\}$'s from

$$\hat{p}_{ij}(t_r) = \frac{q_{ij}(t_r)}{q_i^*(t_r)}. \tag{6}$$

Furthermore, where a series of observations exist over time, the $\{\hat{p}_{ij}(t_r)\}$'s can be computed for each interval in $t_r \epsilon T$, and if the transition probabilities are stationary (time-homogeneous), they can then be regarded as the average or mean of the individual $\{\hat{p}_{ij}(t_r)\}$'s taken over $r = 1, \ldots, T$.

The estimation of the parameters of the multi-way model is directly analogous to that of the two-way design of Eqs. (5) and (6). This may be illustrated by the four-way case; that is, we wish to estimate the transition probabilities for a model of the form $P' = \{p'_{n_1,n_2,n_3,n_4}\}$. Let $\{p'_{n_1,n_2,n_3,n_4}\} = \{p_{ijkl}\}$. Extending Eq. (5), we get

$$\hat{p}_{ijkl} = \frac{q_{ijkl}}{q_{ij}^*} \tag{7}$$

here $q_{ij}^* = \sum\sum_{[kl]} q_{ijkl}$. These are, of course, also subject to the usual probability constraints—i.e.,

$$0 \leq \hat{p}_{ijkl} \leq 1, \tag{8a}$$

$$\sum\sum_{[kl]} \hat{p}_{ijkl} = 1. \tag{8b}$$

This is, then, an extension of the simple two-way (K^2) model for the case where the transition probabilities are conditioned on the movements of two temporally defined variables. In the example discussed below (section 3), the four-way (K^4) model will provide the basis for most of our descriptive and inferential procedures.

(2) Statistical tests for the very general classes of hypotheses discussed above have been treated in detail and will not be restated here. In particular, the tests de-

57. Anderson and Goodman, "Markov Chains"; and Lee et al., *Markov Probability Model.*

58. See J. J. Martin, *Bayesian Decision Problems and Markov Chains* (New York: John Wiley, 1967).

veloped by Anderson and Goodman,[59] Goodman,[60] and Goodman and Kruskal[61] are regarded as the basis of the requisite statistical inference procedures. Additional though less formal inference procedures can also be employed. These include a comparison of mean life in state parameters,[62] the predictive evaluation of the state distribution parameters, and a graphical comparison of transition probabilities.

The methodological program may thus be viewed as being distinctly empiricist in orientation (in that the parameters of the matrices are all derived from the micro-level data). The objective is to develop a theory of residential and social mobility based on observational criteria rather than to provide tests for axiomatically defined constructs. Our contention is that the methodology which has been outlined here is particularly suited to this undertaking. Goodman, for example, has utilized a similar formulation as the foundation for his mobility and interaction studies. In effect, then, we want to know what the empirical relationships are—not simply the hypothetical effects of certain a priori formulations—and to utilize this information to structure the theory; the method of "structured induction" proposed above can be construed as the foundation for such a program of inferences.

3. ANN ARBOR: A CASE STUDY

We turn now to an application of the methods outlined in section 2. More specifically, by using micro-behavioral data on the Ann Arbor, Michigan, Black community, examination will be made of one particular subset of the data, i.e., residential mobility patterns. The restriction of the discussion to locational factors is intended only to provide an example. Although the present research and analysis have not been limited to this one area, one should note that focusing on residential patterns will best illustrate the methods discussed above.

It might be noted at the outset that one of the most interesting results of the study has been that the inferences derived from the structured quantitative analysis have corresponded, for the most part, to the conclusions of the unique case-study approach of the historian. One reason for this is that the history of Ann Arbor was examined and analyzed from the usual written and manuscript sources, and many of the classificatory schemes are predicated on this basic empirical research. But not all of the conclusions were anticipated. Traditional historical methodology failed to reveal, for example, the significance of place of birth in Black residential and social patterns. The form of analysis which has been outlined above (section 2), on the other hand, revealed that the chances for a northern-born Black to move from one

59. Anderson and Goodman, "Markov Chains."

60. L. A. Goodman, "Mover-Stayer Model"; "Processes of Change"; "Social Mobility Tables"; "The Multivariate Analysis of Qualitative Data: Interactions Among Multiple Classifications," *Journal of the American Statistical Association* 65 (1970): 226–56 and "The Analysis of Multidimensional Contingency Tables: Stepwise Procedures and Direct Estimation Methods for Building Models for Multiple Classifications," *Technometrics* 13 (1971): 33–61.

61. L. A. Goodman and W. H. Kruskal, "Measures of Association for Cross Classifications," *Journal of the American Statistical Association* 49 (1954): 732–64; "Measures of Association for Cross Classifications. II: Further Discussion and References," *Journal of the American Statistical Association* 54 (1959): 123–63 and "Measures of Association for Cross Classification. III: Approximate Sampling Theory," *Journal of the American Statistical Association* 58 (1963): 310–64.

62. For a further discussion of this point, see I. G. Adelman, "A Stochastic Analysis of the Size Distribution of Firms," *Journal of the American Statistical Association* 53 (1958): 893–904; see especially p. 897.

part of Ann Arbor to another or for upward social class changes were greater than those of southern-born Negroes.

This point illustrates one of the advantages of the research strategy proposed — the union of historical empiricism and social science methodology. By wedding the historian's concern with the unique and the social scientist's interest in the nomographic, and by combining the humanist's atomization and the scientist's systemization, the attempt has been made to avoid the pitfalls of a monolithic disciplinary orientation while building a thorough, empirical approach to general social theory. If the results at this stage are limited, it should be remembered that the report is on only one part of the data for one community.

3.1 The Data and Their Measurement

The data which will be used to illustrate this argument are drawn from several historical sources (as described in section 2, above). Specifically, from manuscript censuses[63] and city directories,[64] the following information was obtained for the total (recorded) Negro population of Ann Arbor, Michigan, during the period 1870 to 1899 (inclusive): (1) the name of each individual, (2) the year in which the observation was made, (3) age, (4) occupation, (5) sex, (6) whether the individual lived alone or with other members of his family, (7) birth place, and (8) residence. These published records are available for the years 1870, 1880, 1883, 1886, 1888, 1890, 1892, 1894, 1895, 1896, 1897, 1898, and 1899. Clearly, there are discrepancies between the sources, both with respect to the identification of the same properties from two different records as well as the measurement of these variables — e.g., there was a change in the addressing system between 1897 and 1898. Many of these difficulties were, however, accounted for by careful attention to each individual case. In any event, pragmatic justification for their use nevertheless exists, i.e., it is the best that could be provided under the circumstances.

One additional piece of information was obtained for each individual in the study — social class. Unlike the other variables, for which direct evidence was available, the assignment of a measure of social class was indirect. To obtain a measure of this important variable, newspaper articles, personal letters, and other public and non-public sources were searched. Where evidence existed for the relative prominence of an individual, the higher value (middle-class) was given. If a person's name came up at all in the above-mentioned sources, a second value (working class) was usually assigned. All those whose names did not appear (or who appeared in a detrimental context) were put in the lower class. It should be noted that the class assignments here are

63. Manuscript Population Schedules, U.S. Census for Washtenaw County, 1870 and 1880, are available on microfilm from the National Archives; Manuscript Census, Michigan Census for Washtenaw County, 1894, in the Michigan Historical Collections of the University of Michigan.

64. *Ann Arbor City Directories*, 1883, 1886, 1888, 1890, 1892, 1894, 1895, 1896, 1897, 1898, 1899.

made relative to (a) a White man's conception of what are socially relevant activities — e.g., presence at socially relevant activities — and (b) the social structure of the Black community. One interesting observation that one can make immediately is that, almost by definition, no upper-class Blacks remained in the small town of Ann Arbor. Opportunities for non-Whites in small communities were extremely limited during this period and, judging by the number of prominent (upper-class) Blacks in nearby Detroit, the larger cities were able to attract most of the highly (socially) mobile members of this part of society.[65]

Some of the gross properties of the data are presented in tables 1 and 2. Table 1 indicates the total number of individual heads-of-households recorded (as well as the percentage of the total number of observations) for each of the time periods. Table 2 gives three different measures. The first (year$_i$/year$_j$), a sort of "attrition" indicator, is the number of individuals who were present in Ann Arbor in year i but not in year j. The second figure (year$_i$ and year$_j$) indicates the number of in-

Table 1. *Number of Observations in Year i*

	1870	1880	1883	1886	1888	1890	1892	1894	1895	1896	1897	1898	1899
Number of Observations	79	133	94	90	129	109	143	218	167	174	149	150	146
Percentage of Total Observations	4.44	7.47	5.28	5.05	7.24	6.12	8.03	12.24	9.38	9.77	8.37	8.42	8.20

Table 2.

Year i	Year j	Numbers Year i/Year j	Numbers Year i & Year j	Numbers Year j/Year i
1870	1880	49	30	103
1880	1890	98	35	74
1890	1899	48	61	85
1880	1883	84	49	45
1883	1886	50	44	46
1886	1888	31	59	70
1888	1890	64	65	44
1890	1892	20	89	54
1892	1894	31	112	106
1894	1896	85	133	41
1896	1898	44	130	20
1880	1886	91	42	48
1886	1890	47	43	66
1890	1894	29	80	138
1894	1899	97	119	27
1894	1895	69	147	20
1895	1896	39	128	46
1896	1897	40	134	15
1897	1898	19	130	20
1898	1899	24	126	20

65. Because of our working definition of class, specifically in the importance of occupation as the major though not exclusive component of class designation and the assignment of newcomers to the lower class until they had become "reputable," there is a built-in bias against an indication of downward class mobility.

dividuals who are recorded as being present in the system during both year i and year j; these form the basis of the transition matrices. The third item (year$_j$/year$_i$) gives the number of individuals who were not in the system (Ann Arbor) in year i but who entered during the interval and are recorded in year j. This may be conceived of as sort of "birth" or "entrance-to-system" indicator.

Of the nine types of information which were collected, five will be employed in the present illustration: the individuals, the time of the observation, residence, birth place, and social class. Measures were assigned each of these properties in the following manner.

A. The Individuals

Using the name, address, and sometimes relatives as indicators, Black heads-of-households were identified and recorded. The use of only the heads-of-households is suggested by the nature of the problem, that is, the decisions involved in residential mobility are most often a function of the motivations of the decision-making unit of the family.

B. Time of Observation

When an individual's name occurred in any of the records, the time (year) that the source was published was used as a measure of the time of the observation. For the purposes of our example, an approximately two-year interval of observations was employed: 1880, 1883, 1886, 1888, 1890, 1892, 1894, 1896, and 1898.

C. Residence

In addition to the time of the observation, an address was listed for each individual. Using a brute force method—i.e., by placing a transparent sheet of graph paper over a street map of Ann Arbor—these addresses were transformed into Cartesian coordinates. And, by further grouping these on an a priori basis, an assignment was made into one of three residential areas (see figure 1). For the present purpose, the set of residential areas may be functionally defined. Area one (1) included the traditionally Black downtown and industrial sections; area two (2) included the mainly White residential western section of town; and area three (3) included the relatively heterogeneous neighborhood around the University of Michigan. Clearly, other boundaries could have been defined and, in fact, an infinite number are possible. However, the requisites of computational simplicity and the nature of the inferences desired suggested that those chosen have some direct theoretical significance here.

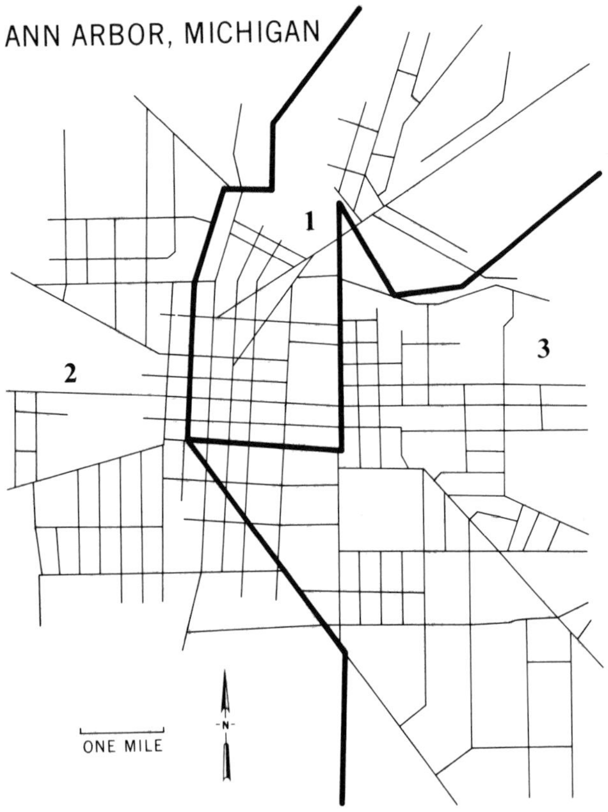

Figure 1. Three cell residence areas, Ann Arbor Negroes, 1870–1899.

D. Birthplace

The birthplace of each individual head-of-household was also recorded. With few exceptions, these could be more broadly categorized as either "born in the North" or "born in the South," and it is this classification which was employed.[66]

E. Social Class

The social class assignments were made as described above. However, in the analytical treatment, a reduced set of two categories was employed: (1) middle plus working class; and (2) lower class.

3.2 An Example: Residential Mobility

In this section we shall present some preliminary results from the above-mentioned study of mobility.[67] Although hypotheses will not be tested in the strict statistical sense, several formal observations will be suggested. This follows from the independent work of Goodman[68] and Selvin and Stuart[69] wherein they discuss the rationale for employing "ransacking" or "data-dredging" procedures in the investigation of mobility tables. It also permits us to side-step the details of particular statistical tests as well as the difficulties incumbent in significance tests with the rather limited population size which was studied. In effect, only those tables which exhibit obvious structural differences will be examined here. It might be noted that since the observed transition matrices were demonstrated to be statistically time-homogeneous (according to the method outlined by Anderson and Goodman),[70] only the average transition probabilities are given. Also, as a matter of convenience, all the matrices are presented in a two-way format.

Now, let us examine the mobility table (table 3) for changes in the residences of Black heads-of-households in Ann Arbor between 1880 and 1899 inclusive. The time interval between observations $(t_r - t_{r-1})$ is approximately two years (see section 3.1 (B), above). The interpretation of the states is as follows: (1) the downtown area (the area with the highest proportion of Negroes); (2) the west side of Ann Arbor; (3) the east side of Ann Arbor (mainly around the university). Note that, although there does not appear to be any significant difference between the mobility patterns exhibited by residents of states (1) and (3), the occupants of state (2) display a higher propensity to move from their homes. The probabilities of moving into area (2) from areas (1) and (3) are also demonstrably low. This, of course, does not say much in itself. But we may attach some significance to this if we note that area (2)—the west side of Ann Arbor—

Table 3. *Average Transition Matrix*

Three-State Residence Changes, Ann Arbor Negroes, 1880–1899

	State j	Time (t)		
State i		1	2	3
T 1		0.87	0.04	0.09
i				
m 2		0.22	0.63	0.15
e				
(t − 1) 3		0.15	0.04	0.81

66. "Born in North": Michigan, New York, New Jersey, Pennsylvania, Ohio, and other traditionally "northern" states. Individuals born in Canada are included in the classification. "Born in South": Kentucky, Virginia, Delaware, Maryland, District of Columbia, and other traditionally "southern" states.

67. Gale, "Probability and Interaction," chap. 4.

68. Goodman, "Social Mobility Tables."

69. H. C. Selvin and A. Stuart, "Data-Dredging Procedures in Survey Analysis," *American Statistician* 20 (1966): 20–23.

70. Anderson and Goodman, "Markov Chains."

Perspectives in Geography 2   Geography of the Ghetto

has traditionally been an area of White working-class residences, populated mainly by German immigrants. We might hypothesize, then, that the high rate of mobility is a function of racial stability in this segment of the community.

It should be evident, though, that these simple mobility parameters are singularly difficult to interpret in terms of the behavior of individuals. In fact, all that is available here is a one-variable surrogate for other, more elemental conditions—such as those linked with social or economic status. With this in mind, we may now consider a four-way residential mobility model in which the simple transition probabilities presented in table 3 are conditioned on other variables.

Consider first the pattern of residential mobility as conditioned on changes in social class (table 4). Once again, the time interval over which the transition probabilities are defined is two years. The states here are defined as follows: (1,1) living in area (1) and being middle class; (1,2) living in area (1) and being lower class; (2,1) living in area (2) and being middle class; (2,2) living in area (2) and being lower class; (3,1) living in area (3) and being middle class; (3,2) living in area (3) and being lower class. Table 4 is thus a break-down of the simple residential mobility parameters (given in table 3) wherein the shifts are predicated on associated changes in social class states over time. For example, $p_{1,1,1,1}$ may be interpreted as the probability of being middle class and living in area (1) at time $t-1$ and remaining in this state at time t; from table 4 we can see that this value is 0.92. On the other hand, the conditional probability $p_{1,1,1,2}$ may be taken as the probability of being middle class and in area (1) at time $t-1$ and shifting to lower class while remaining in area (1) by time t; from table 4 it may be seen that the value of this is zero—i.e., no individuals were observed as exhibiting this type of change.

Several things are apparent from an examination of table 4. First, quite independently of residential shifts, there is a higher propensity for upward than for downward social mobility. This, of course, is to be expected. Second, it can be seen that the probability of changing residences is higher for the lower class than it is for the middle class. This, also, is expected. The lower class is almost by definition comprised of those individuals with fewer roots—e.g., younger families and those most likely to be displaced by small changes in economic conditions. Third, and perhaps most interestingly, there seems to be no direct relationship between residential change and associated shifts in social status, that is, one particular area does not stand out as *the* area for socially upwardly mobile families. From at least one point of view, this is unanticipated. It might be expected that as one moves up the "social ladder," as it were, this would be accompanied by a change in residences—say, to

Table 4. *Average Transition Matrix*

Three-State Residence and Two-State Social Class Changes, Ann Arbor Negroes, 1880–1899

State i / State j		State k / State l	Time (t) 1		2		3	
			1	2	1	2	1	2
Time (t−1) 1	1		0.92	0.00	0.03	0.00	0.04	0.00
	2		0.13	0.64	0.01	0.05	0.02	0.15
2	1		0.09	0.00	0.73	0.00	0.18	0.00
	2		0.11	0.40	0.03	0.40	0.01	0.05
3	1		0.11	0.00	0.05	0.00	0.84	0.00
	2		0.01	0.19	0.00	0.03	0.11	0.66

a "nicer" neighborhood. One possible explanation for the lack of this type of change might be the relative absence of social distinction by residence in the Black community. And this, of course, implies that the number of residences open to Blacks might be so limited as to disallow such a luxury. The absence of residential stratification might, however, be the result of some other set of discriminatory priorities which are not reflected in the measurement of social class (as it has been defined here). Attention is now turned to this point.

Consider first residential change as conditioned upon birthplace (table 5). The same two-year interval is employed as the time of transition. The states are interpreted in the following manner: (1,1) born in the North and living in area (1); (1,2) born in the South and living in area (1); (2,1) born in the North and living in area (2); (2,2) born in the South and living in area (2); (3,1) born in the North and living in area (3); (3,2) born in the South and living in area (3). One aspect of table 5 is immediately apparent; some of the states (in particular, those which have been left blank) are *logically* impossible—i.e., logically equal to zero. And this, of course, is a function of the fact that birthplace does not change over time. For comparative purposes, however, the four-way matrical framework will be retained. The interpretation of the probabilities is similar to that noted above for the conditional movement of residences and social class.

Perhaps the most striking feature of residential mobility as conditioned on place of birth is that there seems to be a clear relationship between birthplace and the propensity for shifts in residence. In all cases, i.e., no matter what the initial area of residence, there is a higher probability of changing residence for northern-born Blacks. This is analogous to the situation which was observed for social class conditioned residential changes. It appears that the relatively anomalous factor of birthplace exerts a distinct influence. While this is not necessarily remarkable, it does suggest that any theory of residential mobility will have to account for this type of conditional relationship. Of course, one possible explanation here is that birthplace itself acts as a surrogate for a structural distinction within the Black community. As has been noted, the employed definition of social class is a function of those conditions which influence social class in the *White* community. Social functions, education, ownership of property—these are the variables which defined social status in this example. Suppose, however, that these are *not* the principal conditions which define social class for Blacks. Perhaps a different set of priorities is important, such as where one is born. In this case, if we employ birthplace as a surrogate for social class, then perhaps we can strengthen our explanatory arguments about a relation-

Table 5. *Average Transition Matrix*

Three-State Residence and Two-State Birthplace Changes, Ann Arbor Negroes, 1880–1899

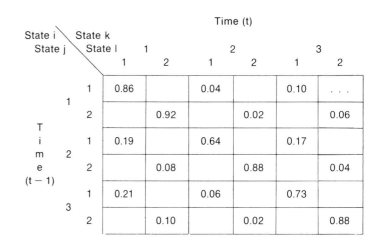

State i / State j (Time t−1)		State k → State l →	1	1	2	2	3	3
			1	2	1	2	1	2
1	1		0.86		0.04		0.10	. . .
1	2			0.92		0.02		0.06
2	1		0.19		0.64		0.17	
2	2			0.08		0.88		0.04
3	1		0.21		0.06		0.73	
3	2			0.10		0.02		0.88

Table 6. *Average Transition Matrix*

Three-State Social Class and Two-State Birthplace Changes,
Ann Arbor Negroes, 1880–1899

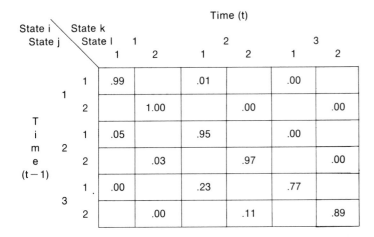

State i / State j (Time t−1)		State k (Time t) 1		2		3	
	State l	1	2	1	2	1	2
1	1	.99		.01		.00	
	2		1.00		.00		.00
2	1	.05		.95		.00	
	2		.03		.97		.00
3	1	.00		.23		.77	
	2		.00		.11		.89

ship between social and residential mobility. Clearly, social conditions do influence residential change. It may be, however, that as far as the Black community is concerned, this "social condition" is more a function of birthplace than of what Whites see as the crucial conditions. In any event, this is one possible way of reasoning and of searching for explanations.

As a final observation, one should note the close relationship exhibited between social mobility and place of birth for the members of the Black community in nineteenth-century Ann Arbor. In particular, consider the parameters of table 6. The same over-all pattern of upward social mobility which was pointed out earlier is apparent. More to the point, however, there also appears to be a distinction between the social mobility patterns of northern-born versus southern-born Blacks. Lower-class heads-of-households who were born in the North exhibit approximately twice the probability of upward social mobility than do Blacks of the same class who were born in the South. The pattern is similar for working-class Blacks, although not so marked. The one anomaly would seem to be for middle-class Blacks, but even here the difference is so small as to make any statistical differentiation impossible (given the number of cases examined). In this regard, there is another observation which would seem to be pertinent: the distinction between the social mobility patterns of northern-born and southern-born Blacks diminished with increased status. This is clearly not an anomaly, and on one level, it might lead to the hypothesis that there exists a propensity for internal discrimination which diminishes with length of stay in the community and general social acceptance. In any event, observed relationships between social class and birthplace do tend to support some of the observations which were noted with respect to residential mobility and birthplace. Although this correlation does not in itself provide conclusive evidence, it does lend strength to our earlier suppositions.

3.3 Some General Remarks

It should be clear from the above discussion that the surface has merely been scratched. The four examples presented here only touch on the possible questions which may be asked about social and residential mobility—even within the context of the very limited set of data which was employed. For reasons of brevity, much of the data of the original study was omitted; many of the observed relationships in the tables were ignored. In addition, a number of the available statistical inference procedures, such as those outlined by Goodman and Cox, have been bypassed in favor of some rather simple observational procedures. Questions as to the best estimation procedures for the transition probabilities—e.g., whether these should be determined in a frequentist or Bayesian manner[71]—have also been side-stepped. The theorems of Markov processes have similarly been ignored in this preliminary discussion. What has been demonstrated, albeit briefly, are some of the possibilities of description, explanation, and hypothesis formulation with the aid of the proposed methodological program.

SUMMARY AND CONCLUSIONS

This paper has outlined a program for exploratory research on Black residential mobility and neighborhood development. The argument was given in three parts. First, the limitations of much of the previous research on the social history and residential and socioeconomic mobility patterns of Blacks in the United States were presented. In the second section, an outline of a comprehensive methodology to account for these limitations was proposed. It included (A) the employment of disaggregated data, and (B) a methodological strategy based on the use of dynamic contingency tables and statistical techniques for analyzing these matrices. The final section provided an illustration of the use of this methodology on some data from a recent study of Black residential mobility in Ann Arbor, Michigan, in the nineteenth century.

Although the conclusions of this investigation are by no means definitive, it is nevertheless possible to offer one or two general observations. The initial stages of any scientific investigation (presumably this includes the study of Black communities) inevitably require careful observation and description. This is taken to be the essence of modern empiricism.[72] Thus, given the types of data that are normally available in the social sciences (i.e., nominal and ordinal) and the difficulties incumbent in employing randomization and other experimental procedures, the obvious methodological program is one which employs a rich classificatory scheme as the foundation for explanatory inferences. This becomes all the more apparent when the descriptive model is also defined with respect to temporal and locational as well as functional attributes. And, of course, the availability of a wide range of estimation and inference procedures makes this course all the more appealing.

From a slightly less pragmatic point of view, however, the proposed methodological program can also be seen as a means of substituting "translucid-box" (or representational) for "black-box" (or phenomenological) models. This point has been discussed at some length in several recent papers;[73] suffice to say here that whereas phenomenological models often preclude or

71. Good, *The Estimation of Probabilities;* T. C. Lee, C. G. Judge, and A. Zellner, "Maximum Likelihood and Bayesian Estimation of Transition Probabilities," *Journal of the American Statistical Association* 63 (1968): 1162–79.

72. For further discussion of this point, see Gale, "Explanation Theory," and P. Suppes, "Models of Data," in E. Nagel, P. Suppes, and A. Tarski, eds. *Logic, Methodology and Philosophy of Science: Proceedings of the 1960 International Congress* (Stanford, California: Stanford University Press, 1962), pp. 252–61.

73. See, for example, Bunge, "Phenomenological Theories," and Gale, "Explanation Theory."

obscure deeper insights into the workings of complex systems, the use of representational models is in quite the opposite spirit. By focusing on relationships, mechanisms of change, and contingent interactions, the aim is to exploit the analogical, heuristic functions of models, i.e., to make the relationships and mechanisms of internal structural change more visible. This is, of course, crucial in the beginning stages of any investigation where the recognition of patterns and formulation of hypotheses are quite as important as the testing of particular theories. And, in terms of the subject of this investigation (Black residential mobility and neighborhood development), in the long-run this is likely to be the strongest justification for the program outlined above.

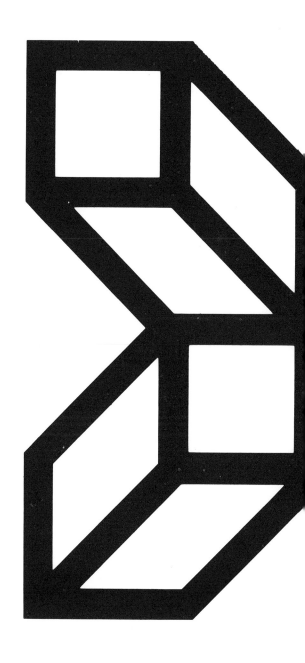

Robert J. Colenutt
Syracuse University

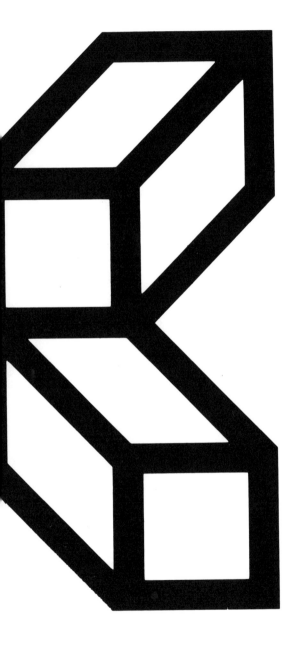

Do Alternatives Exist for Central Cities?

ABSTRACT

Alternative futures for the central areas of American cities may be much more limited than is sometimes assumed. This is because the problems of central cities are caused by structural processes in the American economy and are therefore not solvable by "liberal" planning programs. Four major trends are described which reflect the operation of these structural processes—the tendency for the poor to live in central cities, the reduction in supply of low-income housing, the tendency for businesses to become larger and to locate outside central cities, and the increasing functional separation of central city and suburb. It is argued that liberal planning may not be able to reverse these long-term tendencies. To illustrate the argument, strategies for reviving the tax base, for creating metropolitan governments, or for encouraging community control are analyzed. The conclusion is reached that these strategies show few signs, or indeed capability, of halting or reversing these trends. Therefore, more fundamental policy prescriptions that attack the roots of these trends are suggested.[1]

1. I should like to thank Thomas J. Wilbanks of the Department of Geography, Syracuse University, for his invaluable comments on the first draft of this paper. Thanks are also due to Mike Libee, of Syracuse University, who undertook most of the data analysis. As usual, I must acknowledge the conceptual guidance received over the years from David Harvey of Johns Hopkins University.

It is a commonly held assumption among writers on urban affairs that there are alternative ways in which central cities of metropolitan areas can develop, provided that the correct urban policy is implemented. Thus, there is a widespread belief that good policy-making and good planning can somehow cope with the creeping deterioration of central cities. The purpose of this paper is to challenge this assumption and to argue that the causes of central city problems are not amenable simply to better planning or better ways of governing metropolitan areas but are rooted in the structure of the American economic system and, as such, require more fundamental prescriptions.

The principal reason why planning is seen as a means of salvaging cities is that urban problems are believed to be the result of multiple causes that can be dealt with more or less independently. Hence, there are a number of partial explanations for the dilemmas of central cities. For example, the National Advisory Commission on Civil Disorders (1968) places much of the blame for the living conditions of the poor in central cities on racism in jobs, housing, and education. Downs (1968a) feels that the critical problem is the concentrated distribution of Blacks in metropolitan areas, and he recommends that programs for dispersal be formulated. Other writers see the real villain as sluggishness in the housing market or, alternatively, point at the diminishing tax base of central cities.

Most writers recognize that all of these causes must be dealt with. However, since there is no underlying framework that connects these causes, urban programs often turn out to be conflicting, inconsistent, and generally ineffective. The argument of this paper is that an underlying framework can be detected if some of the long-term trends affecting central cities are investigated. Once there is an understanding of structural processes, it becomes easier to criticize the policies that are being applied to cities and those policies being contemplated.

Thus, in the first part of the paper, four fundamental trends affecting central cities will be analyzed — accumulation of the poor in central cities, reduction in the supply of low-income housing, increasing size of retail and manufacturing establishments, and increasing functional separation of central cities and suburbs. In the second part, three policy frameworks — rebuilding the tax base, metropolitan government, and community control — will be assessed in light of these trends.

THE TRENDS

The Tendency for the Poor to Live in Central Cities

According to Downs (1968b, pp. 13–15), just over half of those in poverty in the United States in 1966 lived in metropolitan areas and, of the estimated 29.7 million total poor at that time, 32 percent lived in central cities. Thus, in the mid-1960s, the poor were almost evenly split between rural and metropolitan areas. Previously, the majority of the poor lived in rural areas; in the future, the majority of the poor will evidently be located in central cities.

Circumstantial evidence for this trend can be obtained by looking at data on the percentage of central city population that is non-White. In 1950, the proportion for all central cities was 12 percent, but by 1966 it had increased to 20 percent. Since the percentage increase was greatest in the largest central cities, it is useful to focus attention on the 48 cities listed by the Bureau of the Census as having Black populations of over 50,000 in 1970. In these cities, the proportion rose from 33.9 percent in 1950 to 45.9 percent in 1970 (table 1). Projections made by the National Commission on Urban Problems (Downs, 1968b, pp. 44–51) suggest that this trend will continue so that by 1985, all central cities will be approximately 31 percent non-White.

Of course, not all non-Whites are poor (only 32 percent in 1966, according to the National Advisory Commission on Civil Disorders, 1968). Therefore, one should not conclude that cities are becoming increasingly poor, judging from non-White trends alone. In fact, over half of the poor in central cities are White. Between 1950 and 1960, over two million people left the counties that the 1964 Commission on Appalachia defined as the Appalachian Region. Almost all of these migrants went to the central cities of metropolitan areas in the Northeast and the Midwest.

A further important qualification about trends in the non-White data should be added. If one examines the *rates* of increase in the non-White population between 1950 and 1960 and between 1960 and 1970, there is an observable decline in the rate of the non-White population increase in the 48 cities listed by the Bureau of the Census (table 1). Thus, although the cities will increasingly contain greater numbers of the poor, very few cities will "go all Black." This is partly because of a reduction in the rates of natural increase and of migration of non-Whites but equally because poor Whites are still entering large cities and because many Whites already there cannot or will not leave. The notion of widespread White emigration in the face of Black immigration is misleading. Many Whites live in very stable areas and could not afford to leave even if they wished to.

However, because those Whites remaining in central cities are generally working-class people, over time there has been a steady decline in the median family income of the central city compared with the rest of the metropolitan area. This is to be expected from the assertion that the central cities are becoming poorer. A

Table 1. *Percentage of Blacks in Cities With a Black Population of 50,000 or More by Rank*

Rank	City	Percentage of Total Pop. 1950	Percentage of Total Pop. 1960	Percentage of Total Pop. 1970	Rate of Change[a] 1950–1960	Rate of Change[b] 1960–1970
1	New York	9.5	14.0	21.2	0.45	0.52
2	Chicago	13.6	22.9	32.7	0.65	0.34
3	Detroit	16.2	28.9	43.7	0.61	0.35
4	Philadelphia	18.2	26.4	33.6	0.41	0.23
5	Washington, D.C.	35.0	53.9	71.1	0.47	0.29
6	Los Angeles	8.7	13.5	17.9	1.20	0.47
7	Baltimore	23.7	34.7	46.4	0.46	0.27
8	Houston	20.9	22.9	25.7	0.72	0.45
9	Cleveland	16.2	28.6	38.3	0.70	0.13
10	New Orleans	31.9·	37.2	45.0	0.29	0.13
11	Atlanta	36.6	38.3	51.3	0.54	0.34
12	St. Louis	18.0	28.6	40.9	0.40	0.16
13	Memphis	37.2	37.0	38.9	0.25	0.31
14	Dallas	13.1	19.0	24.9	1.20	0.61
15	Newark	17.1	34.1	54.2	0.85	0.48
16	Indianapolis	15.0	20.6	18.0	0.53	0.36
17	Birmingham	40.0	39.6	42.0	0.04	0.07
18	Cincinnati	15.5	21.6	27.6	0.39	0.14
19	Oakland	12.4	22.8	34.5	0.76	0.48
20	Jacksonville	26.9	23.2	22.3	0.43	1.45
21	Kansas City	12.2	17.5	22.1	0.50	0.32
22	Milwaukee	3.4	8.4	14.7	1.8	0.67
23	Pittsburgh	12.2	16.7	20.2	0.23	0.03
24	Richmond	31.7	41.8	42.0	0.26	0.13
25	Boston	5.0	9.1	16.3	0.60	0.61
26	Columbus	12.4	16.4	18.5	0.73	0.28
27	San Francisco	5.6	10.0	13.4	1.50	0.29
28	Buffalo	6.4	13.3	20.4	0.93	0.32
29	Gary	29.3	38.8	52.8	2.40	0.28
30	Nashville	20.0	19.1	19.6	0.49	1.67
31	Norfolk	29.4	25.8	28.3	0.72	0.01
32	Louisville	15.6	17.9	23.8	0.22	0.22
33	Ft. Worth	12.9	15.8	19.9	0.57	0.37
34	Miami	16.1	22.4	22.7	0.63	0.15
35	Dayton	14.1	21.8	30.5	0.67	0.28
36	Charlotte	28.1	27.9	30.3	0.50	0.29
37	Mobile	35.4	32.4	35.4	0.38	0.05
38	Shreveport	33.1	34.4	34.1	0.35	0.07
39	Jackson	40.9	35.7	39.7	0.28	0.16
40	Compton	4.5	39.4	71.0	1.00	0.80
41	Tampa	21.9	16.8	19.7	1.80	0.25
42	Jersey City	6.9	13.3	21.0	0.77	0.45
43	Flint	8.7	17.5	28.1	1.40	0.58
44	Savannah	40.4	35.5	44.9	0.10	0.03
45	San Diego	4.4	6.0	7.6	1.30	0.49
46	Toledo	8.0	12.6	13.8	0.64	0.31
47	Oklahoma City	8.6	11.6	13.7	0.80	0.32
48	San Antonio	7.0	7.1	7.6	0.46	0.18

Source: Bureau of the Census, 1970.

[a] Rate of change is calculated by dividing the change of Negro population between 1950–1960 by 1950 Negro population.
[b] Rate of change is calculated by dividing the change of Negro population between 1960–1970 by 1960 Negro population.

comparison of Standard Metropolitan Statistical Area (SMSA) median family income and central city median family income for the 20 largest SMSAs in 1950 and 1960 suggests the general trend (table 2). The average difference between the ratios during this time was 6 percent, meaning that between 1950 and 1960, SMSAs experienced a 6 percent increase in median family income relative to central cities. The largest increases were in Washington, D.C. (14 percent), Detroit (11 percent), and Buffalo (10 percent), whereas the smallest occurred in Houston (− 1 percent), San Antonio (1 percent), and Dallas (2 percent). Generally southern and southwestern cities experienced a smaller increase than northern cities−an important regional variation that will be discussed later in this paper.

The Tendency for the Supply of Low-Income Housing to Diminish

As long as the poor continue to concentrate in central cities there will be a rising demand for low-income housing. According to a commonly accepted housing-market theory, housing for the poor is provided by a filtering down of middle-income housing. There are several reasons why this process cannot provide an adequate supply of housing for the poor. First, not enough middle-income housing is being built to satisfy the increased demand for low-income housing. This is particularly true during an economic recession. Secondly, a rather high percentage of central city housing is already substandard (11 percent in 1960; Smith, 1970, p. 467) or is moving in that direction and will, therefore, eventually be removed from the total housing stock. The low-income housing market is most severely hit by this reduction in supply. Thus, in almost every large central city, vacancy rates for low-income housing are lower than vacancy rates for middle-income housing because of loss through delapidation below minimum standards for occupancy.

Some statistics compiled by the National Advisory Commission on Civil Disorders (1968, p. 467) give an idea of the severity of the problem:

"During the decade of the 1950's when vast numbers of Negroes were migrating to the cities, only 4 million of the 16.8 million new housing units were built in central cities. These additions were counter balanced by the loss of 1.5 million central city units by demolition. The result was an increase in the number of non-whites living in substandard housing (1.4 to 1.8 million between 1950 and 1960) even though the number of substandard units declined."

Demolition or clearance, whether under the name of urban renewal, freeway construction, or other programs,

Table 2. *Ratio of Average Income in SMSA and in Central City for the Twenty Largest United States Cities*

City	1950 Ratio	1960 Ratio
New York	1.05	1.08
Chicago	1.03	1.09
Los Angeles	1.02	1.09
Philadelphia	1.04	1.11
Detroit	1.01	1.12
Baltimore	1.02	1.10
Houston	1.03	1.02
Cleveland	1.10	1.17
Washington, D.C.	1.12	1.26
St. Louis	1.06	1.17
Milwaukee	1.03	1.05
San Francisco	1.00	1.06
Boston	1.08	1.16
Dallas	0.97	0.99
New Orleans	1.01	1.08
Pittsburgh	1.01	1.06
San Antonio	1.01	1.02
San Diego	0.97	0.99
Seattle	0.97	0.99
Buffalo	1.03	1.13

Source: *City and County Data Book,* 1962.

has seriously reduced the supply of low income housing. Furthermore, as Muth (1969, p. 332) points out, the housing that has been removed has not been replaced with similar priced housing. For example, in Syracuse, the number of housing units has risen over the past twenty years and is expected to continue to rise in the future. However, this rise is largely accounted for by middle- and lower-middle-income housing (either new construction or conversion of large houses into multi-family dwellings.)

There are two additional factors which should be remembered. First, the private housing industry is not inclined to build low-income housing because it yields a narrower profit margin than middle-income units. Secondly, public housing which is supposed to augment the decreasing supply of low-income housing has not produced an adequate stock of cheap housing to meet the needs of the different subgroups among the poor and working class nor has it provided structures that satisfy the majority of public housing residents (Smith, pp. 477–80).

The reduction in low-income housing units seems to be a structural trend. Certainly there are no signs of a reversal, and since poverty in central cities is growing we can only assume that the trend will continue. Obviously, this raises important questions regarding the public policy impact on housing for low-income families. For example, one question is whether "opening up the suburbs" will change the situation significantly[2] or whether programs for mass-produced housing will actually increase the supply of housing for all the different kinds of poor families that need housing.

The Tendency for Business Establishments to Become Larger

As the poor accumulate in central cities, there are forces in the economy that make the central cities less attractive to business and industry and which make it more difficult for small entrepreneurs to establish successful businesses there. These developments are related to the tendency for firms and business establishments in a capitalist economy to become larger as the pressures of competition encourage increasing economies of scale, diversification, and vertical integration of production processes. It is almost an axiom of classical economic theory that firms will substitute capital for labor and in other ways reduce the unit costs of production in order to increase or maintain profits.

This process has, however, proved to be rather difficult to measure. The problem appears to lie in the determination of whether a particular firm is independent of other firms. Unless this fact is established, data on the size distribution of firms in a particular industry

2. See, for example, the strong case for opening up the suburbs presented by Linda and Paul Davidoff and Neil Gold in the *New York Times Magazine,* 7 November 1971. However, in this article no definition of "low-income housing" is given, and it is at least probable that if "low-income housing" is built in the suburbs, it will not constitute housing for the poor.

are not trustworthy (Utton, 1970). Since there is an increasing tendency for large firms to integrate vertically, that is, to control an entire production–marketing system from the acquisition of raw materials to the sale of products derived from these materials, the classification of firms by a single function, e.g., automobile manufacturing or food processing, becomes essentially meaningless. Similarly, as large firms continue to diversify by buying out competitors or establishing controlling interests in them, firms become increasingly interlocked.

For these reasons, data on industrial concentration must be interpreted with caution. The most common method of measuring market concentration is to analyze the size distribution of firms in a particular industry, using such measures as proportion of total assets, employment, and value added or profits as indicators of size. Employing this method, most researchers conclude that concentration in nearly all manufacturing industries in the United States and the United Kingdom has increased markedly since 1900 (Hart, 1960; Sheperd, 1961). However, disagreement exists over the continuation of this trend in the United States since World War II. (It is generally agreed that the trend *has* continued in the United Kingdom.)

It is possible that the disagreement is attributable to unreliability in the size distribution method. If vertical integration and diversification have increased since World War II, the method should have become increasingly unreliable. Hence, one may place more faith on the conclusions reached by Collins and Preston (1961) after studying the entry and exit rates of companies to and from the list of the major American firms. They conclude that the list has stabilized significantly since World War II, which, therefore, indicates a tendency toward monopoly or increased concentration.

In what way has all this affected the economic and spatial structure of cities? Probably the most important effects have been on labor-intensive manufacturing and on the competitive position of small retail and service businesses. Manufacturing industry is not only moving out of central cities but is becoming larger and increasingly capitalized. Within any given metropolitan area, therefore, there has been a reduction in the number of firms and establishments producing, distributing, or marketing any particular product (given the size of the market). This reduction has been most severe among the smallest and least capitalized firms with decreasing exit rates as one moves into the larger size classes.

Of course, there has been a steady shift away from manufacturing to service employment, but the same forces are also operating in this sector of the urban economy. There is much evidence of this trend. It is apparent to most city dwellers that stores are being

Table 3. *Retail Sales per Establishment for the Twenty Largest United States Cities (in $000s per Retail Establishment)*

City	City 1950	SMSA–City 1950	City 1960	SMSA–City 1960	SMSA–City Percentage Change 1950–1960	City Percentage Change 1950–1960
New York	77	69	110	142	106	43
Chicago	100	89	156	146	64	56
Los Angeles	102	91	151	161	77	48
Philadelphia	75	71	104	122	72	39
Detroit	114	93	134	158	70	18
Baltimore	84	63	121	133	111	44
Houston	119	57	144	116	104	21
Cleveland	100	91	131	166	82	31
Washington, D.C.	157	122	206	227	86	31
St. Louis	84	71	118	128	80	40
Milwaukee	102	66	125	118	79	23
San Francisco	101	90	117	161	79	16
Boston	109	81	148	134	65	36
Dallas	132	65	177	103	58	34
New Orleans	76	43	130	114	165	71
Pittsburgh	117	70	147	108	54	26
San Antonio	81	38	123	77	103	52
San Diego	100	68	169	129	90	69
Seattle	107	66	162	118	70	51
Buffalo	80	61	113	116	70	41

Source: *City and County Data Book,* 1962.

3. The majority of the differences in the scale of retail operations in the top ten cities and the second ten cities can be explained by the lack of development of suburbs outside the "central city" in the South and the Southwest. Pittsburgh, Buffalo, and Boston are exceptions, however, having extensive suburbs (in a statistical sense) but a relatively small scale of retail operations in these suburban areas. I have no general explanation for these exceptions.

abandoned, that entire commercial strips are deteriorating, and that very large shopping centers are sprouting up in the suburbs and not in the central city.

Partial statistical confirmation of the trend emerges from examination of data on retail sales per retail establishment in the twenty largest United States cities in 1950 and 1960. Perusing the data in table 3 for central cities and suburbs (SMSA-Central City), it is clear that the scale or size of retail operation grew considerably from 1950 to 1960 with an average change of 83 percent for suburban areas. This change only reflects an increase in the average size of establishments and does not reflect increases in chain store activity occurring at the same time.

There is additional evidence from table 3 that the scale of retailing in the suburbs is larger than in the central city. In 1950, the scale of retail activity in central cities was larger than the prevailing scale in the suburbs. This is expected since it was not until the late 1950s that the suburban shopping center boom began in earnest. By 1960, however, the pattern had changed. The scale of operations in suburbia was larger in eight of the ten largest United States cities and in two of the ten second largest cities. It is unclear why the smaller metropolises behave differently from the larger.[3] However, what is important here is that the *shift in the scale of retail activity* in the majority of metropolitan areas is associated with a *spatial shift in location.*

Moreover, change in scale is relatively larger in suburban areas. For example, columns 5 and 6 of table 3, which were constructed by dividing column 2 by column 4 and column 1 by column 3, respectively, show the comparative rate of change in scale between 1950 and 1960 for cities and suburban areas. The rate of increase is, on the average, twice as large in suburban areas as in central cities. Thus, although retail operations are growing all over the metropolitan area, they are not growing so rapidly in the cities as they are in the suburbs.

Further illustration of this trend is given by Brimmer (1969) in a study of the Negro in the American economy. He produces some very revealing data on the decline of Black-owned businesses in the United States (table 4). First, these data demonstrate that self-employed businessmen of all kinds are no longer competitive and that, on the average, Black businesses (which are usually located in central cities) are two or three times less successful than non-Black businesses. Secondly, it is possible to infer from these data that the prospects for the development of a successful business in the poor areas of cities are not promising. In the suburbs, on the other hand, there is a comparatively high probability that a small retail store will survive as long as it is located in a shopping center (as opposed to a commercial strip). In shopping centers, small retail stores can economically take advantage of the proximity to large department stores and supermarkets. These same economies affect the survival of small stores in central business districts.[4] The tendency for businesses to become larger has, therefore, had a fundamental impact on the spatial pattern of employment opportunities and on the spatial structure of retailing in central cities. The main effects appear to be the removal of job opportunities for poorly skilled workers and the creation of barriers to local business initiative.

The Tendency for Central Cities to Become Isolated

One of the results of the continued migration of the poor to central cities and the movement of manufacturing and retail businesses to the suburbs is that the central city is becoming functionally separated from the rest of the SMSA. Thus, central cities are increasingly assuming the characteristics of depressed areas with major differences in social class composition as compared with the suburbs. They have also experienced a decreasing amount of spatial interaction with the suburbs.

There is abundant evidence that there are social class differences between central cities and suburbs and that these differences are increasing. Duncan and Duncan (1960) have shown that there are significant spatial clusterings of various occupational groups; most social

Table 4. *Annual Average Percentage Change in the Number of Self-Employed Businessmen 1950–1960*

Business	Negro Self-employed	All Self-employed
Communications, utilities, and sanitary services	−11.2	−1.2
Trucking and taxis	− 6.5	−2.9
Furniture and house furnishing	− 6.1	−2.9
Apparel and accessories	− 5.9	−3.6
Hardware and building materials	− 3.9	−1.6

Source: Brimmer, Andrew F. 1969. "The Negro in the National Economy," in John F. Kain (ed.), *Race and Poverty*. Englewood Cliffs, N.J.: Prentice-Hall, Inc., p. 91.

4. It is interesting to observe how the competitive advantage of specialty shops in downtown areas (e.g., boutiques, gift shops, organic food stores, etc.) is reduced by the development of speciality "shops" within large department stores.

area analyses have shown clear patterns of separation between social classes in metropolitan areas. Moreover, theories of the urban land market and of the socio-spatial structuring of cities both predict consistent patterns of separation. There are some exceptions, of course, such as the presence of prestige residential areas in the center of many large cities, but the general pattern holds. Some writers, including Brazer (1967) for example, have labeled this inference a "stereotype." Brazer maintains that most metropolitan areas in the United States do not exhibit the expected dichotomy of a poor central city and a rich suburb. She reached this conclusion after a study of the economic and social differences between the central cities and suburbs of 177 metropolitan areas. However, since the proportion of a metropolitan population living in the "central city" varies widely, her conclusion is not really acceptable. In fact, if one examines those cities in the Northeast that have a high proportion of the metropolitan population living outside the central city, the stereotype is clearly confirmed. In Brazer's own words (1967, p. 300):

"In the Northeast the dichotomy is pronounced and conforms to the stereotype: in addition, non-whites, broken families, elderly persons, undereducated youth and adults, low income families and low status occupations are all much more prominent in the cities; while college graduates, high income families, high status occupations and high housing values are disproportionately represented in the suburbs."

Evidence of the widening of the central city–suburb gap is not readily available. We have already seen that the income gap between city and suburb is increasing (table 2) and that the non-White proportion of central city populations is growing. Both of these trends suggest a widening of the gap. In addition, the Taeuber and Taeuber (1965) study of the segregation of Negroes in cities reveals how the pattern of segregation has increased steadily since 1910 and continues to increase, particularly in Southern cities and larger Northeastern cities. Although they were investigating racial segregation, it is not unreasonable to assume that this was highly correlated with class segregation.

Functional separation of central cities and suburbs seems to be following the dispersal of industry, shopping centers, and middle and high income populations throughout the suburbs of metropolitan areas. It is becoming apparent that suburbs tend to interact with each other more than with the central city. This was observed in 1956 by Hoover and Vernon (1959, p. 145) who showed that in the New York Metropolitan Area journey-to-work trip-rates between and within suburban traffic zones were higher than the rates between suburban zones and the central city (although this difference diminished with proximity to the central city). Similar patterns are evident for shopping trips and for social and entertainment trips.

However, the fact that jobs are moving to the suburbs has raised expectations that interaction between central city and suburb will take the form of "reverse commuting." Although reverse commuting is taking place, there are reasons to believe that it will not be so heavy as the suburb-to-city commuting that it is partially replacing. One reason for this is that suburban manufacturing firms are generally more capital intensive than the manufacturing firms that were previously located in the central city and, therefore, employ fewer unskilled and semi-skilled workers. Secondly, there is some evidence that suburban firms are not enthusiastic about hiring central city residents unless these residents have cars.[5] Since the poor own disproportionately fewer cars than the non-poor, hiring practices based on automobile ownership reduce the amount of commuting between central cities and suburbs.

If these interpretations of recent developments are correct, central cities or the centers of large metropolitan areas are likely to function much like depressed regions in the spatial economy. Although the labor force in poor areas will not be completely discarded by the rest of the economy, it is unlikely that it will be developed to the same level as the labor force in other regions of the metropolis. To some degree Turner's (1970, p. 3) statement that in the inner city ". . . the economics of uselessness are replacing the economics of exploitation . . ." may increasingly characterize the function of poor regions within central cities.

The familiar characteristics of depressed areas should ultimately manifest themselves. Younger and better educated persons will be forced to apply their skills outside the region so that the population will gradually become comprised of older persons more likely to be dependent on welfare and government work programs. Neglect of property and services will increase. There is already an abundance of vacant, derelict, and under-used land in central cities. Some areas of central cities are still in demand by expanding institutions (universities, cultural centers, and government buildings) but large areas are not.

LONG- AND SHORT-TERM TRENDS

The four trends cited above appear to be structural, that is, they are related to the way in which the American economy works and is organized in space. Other trends, such as the decline of city tax bases, deterioration of public transportation, and the rise in street crimes, have not been described since they are consequences of the trends outlined above.

5. A study made by students at Syracuse University showed that large suburban manufacturing firms discriminate in their hiring activities against persons without cars.

Table 5. *The Ratio of Central City Population to Total SMSA Population for 46 United States Cities, 1960 and 1970*

City	1960 Ratio	1970 Ratio
New York	0.73	0.68
Chicago	0.57	0.48
Detroit	0.44	0.36
Philadelphia	0.46	0.40
Washington, D.C.	0.37	0.26
Los Angeles	0.47	0.45
Baltimore	0.52	0.44
Houston	0.66	0.62
Cleveland	0.46	0.36
New Orleans	0.69	0.57
Atlanta	0.48	0.35
St. Louis	0.36	0.26
Memphis	0.74	0.81
Dallas	0.61	0.54
Newark	0.24	0.20
Indianapolis	0.50	0.68
Birmingham	0.57	0.41
Cincinnati	0.40	0.33
Jacksonville	0.44	1.00
Kansas City	0.44	0.40
Milwaukee	0.58	0.51
Pittsburgh	0.25	0.22
Richmond	0.50	0.48
Boston	0.27	0.23
Columbus	0.62	0.59
San Francisco	0.42	0.35
Buffalo	0.41	0.34
Gary	0.61	0.52
Nashville	0.37	0.83
Norfolk	0.73	0.60
Louisville	0.54	0.44
Fort Worth	0.62	0.51
Miami	0.31	0.26
Dayton	0.36	0.28
Charlotte	0.64	0.59
Mobile	0.54	0.51
Shreveport	0.58	0.61
Jackson	0.65	0.59
Tampa	0.59	0.49
Jersey City	0.45	0.42
Flint	0.47	0.39
Savannah	0.79	0.62
San Diego	0.55	0.51
Toledo	0.50	0.55
Oklahoma City	0.63	0.58
San Antonio	0.82	0.75

Source: Bureau of the Census, 1970.

Moreover, along with the long-term developments, there are recurrent cycles and short-term trends that have important social consequences. The economic and social geography of the city actually changes significantly during economic upswings and downswings or during booms and recessions in particular sectors of the economy. We have already noted that the supply of housing is sensitive to short-term economic trends. Another example is the profound effect that high rates of unemployment have on the character of neighborhoods. More welfare, less income, and more teenagers without jobs introduce new patterns of social relations into a neighborhood. When there are jobs, the activities and atmosphere are different. On a smaller geographic scale the vicissitudes of the economy create emigration in some regions and overcrowding in others. Such is inevitable in an unplanned spatial economy and is one of the forces that cities have to deal with.

THE GEOGRAPHIC SCALE OF SOCIAL CHANGE

Thus, the condition of cities is related to certain structural relations in the national economy and at the same time is affected by short-term trends and by changing relative location in the spatial economy. If one is serious about coming to terms with the urban condition, then it is necessary to begin exercising control over the processes that cause undesirable trends and inequalities. Control over processes can be exerted at different levels of government and spatial organization. For example, in order to create more low income housing for cities, it is possible to conceive of programs developed at the federal, state, metropolitan, city, or neighborhood levels. It makes a great deal of difference which level is adopted. For example, federal housing subsidies, public housing, or neighborhood housing cooperatives will have quite different impacts on the low-income housing market. As another example, poverty might be tackled more decisively by raising the minimum wage, introducing a national health service, and providing a guaranteed annual income of $6,500 than by encouraging individual cities and communities to attract employers, engage in neighborhood rehabilitation programs, and subsidize local health clinics. All of these programs are probably necessary, but the point is that local programs may well prove ineffective without higher level intervention.

A CRITIQUE OF STRATEGIES FOR CENTRAL CITIES

This section of the paper is a critique of three general strategies for reviving central cities. These approaches will be analyzed in the light of the trends outlined above and also with reference to the geographical scale on which they operate.

Rebuilding the Tax Base

Much attention is being focused on "the flight of the tax base" from central cities; so much so that the problem is being gradually elevated to the status of a principal determinant of urban policy (e.g., urban renewal, subsidies for downtown redevelopment, etc.). It cannot be denied that cities are caught in a cost squeeze caused by a reduction in the tax base and an increase in the demand for services[6] and that, as Netzer (1968, p. 443) points out, central city–suburban tax base disparities are increasing. However, one has to ask (at the risk of sounding callous) what effect an increase in tax base might have; what effect an infusion of money from revenue sharing or from new taxable properties would have on poverty, inequality, or the deterioration of the central city. Such an increase would be ineffective; principally because there is little evidence that cities with large tax bases are tackling poverty any more effectively than cities with small or diminishing tax bases. A sense of the spatial variation in tax bases among cities may be obtained by examining table 5 where city populations are expressed as ratios of total SMSA populations for 46 metropolitan areas. Assuming that this measure is a reasonable indicator of the relative strength of city tax bases, some interesting conclusions can be drawn from the data.

In both 1960 and 1970, those metropolitan areas with large fractions of the total population in the central city were generally located in the South and Southwest: Houston, New Orleans, Memphis, Dallas, Fort Worth, Charlotte, Jackson, Savannah, and San Antonio. Those with the smallest fractions living within the city limits were Northern cities such as Detroit, Cleveland, St. Louis, Newark, Pittsburgh, Boston, and Buffalo. There are exceptions such as New York City, Columbus, and Gary, which have larger than expected percentages for Northern cities, and Atlanta, which has a smaller than expected percentage for a Southern city. However, the dominant pattern is that of relatively smaller city areas in the North compared with the South and Southwest.

It is probably accurate to conclude, then, that large Southern and Southwestern cities do not have a tax base problem of anywhere near the same severity as cities in the North. Yet these cities have many of the same problems as Northern cities—growing accumulation of the poor in central areas, deterioration of housing and services, lack of inner-city employment, inadequate supply of low income housing, etc. These problems exist independently of the tax base.

How can this be explained? First, as Campbell and Sacks (1967) point out, city revenues do not come entirely from the local tax base. In fact, federal and state monies are equally important, and these contributions vary considerably between regions. Also, it seems likely

6. One of the important trends affecting central cities at the moment is that despite a general decrease in central city population, the absolute number of housing units and households is going up. Thus, demands on services are increasing even though the total population is going down. For example, data prepared by John Thompson, Department of Geography, Syracuse University, show that in 1968, 220,600 people were accommodated in 64,500 housing units; in 1970, 197,000 persons were accommodated in 71,800 housing units. Similarly, the number of households has risen. What all this means is that the demand for services is increasing as the sharing of space, services, and public facilities is decreasing.

that a critical issue in city government is not the strength of the tax base but the manner in which city revenues are returned to residents. If services are inequitably distributed and tend to favor the needs of the rich over the needs of the poor,[7] an increase in the tax base will not change the pattern of relative deprivation in the city. Chicago, for example, has made an enormous effort to anchor and rebuild the tax base. However, this effort has not affected the Black neighborhoods on the South side (Woodlawn, for instance) or the Southern White areas of Uptown. In fact, it is possible that the increase in the tax base has been absorbed by the service demands of the new taxable properties themselves.

The tax base question and the policies stemming from it do not, therefore, confront the processes that have created regions of poverty and distress in central cities, although, of course, a tax crisis does not really ameliorate matters.

Metropolitan Government

The push for metropolitan government arises quite naturally from the tax crisis. Faced with internal tax shortages and the possibility that revenue sharing will not provide an adequate supplement to the resource base of the city, as well as with hostility on the part of "upstate" or "downstate" legislators to cities in general, metropolitan government is being recommended as a way of pooling the resources of metropolitan regions.[8]

The other major rationale for metropolitan government is that it creates an opportunity to distribute more equitably spillovers from services and facilities throughout metropolitan regions. Netzer (1970, pp. 131–36), discussing the externalities of solid waste disposal and of air and water pollution, argues that small area governments are entirely inadequate to deal with the regional scale of these problems. It is undoubtedly true that cities, often engaged in a struggle with suburban municipalities for permission to build sewage and waste disposal plants, would welcome with relief a metropolitan solution to these problems.

The claims for metropolitan government are substantial. Danielson (1966, p. 153) states that ". . . metropolitan government threatens to redistribute influence and alter the existing system of public control over the vital parameters of community life." The question is how reasonable this claim may be and whether metropolitan governments can check the forces impinging upon the cities; for example, whether metropolitan governments can make it possible to reduce poverty, improve services, build houses, and provide better schools.

One way in which the impact of metropolitan government could be assessed is the investigation of metropolitan governments that have already been created. In

7. In *Detroit Geographical Expedition Field Notes No. 4,* "The Trumbull Community," there is a study of the inequality of police protection among communities in the city of Detroit. This is one example of the way tax dollars are returned to city residents in an inequitable fashion.

8. The literature on metropolitan government is extensive. See, for example, Bernard J. Frieden, *Metropolitan America: Challenge to Federalism* (Washington, D.C., 1966); The Advisory Commission on Intergovernmental Relations, *Metropolitan Social and Economic Disparities: Implications for Intergovernmental Relations in Central Cities and Suburbs* (Washington, D.C., 1965); Robert O. Warren, *Government in Metropolitan Regions* (Davis, California: Institute of Government Affairs, University of California, 1966).

the United States, one could examine Miami–Dade County (Florida) which became metropolitan between 1953 and 1955 (Sofen, 1966) or Nashville, whose residents voted for metropolitan government in 1963 (Grant, 1966). Comparison could then be made with similar cities that have not adopted this form of government. Alternatively, in the United Kingdom, metropolitan government in the London region could be studied, exploring, for example, the effect of the Greater London Council on the distribution of services and resources among social groups and between social areas in the region.

If such studies were conducted, it is possible that the redistributive effects of metropolitan government would be found to be only as strong as the state, federal, or national policies toward cities and poverty in which the different metropolitan areas find themselves enmeshed. Metropolitan government cannot build low-income housing unless federal subsidies are available nor can metropolitan government develop good city schools unless state aid to schools is equalized. In other words, metropolitan governments by themselves may not be able to reverse inequality in cities. There is still poverty, homelessness, and educational inequality in London despite the efforts of the Greater London Council.

Although these shortcomings do exist, metropolitan government might provide a holding function in the decay of city services and might further increase the pressure for low-income housing in the suburbs (provided that this is backed by federal legislation). However, the precise allocation of the new resource base will depend on the distribution of voting power in the government. Poor inner-city communities might easily be outvoted by more numerous and politically powerful suburban communities. In order to prevent this from happening, a clear social policy of income redistribution would be required as a guide to policy-making. Without such a policy, existing trends would, in fact, be reinforced.

An illuminating example of what happens in the absence of such a policy guide is provided by the Baltimore Metrotown Plan prepared by the Baltimore Regional Planning Council (Boyce, Day, and McDonald, 1970). The Council encompasses the city of Baltimore and the surrounding counties of Baltimore, Howard, and Anne Arundel and is required to develop a regional plan for the Baltimore metropolitan area. The Metrotown Plan, based on projections of population and income for the city and the counties, recommended that a series of satellite centers (or Metrotowns) be built in the counties as a means of introducing some coherence into the pattern of virtually unplanned urban sprawl. The plan, if adopted, would direct large quantities of regional investment and planning effort to the suburbs which would further decrease the relative advantages of the city of Baltimore itself for industry, retail outlets, housing construction, and entertainment centers. In the long run, the structural trends outlined earlier would be strongly and decisively reinforced. Pahl (1970, p. 233) draws the same conclusion from the reports of the South East (England) Economic Planning Council which he finds are characterized by a "confusion about social goals and social policies." Hence, the real danger of the metropolitan regional approach is that the trends that create and sustain poor regions will not be arrested. There is no guarantee whatever that metropolitan government per se will choose to be altruistic.

The conflict between the needs of the central city and those of the rest of the metropolitan region is at the core of the urban problem. Hawley and Zimmer (1970), in a survey of attitudes toward metropolitan government held by a sample of 3,000 persons in cities across the United States, found that suburban residents were strongly resistant to sharing with the central city and that a majority of central city residents were also not at all convinced that metropolitan government would be in their best interests. Thus, neither group believes that investment in one subregion will eventually filter down or filter across metropolitan boundaries. The problem is that what is good for one part of the metropolitan region is not necessarily good for the other part. And even within particular subregions there is no guarantee that benefits from a particular investment (such as a new office building) would filter down to those with the greatest needs. Winnick (1970) characterizes this conflict as one of *place prosperity* versus *people prosperity*—a central city may have an exciting new skyline, but poverty may flourish behind it all.

Community Control

Because high-level policies and programs fail to deal effectively with the problems of central cities, the concept of community control has become popular in one form or another. These forms vary from encouraging neighborhoods to provide needed services through neighborhood government to cultural nationalism and self-determination for the Black communities of central cities. These concepts will be considered along with the work of community groups in inner cities.

Neighborhood and community organizations spread quite rapidly in the United States cities during the 1950s and 1960s. Some of the organizations grew out of the fear of Black invasion, but many were encouraged by city planning commissions in an attempt to persuade local people to become concerned about their own neighborhoods. Leggett (1968), in his study of the attitudes of the working class in Detroit, describes how grass-roots block clubs were organized with the help of the city planning department. A similar policy is now being followed in Syracuse where the mayor has a policy of "transferring power and attention to the neighborhoods and away from downtown."

Since block clubs and neighborhood organizations emphasize conservation and neighborhood improvement, they are supported principally by home owners. However, in areas of the city where the majority of residents are renters and in which it is commonly believed that the neighborhood is declining, neighborhood organizations find support (and success) much harder. In addition, there is little evidence that even the most flourishing neighborhood organizations can reverse the long-term trends of the movement of jobs to the suburbs or the decay of inner city commercial strips, for example. Kotler's (1969) concept of neighborhood government is a natural extension of community organization. He proposes partly self-governing communities within metropolitan regions. Assuming that a neighborhood system could be established, the question for the cities is whether the poor units in the system could meet their own needs.

This dilemma is really the starting point for Harvey's (1971) essay on territorial social justice in which he argues that a neighborhood government system would be unjust unless poor areas were systematically compensated for their lack of resources, greater needs, and greater accumulation of negative spillovers. This approach assumes that relative deprivation can be reduced by ironing out some of the environmental differences between subregions in the city. However, it is uncertain whether inequalities in the spatial distribution of income and occupations will be reduced by this procedure. Since it was these inequalities that placed people in disadvantaged locations in the first place, it seems necessary to investigate whether they could be altered by territorial redistribution of resources.

Although neighborhood government has not been adopted in any American city, the "community" has become the focus for most of the serious action programs concerned with saving the inner city. Two positions will be discussed here—the development of community organizations for survival reasons and the attempt to rebuild communities by community effort. The first position is really a holding action; the second is much more ambitious and envisages comprehensive community redevelopment.

Survival for the poor communities of American cities is a real issue. These communities are threatened by the expansion of institutions, by urban renewal, by the neglect of landlords and city services, and by inadequate police protection. Studies of the Trumbull community in Detroit (made by the Trumbull Community Center and the Detroit Geographical Expedition in the summer of 1971) showed that the deterioration of the neighborhood over the preceding ten years was due largely to the activities of the Detroit Housing Authority.[9] The Authority has been steadily buying up property in the community and allowing it to deteriorate in order that the area can be eventually cleared. Fear of renewal has caused home owners to move, thus further undermining the strength of the community. At the same time, local commercial establishments faced with declining demand are being forced to close. Meanwhile, the city of Detroit refuses to improve services in the area because they do not expect the community to exist much longer. This is an example of a crisis of community survival.

The Trumbull community organization has come to play a more vital role in the neighborhood as the crisis has deepened. It has challenged the urban renewal plans and has begun to provide community services that the city would not supply. Free health services, a housing relocation service, and free courses in law and community planning are now available in the community. There are also plans to start a housing cooperative. For the first time, Trumbull is beginning to exert some control over its destiny. This is really the issue in many central city neighborhoods. Previously, powerful business and institutional interests have been making plans for them which have not always been in the best interests of the neighborhoods. These plans improve the bargaining power of the community and ensure local participation in city or institutional planning that might effect the neighborhood. The hope is that counter plans prepared in time can obstruct developments that threaten the community. These expressions of community resistance and initiative are increasingly seen (especially by community organizers) as the beginning of the long struggle for community control.

However, it would be unwise to romanticize about the power or effectiveness of groups such as the Trumbull community organization. They are necessary but are not inevitably effective. In many of the struggles against freeways, university expansion plans, and police harassment, poor communities have not been successful. Community action does not provide any long-term alternative to more sweeping higher level programs for cities. It provides pressure for radical change but should be viewed only as a transitional phase in the struggle for power in metropolitan communities and in society as a whole.

Community redevelopment, on the other hand, is more ambitious and is, in a sense, less politically radical. It begins with the assumption that inner city communities can be rebuilt within the framework of American capitalism. The most recent account of such a redevelopment strategy for the ghetto is the book by Vietorisz and Harrison on economic development in Harlem (1970). They

9. See *Detroit Geographical Expedition Field Notes No. 4,* "The Trumbull Community," February 1972.

106

argue that a set of community owned and operated greenhouse industries (industries that produce goods and services needed by the local community, provide job training opportunities, and stimulate other industries) could build an economic base for Central Harlem that would ultimately generate jobs, services, housing, and political power for its residents.

The theoretical key to the plan is an idea called "backward integration." Some simple examples will serve to explain this concept. Every greenhouse industry in the community (automobile, food, or clothing cooperatives) needs supplies at low prices (food, cans, spare parts) from other business establishments. At the moment these supplies come from outside the community; but if they could be produced locally, one more piece of the Harlem economy could come under the control of the community. If there is a sufficient demand for food, for example, a canning plant might well be a feasible local industry. Vietorisz and Harrison contend that with luck and a large amount of initial capital, a process of backward integration could spawn stores, warehouses, factories, banks, and housing construction.

The task is formidable. In November 1966, when Vietorisz and Harrison studied the economy of Harlem, they found that there was an official unemployment rate of 8.3 percent (30 percent for males 16–19 years old) and a subemployment rate of 35 percent.[10] To make any real dent in this crisis situation, a large amount of money would be needed to get things moving, and local and federal legislation would be necessary to complement the activities of the Harlem development corporation. Vietorisz and Harrison note, for example, that a minimum wage of $3.50 an hour would be necessary in order to raise employed workers out of poverty. Even if this were forthcoming, it is difficult to envisage a renewed Harlem that would be an attractive alternative to those that have the resources to live elsewhere.

Writers on community development such as Roberts (1970) and Tabb (1970) argue that Black capitalist or co-operative enterprises (e.g., the Harlem project) cannot possibly reduce the relative deprivation of the poor. They point out that Black businesses or cooperatives can never provide goods and services that are truly competitive with White corporations, even if the community enthusiastically supports local enterprise. They also infer that the subemployment of Central Harlem is necessary for the smooth functioning of American capitalism and, therefore, a substantial improvement of poor areas of cities would not be feasible within the existing economic system. Consequently, these authors do not feel that it is possible to elevate the poor to the non-poor class without restructuring the economic system itself.

10. "Subemployment" is defined by the Labor Department as the sum of those who work but hold marginal jobs, those who are employed part-time but would prefer full-time work, and those who earn poverty wages.

CONCLUSION

The argument of this paper has been that the crisis of central cities is rooted in the way the American economy operates. The economy has shifted the poor from the countryside and from Appalachia (Peet, 1970) but it has not reduced relative deprivation. It has only changed the geographical distribution of the poor. All of the economic indicators for the South, for example, look healthier now than 30 years ago. However, this is not because the Southern poor have been able to escape from poverty in the South itself, but simply because large numbers of the poor have abandoned the region and are being replaced by segments of the non-poor population.

Hence, one cannot expect the economy to raise the poor out of poverty just because they are now located in central cities. If it was ever true in the past that cities acted as ladders for social mobility, it is less true now when there are more of the poor living in cities. Also the same forces of capitalization and concentration and the systematic bias against powerless communities that drove the poor out of the rural South are maintaining poverty in metropolitan areas.

A critical question, therefore, is whether some governmental intervention could alter this situation. The three general strategies discussed above provide possible means for improving the situation in the central cities by a small amount. However, they provide little assurance that relative deprivation will be reduced substantially. Current policies are aimed at only a small degree of redistribution, and they do not challenge the processes in the economy which create spatially inequitable patterns of social and economic opportunity in the first place. Such a challenge is necessary if we wish to find just alternatives for central city residents.

REFERENCES CITED

Boyce, Ronald, Day, Michael, and McDonald, Chris. 1970. *Metropolitan Plan Making*. Philadelphia: Regional Science Research Institute.

Brazer, Marjorie. 1967. "Economic and Social Disparities Between Central Cities and Their Suburbs." *Land Economics* 43:294–302.

Brimmer, Andrew F. 1969. "The Negro in the American Economy." In John F. Kain, ed. *Race and Poverty*. Englewood Cliffs, N.J.: Prentice-Hall.

Campbell, Alan K., and Sacks, Seymour. 1967. *Metropolitan America*. New York: The Free Press of Glencoe.

Collins, N. R., and Preston, L. E. 1961. "The Size Structure of the Largest Industrial Firms, 1909–1958." *American Economic Review* 51:986–1011.

Danielson, Michael N. 1966. *Metropolitan Politics*. Boston: Little, Brown and Co.

Downs, Anthony. 1968a. *Who Are the Urban Poor?* New York: Committee for Economic Development.

———. 1968b. "Alternative Futures for the American Ghetto." *Daedalus* 97:1331–78.

Duncan, Beverly, and Duncan, Otis D. 1960. "The Measurement of Intra-City Locational and Residential Patterns." *Journal of Regional Science* 2:37–54.

Grant, Daniel R. 1966. "Nashville's Politicians and Metro." In Michael N. Danielson, ed. *Metropolitan Politics*. Boston: Little, Brown and Co.

Hart, P. E. 1960. "Business Concentration in the United Kingdom." Journal of the Royal Statistical Society 123:50–58.

Harvey, David. 1971. "Social Justice in Spatial Systems." Paper presented to the Association of American Geographers, April 1971, Boston.

Hawley, Amos H., and Zimmer, Basil G. 1970. *Metropolitan Community.* Beverly Hills: Sage Publications.

Hoover, Edgar M., and Vernon, Raymond. 1959. *Anatomy of a Metropolis.* Cambridge: Harvard University Press.

Kotler, Milton. 1969. *Neighborhood Government.* New York: Bobbs-Merrill Co.

Leggett, John C. 1968. *Class, Race and Labour.* London: Oxford University Press.

Muth, Richard F. 1969. *Cities and Housing.* Chicago: University of Chicago Press.

Netzer, Dick. 1968. "Federal, State, and Local Finance in a Metropolitan Context." In Harvey S. Perloff and Lowdon Wingo, Jr., eds. *Issues in Urban Economics.* Baltimore: Johns Hopkins University Press.

———. 1970. *Economic and Urban Problems.* New York: Basic Books.

Pahl, R. E. 1970. *Whose City?* London: Longmans Group.

Peet, Richard. 1970. "The Geography of American Poverty." *Antipode* 2:1–34.

Report of the National Advisory Commission on Civil Disorders. 1968. New York: Bantam Books.

Roberts, Dick. 1970. *The Fraud of Black Capitalism.* New York: Pathfinder Press.

Shepherd, W. G. 1961. "A Comparison of Industrial Concentration in the United States and Britain." *Review of Economics and Statistics* 43:70–75.

Smith, W. F. 1971. *Housing: The Social and Economic Elements.* Berkeley: University of California Press.

Sofen, Edward. 1966. "Reflections on the Creation of Miami's Metro." In Michael N. Danielson, ed. *Metropolitan Politics.* Boston: Little, Brown and Co.

Tabb, William K. 1970. *The Political Economy of the Black Ghetto.* New York: W. W. Norton and Co., Inc.

Taeuber, Karl E., and Taeuber, Alma F. 1965. *Negroes in Cities.* Chicago: Aldine Publishing Co.

Turner, James. 1970. "Blacks in Cities: Land and Self-Determination." *Black Scholar* 1:9–20.

Utton, M. A. 1970. *Industrial Concentration.* Baltimore: Penguin Books.

Vietorisz, Thomas, and Harrison, Bennett. 1970. *The Economic Development of Harlem.* New York: Praeger Books.

Winnick, Louis. 1969. "Place Prosperity vs. People Prosperity." Unpublished paper.

5

PATTERNS OF BLACK
INTRAURBAN MOBILITY
AND RESTRICTED
RELOCATION OPPORTUNITIES

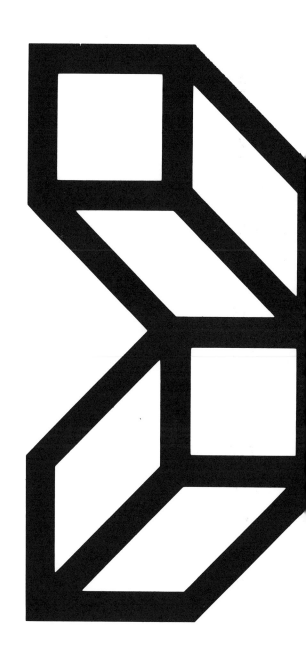

W. A. V. Clark
University of California, Los Angeles

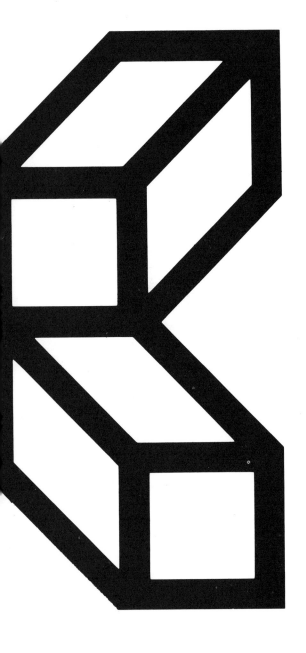

Patterns of Black Intraurban Mobility and Restricted Relocation Opportunities

ABSTRACT

This paper focuses on a sample of Black households which moved within the Milwaukee region during the period 1950–1962. A data set consisting of residence histories for the years 1952, 1954, 1956, 1958, 1960, and 1962 was used to examine two hypotheses regarding the nature of the residential mobility of Black households. The results of the tests suggest that Black households move shorter distances than other households as a whole and that those Black households moving longer distances often have higher family incomes and more extensive educational backgrounds. Additional evidence on the movements of Black households was obtained by a Markov Chain analysis. The difficulties of using Markov Chain analysis in situations involving both time and space dimensions are recognized. However, in this case, a methodology may be employed to overcome such problems. After the two-dimensional locational matrix was collapsed into North–South and East–West components, transition probability matrices and matrices of mean first passage times were computed. The results confirmed the circular nature of residential movements within the ghetto. The implications of this research emphasize the restricted relocation opportunities for Black households. While White households often change residences to achieve gains in neighborhood status and improved community facilities, including schooling, this seems less plausible for Blacks.[1]

1. This study was supported by a grant from the University of California. The use of the UCLA Campus Computing Network is acknowledged.

While there is increasing information in the literature about the movement of urban households as a whole within cities, there remains a lack of detail on the movement of specific minority groups. In particular, there is almost no information on the intra-city migration of Black households. Hunter (1964) has suggested, "A hypothetical view of the slum would show it with much movement back and forth and in circles but not much out of the area . . . (moreover) there are no studies showing the exact nature of this phenomenon authoritatively and exhaustively. . . ." The documented studies indicate only the general pattern of mobility. A study of the East Woodlawn area of Chicago (Hunter, 1964) indicated that only 23.7 percent of Blacks five years old and older had resided at the same address for five years or longer at the time of the 1960 census. Another study in Newark (Hunter, 1964) showed that while only 62 percent of White households studied had moved at least once in ten years, 84 percent of the Black households *had* moved in the same ten-year period. The impact of this type of mobility increases the pressures on the continuity of family life and is deemed particularly detrimental to the establishment of schooling patterns and the progress of children through the elementary school grades and into high school. In some ghetto areas, schools registered more transfers than pupils actually attending school. For example, in 1962, the Hough Elementary School in Cleveland had an enrollment of 1,478 and 1,648 transfers (Cleveland Board of Education, 1962). Thus, mobility within ghetto areas may have a decisive and regressive effect on the development of the Black population. It is, therefore, of prime importance to establish the extent to which mobility occurs within the ghetto.

Although research on intraurban mobility to date has established a number of important generalizations, it is presently unknown whether the generalizations apply specifically to minority populations. In addition, the generalizations are focused on the reasons for changing residences rather than on the spatial elements of the relocations of households. The importance of the life cycle, of neighborhood and environmental factors, and of forced relocation in the movement of minority households is as yet not determined. While it is expected that life cycle factors are important considerations in the relocation of Black households, the same life cycle factors may be overridden by the desire to find better housing within or outside the ghetto.

Similarly, several models (Wolpert, 1965; Brown and Moore, 1970; McGinnis, 1968) of the residential location process have been proposed, but none of these models has included a specific minority component. This is partially understandable since there has been a lack of empirically derived information which could be used to suggest ways in which the models may be elaborated. Recently, a comprehensive general model of mobility has focused on the mobility process within a Markov Chain framework and has suggested that the movement of households can be examined within and between states characterized with particular socio-economic descriptions (McGinnis, 1968). However, extensions of this model have criticized the Markov approach and have substituted for it a general stochastic model (McGinnis, 1968). Despite the promising avenues of approach opened by the mobility models, there is insufficient evidence to suggest that they will be generally applicable, and in any case, all the modeling approaches require considerable modification and development. Hence, the main task in this paper is to test two hypotheses of intraurban movement of Black households. It is hoped that the analysis will elicit information which will be useful in the development of more general and applicable models, particularly with extensions to minority groups. The hypotheses refer directly to the statement by Hunter (1964) cited above. First, it is theorized that because of a restricted housing opportunity set—restricted through discrimination, lower incomes, and underemployment (if not unemployment) —Black households will have a significantly more restricted pattern of intraurban mobility than White households. Thus, Black households, as a subset of all intraurban migrants, will move shorter distances than White households. A comparison of the frequency and the distance of Black and White household moves will allow this hypothesis to be tested. Secondly, those Black households which move distances comparable with White households, or more specifically those Black households that move away from the heart of the ghetto area, are households with higher incomes and higher levels of education than the Black population as a whole and also buy rather than rent homes. Most likely these Black households fill professional occupations and thus may be able to fulfill the desire for escape suggested by a respondent quoted by Gottlieb (1969): "He wants out of the slums. He wants out of unemployment. He wants out of a physical setting which restricts mobility and maximizes personal defeat." In addition to tests of the two hypotheses, it is possible to offer some observations on the extent to which Black households are more mobile than White households, and, by inference, the extent to which Black families are in a trauma of mobility—with corresponding detrimental effects on the schooling of their children.

Hunter (1964) has suggested that the spatial consequences of Black mobility include a great deal of circular movement within the ghetto and little movement out of the ghetto. This leads to the suggestion that much movement within the ghetto is indicative of a random

Table 1. *Percentage of Black Households Moving Specified Distances (by Number of Moves)**

Distance (Miles)	One Move (288)	Two Moves (133)	Three Moves (43)	Four Moves (10)	Five Moves (1)
0– .5	12.5	16.92	14.73	10.00	20.00
.5– 1.0	37.15	35.71	34.11	40.00	20.00
1.0– 1.5	26.39	19.17	30.23	17.50	
1.5– 2.0	7.29	7.52	4.65	12.50	40.00
2.0– 2.5	2.43	4.51	6.98	2.50	20.00
2.5– 3.0	1.04	1.88			
3.0– 3.5	1.04	1.13	1.55		
3.5– 4.0	.69	.75			
4.0– 4.5	.69			5.00	
4.5– 5.0	.35		1.55		
5.0– 5.5		.38			
5.5– 6.0	.35				
6.0– 6.5	.69	.38			
6.5– 7.0	.35	.75	.78		
7.0– 7.5					
7.5– 8.0	.35				
8.0– 8.5					
8.5– 9.0	.35				
9.0– 9.5		.38			
9.5–10.0	.35				
10.0–10.5	.35			5.00	
10.5–11.0		1.88			
11.0–11.5		.38			
11.5–12.0					
12.0–12.5					
12.5–13.0					
13.0–13.5	.35	.38			
13.5–14.0		.38			
14.0–14.5					
14.5–15.0					
15.0–15.5				.78	2.50
20+	7.29	8.27	4.65	7.50	

*The number of households in each group is indicated in parentheses.

2. I would like to thank the South–East Wisconsin Regional Planning Commission for permission to use the data.

3. Place of residence is defined in state plane co-ordinates and is accurate to the nearest one-half mile. Thus, residences for specified areas have the same co-ordinates. The accuracy is probably the equivalent of average block locations.

4. The data used in the calculations for table 1 include those households which moved into the region at any date later than 1950. The calculations for figure 2 and tables 8–12 include only households with full residence location histories 1950–1962.

spatial process. A simple variant of a Markov process is suggested and tested with the same data which are used to assess the hypotheses already elaborated.

SAMPLE DATA

The information used in this analysis was collected by the South-East Wisconsin Regional Planning Commission as part of a larger study of traffic movements within the region.[2] The data pertain to a 10 percent sample of all households within the southeastern Wisconsin metropolitan region, comprised of Washington, Milwaukee, Walworth, Racine, and Kenosha counties. In all, data on approximately 16,000 households were collected. Data on occupation, education, income, housing value, reasons for moving, and age, in addition to place of residence for two-year intervals for the period 1950–1962 were gathered from the sample.[3] Such longitudinal data are relatively rare. Their inclusion here allows detailed analysis of the movements of households over a period of time. Heretofore such an analysis has been virtually impossible. From this large data file 716 Black households were selected. Obviously the total number of Black households in Milwaukee was underrepresented in the sample, but this is not viewed as a serious hindrance to this research.

DISTANCES AND PATTERNS OF MOBILITY

The basic information for the number of moves by distance for households which moved one or more times in the period 1950–1962 is presented in tables 1 and 2.[4] Seventy-five percent of the Black households which had moved at some time between 1950 and 1962 moved less than 1.5 miles. When both Black and White households are combined, only 28 percent of the total number moved the same distance, clearly illustrative of a constrained pattern of movement by Black households. Thus, there is some preliminary evidence to support Hunter's (1964) statement. A plot of 71 of the 75 Black households (figure 1) that moved within the city of Milwaukee in the period 1960–1962 reinforces the impression of constrained movement. Apart from a few cross-city moves, almost all Black household moves occurred within the confines of an area identified as the ghetto (Rose, 1970; Hansell and Clark, 1970). The concentration of moves is striking with a dense pattern of origins and destinations tightly clustered within a very small area (figure 2).

RELATIONSHIPS OF INCOME–EDUCATION–OCCUPATION AND MOBILITY

The second hypothesis is that Black households that move longer distances, possibly breaking the ties

Table 2. *Percentage of All Households Originating in Milwaukee County and Moving Specified Distances (by Number of Moves)**

Distance (Miles)	One Move (3009)	Two Moves (994)	Three Moves (313)	Four Moves (68)	Five Moves (16)
0– .5	4.96	5.68	5.75	5.51	2.86
.5– 1.0	10.91	12.42	12.67	10.29	12.86
1.0– 1.5	11.83	13.03	15.12	8.46	17.14
1.5– 2.0	7.74	8.35	6.92	11.40	4.29
2.0– 2.5	7.80	7.70	9.27	6.25	12.86
2.5– 3.0	7.93	6.74	5.54	4.41	4.29
3.0– 3.5	5.85	4.83	4.90	3.31	1.43
3.5– 4.0	5.22	4.98	4.67	5.88	10.00
4.0– 4.5	5.49	4.83	3.94	7.35	1.43
4.5– 5.0	4.72	4.18	3.51	2.94	2.86
5.0– 5.5	4.46	3.77	3.09	5.51	2.86
5.5– 6.0	3.54	2.87	2.56	.74	4.29
6.0– 6.5	2.74	2.82	2.13	2.21	1.43
6.5– 7.0	2.47	1.96	1.28	1.47	.00
7.0– 7.5	1.59	1.76	1.70	2.94	.00
7.5– 8.0	1.52	1.41	2.24	1.10	1.43
8.0– 8.5	1.19	.86	1.17	1.47	4.29
8.5– 9.0	1.32	1.01	.85	.37	1.43
9.0– 9.5	.70	.55	1.06	1.84	.00
9.5–10.0	1.00	.75	.53	.74	.00
10.0–10.5	1.00	.86	1.70	1.10	.00
10.5–11.0	.37	.80	.43	.37	.00
11.0–11.5	.37	.40	.11	.74	1.43
11.5–12.0	.20	.80	.53	.00	1.43
12.0–12.5	.40	.45	.11	.00	2.86
12.5–13.0	.60	.20	.32	.00	.00
13.0–13.5	.27	.10	.21	.00	.00
13.5–14.0	.23	.25	.11	.00	1.43
14.0–14.5	.17	.15	.11	.37	.00
14.5–15.0	.20	.30	.43	1.10	.00
15.0–15.5	.20	.20	.43	.74	.00
15.5–16.0	.10	.25	.21	.00	.00
16.0–16.5	.27	.05	.00	.00	1.43
16.5–17.0	.07	.05	.21	.00	.00
17.0–17.5	.10	.10	.00	.00	.00
17.5–18.0	.10	.15	.21	.00	.00
18.0–18.5	.07	.10	.00	.37	1.43
18.5–19.0	.07	.10	.00	.00	.00
19.0–19.5	.03	.00	.32	.00	.00
20+	2.26	4.18	5.64	11.03	4.29

*The number of households in each group is indicated in parentheses.

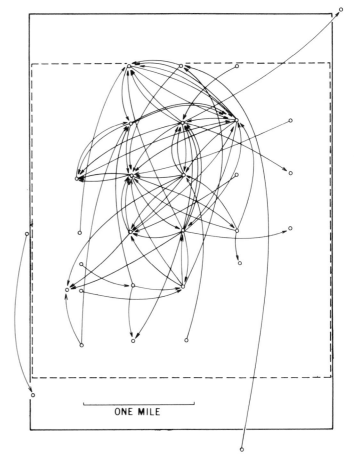

Figure 1. Plot of Black households which moved between 1960 and 1962. Both origins and destinations are given in state plane co-ordinates to the nearest one-half mile. The superimposed, dashed square indicates the area to which the Markov Chain analysis applies.

ONE MILE

117

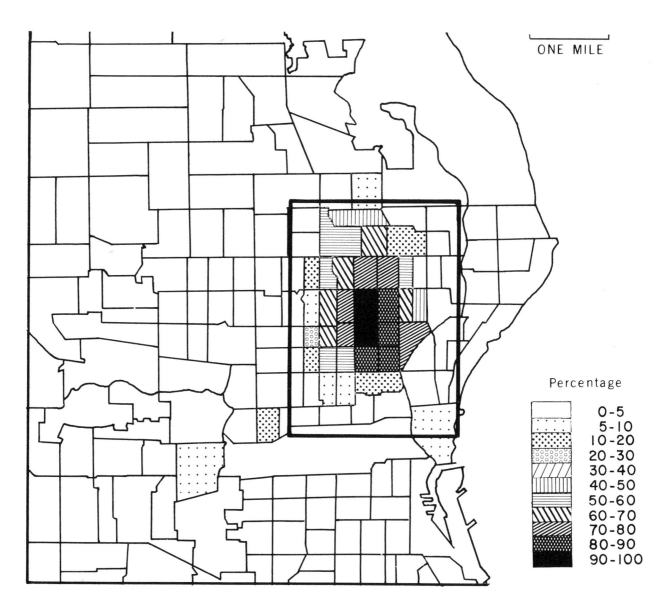

Figure 2. Black population as a percentage of total population by census tract for 1960. The superimposed rectangle indicates the area to which figure 1 applies.

of the ghetto or at least moving away from the core of the ghetto, come from groups with higher incomes. Other studies have shown that a strong correlation exists among income, occupation, and education in a number of urban areas (Reid, 1962). To test the hypothesis, Black households were divided into three groups. The first group consisted entirely of families that had not moved during the period 1950–1962. The second group comprised Black households that had moved two miles or less at any time between 1950 and 1962; that is, if the household made more than one move, all of the moves had to be two miles or less. The third group consisted of Black families who made at least one move of more than two miles. The assumption is that multiple movers are likely to move short distances, and it is thus unlikely that the bias of one long move and many short moves will be a problem. Indeed, a total of only 54 households moved three or more times. Frequency tables for occupation, income, value of housing or rent paid, and age were prepared for each group (tables 3–7).

Descriptively, these tables show that the movers, particularly the households moving distances greater than two miles, have higher incomes, are often high school graduates, and are craftsmen and foremen rather than operatives. Specifically, 27 percent of the households moving over two miles had incomes in excess of 6,000 dollars, whereas only 19 percent of those moving less than two miles had incomes in this category. Similar results were found for educational levels. In addition, a relatively high percentage of the household heads were in professional occupations. These results for education and occupation are as expected when income is viewed as an explanatory variable. Related to the above conclusions is the observation that those households moving longer distances occupy higher value homes. Therefore, the hypothesis of a better educated, higher income elite within the Black population which can afford to move greater distances and can thus break the narrow constraints of the ghetto is upheld.

To substantiate these descriptive results, chi-square tests (table 8) of the groups of households that moved less than two miles and those that moved more than two miles were conducted for income, occupation, education, and house value—rent paid.[5] In this way, attention is given to the whole distribution rather than to the extremes of the distribution. The results are reported for all three groups, although the hypothesis being tested relates specifically to moves longer than or shorter than two miles. Although only education and income have χ^2 values significant at the 0.05 level, both occupation and house value or rent show significant differences at the 0.10 level. The evidence is thus relatively strong that those households moving greater distances

Table 3. *Percentage of Black Households by Distance Moved and Occupation Type*

Occupation	No Move	0–2.0 Miles	≥2.1 Miles
Professional	5	3	6
Managers, officials	4	1	1
Clerical and kindred	1	4	6
Sales workers	1	1	1
Craftsmen and foremen	9	10	16
Operatives	27	39	30
Private household	3	3	0
Other service	9	8	7
Laborers	15	12	14
Farmers, farm managers	1	1	2
Housewives	14	11	11
Students	0	0	0
Unemployed	7	6	5
Retired	8	3	2
Unknown	0	0	0

Table 4. *Percentage of Black Households by Distance Moved and Years of Education*

Educational Level	No Move	0–2.0 Miles	≥2.1 Miles
Grade school not completed	22	16	16
Grade school completed	20	29	20
High school not completed	26	26	19
High school completed	20	19	24
Business or technical school	4	3	7
College not completed	5	4	4
College completed	1	1	3
Graduate school	2	1	3
Unrecorded	2	1	4

Table 5. *Percentage of Black Households by Distance Moved and Family Income*

Income ($)	No Move	0–2.0 Miles	≥2.1 Miles
0– 2,000	21	11	10
2,000– 4,000	19	18	21
4,000– 6,000	27	33	22
6,000– 8,000	7	10	17
8,000–10,000	3	5	5
10,000–12,000	2	2	2
12,000–14,000	1	2	0
14,000–16,000	0	0	1
16,000–20,000	0	0	1
20,000 and over	1	0	0
Unrecorded	21	19	22

5. The actual frequencies and not percentages were used in the calculations for the chi-square tests.

Table 6. *Percentage of Black Households by Distance Moved and Rent Paid or House Value*

Value ($)	No Move	0–2.0 Miles	⩾2.1 Miles
0– 5,000	3	0	2
5,000–10,000	15	8	9
10,000–15,000	16	9	9
15,000–20,000	1	2	5
20,000–25,000	0	0	2
25,000 and over	1	0	1
Rent			
0– 60	28	23	19
60–100	28	50	43
100–150	0	0	0
150 and over	0	0	0
Unrecorded	10	6	8

Table 7. *Percentage of Black Households by Distance Moved and Age of Head of Household*

Age (Years)	No Move	0–2.0 Miles	⩾2.1 Mile
15–19	3	0	0
20–24	10	5	3
25–29	10	14	19
30–34	12	18	21
35–44	26	32	40
45–54	18	18	10
55–64	13	7	4
65 and over	7	4	3
Unrecorded	2	1	0

Table 8. *Chi Square Tests on Distance Groupings and Socio-economic Status*

Socio-economic Status	Nonmove vs. Moves Two Miles and Under	Nonmove vs. Moves Over Two Miles	Move Two Miles and Under vs. Moves Over Two Miles
Education	9.6 (7)**	6.1 (7)	15.6* (7)
Occupation	35.4* (12)	22.8* (12)	18.5 (12)
Income	21.3* (6)	18.1* (6)	47.0* (6)
House value or rent	40.2* (8)	25.2* (8)	13.3 (8)

* Statistically significant at the .05 level.
** Degrees of freedom are indicated in parentheses.

consist of the better educated, higher income earners and generally confirms the hypothesis outlined earlier in the paper.

STOCHASTIC MODELS OF MOBILITY

While we have been able to offer some support for the hypotheses suggested earlier in the paper and drawn from the work of Hunter (1964) and others, it seems indicative of the state of knowledge concerning Black areas within cities that we are unable to present any model formulation for the conceptual knowledge of the ghetto. Rose (1970) and Morrill (1965) have experimented with simulation models of ghetto expansion. In continuing, a very speculative look will be taken at a stochastic model which might be used to explain the movements of households in general but will be particularly applicable to the movements of Black households within the ghetto.

Initial attempts to build a model of the spatial movements of Black households utilized two-dimensional random-walk processes. The results were not encouraging. It must be emphasized that the intention here is to build a simple, rather than complex, spatial model which will account for all aspects of the residential relocation process. The model to be outlined, while far from complete, does build on already suggested methods (Brown and Longbrake, 1970; McGinnis, 1968) and also attempts, albeit clumsily, to integrate the time and space dimensions into a Markov Chain.

Assume that the Black household is indeed moving within a confined area in a fashion which may be described as Hunter's "back and forth" movement. That is, there is a great deal of circular movement within the ghetto area but very little movement which ultimately breaks the bounds of the ghetto. As such, there exists a set of movements which, at least in the aggregate, can be described as a set of random movements entailing origins and destinations. The conditions necessary for satisfying a Markov process are that the movements not be planned in any systematic fashion and that the movements in period t are related only to the locations in t — 1 or the previous time period. To reiterate, a Markov process is one in which the movement of an individual from one "state" to another is dependent only on the "state" occupied in the previous time period.

It is important at this point to identify two problems. First, the development of Markov Chain models has been criticized because the models do not take into account a time sequence of movements and that there are some people who are chronic movers. Obviously we cannot consider the movements of people independently of time. Where there is substantial empirical evidence to support this view, there have been no adequate theoreti-

Table 9. *North–South Positions of Black Households*

Migration Positions for North–South Directions

	1	2	3	4	5	6
1	8	1	0	1	1	1
2	2	58	12	7	6	4
3	2	9	68	15	5	3
4	0	6	15	79	16	3
5	0	2	3	10	52	6
6	0	0	2	2	4	27

Transition Probabilities for North–South Directions

	1	2	3	4	5	6
1	.667	.083	.0	.083	.083	.083
2	.022	.652	.135	.079	.067	.045
3	.020	.089	.667	.147	.049	.029
4	.0	.050	.127	.664	.134	.025
5	.0	.027	.041	.137	.712	.082
6	.0	.0	.057	.057	.114	.771

Mean First-Passage Times

	1	2	3	4	5	6
1	52.13	22.02	15.56	10.38	10.91	18.97
2	144.99	9.03	10.93	9.91	11.77	21.76
3	146.33	20.58	5.02	8.48	12.04	22.71
4	154.09	22.90	11.24	4.02	9.99	22.57
5	156.66	25.29	13.91	8.74	4.00	19.54
6	157.81	27.89	14.14	10.86	9.88	5.82

Equilibrium Distribution

1	2	3	4	5	6
.019	.111	.199	.249	.250	.172

Table 10. *East–West Positions of Black Households*

Migration Positions for East–West Directions

	1	2	3	4	5	6
1	11	3	0	3	1	0
2	3	69	1	5	8	1
3	2	3	19	5	0	0
4	4	31	10	186	12	1
5	4	3	1	10	27	0
6	0	1	0	3	0	3

Transition Probabilities for East–West Directions

	1	2	3	4	5	6
1	.611	.167	.0	.167	.056	.0
2	.034	.793	.011	.057	.092	.011
3	.069	.103	.655	.172	.0	.0
4	.016	.127	.041	.762	.049	.004
5	.089	.067	.022	.222	.600	.0
6	.0	.143	.0	.429	.0	.429

Mean First-Passage Times

	1	2	3	4	5	6
1	11.25	7.40	46.98	7.50	15.39	180.31
2	25.98	2.76	46.58	9.44	13.83	175.26
3	24.53	8.49	16.35	7.23	18.17	181.06
4	27.69	8.22	42.29	2.94	16.09	179.04
5	23.57	9.18	44.21	6.14	7.27	181.30
6	29.01	7.91	45.12	4.11	17.27	102.77

Equilibrium Distribution

1	2	3	4	5	6
.089	.332	.061	.340	.138	.010

6. At least partly because of the violation of the stationarity assumption of the Markov Chain, Collins (1971) and Olsson and Gale (1968) have observed that there is a stronger theoretical justification for adopting a Markov framework in the analysis of structural changes than in the analysis of spatial systems. However, the conclusion (Collins, 1971) that the results obtained from the spatial and structural matrices are markedly similar offers some support for the speculative investigations undertaken in this paper.

cal explanations of the phenomena of the mover-stayer framework. A discussion of the mover-stayer relationship can be found in papers by Land (1969), Morrison (1967), and Taeuber et al. (1961). In this study, however, there are only eleven households that moved four or more times.

The other problem in the development of a Markov model is more difficult, and the measures used in the development of the present approach may be subject to criticism. However, the approach is presented for its partial, if not ultimate, solution to the problem of the temporal-spatial Markov Chain (Olsson and Gale, 1968).[6] Observation shows that in dealing with the movements of a population or of some other phenomenon over space and time, there is an additional dimension to the problem of constructing states and deriving the transition probabilities for the movements between these states. The problems are easily outlined; however, the solutions are not. If, for example, the prob-

Table 11. *North–South Movements of Black Households*

Migration Movements for North–South Directions

	1	2	3	4	5	6
1	0	2	0	1	1	1
2	2	10	14	9	6	4
3	2	11	7	19	9	3
4	0	7	16	11	17	3
5	0	2	3	10	5	7
6	0	0	2	2	4	3

Transition Probabilities for North–South Directions

	1	2	3	4	5	6
1	.0	.400	.0	.200	.200	.200
2	.044	.222	.311	.200	.133	.089
3	.039	.216	.137	.373	.176	.059
4	.0	.130	.296	.204	.315	.056
5	.0	.074	.111	.370	.185	.259
6	.0	.0	.182	.182	.364	.273

Mean First-Passage Times

	1	2	3	4	5	6
1	72.23	6.66	5.59	3.90	4.38	7.94
2	69.09	7.62	4.19	3.77	4.74	9.07
3	70.00	7.81	4.95	3.19	4.48	9.25
4	72.84	8.61	4.34	3.65	3.94	9.12
5	73.68	9.46	5.19	3.21	4.21	7.46
6	73.92	10.21	5.06	3.78	3.48	7.05

Equilibrium Distribution

1	2	3	4	5	6
.014	.131	.202	.274	.238	.142

Table 12. *East–West Movements of Black Households*

Migration Movements for East–West Directions

	1	2	3	4	5	6
1	1	3	0	4	1	0
2	3	10	1	6	8	1
3	2	3	0	5	0	0
4	4	36	12	49	12	2
5	4	4	1	16	1	0
6	0	1	0	3	0	0

Transition Probabilities for East–West Directions

	1	2	3	4	5	6
1	.111	.333	.0	.444	.111	.0
2	.103	.345	.034	.207	.276	.034
3	.200	.300	.0	.500	.0	.0
4	.035	.313	.104	.426	.104	.017
5	.154	.154	.038	.615	.038	.0
6	.0	.250	.0	.750	.0	.0

Mean First-Passage Times

	1	2	3	4	5	6
1	11.46	3.28	17.42	2.49	6.47	58.21
2	11.32	3.33	17.09	2.98	5.41	56.44
3	10.52	3.33	17.43	2.39	7.23	58.20
4	12.25	3.35	15.64	2.51	6.62	57.25
5	11.12	3.84	16.57	2.01	7.18	58.36
6	13.02	3.51	17.00	1.74	7.32	58.05

Equilibrium Distances

1	2	3	4	5	6
.087	.300	.057	.398	.139	.017

lem is to examine the movements of firms through certain size classes (Adelman, 1958) or the movements of aggregate tracts through some classes of rental value (Clark, 1965) or any of a number of similar one-dimensional problems, there is no technical difficulty in the calculation of the transition probabilities. However, when the interest lies in the movement from one location to another (that is, when the states are two dimensional), the problem is more complicated. The difficulties can be illustrated in the following manner.

Imagine a square region divided into 100 subregions or zones (for example, neighborhoods or communities within a city). The square region has ten divisions along the North–South and East–West co-ordinates. Now, consider a family's moving from the upper northwestern zone to the zone directly to the east. The movement is to an immediately neighboring state. Moreover, the state to the immediate south of the first zone is also a neighboring state. This means that when the transition probability matrix is formed there is no way to develop a matrix that will yield a single diagonal equilibrium matrix. Any matrix from a 10 × 10 region would have to be a 100 × 100 matrix to account for all of the possible interconnections. In attempting to solve this problem and still conduct the analysis within a Markovian framework, the following alternatives are suggested. (The data on the movements of Black households are processed through the first of the alternatives.)

A simple solution which yields interpretable results involves a collapse of the two-dimensional spatial array to a single dimension. However, in order to maintain the spatial impact of the movements, the region, in this case the ghetto, could be collapsed in the following way: first set up a series of states where the states are parallel rows (figure 3); then, a set of additional column states is set up (fig. 3). Transition probabilities and equilibrium vectors are subsequently calculated for each dimension of the region.

A more appealing approach is to construct a series of pie-shaped (sector) zones covering the region. Of course, for these to be of equal size, the initial region must be circular or nearly circular in shape (fig. 3). Initially, it was intended to use the sector-shaped units as simple states and carry out the analysis within these states. However, until a function can be developed which will take account of the fact that the probability of changing states is not equal throughout the lineal extent of the sector, this alternative approach will be of conceptual interest only. The actual model is outlined in the following section.

MARKOV MODELS OF BLACK HOUSEHOLD RELOCATIONS

The following approach was undertaken in using the modification of the Markov model already outlined. All Black households which moved at least twice between 1950–1962 and which moved only within the area bounded by a dotted line in figures 1 and 2 were selected from the file of 716 Black households for the South–East Wisconsin Region. Of the eligible households which moved twice and which lived in the Milwaukee Region in 1950, 76 originated in the defined area and 93 percent of these remained in this region in 1962. The choice of households which moved at least twice ensures that the Markov Chain model is more than an enumeration of simple origins and destinations. Obviously some households moved more often than others. Moreover, it is also apparent that those households which moved two or three times did not all move at the same time. To circumvent these problems, two analyses were undertaken. First, an analysis of the households was conducted for every time period. This means, of

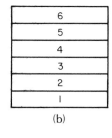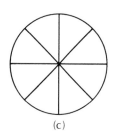

Figure 3. Diagrammatic representation of the states for the Markov Chain analysis.
(a) East–West alignment of states.
(b) North–South alignment of states.
(c) Possible arrangement of states for a sector Markov model.

course, that the household was counted at its location at each point in time, whether or not the household moved, moved within the same zone, or moved from one zone to another. The second analysis included only those households which *moved* either within the same zone or to another zone. The second method thus eliminated those families which stayed in the same location over a number of time periods. As will be noted later, the main difference in the two methods of analysis relates to the composition of the diagonal values of the transition probability matrix. The North–South zones and the East–West zones used in the analysis are identified in figure 3.

When the transition probability matrices for the positions of households at all time periods are examined, the influence of the households that held the same residence for considerable periods of time heavily weights the diagonal values. However, the tendency for movements to occur within the same zone or to neighboring zones is apparent for both North–South and East–West directions. The matrix of mean first-passage times may be viewed as a measure of the most desirable zones from among the North–South or East–West breakdown of zones. For the North–South breakdown within the ghetto, zone four emerges as the main zone; and for the East–West zones, both zones two and four emerge — although zone four is perhaps the more important. In the long run, as indicated by the equilibrium vector, zones two and four in the East–West breakdown and four and five in the North–South breakdown emerge as those zones likely to be most important in the movements of the households. Nevertheless, the main implication of these results and the major intent of this paper is to indicate that, over a substantial period of time, the positions of the Black households within the ghetto area of Milwaukee are likely to reflect the positions of those households at the beginning of the time period. Thus, the model confirms the suggestions that Hunter (1964) makes about the internal to-and-fro movement.

When the analysis is restricted to the actual movements of households, one gains a slightly different perspective, although the conclusions reinforce the results already reported. The diagonals of the transition probability matrices are less dominant, and the off-diagonal elements assume greater importance. Significantly it is the off-diagonal elements which are closest to the diagonals that emerge as equal in importance to the diagonal values. A careful examination of the East–West transition probability matrix for movements only reveals an interesting and telling situation. Very little movement occurs from zone two to zone one, that is, toward the edge of the area identified as the ghetto. In addition, virtually no movement occurs within and between zones five and six at the other end of the East–West zones. Consequently, more of the movement occurs within zones two through four, thus confirming the general conclusion already posited for the analysis of the positions of all Black households. The results of the analysis for the mean first-passage times and the equilibrium vectors also indicate results similar to those already described for the positions of all households.

CONCLUSION

Quite simply, the intent of this paper has been to offer documentation for certain statements concerning the general movement of Black households within a ghetto area. The ghetto area of Milwaukee was chosen mainly because a set of detailed longitudinal data was available, allowing an analysis of both the time sequence of movements and the spatial expression of these movements. An hypothesis of many short-distance movements by Black households and constrained within a limited spatial extent was generally accepted. In addition, evidence was presented to uphold the theory that Black households which moved longer than average distances in the period 1950–1962 had higher incomes and higher levels of education than the other Black households.

The Markov Chain analysis employed a methodology to overcome the problems inherent in subjecting both temporal and spatial data to such an analysis. While the division of the two-dimensional spatial sequence into two one-dimensional sequences may not meet with general acceptance, it did permit analysis of the movements of Black households in a spatial context, and meaningful results were generated. When the positions of the Black households at each time period were considered (whether or not the households actually relocated) or when only relocations or movements were considered, the results were basically similar and confirmed the hypothesis of considerable internal movement within the ghetto and little movement toward the boundaries of the ghetto area.

The implications of the analysis are obviously far reaching. First, there are the implications of constrained opportunities for housing, but this is a topic which has been discussed extensively. More significant are the educational implications. When much of the movement occurs within a confined area, the movement does not relate to an improvement in socio-economic position. The move often actually results in no more than a disruption of educational patterns and the exchange of one poor school for another. If the pattern described by Hunter (1964) and confirmed to a large extent in this analysis is true of most minority concentrations, then the possibility for minority groups to achieve equality in housing or schooling is constrained at the basic neighborhood level. This is an area for further research: the patterns of mobility are relatively easily documented; their implications are, however, less easily identified.

REFERENCES CITED

Adelman, I. 1958. "A Stochastic Analysis of the Size Distribution of Firms." *Journal of the American Statistical Association* 53:893–904.

Brown, L. A. 1970. "On the Use of Markov Chains in Movement Research." *Economic Geography* 46 (Supplement): 393–403.

————, and Longbrake, D. B. 1970. "Migration Flows in Intra-Urban Space: Place Utility Considerations." *Annals of the Association of American Geographers.* 60:368–84.

————, and Moore, E. 1970. "The Intra-Urban Migration Process: A Perspective." *Geografiska Annaler* 52, ser. B:1–13.

Clark, W. A. V. 1965. "Markov Chain Analysis in Geography: An Application to the Movement of Rental Housing Areas." *Annals of the Association of American Geographers* 55:351–59.

————. 1970. "Measurement and Explanation in Intra-Urban Residential Mobility." *Tijdschrift voor Economische en Socialegeographie* 61:49–57.

Cleveland Board of Education. 1962. Bureau of Educational Research, Memorandum.

Collins, L. 1971. "Some Limitations of Markov Chain Analysis in Geographic Research." Unpublished paper, Department of Geography, University of Edinburgh.

Gottlieb, D. 1969. "Poor Youth: A Study in Forced Alienation." *Journal of Social Issues* 25:91.

Hansell, C., and Clark, W. A. V. 1970. "The Expansion of the Negro Ghetto in Milwaukee: A Description and Simulation Model." *Tijdschrift voor Economische en Socialegeographie* 61:267–77.

Hunter, D. 1964. *The Slums: Challenge and Response.* New York: The Free Press of Glencoe.

Land, K. C. 1969. "Duration of Residence and Prospective Migration: Further Evidence." *Demography* 6:133–40.

McGinnis, R. 1968. "A Stochastic Model of Social Mobility." *American Sociological Review* 33:712–22.

Morrill, R. L. 1965. "The Negro Ghetto: Problems and Alternatives." *Geographical Review* 55:339–61.

Morrison, P. A. 1967. "Duration of Residence and Prospective Migration: The Evaluation of a Stochastic Model." *Demography* 4:559–60.

Olsson, G., and Gale, S. 1968. "Spatial Theory and Human Behavior." *Papers of the Regional Science Association* 21:229–42.

Reid, M. G. 1962. *Housing and Income.* Chicago: University of Chicago Press.

Rose, H. M. 1970. "The Development of an Urban Subsystem: The Case of the Negro Ghetto." *Annals of the Association of American Geographers* 60:1–17.

Taeuber, K. E., et al. 1961. "Residence Histories and Exposure Residences for the United States Population." *Journal of the American Statistical Association* 56:824–34.

Wolpert, J. 1965. "Behavioral Aspects of the Decision to Migrate." *Papers of the Regional Science Association* 15:159–69.

6

IMPLICATIONS OF SOME
RECOMMENDED ALTERNATIVE URBAN
STRATEGIES FOR BLACK RESIDENTIAL
CHOICE

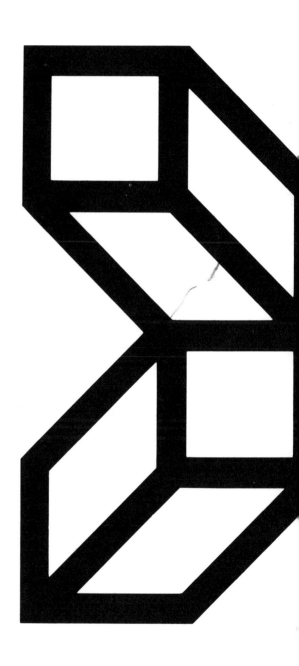

David R. Meyer
University of Massachusetts, Amherst

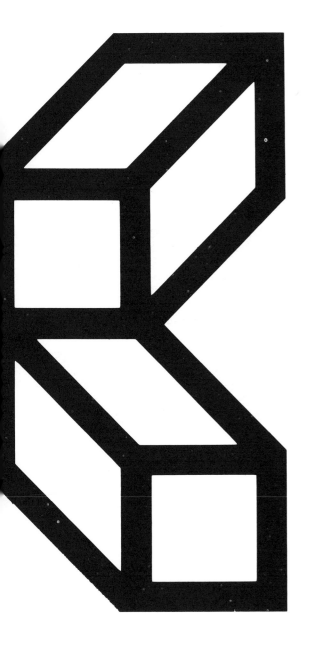

Implications of Some Recommended Alternative Urban Strategies for Black Residential Choice

ABSTRACT

Since strategies dealing with existing racial patterns in cities concern the residential locations of Black households, the residential choices of these households are affected by the implementation of the strategies. Five, basic, alternative strategies include: (1) present policies, (2) enrichment only, (3) integrated core, (4) segregated dispersal, and (5) integrated dispersal. Each strategy is examined in the context of its implications for Black residential choice.[1]

---

1. The author wishes to thank Judith M. Meyer, Mount Holyoke College, for her valuable comments on the manuscript.

Concentration in the United States of Afro-Americans within parts of metropolitan areas, especially in central cities, has been recognized as a problem of crucial national importance (*Report of the National Advisory Commission,* 1968). Several strategies have been proposed to deal with these clustered racial patterns. It would seem that the implementation of these strategies would have significant effects on the residential choices of Black households. These effects must be considered if the strategies are to be truely beneficial to Blacks. In the following discussion the present racial patterns of cities will be summarized briefly. Some propositions concerning Black residential choice will then be set forth. Following this, alternative strategies dealing with racial patterns of cities are discussed. Five basic alternative strategies are then analyzed in terms of their implications for Black residential choice.

PRESENT RACIAL PATTERNS OF CITIES

In 1960, 80 percent of the Afro-Americans in metropolitan areas lived in central cities, and by 1969 this had declined only slightly to 79 percent. During this period, 77 percent of the increase in the Black metropolitan population occurred in the central cities. At the same time, *all* of the increase in the White metropolitan population occurred outside of the central city. Moreover, there was actually a 5 percent decline in the central city White population from 1960–1969. As a result of these changes, the Black proportion of the central city population increased from 16 percent in 1960 to 21 percent in 1969. However, these figures mask the fact that Blacks are particularly concentrated in the larger metropolitan areas. In 1969, Afro-Americans comprised 26 percent of the central city populations in metropolitan areas of one million or more persons and 16 percent of central city populations in metropolitan areas under one million population (U.S. Bureau of Census, 1970, p. 2). By 1985, Blacks may exceed 50 percent of the population in thirteen major central cities in the United States (*Report of the National Advisory Commission,* 1968, p. 391).

Beneath the gross dichotomy of central city and non-central city, there exists almost complete separation of Black and White residences. Using block data, the Taeubers have shown that urban residential segregation of Blacks and Whites has been maintained at a high level from 1940 to 1960 in all regions of the United States (Taeuber and Taeuber, 1965, pp. 31–43). Further analysis of a smaller set of cities in the mid-1960s suggests that the segregation pattern has not changed (Farley and Taeuber, 1968).

White discriminatory practices, including both personal prejudices and institutionalized practices of such groups as banks, housing developers, real estate brokers, and government agencies have been a major factor in enforcing almost total residential separation between Blacks and Whites (Denton, 1967; McEntire, 1960; Ohio Civil Rights Commission, 1963; Weaver, 1948). The notion that Blacks are segregated from non-Blacks merely because Black people have a lower socio-economic status has not withstood analytical scrutiny. Only a small part of the segregation of Afro-Americans can be attributed to their lower socio-economic status (Berry et al., 1969, pp. 31–39; Taeuber and Taeuber, 1965, pp. 78–95).

PROPOSITIONS ABOUT BLACK RESIDENTIAL CHOICE

A basic proposition about Black residential choice is that Black households cannot freely exercise their residential preferences. The previously noted literature on White discriminatory practices is but a small part of a large literature which supports this proposition. Although White discriminatory practices are significant inhibitors of Black residential choice, other propositions can also be stated. These are based on the view that the environment within which a household may choose a residence consists of three components: characteristics of dwelling units, neighborhoods, and location of dwelling units with respect to the household's movement patterns (Brown and Moore, 1970, p. 2). The general literature on residential choice and specific references to Black residential choice from diverse sources suggest that the following are reasonable propositions concerning Black households' preferences for residence.

First, at the individual dwelling level, the higher the income of the Black household, the more money spent for housing, the better the quality of housing purchased, and the more likely the household will want to own its dwelling. Furthermore, families with children tend to prefer single-family dwellings while young and elderly single people may prefer apartments. Secondly, at the neighborhood level, Black households desire that the neighborhood be relatively homogeneous in socio-economic status. In addition, although Black households have gone on record as favoring residential integration, many Blacks do not wish to be isolated in White residential areas but prefer to live near other Blacks. Thirdly, Black households prefer to balance their journey to work with their preference for locations with open space; new, standard quality housing; and large dwellings (Erskine, 1967; Meyer, 1970, pp. 6–22; Muth, 1969; Simmons, 1968; Watts et al., 1964).

ALTERNATIVE URBAN STRATEGIES

Current Black residential choices are made within the context of the previously described racial patterns of American cities. Most alternative urban strategies which have been proposed are designed to alter these existing racial patterns. They are generally intended to remedy negative aspects of the large Black ghettos in cities. It has been suggested that these negative aspects include such attributes as (1) the compounding of human problems and frustrations; (2) the high incidence of crime; (3) the economic viability of central business districts threatened by encroachment of social and economic deprivation; (4) the psychological damage of undesirability and inferiority as perceived by residents forced to live apart from the White majority; (5) increasing local governmental expenditures for poverty-linked services, combined with decreasing ability to raise revenues; (6) inadequate access to the job market; (7) *de facto* school segregation with a concomitant lower quality of education; (8) substandard housing; and (9) Black hatred of the ghetto (Funnye and Shiffman, 1967; Grier, 1967; Kain and Persky, 1969; Taeuber, 1968). These may not be the only problems of the central city ghetto, nor is there necessarily agreement that all of the above are perceived as problems by Blacks.

Regardless of whether there is agreement on the foregoing problems, those strategies which have been put forward to deal with existing racial patterns generally propose some form of residential racial mixing. However, there is little agreement that whatever is undesirable about existing racial patterns will be remedied by residential racial mixing. As an example, Piven and Cloward (1967) maintain that attempts to desegregate housing have failed to provide better urban housing for Blacks. Furthermore, emphasis on racial mixing detracts from the development of separatist institutions through which Afro-Americans can acquire power over their lives. Thus, many Blacks have suggested that residential desegregation should not be pursued and, instead, Black communal organizations should be developed and strengthened within the Black living areas. Black control over all institutions within Black areas in cities is viewed by Turner (1970) as an essential component of Black liberation. In fact, Turner (1970, pp. 12–13) suggests that these areas might be claimed to be autonomous city states.

Downs (1968, p. 1344) has succinctly isolated five alternative strategies dealing with existing racial patterns. These strategies are derived from a combination of the following alternatives.

Degree-of-Concentration Alternatives: (1) Continue to concentrate non-White population growth in central cities or perhaps in a few older suburbs next to central cities (*concentration*); (2) disperse non-White population growth throughout all parts of metropolitan areas (*dispersal*).

Degree-of-Segregation Alternatives: (1) Continue to cluster Whites and non-Whites in residentially segregated neighborhoods, regardless of location within the metropolitan area (*segregation*); (2) scatter the non-White population, or at least a significant fraction of it, "randomly" among White residential areas to achieve at least partial residential integration (*integration*).

Degree-of-Enrichment Alternatives: (1) Continue to provide relatively low-level welfare, education, housing, job training, and other social services to the most deprived groups in the population—both those who are incapable of working, such as the vast majority of public-aid recipients and those who might possibly work but are unemployed because of lack of skills, discrimination, lack of desire, or other reasons (*non-enrichment*); (2) greatly increase the level of support to welfare, education, housing, job training, and other programs for the most deprived groups, largely through federally aided programs (*enrichment*).

Some of the eight possible combinations of the alternatives are internally inconsistent in practice. By a process of elimination, Downs (1968, p. 1345) isolates five, basic, alternative strategies: (1) *present policies:* concentration, segregation, non-enrichment; (2) *enrichment only:* concentration, segregation, enrichment; (3) *integrated core:* concentration, integration (in the center only), enrichment; (4) *segregated dispersal:* dispersal, segregation, enrichment; (5) *integrated dispersal:* dispersal, integration, enrichment.

As Downs emphasizes, different strategies might be adopted in different metropolitan areas. Furthermore, each strategy is a "pure" form. In practice a strategy might consist of a mixture of several alternatives. Downs examined the impact of the five strategies on the future of American cities. The following discussion represents an extension of Downs's analysis to the specific case of the impact of the alternative strategies on Black residential choice.

EFFECTS OF ALTERNATIVE STRATEGIES

The *present policies strategy* assumes that federal and local programs are inadequate to change the existing racial patterns of cities (Downs, 1968, p. 1346). Downs contends that this would result in relatively little change in the existing concentration of Black households in the central cities or older suburbs, in the residential segregation between Blacks and Whites, and in the non-viable socio-economic conditions within the Black residential concentrations. This means that most Black households will continue to exercise their residential choices within the confines of Black residential areas. Black households will differentiate themselves in these residential areas such that Black family income will vary directly with the value and rent of dwellings, owner occupancy, and quality of housing (Meyer, 1970, pp. 27–47). However, the meager available evidence suggests that Black households may not be so successful as White households in attaining internally homogeneous residential areas according to such criteria as socio-economic status (Frazier, 1932, pp. 109–12). The addition of housing stock to the Black housing market will mainly come on the periphery of the all-Black living areas as Black households replace White households (Morrill, 1965; Rose, 1970).

Since single-family dwellings and new housing tend to be located toward the periphery of the metropolitan area while multi-family and older housing are usually concentrated near the center, Black households will continue to be limited in their choice of single-family dwellings and new housing. Only as the growth of Black residential areas reaches single-family dwelling areas will this type of housing become available in large numbers. New dwellings will seldom be accessible to Black households because by the time Black residential areas expand to a particular point, the housing will have already aged ten, twenty, or more years. Public housing is one of the few categories of new housing available to low-income Black households.

Because most Black households are restricted to older housing in the central cities, their access to standard housing is limited. When Black households are compared with White households of similar income, rental levels, and size of housing units, it has generally been shown that Blacks receive lower quality housing (McEntire, 1960, pp. 136–50; Rapkin, 1966). However, Muth dissents from this view and claims that there is little difference in housing quality received by Blacks and Whites when *all* important factors are considered (Muth, 1969, pp. 250–80).

Since the Black population is spatially concentrated into only a few areas of cities whereas employment, though especially large in the CBD (Central Business District), is spread over the entire metropolitan area, not all Black workers are able to choose desirable residential locations with respect to their employment locations. Black workers employed in suburban locations are generally unable to choose residences near their workplace. Furthermore, those Black workers employed in the CBD must live in the central city. This may be desirable if the household has a low income. However, if the household has a high income and would prefer a home in the suburbs, despite higher transportation costs, the household cannot satisfy such a demand. Instead, the high-income Black household is forced to live in the central city (Meyer et al., 1965, pp. 156–59). As employment continues to move to and/or grow on the metropolitan periphery, Black households will remain in increasingly poor residential locations with respect to their workplace locations (Deskins, 1970).

In the *enrichment-only strategy,* federal programs improving education, housing, incomes, employment and job training, and social services received by Black households are vastly revised, broadened, and expanded. Specific housing programs might include rent or ownership supplements for poor families. The aim is to improve dramatically the quality of life within present Black residential concentrations and leave residential segregation unchanged (Downs, 1968, pp. 1346–47).

Raising the income of poor Black families will undoubtedly enable them to increase their consumption of standard housing. Subsequent increased demand should provide an incentive for apartment owners to improve the quality of their property. However, there is a limit to how much improvement in quality is possible. Many dwelling units in the central city are extremely old and structurally unsound. Hence, the increased price the families are able to pay may not be sufficient to cover the expenses of renovation. The quality of housing available to Black households relative to Whites may still not be comparable. Regardless of how much more money Black households receive, they are restricted to choosing among older, more deteriorated housing. Black households with increased incomes may satisfy their demand for standard housing by moving to the periphery of the all-Black living areas. However, unless the rate of ghetto expansion is sufficiently rapid, the increased demand for better quality housing may only result in higher prices for all Black households.

The only way in which the enrichment-only strategy will enable Black households to have greater access to new housing is to tear down existing housing and build new. Since the construction costs of such housing must necessarily include destroying the existing buildings, it is more expensive to build than new housing on vacant land on the metropolitan periphery. Only massive subsidies would make it economically feasible to build for Blacks in the central cities. Unless the subsidies are available to middle- and upper-income Black households in addition to low-income households (some of whom already have access to new public housing), the middle- and upper-income Black households will not be able to acquire new housing.

These comments on the expense of building new housing also apply to single-family dwellings. Since the all-Black living areas are frequently composed of multi-family dwellings, there is little possibility of making single family dwellings available to Blacks. To tear down multi-family dwellings and erect single-family dwellings on the same sites would price the single family dwellings beyond the reach of all but the most wealthy, unless large subsidies were forthcoming. Furthermore, the substitution of single-family dwellings for multi-family dwellings would lead to a net decrease in the housing stock unless additional housing were made available. It would appear that the only realistic way single-family dwellings could be made available to Black households under the enrichment-only strategy is by peripheral expansion of the Black residential areas. Finally, the adoption of an enrichment-only strategy means that the poor location of some Black households with respect to their workplace would not be improved. The situation existing under the present-policies strategy would be maintained.

According to Downs (1968, pp. 1347–48), the *integrated-core strategy* is

"Similar to the enrichment-only strategy because both would attempt to upgrade the quality of life in central-city ghettos through massive federally assisted programs. The integrated-core strategy would also seek, however, to eliminate racial segregation in an ever expanding core of the city by creating a socially, economically, and racially integrated community there. This integrated core would be built up through large-scale urban renewal programs, with the land re-uses including scattered-site public housing, middle-income housing suitable for families with children, and high-quality public services—expecially schools."

Downs goes on to suggest that such a strategy is only feasible if the racial balance in the core can be controlled. Achievement of this strategy would enable some Black households to acquire new, high quality housing. However, as Downs (1968, p. 1348) admits, achievement of the strategy will probably necessitate maintaining a majority of Whites, otherwise no Whites would be attracted. Since the amount of integrated housing would probably not be large, the proportion or number of Black households benefitting from this strategy would probably be low.

There is also some question whether middle- and upper-income Blacks with children can be attracted to the core in large numbers because these households have sufficient income to purchase single-family dwellings as it becomes available on the periphery of the expanding Black residential areas. This housing may be more attractive to the middle- and upper-income households with children because of the large amounts of interior space and private yards that come with single-family dwellings. In the core, the "integrated" housing would probably consist of apartment buildings and townhouses—the land being too expensive to construct single-family units. Those middle- and upper-income

Blacks most likely to be attracted to the core would consist of single people and married couples without children. These households may be more interested in the cultural and recreational facilities available in the core than in living in single-family dwellings.

If the area in which the integrated-core strategy is implemented was previously all-Black, this strategy would result in a net reduction in housing units available to Blacks in the core, since the "integrated" housing would probably not be constructed at a density higher than that of the previous housing. Even if it were, the density would surely not be so high as to contain the same number of Black households as previously lived there *plus* the number of Whites needed to have a White majority. Therefore, the end result of the integrated-core strategy would be to force some Black households to move outside of the core which, in turn, would necessitate that other Black households acquire housing in previously White residential areas. As with the previous strategies, the integrated-core strategy would not improve the poor residential locations of some Blacks with respect to their workplaces.

The outcome of the *segregated-dispersal strategy* would be clusters of Black households widely scattered throughout the metropolitan area. Whether or not the original few large concentrations in the central cities would remain depends on the success of the strategy. In this strategy, however, there are numerous implications for Black residential choice. A greatly enlarged range of housing would presumably become available to Blacks. Such housing would include newer housing than that available near the center of the city. If a cluster consists of a new housing development on the periphery, this would open up newer housing previously seldom attainable by Black households, especially in northern metropolitan areas. The increase in availability of newer housing would also mean that the amount of standard housing from which Black households could choose would increase. Hence, many Blacks could acquire the quality which they desire without investing large amounts of money for renovating deteriorated structures. Furthermore, the scattered clusters would contain mostly single-family dwellings, since these are the typical dwellings outside of the central city, making it possible to satisfy the demands of those Blacks who can afford to purchase single-family dwellings.

Another implication for Black residential choice may be that Blacks could increase their differentiation among residential areas. At the present time, most middle- and upper-income Black households can never move far from low-income Black households. As the low-income housing areas have continued to grow, the middle- and upper-income Blacks have had to constantly move.

With the implementation of the segregated-dispersal strategy, these households could move to residential areas unlikely to change for long periods of time. At the same time, this strategy would enable Blacks to choose housing in close proximity to other Blacks.

Finally, the dispersed clusters would make it feasible for Blacks to choose dwellings which are located so that the household could suitably balance its housing needs with the journey to work. The blue-collar worker employed in the suburbs could choose a home near his workplace. On the other hand, the high-income worker employed in the CBD could choose more desirable housing in the suburbs even though paying more for transportation.

The *integrated-dispersal strategy* postulates that Black households would be widely dispersed throughout the metropolitan area with no clusters other than perhaps the original concentration existing before the strategy was implemented.

The implications of this strategy for Black residential choice are similar to the implications of the segregated-dispersal strategy. The only real difference is that under an integrated-dispersal strategy the entire range of housing in the metropolitan area would be available to Blacks rather than the somewhat more limited range available in the segregated-dispersal strategy. In effect, all residential sites are potential locations for Black households since they would have complete freedom of choice. However, this strategy would be extremely difficult to implement. Existing laws prohibiting discrimination in housing have not significantly opened White residential areas to Black households. The laws are frequently not enforced. At the same time, discriminatory practices become more subtle but no less effective. Given the difficulties of implementing this strategy, the supply of housing opened to Black households would be dwarfed by the supply of housing added by the peripheral expansion of Black residential areas. For example, data from Chicago suggest that for each Black household for whom fair-housing groups found homes in the suburbs from 1960–1967, over 100 Black households found their own housing on the periphery of the Black residential areas (Berry et al., 1969, pp. 101–115).

CONCLUSIONS

Each of the methods discussed above has been mentioned as a possible strategy by governmental and private organizations or by individuals who advocate a policy position. With the exception of the integrated-dispersal strategy, all of the methods represent, in some way, compromises with a dominant fact of American life —racist attitudes and practices of Whites. The integrated-dispersal strategy, which is not a compromise, is probably the strategy least likely to be implemented successfully over a short term. White discriminatory practices are too deeply embedded in American life. At the same time, increased emphasis on Black unity may lead to decreasing proportions of Blacks willing to be "integrators" of White neighborhoods.

If any strategy is to deal successfully with racial patterns in cities and at the same time benefit Black households in their residential choices, it will probably have to consist of a composite of the strategies which have been discussed. Because of its injustice, White discrimination in housing must be vigorously eliminated. However, this will be a long-term process and does not by itself take into account the preferences some Blacks may have for living in close proximity with other Blacks. Therefore, other alternatives need to be pursued to widen the choices available to Black households. Of the other strategies discussed, the segregated-dispersal strategy seems to be the most effective way of expanding housing choices. Since this strategy may also be difficult to implement, the improvement of housing within the major Black concentrations may provide short-term benefits while the segregated-dispersal strategy is being implemented. Whatever composite of strategies is pursued, most housing needs of Blacks for the immediate future will be met, although imperfectly, by the peripheral expansion of Black residential areas.

REFERENCES CITED

Berry, Brian J. L., Smith, Katherine B., Vorwaller, Darrel J., and Wertymer, John. 1969. Unpublished paper, Center for Urban Studies, University of Chicago.

Brown, Lawrence A., and Moore, Eric G. 1970. "The Intra-Urban Migration Process: A Perspective," *Geografiska Annaler* 52, ser. B: 1–13.

Denton, John H. 1967. *Apartheid American Style.* Berkeley, Calif.: Diablo Press.

Deskins, Donald R., Jr. 1970. "Residence-Workplace Interaction Vectors for the Detroit Metropolitan Area: 1953 to 1965." In *Interaction Patterns and the Spatial Form of the Ghetto.* (Special Publication No. 3) Evanston, Ill.: Department of Geography, Northwestern University, pp. 1–23.

Downs, Anthony. 1968. "Alternative Futures for the American Ghetto." *Daedalus* 97:1331–78.

Erskine, Hazel. 1967. "The Polls: Negro Housing." *Public Opinion Quarterly* 31:482–98.

Farley, Reynolds, and Taeuber, Karl E. 1968. "Population Trends and Residential Segregation Since 1960." *Science* 159:953–56.

Frazier, E. Franklin. 1932. *The Negro Family in Chicago.* Chicago: University of Chicago Press.

Funnye, Charles, and Shiffman, Ronald. 1967. "The Imperative of Deghettoization: An Answer to Piven and Cloward," *Social Work* 12:5–11.

Grier, George W. 1967. "The Negro Ghettos and Federal Housing Policy." *Law and Contemporary Problems* 32:550–60.

Kain, John F., and Persky, Joseph J. 1969. "Alternatives to the Gilded Ghetto." *Public Interest* 14:74–87.

McEntire, Davis. 1960. *Residence and Race.* Berkeley and Los Angeles: University of California Press.

Meyer, David R. 1970. *Spatial Variation of Black Urban Households* (Department of Geography Research Paper No. 129) Chicago: University of Chicago.

Meyer, J. R., Kain, J. F., and Wohl, M. 1965. *The Urban Transportation Problem.* Cambridge: Harvard University Press.

Morrill, Richard. 1965. "The Negro Ghetto: Problems and Alternatives." *Geographical Review* 55:339–61.

Muth, Richard F. 1969. *Cities and Housing.* Chicago: University of Chicago Press.

Ohio Civil Rights Commission. 1963. *Discrimination in Housing in Ohio.* Columbus, Ohio.

Piven, Frances F., and Cloward, Richard A. 1967. "The Case Against Urban Desegregation." *Social Work* 12:12–21.

Rapkin, Chester. 1966. "Price Discrimination Against Negroes in the Rental Housing Market." In *Essays in Urban Land Economics.* Los Angeles: Real Estate Research Program, University of California, pp. 333–45.

Report of the National Advisory Commission on Civil Disorders. 1968. New York: Bantam Books.

Rose, Harold M. 1970. "The Development of an Urban Subsystem: The Case of the Negro Ghetto." *Annals of the Association of American Geographers* 60:1–17.

Simmons, James W. 1968. "Changing Residence in the City: A Review of Intra-urban Mobility." *Geographical Review* 58:622–51.

Taeuber, Karl E. 1968. "The Problem of Residential Segregation." *Academy of Political Science, Proceedings* 29:101–110.

_____, and Taeuber, Alma F. 1965. *Negroes in Cities.* Chicago: Aldine Publishing Co.

Turner, James. 1970. "Blacks in the Cities: Land and Self-Determination." *Black Scholar* 1:9–13.

U.S. Bureau of the Census. 1970. "Trends in Social and Economic Conditions in Metropolitan and Non-metropolitan Areas." *Current Population Reports.* Series P–23, no. 33.

Watts, Lewis G., Freeman, Howard E., Hughes, Helen M., Morris, Robert, and Pettigrew, Thomas F. 1964. *The Middle-Income Negro Family Faces Urban Renewal.* Waltham, Mass.: Brandeis University.

Weaver, Robert C. 1948. *The Negro Ghetto.* New York: Harcourt, Brace and Co.

7

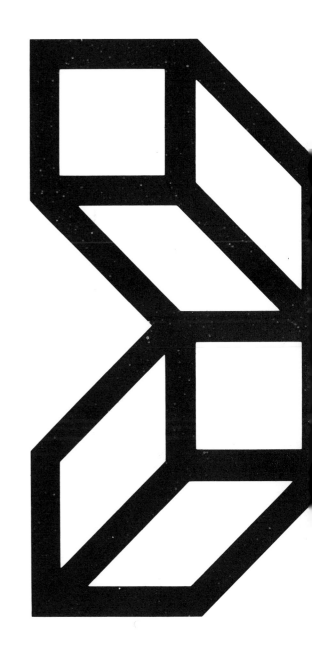

John Mercer
University of Iowa

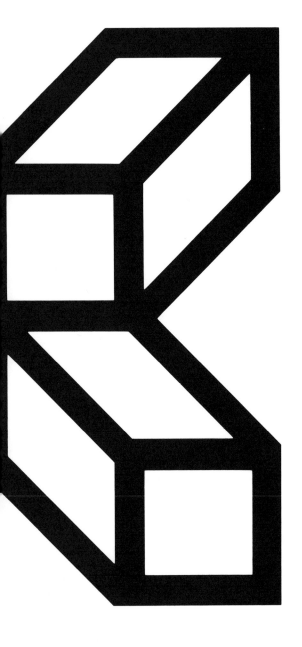

Housing Quality and the Ghetto

ABSTRACT

This essay deals with the spatial relationships between areas of Black residence and areas of substandard housing in American cities. After noting the strength and persistence of the relationship, some possible explanations are considered. Evidence from available studies, including some recent multivariate analyses, suggests that the low income of the Black population together with the very real discrimination which occurs in the operation of the housing market are principal contributing factors. We still lack sufficient data to make any incisive statements about possible attitudinal causes. The "costs" of living in such accommodations are illustrated by a discussion of the socio-psychological "costs" of living in blighted housing and also of the monetary cost, particularly where public programs, such as urban renewal and public housing, have brought about forced relocation. One major conclusion that emerges is that we have barely begun to investigate this critical topic, limited as we are by the data and available methodology.

Whatever the ghetto may be—a city within a city (Drake and Cayton, 1945), an "airtight cage" (Lyford, 1966), or a colony exploited by racist institutions and individuals (Harrison, 1968)—it is above all a residential area.[1] Generally, however, it is one of the lowest quality residential areas in any metropolitan area, if not the poorest. There is a persistent and strong spatial relationship between the location of Black residences and substandard housing. The extensive pre-1960 literature on the poor quality of housing occupied by Blacks is well summarized in the *Final Report to the Commission on Race and Housing* (McEntire, 1960). This relationship also occurs with respect to other ethnic minorities, such as Puerto Ricans in New York (Sexton, 1965). The persistence of this relationship is clear. There is evidence of the poor housing conditions of urban Blacks in the 1850s (Meier and Rudwick, 1966, p. 82) and again in the 1960s (*Report of the National Advisory Commission on Civil Disorders,* 1968, pp. 467–74). There is no reason to expect that this relationship will not be further substantiated via evidence from the 1970 census data.[2]

This essay considers some possible explanations for this relationship and some implications of its continuation. There is little doubt that the Black population is concerned about housing conditions, since Blacks frequently identify this as a major problem area along with such factors as lack of employment, poor educational opportunities, and others. This is true whether one considers statements by Black leaders (McKissick, 1966; Black Panther Party, 1966) or private individuals (*Report of the National Advisory Commission on Civil Disorders,* 1968, pp. 143–44).[3] This issue is not only of immediate importance to the people who are currently living and raising families in substandard dwelling units, but it is also of importance in the social science community as we seek increased understanding of urban reality. For example, can we attribute poor housing conditions to the occupants' inability to look after the property—the "they live like animals" syndrome; or is it the lack of maintenance on the part of landlords—the "vicious, grasping slumlord" syndrome; or is it the poverty of the inhabitants or racial discrimination?

If one assumes, for the moment, that the relationship between residential blight and ghettos is produced by an unknown number of spatial and aspatial factors which operate together, then a necessary research task is the identification of the various interrelationships and the contribution of each factor to the relationship. From this perspective, certain recommendations must then be made as to the appropriate kinds of policy and *action* that are required. Such a position may leave one open to a charge of incredible naïveté, since the cynic will be quick to observe that slums and residential blight

1. For the purposes of this essay, ghetto is defined as a segment of urban space predominantly occupied by Black people. It is sustained by both household choice and discriminatory practices, the interrelationships not being exactly known.

2. The only evidence of this relationship that I have seen for 1970 is from Cedar Rapids, Iowa. The population in one census tract is 30.67 percent Black, while the next highest percentage is 3.44 percent. This same tract ranks first in overcrowding (percentage of the housing stock with more than one person per room) and fourth in plumbing deficiencies (percentage of the housing stock lacking one or more plumbing facilities).

3. From more than 1,200 interviews in riot cities, the Advisory Commission staff ranked the major grievances of respondents. Inadequate housing along with police practices, unemployment, and underemployment comprised the first level of intensity.

are an enduring characteristic of urban areas and that such areas have been the "traditional home" of the oppressed, disadvantaged minorities throughout history. Nonetheless, a problem-solving orientation is clearly desirable in geography and other social sciences (Chisholm, 1971). To paraphrase Harvey's (1971) position, it is time cities were spatially organized to maximize social justice rather than efficiency and/or profitability. This is a goal worth striving for and the continuation of the Black—poor-quality housing relationship is contradictory to any notion of social justice.

SOME PROBLEMS IN RESEARCH DESIGN

A quick inventory of the stock of knowledge reveals that we, as geographers, have been largely content to leave the study of the ghetto to other social scientists. There are, of course, notable exceptions (Rose, 1969, 1970; Morrill, 1965; Adams and Sanders, 1969; Ward, 1971). In spite of our noncontribution, an impressive amount of material has been amassed concerning the nature of the ghetto, life styles in the ghetto, and various other aspects of ghetto life. This material is too extensive to document here. Although the ghetto occupies a significant amount of space within the central city— evidence now also points to "mini-ghettos" in some suburban areas—and of course, the spread of the ghetto has strong spatial connotations. Where have we been? Is our sense of priorities so distorted that we neglect this topic?

A similar lament can be raised when it comes to the other side of the coin. "Slums" and/or areas of residential blight are also important spatial elements in the internal structure of the city. Also, language such as "the insidious spread of urban blight across the city" may be conjured up. Again, however, geographers have been conspicuously absent from research in this area. There are some exceptions (Knos, 1959; Pownall, 1960; Berry and Murdie, 1965; Robson, 1966; Hartshorn, 1968, 1971; Mercer, 1971). For purposes of this essay, the concept of a "slum" will not be utilized. This avoids difficult definitional problems, particularly in a socio-psychological context. We cannot deny, however, that there are also difficult problems associated with the measurement of residential blight (Wellar, 1968; Wexler, 1965; U.S. Bureau of the Census, 1967).[4]

One limitation of the research carried out in this area by those with a spatial perspective is that it is mostly at an aggregate level of analysis (Tilly et al., 1965; Muth, 1969; Robson, 1966). This reflects a dependency on national censuses as a source of data. Another necessary procedure is the acquisition of data on individuals whose decision-making is a critical part of the process whereby residential blight is generated. Furthermore,

4. Throughout this essay, residential blight is thought of in terms of such census variables as dilapidated, deteriorating, and overcrowded.

these data must be locationally codified, so that they may be used in conjunction with the kinds of aggregate spatial data that are readily available. In this way, some of the contextual relationships between individuals and their "action-space" may be specified.

Thus, for example, contagion is often regarded as an important causative factor when considering the spread of residential blight. Most are familiar with the phrase so beloved of planning documents—"blighting influences." Just how "blighting influences" work is rarely spelled out in any rigorous fashion. It would seem most likely that the decision on upkeep of a property is made at the individual level—by the owner–occupier, the landlord (or his representative), or by a decision-maker in a local public authority agency which owns the property. Now, he (or she) may perceive, or is led to believe, that immediate proximity to some element of the physical urban stock such as a truck terminal, a glue factory, or an elevated transit line is injurious to the value of the property. (This assumes that the location of the facility in each case is subsequent to the existence of the residential property.) Proximity to some "noxious" element is perceived as reducing the value of the house in the eyes of prospective purchasers. Should capital then be invested in this property in the form of maintenance expenditures? If the owner decides against further investment and the property subsequently deteriorates in terms of physical condition, it may enter the "blighted" category.[5] If this situation occurs with a number of properties (as seems possible since owners of other adjacent properties may independently arrive at a similar decision), then we are told that "such and such" a facility is a "blighting influence" on the neighborhood. Therefore, the effect of decisions made at the individual level are observable at a neighborhood level, and the cause is attributed to the facility when, in fact, the effects are brought about by individual maintenance decisions. These decisions are being made, however, with respect to a neighborhood attribute. The area within which a facility is regarded as having negative externalities is perhaps critical for an understanding of "blighting influences." Some research on the spatial range of both positive and negative externalities is long overdue.

It is possible to translate this example into a social context. Instead of a facility having negative externalities, one can conceive of concentrations of Blacks (or other groups) having negative externalities. Perception of this externality and the range of the externality (one would expect that as distance from the source of the externality increased, the "negativeness" would decrease) would prompt some kind of decision by an individual home-owner or landlord. If the spatial concentration of Blacks is large enough, then the well-known "tipping point" effect comes into play (Wolf, 1963).

5. One might think that the decision itself has a negative externality, but this could only be assessed once the decision produced an observable outcome.

The egress of the White population is a relatively short-run action and may have no immediate impact on housing quality. If the concentration was significant (in a perceptual sense), but did not reach the critical level of the tipping point, then it might be possible to hypothesize behavior such as was described for the owner adjacent to the noxious facility.

This discussion illustrates one problem of using aggregate data such as the census, since they "lock" the researcher into ten-year time periods and a "comparative statics" approach, if any attempt is made to consider change. This is clearly inadequate in attempting to understand the dynamics of the housing market. What is needed is information on a small time-interval basis so that the lag between a decision or event and the observable effect can be better assessed.

POSSIBLE RESEARCH FRAMEWORKS

There is no easy approach, then, to considering the question of why there is a spatial relationship between areas of Black residence and areas of poor housing quality. There appears to be no single study that addresses the question at both the macro- and the micro-level with data available for short intervals over a reasonable time span. Until this grand design is executed, it is necessary to synthesize what is available.

One framework for explaining the relationship is developed in a study of race and residence in Wilmington (Tilly et al., 1965). There are, it is suggested, four categories of factors—(A) land use, (B) external controls, (C) resources, and (D) criteria of choice. Land use, including the distribution of land values, is the basic urban pattern facing the decision-maker. External controls result from decisions made by non-members of the minority group such as property owners, real estate agents, mortgage brokers, and governmental agencies. Resources are distributed within the group and include funds, borrowing power, and knowledge of the market. Criteria of choice are the decision rules employed by the minority group members. After reviewing how various factors in these categories interact, the authors present a series of block maps of housing quality and Black residence and conclude that Black housing is indeed spatially correlated with areas of poor quality. There is, however, no attempt to utilize a multivariate model to assess this relationship or the utility of the suggested framework. The multivariate approach to the analysis of housing quality has been adopted by others (Muth, 1969; Mercer, 1971). These studies are also carried out at the aggregate level using census data. The following appears to summarize Muth's basic thesis. Most arguments that purport to explain the spatial pattern of residential blight are "defective" since they ignore the poverty or low incomes of the occupants. Furthermore, the traditional arguments, such as declining demand for housing in the older, more central parts of cities, are not consistent with some facts: (1) slum housing seems to be expensive in relation to its quality, (2) urban renewal projects lose money, and (3) housing quality markedly improved from 1950 to 1960.

In proposing his alternative theory, Muth (1969) observes that housing demand increases in proportion to income. Higher income households consume better quality housing commensurate with their increases in income. Relatively, then, the low-income households would tend to occupy poorer quality housing and consume less space per person. This leads Muth to argue that the critical factor is the location of low-income households and that blight results from the housing stock in low-income neighborhoods being adapted by the deferral of maintenance and repairs in response to the poverty of the inhabitants. A rise in the relative price of housing is also a factor which he suggests is positively related to poor quality housing through the low per household consumption of housing. Muth's reasoning does seem to sit well with the three empirical facts cited above.

In his empirical analyses, Muth found a strong and consistent relationship between median income and the proportion of dwelling units which are substandard.[6] An increase in income would lead to an increase in housing quality. Muth's results also lead him to suggest that the reason more Blacks than Whites live in poorer quality housing is that they are poorer (Muth, 1969, pp. 278–80). Unfortunately, Muth does not attempt to broaden the scope of his research by integrating his findings with those of others; in fact, he conspicuously ignores empirical results that appear related to his work. An appropriate criticism of Muth's position appeared in a recent review which stated, "he does not give sufficient weight to the role of racial discrimination in restricting location of black residences" (Shafer, 1971, p. 351).

The author's own perspective suggests that the spatial choice of residence by the occupants and maintenance behavior by the landlords and owner-occupiers are the keys to explaining the relationship. This interaction occurs, however, within an environmental context which includes the existing stock of housing, sources of possible negative externalities, and the attitudes (and decisions) of public and private institutions and individuals. There is some comparability here with the Tilly et al. (1965) categories of land use and external control.

While one can also agree with Tilly et al. that knowledge of attitudes toward housing and preference structures is a necessary input to a conceptual framework, measuring the appropriate variables and utilizing these

6. Muth's (1969) results are largely derived from his analysis of 1950 and 1960 census data for a limited area on the South Side of Chicago. A sample of 69 tracts drawn from six groups of community areas is used. The basis for grouping is less than clear (p. 249).

is an altogether different matter. For example, there has been a tendency to infer that because so many people move to "suburbia" and live in single-family dwelling units set in a low density residential environment that this is the most preferred type of housing unit. Some national survey data suggest that, freed of any income constraint, most people do express a preference for this form of residential bundle (Lansing and Hendricks, 1967, pp. 102–126). Similarly, some writers have attributed the recent dramatic increase in apartment living to changes in preferences (Bourne, 1968, p. 214). However, the revealed preference is constrained by the available opportunity set; a preference for a particular residential bundle cannot be *revealed* if it does not exist. Furthermore, although the particular residential bundle which a household most prefers may exist, consumption (or occupancy) may be severely constrained by the financial resources available to the household.

A small modification to Alonso's (1965) basic budget equation demonstrates that the cost of housing is a function of the amount of disposable income (i.e., after tax), the expenditures for commuting to the workplace, and the expenditures on all other goods.

$$c = y - k - a \qquad (1)$$

Where c is the cost of housing, y is the disposable household income, k is the household commuting cost, and a is the cost of purchasing all other goods. Now c, the cost of housing, has two components—one represents the cost of actual dwelling unit or structure, c_s, and the other represents the amount of land consumed, or cost of the lot, c_l. Thus,

$$c_s + c_l = y - k - a \qquad (2)$$

c_s reflects both amount of internal space consumed and the quality of the unit. It is assumed that any neighborhood effects are reflected in the cost of the land— c_l. Equation (2) can then be rewritten

$$c_s = y - (k + a + c_l) \qquad (3)$$

To obtain data on the variables k, a, and c_l is extremely difficult, particularly at a household level. Even obtaining reliable data on income is difficult in survey work. Given a prior commitment to aggregate data in the research design, median income was used as a surrogate to measure resources in this empirical analysis.

In terms of Eq. (3), if y, disposable income, increases, the expectation is an increase in the quality of goods consumed as well as a possible expansion of the range of goods consumed. Exactly which goods this affects and how depends on the preference structure of the household. A positive relationship between income and housing quality is thus expected. However, at some point, the utility derived from additional expenditures

Table 1. *Multiple Regression Analyses: Summary*

Dependent Variable*	Multiple Correlation Coefficient	Standard Error of Estimate	Percentage Explained— Sum of Squares	N
	1950			
NPBORD	0.764	14.04	58.32	1060
PERPRM	0.866	4.92	74.94	1060
	1960			
PERPRM	0.813	5.18	66.03	1216
RB1950	0.735	11.71	54.05	1216
DILAP	0.477	7.18	22.76	1216

*PERPRM: percentage of the dwelling units with a person per room ratio greater than one.

NPBORD: percentage of the dwelling units with no private bath or units which are dilapidated.

DILAP: percentage of the dwelling units which are dilapidated.

RB1950: percentage of the dwelling units which are dilapidated, deteriorating, and lacking in plumbing facilities, and sound but lacking in plumbing facilities. This category is thus similar to the 1950 category, no private bath and dilapidated.

on housing quality will begin to decline and further expenditures on housing quality will not be made.

If y is fixed, on the other hand, there arises a problem of substitution. Thus, if the cost of any expenditure on the right-hand side of Eq. (3) increases, then one possible compensation would be reduced expenditures on c_s (or quality and/or internal space). It is equally possible, however, that the necessary compensatory cut would be on another factor. Again, the substitution relationships here are a function of household preference structures and the demands of the household. Substitutions within the framework of Eq. (3) are more easily made when the income is high. If income falls, then substituting at some point any other factor for housing becomes increasingly difficult. There is a minimum of shelter that can be regarded as necessary by most people. Winnick and Blank (1953, p. 183) comment on this difficulty of substitution: "While other goods and services may be substitutes for the quantity and quality of a family's housing, only rarely can this important item be entirely displaced from the family budget."

They also discuss the problem of substitution *within* housing markets, noting that a large number of clusters of substitutes can be developed using a variety of characteristics such as location, tenure, type of structure, etc. Therefore, a house in another part of the urban area may not be a feasible substitute for the presently occupied unit. Also, a five-room apartment may be preferred as a substitute for a five-room single-family dwelling unit, as compared to a six-room house of the same type. Furthermore, in reducing housing costs, some tradeoff between internal space and quality is also possible. These substitution relationships are another necessary research area. However, command of resources is not the only constraint on choice of residence.

Reviewing the available literature, there is a consensus that non-White minorities are discriminated against in the housing market. Tilly et al. (1965) quote a conclusion of the 1959 United States Commission on Civil Rights: "a considerable number of Americans, by reason of their color or race, are being denied equal opportunity in housing."

In other words, ability to pay (or the possession of resources) is not sufficient to ensure freedom of choice. An important study finds that restrictive racial practices operating through the actions of real estate brokers existed in Chicago in 1955–1956 and that they persisted in 1964–1965 (Helper, 1969). Additional evidence is presented concerning similar behavior in other United States cities. Tilly et al. (1965) also review evidence of discrimination by real estate agents, property-owner associations, and public agencies. The policies of federal and private lending agencies in the housing field are well known—e.g., requiring larger down payments and less attractive terms of Black applicants.

Given the tremendous inflow of non-White migrants into the urban areas of the United States, this lack of free choice has produced extreme concentrations of Black people in certain sections of the city—the desire for social cohesion among Blacks notwithstanding. The increasing segregation of the Black population is shown by the work of the Taeubers and others (Taeuber and Taeuber, 1965). This, then, raises the question of the quality of housing occupied by this segregated group. Is the housing already substandard when occupied? The filtering concept would not have us believe so, especially when Blacks move into an area recently vacated by Whites. Does it become substandard, or blighted, as non-White occupancy persists? Muth suggests this is so, for he argues that housing occupied by low-income households is adapted to their circumstances by conversion and deferral of repairs (here, low-income households are equated with Black households—a gross but realistic comparison). Some additional evidence on the important interrelationships between income or resources, quality of housing, and color is provided in a previous study of housing quality in the Chicago metropolitan area (Mercer, 1971). One of the objectives of this study is to explain the spatial variation of residential blight (as measured by certain census variables). Other socio-economic variables are drawn from the census and are used as predictors in a number of regression analyses. Census tracts are the areal units of analysis; 1,060 and 1,216 tracts are used for 1950 and 1960, respectively.

The over-all regression results for five dependent variables are shown in table 1. The contribution of the independent variables is shown in table 2. The major contributors to the reduction of sums of squares are BLACK and INCOME; the other independent variables contribute little. As expected, the relationship between INCOME and the various measures of residential blight is negative. Thus, as income increases in an area, the amount of low-quality housing decreases. This is consistent with Muth's findings. The relationship between BLACK and the same measures is positive, except in one case. This was also predictable, and it confirms the hypothesis that there is a strong, positive relationship between areas of Black residence and areas of poor-quality housing. A persistent pattern emerges from these results, however. When the dependent variable is a combination of structural condition and plumbing deficiency, then INCOME is the principal explanatory variable. When PERPRM, the overcrowding variable, is the dependent variable, then BLACK is the principal explanatory variable. This is also true for DILAP which is a measure of structural condition; however, the over-all results for the DILAP regression equation are less satisfactory than for the others. This is again consistent with Muth's results since income was the powerful ex-

Table 2. *The Independent Variables*

Independent Variables*	Dependent Variable	Beta Weight	Percentage Sum of Squares Reduced by Each Variable
BLACK	PERPRM-1950	0.548	63.3
	NPBORD	0.347	8.1
	PERPRM-1960	0.358	56.8
	RB1950	−0.090	0.1
	DILAP	0.194	14.5
INCOME	PERPRM-1950	−0.329	10.3
	NPBORD	−0.347	45.4
	PERPRM-1960	−0.501	5.5
	RB1950	−0.257	40.2
	DILAP	−0.199	2.4
OWNED	PERPRM-1950	−0.388	1.1
	NPBORD	−1.688	0.2
	PERPRM-1960	0.101	0.4
	RB1950	−0.336	3.5
	DILAP	−0.117	0.2
RENTED	PERPRM-1950	−0.253	0.1
	NPBORD	−1.602	1.4
	PERPRM-1960	−0.060	0.1
	RB1950	−0.090	0.5
	DILAP	−0.126	0.3
MIGRNT	PERPRM-1950	0.013	0.0
	NPBORD	0.063	0.8
	PERPRM-1960	0.005	0.0
	RB1950	−0.076	0.2
	DILAP	−0.026	0.0
FORBRN	PERPRM-1950	−0.060	0.1
	NPBORD	−0.018	0.0
FORSTK	PERPRM-1960	−0.245	1.9
	RB1950	−0.397	3.7
	DILAP	−0.132	0.2

*BLACK: percentage of the population which is Negro.
INCOME: median income for families and unrelated individuals.
OWNED: percentage of dwelling units which are owner-occupied.
RENTED: percentage of dwelling units which are rented.
MIGRNT: percentage of the population over one year old which resided in a different county or abroad in 1949 (1950 definition) and percentage of the population over five years old which lived in a different house, outside the SMSA in 1955 (1960 definition).
FORBRN: percentage of the population born outside the United States.
FORSTK: percentage of the population born in the United States, one or both of whose parents are foreign born, and those who are foreign born.

For other abbreviations, see table 1.

Table 3. *Partial Correlation Analysis*

1950

BLACK = 1, INCOME = 2, NPBORD = 3, PERPRM = 4

$r_{12} = -0.52$, $r_{13} = 0.59$, $r_{14} = 0.80$, $r_{23} = -0.67$, $r_{24} = -0.69$, $r_{34} = 0.75$

Partial Correlation Coefficients

$r_{13.2} = 0.38$, $r_{14.2} = 0.71$, $r_{23.1} = -0.51$, $r_{24.1} = -0.52$

1960

BLACK = 1, INCOME = 2, RB1950 = 3, DILAP = 4, PERPRM = 5

$r_{12} = -0.52$, $r_{13} = 0.45$, $r_{14} = 0.38$, $r_{15} = 0.75$, $r_{23} = -0.63$, $r_{24} = -0.36$, $r_{25} = -0.59$, $r_{34} = 0.64$, $r_{35} = 0.51$, $r_{45} = 0.40$

Partial Correlation Coefficients

$r_{13.2} = 0.18$, $r_{14.2} = 0.24$, $r_{15.2} = 0.65$, $r_{23.1} = -0.59$, $r_{24.1} = -0.21$, $r_{25.1} = -0.35$

For abbreviations, see tables 1 and 2.

planatory variable when he examined the percentage of substandard housing (equivalent to NPBORD). Muth did not use DILAP or PERPRM as dependent variables.

The relationship observed between BLACK and housing quality appears to be independent of income (see table 3). One would expect substantial reductions in the correlation coefficients between BLACK and the measures of residential blight when INCOME is controlled, if the relationship were attributable to the income conditions of the Black population. Only in one case is the reduction substantial—in 1960, $r_{13} = 0.45$ (BLACK and RB1950) is reduced to $r_{13.2} = 0.18$. These results are at variance with Muth's conclusion that low income explains the observed relationship.

While these results confirm some previous findings, they do not permit any causal inferences to be drawn. Confirmation of the aggregate relationships with data at the individual level must be found. Such data might also allow us to test more meaningful, powerful hypotheses.

The relationship between housing quality and income has been further considered in a multivariate framework (Schmitt, 1971). Observing that the use of measures of occupation and education reduces the significance of income as a determinant of dwelling unit condition in Muth's work, Schmitt examined census data for the central city of Pittsburgh, focusing on the relationships between the educational and occupational variables, income, and housing condition. If his premise that income is a surrogate for material resources and that education is a gross indicator of life style is accepted, then the results indicate that life-style differences are more important than income in accounting for the variation between occupational groups and housing quality.[7] Therefore, although income cannot be discounted, the desire for groups to live with other groups of similar status and life style is an important factor in understanding spatial variation in housing quality. These findings, while limited, are consistent with (A) a sequence which runs from level of education to job opportunity to income available, and (B) the realization that residential segregation occurs for other than racial reasons in American cities.

SOME KEY QUESTIONS

In general, all housing moves toward the condition of blight as time passes. Wolfe (1967) has presented a simple model which describes this process. This is only to be expected given normal or subnormal maintenance expenditures. But the more critical questions are, for example, whether Blacks allocate sufficient resources to obtain standard housing. Does standard housing occupy a lower position on their preference

7. There are, however, problems of controlling for possible interactions between such variables as occupation, education, and income.

scale than, say, automobiles or drugs? Does crowding produce physical dilapidation and is crowding a response to allocation decisions or lack of resources? Finally, do property owners exhibit particular kinds of maintenance behavior in different market contexts?

This final question raises the spectre of the "slumlord." It is not uncommon for the communications media and others to attribute the continued existence of blighted housing to the desire of "slumlords" to maximize their profits from this section of the housing stock. Information on the profitability of such housing is extremely difficult to obtain, Sternlieb (1966), in his authoritative work on the tenement landlord in Newark, New Jersey, observes that slum property is not profitable for some classes of landlords. Such landlords are often "saddled" with the property, since no other entrepreneur is willing to purchase it. Such owners can only look forward to a public "slum-clearance," or urban-renewal project to be freed of the burden. In contrast, other owners are able to achieve substantial rates of return (Sporn, 1960; Nakagawa, 1957). The latter situation occurs particularly where there is a spatially concentrated, heavy demand for low-cost housing. In most cases, the supply is fixed and may even be declining. One would expect, under the notions of equilibrium theory, that suppliers would be attracted into the market to provide low-cost housing. However, it would appear that the provision of low-cost housing is beyond the capability of the housing industry unless there is government subsidy. Alternative sources of profits with less risk attached may, of course, divert the suppliers elsewhere, e.g., luxury central redevelopment or new residential construction on the urban periphery.

In the situation described above—a "tight" market—property owners will be motivated to charge as much rent as possible for rent-bearing units, and maintenance costs can be deferred without risking increased vacancy rates. In this kind of situation, some conversion of large old dwellings is likely to occur, while non-residential properties may be turned into residences, e.g., storefronts, garages, basements. The subsequent increase in supply is limited, however, and must ultimately diminish (see table 4). In such market conditions, overcrowding is also a likely consequence. If the rent demanded is high relative to the household budget, then the addition of relatives and friends or lodgers to assist in paying the rent is common. In such circumstances, there is likely to be considerable strain on the facilities of the dwelling unit, e.g., plumbing, wiring, and the structure itself. There is evidence to support this point (see table 5).

Comparison of maps on overcrowding in the central city of Chicago for 1940 and 1950 (Mercer, 1971) shows that overcrowding was less extensive in 1950 than in 1940 but that it was more highly concentrated (and more

Table 4. *Addition to Housing Stock by Conversion: Wilmington, Delaware*

| | Proportion Of All Dwelling Units Added (Percentage) | |
	Conversion	New Apartments
1936–40	45.9	17.9
1941–45	30.5	20.4
1946–50	36.2	1.5
1951–55	28.9	23.9
1956–60	14.4	71.3
TOTAL	31.1	28.2

Source: Tilly et al. (1965).

Table 5. *Some Family Living Arrangements: Wilmington, 1940 and 1950**

| | Percentage | |
	White	Non-White
Proportion of members of private households who were lodgers, 1940	4.9	18.4
Proportion of married couples without own household, 1950	9.6	20.7

Source: Tilly et al. (1965).

*No comparable data exist for 1960.

Table 6. *Overcrowding in Wilmington*

Persons Per Room	1950 White (%)	1950 Non-White (%)	1960 White (%)	1960 Non-White (%)
1.00 or less	92.1	79.6	94.9	82.5
1.01 to 1.50	6.1	12.1	4.2	12.5
1.51 or more	1.8	8.3	0.9	5.0

Source: Tilly et al. (1965).

severe) in certain areas of the city, notably in those areas which were experiencing considerable Black in-migration over this period (Duncan and Duncan, 1957, figures 7, 8). Spear observes that overcrowding was not a particularly serious problem in Chicago during the period 1900–1920 but that it was widespread in Black residential areas in 1920–1940, a period of considerable in-migration (Spear, 1967, pp. 149–50). Similar patterns of overcrowding are observed in areas of colored migration within British cities (Glass, 1960, pp. 54–58; Rex and Moore, 1967, pp. 133–37).

Overcrowding may also reflect the current vacancy rates in the local housing market. The market does appear to have weakened by 1960. In the Chicago metropolitan area, the mean percentage of dwelling units which were vacant rose from 0.80 percent in 1950 to 3.26 percent in 1960. Sternlieb (1966) and Tilly et al. (1965) also note this change in their respective studies. Not unexpectedly, overcrowding decreased to some extent (see table 6) but was still more severe for the non-White population. In the Chicago area, the mean percentage of all dwelling units with more than 1.01 persons per room declined from 14.18 in 1950 to 10.90 in 1960 (Mercer, 1971, pp. 97–98). The number of census tracts which had over 25 percent of the housing stock classified as overcrowded also declined from 152 in 1950 to 109 in 1960. More importantly, perhaps, the areas with the highest percentages of the housing stock classed as overcrowded are to be found at the "leading edge" of the ghetto in such districts as Woodlawn, Englewood, and North Lawndale.

While it is also true that housing quality (as measured by structural and plumbing conditions) improved over the period 1950 to 1960 in a weakening market context, Sternlieb (1966) points out that landlord behavior in this context in Newark again resulted, in some cases, in deferral of maintenance expenditures as landlords sought to reduce costs when faced with declining revenues and increasing vacancy rates. Vacant property is also likely to deteriorate further through neglect and vandalism. The author's own findings in Chicago indicate that while there was an over-all decrease in residential blight from 1950 to 1960, about 7 percent of the central city tracts showed increases in residential blight of over 6 percent (i.e., the difference between the percentage of the stock blighted in 1950 and in 1960 was larger than 6). Thus, in spite of a weakening market, blight persists and is even on the increase in certain areas. Considerable stress has been placed on the maintenance behavior of landlords since this appears to be critical in an explanation of the relationship under consideration here. Most Black people live in rented dwelling units, and there seems to be little prospect of this situation's changing substantially. Indeed, the landlord-tenant relationship has become a focal point of racial conflict in the central city (Lipsky, 1970).

Given the fact of substantial overcrowding in non-White households, does this in itself lead to structural deterioration? An intuitive answer would be "yes, unless sufficient maintenance expenditures are made to offset the 'wear and tear' on the structure." There are some aggregate data which suggest that as Black people move into an area there is an increase in overcrowding, subsequent to which there is an increase in residential blight. This relationship has been examined for seven selected community districts in Chicago from 1940 to 1960 (Mercer, 1971, pp. 87–90). The data are shown in table 7, and while these do not represent the whole data set, they are illustrative. The four community areas listed in table 7 have experienced racial change. Three other areas which did not experience significant racial change are used for comparative purposes.

A general conclusion is that the tracts which undergo racial change also show increases in overcrowding and poor housing condition, although the pattern is less

Table 7. *Racial Change and Change in Housing Quality*

	Tract no.	1940		1950			1960		
		PERPRM	BLACK	NPBORD	PERPRM	BLACK	BLIGHT	PERPRM	BLACK
Englewood									
	872	13.0	26.0	10.5	21.4	61.4	11.1	23.5	96.8
	878	18.2	0.3	17.4	29.9	79.5	20.1	26.5	94.7
	881	21.4	1.9	7.2	9.7	6.9	3.7	22.5	91.9
	875	13.9	0.0	14.1	13.9	0.1	13.2	11.1	9.5
	884	13.5	0.2	10.4	9.9	0.1	5.4	13.5	53.6
Near North Side									
	121	17.8	4.5	59.2	24.1	36.7	39.4	26.4	80.7
	128	20.6	30.5	52.9	34.3	80.4	71.6	26.7	85.4
	134	13.9	33.3	67.2	32.9	63.1	46.2	20.7	70.4
	135	20.3	0.8	60.3	34.7	12.2	77.3	9.9	13.0
North Lawndale									
	464	18.8	0.2	2.1	8.9	0.3	6.47	7.5	0.1
	467	10.4	0.0	1.9	8.3	6.3	11.4	30.8	94.5
	461	21.8	0.3	3.7	13.3	3.0	2.8	38.5	97.8
	459	52.2	0.0	19.6	9.3	0.1	9.2	9.2	0.0
	460	12.7	0.0	7.7	13.3	0.0	4.2	38.4	96.2
Woodlawn									
	626	24.3	0.1	25.5	17.2	2.9	41.2	22.7	76.5
	631	20.5	0.1	27.6	16.5	1.8	27.3	26.4	88.8
	623	3.9	15.3	39.0	25.8	99.4	16.0	12.4	99.7
	632	21.4	0.0	32.0	22.2	0.4	35.1	23.6	66.9

For abbreviations, see tables 1 and 2.

Table 8. *Substandard Housing and Color, Controlling for Overcrowding, 1950 and 1960*

| BLACK = 1, NPBORD = 2, PERPRM = 3 (1950) |
| BLACK = 1, RB1950 = 2, DILAP = 3, PERPRM = 4 (1960) |

$r_{12} = 0.59$	$r_{12.3} = -0.03$	(1950)
$r_{12} = 0.45$	$r_{12.4} = 0.12$	(1960)
$r_{13} = 0.38$	$r_{13.4} = 0.13$	(1960)

For abbreviations, see tables 1 and 2.

consistent for the latter variable. Examination of the whole data set reveals that the tracts within the all-White community areas—and the predominantly White tracts in communities undergoing racial change—either show little change or a decline in the amount of overcrowding and proportion of poor housing. This tendency is most marked for change in overcrowding from 1940 to 1950, where almost all tracts undergoing racial change also showed increases in overcrowding. An exception is in North Lawndale where sizeable decreases occurred in tracts which were invaded by Blacks and abandoned by Polish and Russian Jews.

The tendency is weaker in the period 1950 to 1960. The conditions in Woodlawn and the Near North Side appear to be the major contribution to the weakening of the relationship. Unlike tracts in other areas, those on the Near North Side show highly variable amounts of increase and decrease, although the majority of the tracts show a decrease. In Woodlawn, those census tracts which have little or no further racial change from 1950 to 1960 show decreases in both overcrowding and residential blight. These tracts were already 97–99 percent Black in population by 1950. It is perhaps too early (in 1960) to observe deterioration in housing condition in the areas of recent Black in-migration. Although overcrowding is widespread, blighted housing does not occur extensively in these areas. Subsequent evidence (Satter, 1966; Department of Urban Renewal, 1967), however, shows that physical deterioration did increase. There are also some striking absolute differences in housing quality between the all-White areas and the tracts experiencing racial change.

Too little is known about other possible factors which may be operating in these situations to make any strong inferences or causal connections. Nonetheless, there does seem to be a positive relationship between racial change and a reduction in the quality of available housing. In contrast, once racial change has stabilized, the degree of overcrowding declines as does the proportion of poor housing. The evidence to support this last point is, however, slender. This type of data does not permit us to assess whether overcrowding per se brings about physical deterioration. However, the implication that racial change and overcrowding occur together and that structural decay follows is intuitively appealing.

It may be, therefore, that the relationship observed between color and poor physical condition of housing in Chicago is due to their common relationship with overcrowding. This hypothesis appears to have some merit (see table 8). Controlling for overcrowding reduces the correlation between BLACK and NPBORD almost to zero; in 1960, there is also substantial reduction of the correlation coefficients. Again, however, to truly test the relationship here, information is needed on the reaction of landlords to the Black–overcrowding relationship. These landlords *may* take this as a cue to a "tight market" situation in which they can begin to reduce maintenance and repairs.

The area of preference structures of Black households, particularly with reference to residential environment, remains an "underdeveloped region" in social science research. However, data are available on expenditures. These national data are useful in a limited way in answering the question of what resources Blacks are willing to allocate to housing. Review will also be made of some survey data on expenditures obtained in conjunction with research on urban renewal and public housing relocation schemes, projects which have had a considerable impact on the Black population.

Data are available from the Bureau of Labor Statistics for family expenditures. Table 9A shows that in the United States as a whole, and in each of four designated regions, Black households spend a larger proportion of their income on "shelter, fuel, light, refrigeration and water" than do White households. In 1950, however, on a national basis, the percentage allocation was exactly the same for both classes of households. Thus, it is reasonable to attribute some of the over-all national gain in housing quality for Blacks to increased expenditures on housing. The data in table 9B suggest, however, that the lower-income Blacks consistently spend less on housing than their White counterparts. This may reflect different attitudes toward housing within the Black population itself, since middle- and upper-income

Table 9. *Percentage of Income Expended by Families*

A. On "Shelter, Fuel, Light, Refrigeration, Water" — Urban United States, 1960–61 (Annual Average)

United States		Northeast		North Central		South		West	
Negro	White	Negro	White	Negro	White	Negro	White	Negro	White
20	18	20	19	21	19	19	17	20	18

B. By Income Class, 1950 and 1960–61

1950					
Under $2,000		$2,000–5,999		$6,000 and Over	
Negro	White	Negro	White	Negro	White
21	23	15	16	13	14

1960–61					
Under $3,000		$3,000–7,499		$7,500 and Over	
Negro	White	Negro	White	Negro	White
25	27	19	19	16	16

Source: U.S. Department of Labor, Bureau of Labor Statistics.

159

Blacks must be spending more than their White counterparts (in 1960–1961) in order to account for the national difference of 20 to 18 percent. These data are consistent with Rapkin's (1969) findings that the degree of price discrimination increases noticeably as the Black household approaches middle-class status.

When the percentages in table 9A and B are expressed in absolute dollar terms, the differences in magnitude are striking, although not unexpected (see table 10). A comparison of 1950 with 1960–1961 data shows that Black households are allocating more resources for housing, an increase from 16 to 20 percent of their income, but that they are spending only $61 per month as compared to $85.75 for White households (1960 data). Although Blacks are spending more of their income on housing and related costs than before and even though they allocate more to housing than their White counterparts, they still spend $25 per month less in absolute dollar amounts. In order for a Black household to "compete" with a White household on equal terms, i.e., to allocate $85.75 per month for housing costs, it would, of necessity, have to allocate 37 percent of its income after taxes to this expenditure (1960 data). It is not surprising that $61 per month obtains poorer quality housing and/or less internal space than $85.75 per month.

It is doubtful that any inferences about preferences can be made from the pattern of family expenditures. It might be noted that in both 1950 and 1960 the over-all pattern of expenditures for Black and White consumers was essentially similar. Perhaps the most significant difference is that in both years Black households spent a larger proportion of their income on what the Bureau of Labor Statistics calls "three basic expenses"—food, shelter, etc., and clothing, including upkeep.

URBAN RENEWAL AND PUBLIC HOUSING

Some of the national data on expenditures and consumption inevitably obscure the individual family or household situation. This can be partially gleaned from

Table 10. *Dollar Amounts Expended by Families on "Shelter, Fuel, Light, Refrigeration, Water"—Urban United States, 1950 and 1960–1961 (Annual Average)*

Expenditure	1950 (Current Dollars)			1960–61 (Current Dollars)		
			Percentage—Negro of			Percentage—Negro of
	Negro	White	White	Negro	White	White
Shelter, fuel, light, refrigeration, and water	428	614	70	732	1028	71

Source: U.S. Department of Labor, Bureau of Labor Statistics.

survey data. These data also allow a brief discussion of the impact of two public programs on housing quality in the ghetto—urban renewal and public housing (Department of City Planning, 1960; Wolf and Lebeaux, 1969). The urban renewal program has earned for itself the synonym of "Negro removal." In the Detroit study cited above, 52 percent of the respondents attributed a racial motive to urban renewal—"to push the colored people out." The public housing program has also created a relocation problem. In the early days of these programs, relocation was a haphazard affair; indeed in the case of urban renewal, the task was handed over to the developer. The consequences can be easily imagined.

Both programs have been criticized for effectively reducing the supply of low-rent housing and, by displacing sizeable numbers of households, for increasing pressure (i.e., creating a tight housing market) in other low-rent districts of the city—districts, moreover, that may themselves be renewed soon (Gans, 1962). The relocatees from such public activities are generally housed in "standard" housing after relocation. Although the gains are sometimes overdramatized by those responsible for the administration of the programs, it is likely that the over-all gain in quality is real enough. Thus, superficially, the conclusion that such programs benefit the Black population and will do much to weaken the persistence of the relationship under discussion is a tempting one.

However, the gains in quality are not made without substantial costs. There is now a body of literature on the socio-psychological impact of urban renewal and relocation. The Detroit data also indicate that a substantial percentage—"probably more than a third but less than a half of all interviewed locatees"—still possessed a sense of loss two years after leaving the project area (Wolf and Lebeaux, 1969, p. 428). Time had, however, lessened the sense of loss experienced in the short-run.

An equally important cost is the possible change in housing cost that relocation may bring. This is important on two points: (1) the ability to maintain new property if purchased and (2) the likelihood of continuing to live in a "standard" quality dwelling unit at a higher cost. In commenting on other studies, the Detroit study observes that "relocation has been accompanied, almost invariably, by increased housing costs" (Wolf and Lebeaux, 1969, p. 409). This is particularly critical for those living on fixed incomes; almost 25 percent of the Detroit respondents were on some form of public assistance. In both Detroit and Chicago, the relocatees were paying more after relocation, although there was a real (and perceived) improvement in housing quality. In Detroit, 57 percent of the respondents reported an increase in housing expenditure, 30 percent experienced a decrease, while 10 percent reported no change. More importantly, 37 percent of the respondents experienced an increase of over 20 percent in their housing expenditures—"Net housing expenditures accounted for a median of 30 percent of gross income" (Wolf and Lebeaux, 1969, p. 413). In more general terms, almost two-thirds of the respondents reported an increase in the cost of living in the new home, and almost half did not feel that this new home was worth the difference.[8]

In the Chicago case, those relocatees who were tenants experienced a 32 percent increase in gross rent. Sixty-five percent of the relocatee tenants were paying more than 24 percent of their income for rent after relocation, and those in the lowest income bracket (under $3,000 annual income) were paying 46 percent of their income for rent. A majority of relocatees who purchased homes (57 percent) were making monthly payments which represented 31 percent of the median owner—occupier income. Furthermore, the median purchase price for the homes was $21,500 as compared with $10,400, which was the median price received for the former residence.

While these figures are only illustrative, they focus attention on an important point—such programs may yield a better quality residence but at some socio-psychological cost and at a necessary cutback in other areas of family expenditure, *unless* family income also increases. Also, for some respondents, there may even be a deterioration in housing quality after relocation.

Can these data tell us anything about housing quality in the receptor areas, usually other parts of the ghetto? A little, yes; but careful research of the impact of relocatees on receptor areas is still urgently required. The Detroit study indicates that the relocatees were poorer than those living in the receptor areas; in spite of this, they appeared to maintain their property as well as existing residents. Most, however, were renters (84 percent) and hence, property maintenance would be primarily a landlord decision.

Since the Chicago study identifies the census tracts to which relocatees went, the notion that "spillovers" from public programs are associated with poor housing quality can be examined. The relocation occurred in Chicago in 1957–1958. In 1960, 72 percent of the reception tracts showed a decline in substandard housing, but 54 percent showed an increase in overcrowding (1950–1960 data). When the five census tracts that received almost a quarter of the relocatees are examined, they all showed an increase in overcrowding, while two increased and three decreased in the percentage of housing which was substandard. This is suggestive, but the data do not allow any strong conclusions. First, 197 households moved into 82 different tracts and, secondly, many other variables are not being controlled.

A brief comment on the end product of another pub-

8. Another important point to emerge from the Detroit data is that over 60 percent of the respondents found housing which they preferred and was available but which was "beyond their means." Thus, their currently occupied housing does not reveal their true preference.

lic program is warranted. Since racial discrimination has permitted little public housing to be constructed beyond the ghetto, the public housing projects are an integral part of the ghetto and its housing stock (Meyerson and Banfield, 1955). Although public housing is meant to be standard housing (according to census definitions previously outlined in this essay), some critics argue that we are creating social and psychological disaster areas. Thus, a recent statement concludes that "public housing is a system which, by its very character, functions to create ghetto slums under public management" (Redfield, 1971, p. 309). Titles of other studies of public housing are illustrative— *The Vertical Ghetto* and *Behind Ghetto Walls: Black Family Life in a Federal Slum* (Moore, 1969; Rainwater, 1970). These studies make harrowing reading, as does other non-academic literature on life in the projects.

Perhaps the important distinction between public housing and other forms of ghetto housing is that the tenants in the projects consider the actual dwelling unit and its internal characteristics more favorably than the immediate external environment (Rainwater, 1970; Hartmann, 1963). The urban relocation literature suggests that, in many cases, the pre-relocation environment (including such things as friends and kin as part of the environment) is regarded more favorably than the dwelling unit. Thus, while public housing programs may produce improved living accommodations, they simultaneously produce a different and very difficult residential environment within the ghetto.

SOCIO-PSYCHOLOGICAL IMPLICATIONS OF THE RELATIONSHIP

Intuitively, one might expect that the persistence of the relationship between low quality housing and the Black population would be reflected in certain measures of behavioral stress in the population. The working premise here is that living in poor quality dwelling units affects the occupants in some harmful manner. This premise, in fact, partly underlies current housing policy which aims to provide a "decent" residential environment for all people.

While some consequences of living in blighted housing can be hypothesized, it has proved enormously difficult to demonstrate relationships other than spatial association. Much of the early stimulus here came from human ecologists who strongly emphasized correlation analysis (Faris and Dunham, 1939). A review of the existing propositions concerning housing quality and its effect on people indicates that there is (1) no systematic choice of housing attributes and behavioral characteristics, which makes comparison difficult— more parsimonious procedures are also necessary; and (2) there are inconsistencies in the findings, e.g., relationships going in opposite directions and conflicting conclusions derived from the same pair of variables (Moore et al., 1968, pp. 12–17). The review concludes that the research emphasis must be on relationships among *specific* dwelling unit attributes and such factors as "indices of disorganization, rates of social interaction and perceived neighborhood desirability" rather than on general housing variables (e.g., slums). Also, since other factors can influence these various behavioral characteristics, there is a need for "rigorous experimental designs utilizing control groups" (Moore et al., 1968, pp. 16–17).

Even with such attempted designs, the findings are less than satisfactory. Characterized as "the most careful of the few relevant studies" (Clark, 1965, p. 32), a longitudinal study in Baltimore attempted to assess the effect of housing on morbidity and mental health by obtaining a variety of measures on a test group and a control group (Wilner et al., 1962). Both samples consisted of low-income Black families and were matched for a number of demographic, initial health, and initial adjustment attributes. The test group of 300 families had earlier lived in a "slum" but had since moved to a new public housing project; the control group (also of 300 families) remained in the "slum." The conclusions are that living in substandard housing does have an adverse influence but only for *some* age groups and only for *some* health and morbidity measures. The relationships are not well established, however. With respect to social adjustment, the direction of the relationships was as expected. However, no confidence could be placed in their strength.

While the results are discouraging, certain tendencies have been observed; namely, that poor housing tends to be spatially associated with poor health and difficulties of social adjustment. One major review concludes that quality of housing, particularly if it is desperately inadequate, does have an effect on health, behavior, and attitudes (Schorr, 1964). Clearly, more work is needed in this area and the help of urban-oriented social psychologists is essential. Although it is difficult to measure the relationship, other items such as frequency of rat bites, frequency of incidents of lead poisoning, and frequency of fire are measurable and attest to the potential health and life hazards that exist in areas of blighted housing.

SUMMARY AND CONCLUSION

This essay has considered the strong and persistent spatial association between Black residential areas and areas of low residential quality. It has accused geographers, not of benign, but of critical neglect in this area. It has briefly commented on the need for certain kinds of research on preference structures, the housing attribute–behavioral characteristic relationship, and the identification of lag effects. There are serious data collection problems and problems of appropriate scale.

Frameworks that may have some utility were considered together with their empirical findings. Some key questions were raised and some partial evidence brought to bear on these. The impact of two public programs was briefly discussed and found to be disturbing. Nothing was resolved in this essay nor should this be expected, since much research still needs to be done. Are our designs adequate? Do we have the data? Do we have the ability to measure precisely? Do we have the commitment? Can we make a meaningful contribution to an understanding and explanation of this relationship? It is the author's opinion that we can, but can we then generate action to ensure social justice? It is depressing indeed to consider the geographer's contribution with respect to an understanding of a spatial association that is as cruel and vicious as the society that has permitted it to persist for so long.

REFERENCES CITED

Adams, J. S. and Sanders, R. 1969. "Urban Residential Structure and the Location of Stress in Ghettos." *Earth and Mineral Sciences* 38:20–33.

Alonso, W. 1965. *Location and Land Use.* Cambridge, Mass.: Harvard University Press.

Berry, B. J. L. and Murdie, R. A. 1965. *Socio-economic Correlates of Housing Condition.* Toronto: Metropolitan Toronto Planning Board.

Black Panther Party. 1966. "Black Panther Party Platform and Program: What We Want, What We Believe." In S. Cahill, and M. F. Cooper, eds. *The Urban Reader.* pp. 272–274. Englewood Cliffs, N.J.: Prentice-Hall, Inc.

Blank, D. M. and Winnick, L. 1953. "Structure of the Housing Market." *Quarterly Journal of Economics* 67:181–208.

Bourne, L. 1968. "Market, Location and Site Selection in Apartment Construction." *Canadian Geographer* 12:211–26.

Chisholm, M. 1971. "Geography and the Question of Relevance." *Area* 3:65–68.

Clark, K. B. 1965. *Dark Ghetto.* New York: Harper and Row.

Department of City Planning. 1960. Rehousing Residents Displaced from Public Housing Clearance Sites in Chicago, 1957–58. Special Report, City of Chicago.

Department of Urban Renewal. 1967. Community Improvement Program: Proposals for Program Expansion. City of Chicago.

Drake, St. C., and Cayton, H. 1945. *Black Metropolis.* New York: Harcourt, Brace and Co.

Duncan, O. D., and Duncan, B. 1957. *The Negro Population of Chicago.* Chicago: University of Chicago Press.

Faris, R. E., and Dunham, H. W. 1939. *Mental Disorders in Urban Areas.* Chicago: University of Chicago Press.

Gans, H. 1962. *The Urban Villagers.* New York: Free Press of Glencoe.

Glass, R. 1961. *London's Newcomers.* Cambridge, Mass.: Harvard University Press.

Harrison, B. 1968. "A Pilot Project in Economic Development Planning for American Urban Slums." *International Development Review* 10:23–29.

Hartman, C. 1963. "The Limitations of Public Housing." *Journal of the American Institute of Planners* 29–30:283–96.

Hartshorne, T. A. 1971. "Inner City Residential Structure and Decline." *Annals of the Association of American Geographers* 61:72–96.

_____. 1968. "Urban Residential Blight: The Structure and Change of Substandard Housing in Cedar Rapids, Iowa, 1940–1960." Ph.D. dissertation, University of Iowa.

Harvey, D. 1971. "Social Justice in Spatial Systems." Paper given before Association of American Geographers Annual Meeting, Boston, Massachusetts.

Helper, R. 1969. *Racial Policies and Practices of Real Estate Brokers.* Minneapolis: University of Minnesota Press.

Jones, E. 1960. *Social Geography of Belfast.* London: Oxford University Press.

Knos, D. S. 1959. "Substandard Housing in Kansas City, Missouri." Ph.D. dissertation, University of Iowa.

Lansing, J. B., and Hendricks, G. 1967. "Automobile Ownership and Residential Density." Ann Arbor, Michigan: Institute for Social Research, University of Michigan.

Lipsky, M. 1970. *Protest in City Politics: Rent, Strikes, Housing, and the Power of the Poor.* Chicago: Rand McNally.

Lyford, J. P. 1966. *The Airtight Cage.* New York: Harper and Row.

McEntire, D. 1960. *Residence and Race.* Berkeley: University of California Press.

McKissick, F. B. 1966. "Presentation in Hearings Before the U.S. Senate, Subcommittee on Executive Reorganization Committee on Government Operations." In T. Venetoulis, and W. Eisenhauer, eds. *Up Against the Urban Wall,* pp. 476–86. Englewood Cliffs, N.J.: Prentice-Hall, Inc.

Meier, A., and Rudwick, E. 1966. *From Plantation to Ghetto.* New York: Hill and Wang.

Mercer, J. 1971. "The Spatial Pattern of Urban Residential Blight." Ph.D. dissertation, McMaster University.

Meyerson, H., and Banfield, E. 1955. *Politics, Planning and the Public Interest.* New York: Free Press of Glencoe.

Moore, E. G., Betak, J. F., Wellar, B. S., and Manji, A. S. 1968. "Comments on the Definition and Measurement of Housing Quality." Research Report No. 46. Northwestern University, Department of Geography.

Moore, W. 1969. *The Vertical Ghetto.* New York: Random House.

Morrill, R. L. 1965. "The Negro Ghetto: Alternatives and Consequences." *Geographic Review* 55:221–38.

Muth, R. F. 1969. *Cities and Housing: The Spatial Pattern of Urban Residential Land Use.* Chicago: University of Chicago Press.

Nakagawa, A. 1957. "The Profitability of Slums." *Synthesis* 1:45.

Pownall, L. L. 1960. "Low Value Housing in Two New Zealand Cities." *Annals of the Association of American Geographers* 50:439–60.

Rainwater, L. 1970. *Behind Ghetto Walls: Black Family Life in a Federal Slum.* Chicago: Aldine Publishing Co.

Rapkin, C. 1969. "Price Discrimination Against Negroes in the Rental Housing Market." In J. F. Kain, ed. *Race and Poverty: The Economics of Discrimination,* pp. 112–21. Englewood Cliffs, N.J.: Prentice-Hall.

Redfield, Peattie L. 1971. "Public Housing: Urban Slums Under Public Management." In P. Orleans and Ellis W. Russell, eds. *Race, Change, and Urban Society,* p. 285–310. Beverly Hills, Calif.: Sage Publications.

Report by the National Advisory Commission on Civil Disorders. 1968. New York: Bantam Books.

Rex, J., and Moore, R. 1967. *Race Community and Conflict.* London: Oxford University Press.

Robson, B. T. 1966. "An Ecological Analysis of the Evolution of Residential Areas in Sunderland." *Urban Studies* 3:120–42.

Rose, H. 1969. "Social Processes in the City: Race and Urban Residential Choice." Association of the American Geographers, Committee on College Geography. Resource Paper No. 6.

_____. 1970. "The Development of an Urban Subsystem: The Case of the Negro Ghetto." *Annals of the Association of American Geographers* 60:1–17.

Satter, D. A. 1966. "West Side Story." *New Republic* 155:15–19.

Schafer, R. 1971. "Slum Formation, Race and an Income Strategy." *Journal of the American Institute of Planners* 37:347–53.

Schmitt, Robert. 1971. "An Examination of the Association Between Occupation and Housing." Department of Geography, University of Iowa. Mimeograph.

Schorr, A. L. 1964. *Slums and Social Insecurity.* London: Thomas Nelson.

Sexton, P. 1965. *Spanish Harlem: An Anatomy of Poverty.* New York: Harper and Row.

Spear, A. H. 1967. *Black Chicago: The Making of a Negro Ghetto.* Chicago: University of Chicago Press.

Sporn, A. D. 1960. "Empirical Studies in the Economics of Slum Ownerships." *Land Economics* 36:333–40.

Sternlieb, G. 1966. *The Tenement Landlord.* New Brunswick, N.J.: Rutgers University Press.

Taeuber, K. E., and Taeuber, A. F. 1965. *Negroes in Cities.* Chicago: Aldine Publishing Co.

Tilly, C., Jackon, W. D., and Kay, B. 1965. *Race and Residence in Wilmington, Delaware.* New York Bureau of Publications, Teachers College, Columbia University.

U.S. Bureau of the Census. 1967. "Measuring the Quality of Housing: An Appraisal of Census Statistics and Methods." Working Paper No. 25, Washington, D.C.

Ward, D. 1971. *Cities and Immigrants: A Geography of Change in Nineteenth Century America.* New York: Oxford University Press.

Wellar, B. 1968. "The Utilization of Multi-band Aerial Photographs in Urban Housing Quality Studies." Unpublished report. Northwestern University, Department of Geography.

Wexler, L. 1965. "Housing Census Inadequacies." *Journal of Housing* 9:495–97.

Wilner, D. M.; Walkey, R. P.; Pinkerton, T. C.; and Tayback, M. 1962. *The Housing Environment and Family Life.* Baltimore: Johns Hopkins Press.

Wolf, E. P. 1963. "The Tipping Point in Racially Changing Neighborhoods." *Journal of the American Institute of Planners* 29:217–22.

_____ and Lebeaux, C. N. 1969. *Change and Renewal in an Urban Community.* New York: Frederick A. Praeger.

Wolfe, H. 1967. "Models for Condition Aging of Residential Structures." *Journal of the American Institute of Planners* 33:192–96.

8

THE REVERSE COMMUTER
TRANSIT PROBLEM
IN INDIANAPOLIS

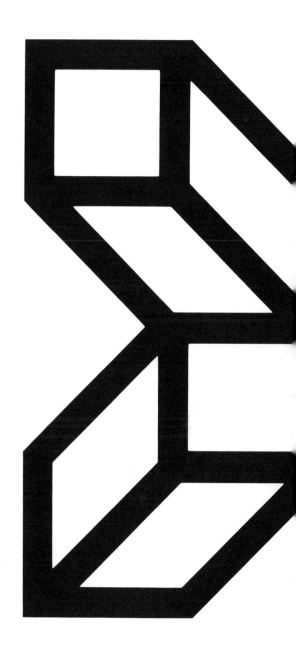

Shane Davies
University of Texas, Austin

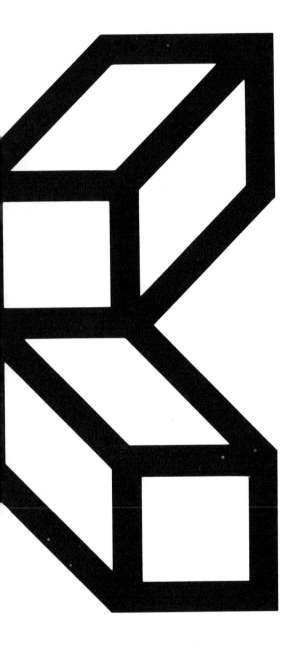

The Reverse Commuter Transit Problem in Indianapolis

ABSTRACT

The reverse commuter transit problem is concerned with the resultant barrier effects of increasing distance between inner city residents and decentralizing workplace locations. The interrelationships of postwar metropolitan changes in job locations and residences and deficiencies in public transit systems significantly affect the employment opportunities of the inner city poor. The difficulty or impossibility of ghetto dwellers' using public transit to reach outlying jobs is found to be an important factor contributing to their high rates of unemployment.

The major objective of this paper is to outline in detail a short-run strategy designed to link ghetto dwellers with suburban job locations. The paper is organized to deal with the reverse commuter transit problem in three major phases. The first section substantiates that there is an increasing gap in Indianapolis between the inner city resident and his prospective places of work. Restrictive residential practices and economic decentralization are shown to rank foremost among the forces which have contributed to this gap. The second phase provides evidence that specific deficiencies in the linkage or route distribution of the Indianapolis Transit System restrict the employment choice of inner city residents who do not own automobiles. An investigation of this more restricted action space provides a comprehensive profile of the work trip patterns of the inner city poor. Variations in wage rates and job retention span are examined when qualified by transit mode and socio-economic characteristics.

The final phase of the study is concerned with delineating the disparities in the route distribution of the Indianapolis Transit System in terms of the residential location and improved job opportunities for the hardcore unemployed. From a series of alternative solutions to the mobility problem of ghetto residents, a transit design is suggested for Indianapolis. This solution is analyzed to show the benefits that would accrue to the disadvantaged by the adoption of this system.[1]

1. This study was made possible through a fellowship award from the Center of Urban Affairs and a grant from the Research and Advance Studies Center, both of Indiana University. The author is indebted to Professor Michael L. McNulty, Department of Geography, University of Iowa, and Professor Jerome W. Milliman, Department of Economics, Indiana University, for their careful supervision of the study.

Reverse commuters are those individuals whose journey to work entails a trip from a central city residence to a job located in the suburbs. The interrelationships of metropolitan changes in job locations and residences and deficiencies in public transit systems have been found to adversely affect the employment opportunities of the inner city poor (Conference on Poverty and Transportation, 1968). Together with poor educational attainment, skill deficiencies, low motivation, and discriminatory hiring practices, the reverse commuter transit problem has been offered as an additional causal factor behind the high unemployment levels of low-income, inner city groups.[2] This paper focuses upon the reverse commuter transit situation in Indianapolis where central city unemployment is a major problem (Davies, 1970). The Indianapolis Manpower Coordinating Committee (1969, p. 9) found that "... many of the unemployed and underemployed groups could qualify for current job openings if they had transportation available on either a personal or public basis. The locations of many major industrial plants are far removed from the target areas [poverty pockets] and many of them have no adequate public transportation facilities." The major complaints recorded by the Transportation Task Force Committee of Indianapolis were inadequate service to a specific location, lack of night and early morning buses, the inconvenience of downtown transfers, and inadequate protection (Indianapolis Transportation Committee, 1969).

This paper investigates first the effects of the interrelationships of residential segregation and decentralized job opportunities on the job distribution of low-skilled workers in Indianapolis who do or do not own motor vehicles. A second objective is to examine how effective the Indianapolis Public Transit system is in serving the employment needs of the disadvantaged. The third objective is to suggest how present transit services can be restructured or supplemented to provide solutions to the reverse commuter transit problem. Ultimate solutions to the problems of central city dwellers will depend upon the effectiveness of long-range programs for education and health, residential desegregation, and elimination of discriminatory hiring practices. In the meantime, short-term programs can be designed to supplement these long-term goals. The major objective of this paper is to outline in detail one such short-run strategy. This strategy is designed to link low-income inner city residents with suburban job locations.

NATURE OF THE DATA

Supporting data for this study are divided into two parts. The first data source comprises personal information on 4,840 job seekers who filed Employment Security

2. In the Indianapolis SMSA, the generally tight labor market conditions have alleviated some of these unemployment problems. The normally restrictive hiring criteria of employers have been somewhat relaxed by the high over-all demand for labor. Increases in consumer demand and higher production goals have created an urgency in filling job vacancies. This has produced a greater probability that the unskilled worker in the lower preference ranks will be hired. Yet, even under these improved labor market conditions, severe levels of unemployment still exist within the central city of Indianapolis. A household survey conducted by the Indianapolis Employment Security Division (IESD) and designed to ascertain the labor force status of residents 16 years of age and older in three of the city's low-income areas—Broadway (3), Methodist (16), and Hillside (1)—found that whereas the seasonal adjusted employment rate for the Indianapolis SMSA was 2.6 percent in July 1968, the average rate for the three neighborhoods was 11.7 percent. The Black unemployment rate was 12.3 percent, the White was 9.3 percent. The unemployment rate for youths 16 to 21 years old was 23.5 percent and 33.7 percent when summer job seekers were included. See Indianapolis Employment Security Division (IESD), "Labor Force Status in Three Indianapolis Neighborhoods: Broadway, Hillside and Methodist, Summer, 1968," Report by the Research and Statistics Dept., January 1969.

511Y job application forms in Employment Outreach Centers between August 1967 and October 1968. These centers operate in each of the city's eleven centrally located poverty pockets (Community Service Council Indianapolis, 1966). The individuals composing the sampled population are classified as "disadvantaged persons" or "hard core" unemployed (Manpower Administration, 1968). Social data registered for this population include race (Indianapolis Employment Division, 1967), age, marital status, household size, present residence and recency of residence. The economic data record the applicant's mode of transit to work; his labor force status; the location, wage rate, and period worked for each of his last three jobs; and finally, his occupational code. The second data source consists of low-skilled manufacturing, miscellaneous, clerical, sales, and service job opportunities filed by firms with the Indianapolis Employment Security Division during the same period. These jobs were selected because they matched the skill levels of the applicants.

RESIDENTIAL PATTERNS

As a prelude to a more complete understanding of those individuals most strongly affected by isolation from job opportunities and discrepancies in the public transit system, the following section discusses the spatial characteristics of Black and White residential patterns in the Indianapolis Standard Metropolitan Statistical Area (SMSA).

Indianapolis exhibits two residential processes common to United States cities today: the exodus of middle- and upper-income Whites to the suburbs and the influx of a poor, principally Black population to areas in the central city (Taeuber and Taeuber, 1965, p. 30). Low-income White and Black inner city residents, through socio-economic and attitudinal segregation, are residentially confined to specific areas of older housing in the city. In these low-income areas the family pattern is "extended" rather than "nuclear" as in the suburbs. Close-knit neighborhoods centered around local stores, churches, taverns, and pool halls are evident. The carless poor satisfy the majority of their social needs within the narrow confines of these poverty pockets. They generate shorter work, shopping, and recreational trips than suburbanites, and their limited movement has been found to reduce their propensity to seek improved positions of employment (Fellman and Rosenblatt, 1968).

Restrictive forms of residential zoning ordinances, house purchasing covenants, and White hostility to Black residential encroachment (Thornbrough, 1963) have created segregated Black housing patterns in Indianapolis (figure 1). The housing market accessible to Blacks has been tightened by the construction of the

173

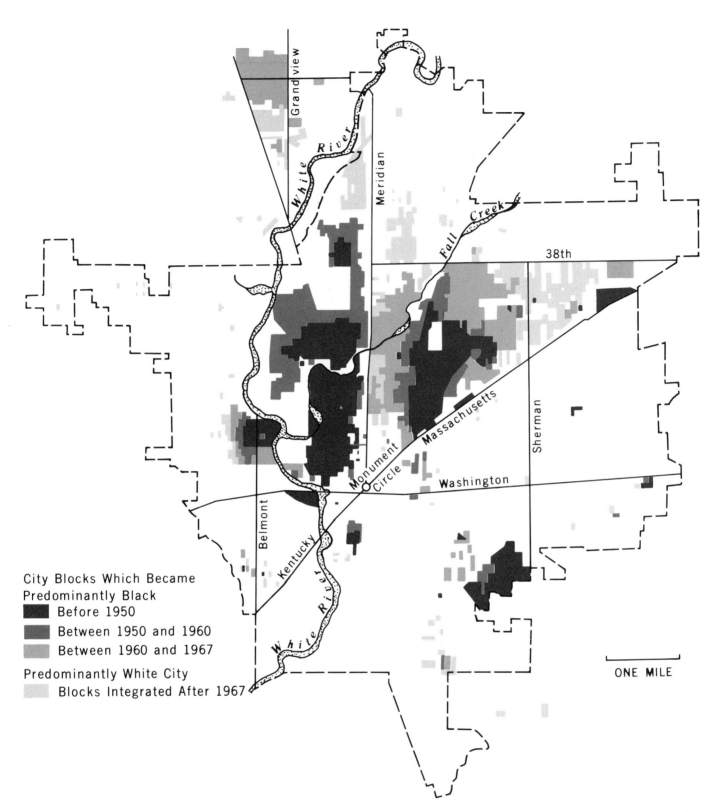

City Blocks Which Became
Predominantly Black
▮ Before 1950
▮ Between 1950 and 1960
▮ Between 1960 and 1967

Predominantly White City
▮ Blocks Integrated After 1967

ONE MILE

Figure 1. Black residential areas in Indianapolis. (Source: Indiana
Civil Rights Commission, 1967.)

inner loop freeway system, Indiana University expansion, and urban renewal which dislocated 7,800 families between 1964 and 1970 (Community Service Council, 1964). Black relocation into White neighborhoods distant from all-Black areas has accounted for less than 1 percent of all Black residential moves during this period (Metropolitan Planning Commission of Indianapolis, 1967, p. 26). Suburban dispersal would have improved accessibility to decentralizing job opportunities and relieved overcrowded housing units while promoting integration. While these forces restricted the development of new Black housing units, the income of Blacks rose and the total population of young Black adults sharply increased.[3] As a consequence, there exists a repressed net demand for 5,000 standard housing units. Black persons per household increased from an estimated average of 3.54 in 1960 to 3.63 in 1967. During the same time period, White household size decreased from 3.18 to 3.00 persons (Metropolitan Planning Department, Marion County, 1968, p. 9).

The exodus of middle- and upper-income Whites to the suburbs is primarily a result of the flight from the external dyseconomies associated with the low wealth, higher expenditures, and higher property taxes of central city jurisdictions. This movement has made inaccessible what was previously an important, if menial, source of basic entry jobs for female domestics and male yard workers. Further, the more suburban shopping malls which accompanied this outward movement are finding it difficult to obtain the required low-skilled help. This difficulty can be partially attributed to either the lack of transportation facilities or inadequate transit schedules. These factors contribute to the high degree of female and teenage unemployment found in the poverty pockets. It could be argued that the outward movement of Whites when correlated with the economic decentralization of jobs would improve the Blacks' chance of bidding more competitively for the remaining central city employment. However, since the central city is becoming more demanding in skill levels, this constitutes a negligible short-term benefit.

Present federally subsidized transportation systems between suburb and CBD produce a negative transfer of incomes (Doeringer, 1968). The subsidies are generally used for aiding the already affluent and more politically effective suburbanite in his journey to work. Federally subsidized transit programs for the reverse commuter are minimal and have only recently been put into effect.

SUBURBANIZATION OF EMPLOYMENT

The dispersal of Whites to the suburbs and the polarization of Blacks in the inner city is a well-established

3. There are signs of a more relaxed atmosphere and a greater understanding between Whites and Blacks as evidenced by an increase in the number and size of neighborhood associations. These have been created in certain areas where there is a Black influx in order to stabilize racial balance. These organizations attempt to arrest panic sellings and prevent discriminatory real estate practices. See Metropolitan Planning Department, "Mapleton-Fall Creek Neighborhood Land Use Plan: Summary of Policy Recommendations," April 1969.

trend which shows almost no signs of reversal. Concurrent with these movements, there has been an outward dispersion of industrial activities. The movement of jobs to suburban locations in Indianapolis has been considerable. In 1967, 43 percent of the jobs in the metropolitan area were located in outlying areas as compared with only 32 percent in 1961. The downtown proportion of over-all employment fell from 33 percent to 25 percent, registering the only negative change. This decline occurred even though the total number of jobs in the Indianapolis SMSA increased by 61,000 (Indianapolis Employment Security Division, 1967).

A further study examined 922 affiliated members of the Chamber of Commerce between 1947 and 1968 for shifts in the location of their industrial activities. Two hundred twenty-eight of these firms changed their location during this period. These decentralizing firms generated 11,304 job opportunities. The 17 firms which moved in toward the central city generated only 440 jobs and required a small and professionalized work force. The average outward distance moved for all firms exceeded three miles. Manufacturing firms, a main supplier of low-skilled basic entry jobs, moved 3.9 miles on the average in an outward direction in this period (Davies, 1970, pp. 34–38).

The hard-core unemployed in this study are presently capable of filling only the lowest skilled occupations. It is therefore more important to analyze employment shifts differentiated by skill levels than undifferentiated job changes at the aggregate level. In similar investigations, Hamilton, Mooney, Kain, and Persky utilized aggregate job statistics with no distinction by type. This raises questions as to the validity and usefulness of their results in developing transit policy for the disadvantaged (Hamilton, 1968, pp. 5–8). Only by ascertaining the geographic distribution of basic entry jobs for the Indianapolis SMSA can the spatial barrier affecting the placement of low-skilled inner city residents be readily assessed. The spatial distribution of low-skilled manufacturing and miscellaneous (2,790), clerical (3,280), sales (810), and service (2,475) jobs provides an insight into those locations most suitable for the placement of the hard core unemployed.

Of the low-skilled job opportunities, clerical jobs, which the inner city residents are least capable of filling, are located nearest to their place of residence and are as well the most accessible by public transportation. Clerical and sales jobs require far higher entry qualifications than manufacturing, which are the least accessible to the disadvantaged (Georgia Institute of Technology, 1969). Clerical positions peak in the 0–10 minute zone, drop sharply, and then gradually decline outwards, whereas manufacturing demand retains a fairly constant level out to the peripheral time zones (figure 2).

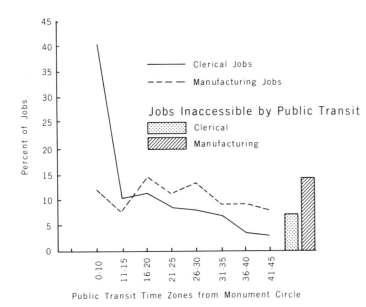

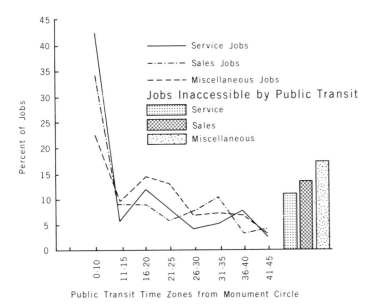

Figure 2. The distribution of low-skilled clerical, manufacturing, service, sales, and miscellaneous jobs over public transit time zones in Marion County, 1968. (Data furnished by the Indianapolis Employment Security Division.)

The shift of manufacturing from the central city to peripheral areas isolated from the public transit system is indicative of an apparent assumption by industrial employers that automobiles are generally available to their labor force. Since automobiles are becoming more important for the work trip, the non-vehicle-owning job seeker is becoming increasingly handicapped (U.S. Department of Commerce, 1967, p. 65). Therefore, carless job seekers are particularly dependent on the spatial distribution of the facilities of the Indianapolis Transit System (ITS). Increasing or decreasing the geographic bounds of this network increases or decreases the disadvantaged job seeker's market for basic entry jobs.

Two spatially opposed processes, residential nucleation and industrial dispersion, interact to increase the distance between the disadvantaged's place of residence and his prospective places of work. This contributes to the job seeker's sense of geographic isolation and job inaccessibility. This spatial barrier has two consequences for the supply side of the labor market. First, the usual channels of labor market information are no longer effective because of the increased physical distance. Secondly, those inner city unemployed who do succeed in finding employment in peripheral job locations are adversely affected by lack of transportation, inadequate routing of public transit, and excessive costs in time and money. The problem is further aggravated by the present national trend toward white collar employment and the movement away from unskilled and semi-skilled jobs. If present trends continue, the work-residence spatial separation will increase and further constrain the potential catchment area of low-skilled employment opportunities for the hard-core unemployed who do not own vehicles.

PUBLIC TRANSIT

Public transit in this study refers to bus travel; Indianapolis has no commuter rail facilities. The inner city poverty pockets are particularly well serviced by CBD–oriented lines. However, the utility of these lines is considerably lessened by the lack of crosstown and outward-bound buses serving peripheral work place locations. Except for one east-west crosstown route, all 26 public transit routes are radial in character and converge on the CBD. This deficiency in crosstown transport forces the disadvantaged to journey downtown prior to any outward movement. Slow bus speeds and the necessity of downtown transfers extends the length of many peripheral journeys beyond profitable limits. The prolonged length of time between buses and the lack of late and early morning services coincident with shift times are major complaints of industries in the Indianapolis SMSA

(Indianapolis Regional Transportation and Development Study, 1966).

Present trends indicate that bus travel in Indianapolis will continue to decline and eventually offer a more restricted route distribution for its patrons. Increases in car ownership and transit operating costs do not show signs of changing direction in the foreseeable future. Inner city residents who work at downtown locations will probably continue to receive good service if the route structure of the ITS does not change from its current orientation. Those who wish to obtain access to suburban industrial parks, recreational facilities, and rural areas will encounter increased difficulties.

One means of expanding the action space of the disadvantaged would be to make them more cognizant of existing transit facilities. The employment bureau needs to be sensitive to the culturally conditioned responses to space manifest in the related behavior of the disadvantaged. Interpretation of complex transit maps and tables is difficult, if not impossible, for many of the hard-core unemployed—some of whom are functional illiterates, unable to read or relate themselves geographically to prospective places of employment. As a consequence, some job seekers lose their way to job interviews and actual employment opportunities. Since present transit maps and schedules are too complex for the disadvantaged to comprehend, symbolic maps which represent the urban structure in terms comprehensible to them are an imperative need. Space, distance, and place are perceived by the disadvantaged in a manner foreign to the nature of present transit maps.

MOBILITY CHARACTERISTICS OF THE DISADVANTAGED

As noted previously, the disadvantaged lack automobiles for transportation to work. Eighty-two percent of the 4,840 job applicants depend upon public transportation for the work trip (table 1). Moreover, 87 percent are Black, and 84.4 percent of this group depend on the bus system. The high proportion of the hard-core unemployed lacking cars suggests that automobile ownership is a variable related to the acquisition of some suitable form of employment. Automobile ownership seems to be a necessary factor for obtaining job interviews and a crucial factor for retaining a job. The "captive riders" are forced to find employment either in the immediate vicinity of their homes or to depend upon job opportunities along the routes of the Indianapolis Transit System.

No significant trip length disparities are found among reverse commuter groups commuting to work by bus; irrespective of sex or race, the mean trip length is 2.2 miles (table 2). This implies that inner city residents of

Table 1. *Distribution of IESD Job Applicants by Age, Race, Sex, and Mode of Transit for the Journey to Work, August 1967—August 1968*

| | Percentage Distribution | | | |
| | White | | Black | |
Age of Worker and Method of Transportation	Male	Female	Male	Female
Workers commuting by auto				
All age groups, sample size	124	58	376	276
Distribution by age (%)				
Under 21	40	12	29	18
21–30	32	41	41	34
31–45	18	27	20	39
46–60	10	17	9	9
61 and over	0	1	1	0
Workers commuting by public transportation				
All age groups, sample size	194	253	1262	2277
Distribution by age (%)				
Under 21	50	29	51	38
21–30	23	27	30	29
31–45	16	22	12	24
46–60	9	17	5	8
61 and over	2	5	2	1

Source: Indianapolis Employment Security Division ES–511Y forms, 1968.

both races might proportionately benefit from improved transit facilities. Though low-income Whites experience less discrimination in housing and jobs, they record equally restricted work-trip distances. It might be stressed, however, that greater attention should be focused on Black neighborhoods, since the data reflect a more acute unemployment problem in this group. Furthermore, additional transit facilities linking Blacks with suburban jobs may provide the greatest traveler and community benefits.

No journey–to–work trip length differences by race are observed for disadvantaged male car users. The mean work trip is 3.32 miles for Black males, 3.04 miles for White males. Disparities exist between the trip lengths of car and bus users, both within and between racial groups. The mean work-trip length of Black male car owners is 1.1 miles longer than trips of bus users. A similar relationship exists for White male car owners.

The reverse commuter work-trip patterns of the "hard core" are not very extensive, regardless of the vehicular mode available, especially when these patterns are compared with trip lengths of suburban CBD-oriented commuters. Suburban commuters have longer work-trips when measured in miles but shorter when measured in time, mainly due to the difference between car and bus travel (Deskins, 1970).

The confined travel behavior of the disadvantaged is a manifestation of their spatially restrictive job opportunities. Their ability to obtain jobs is affected by their misconception of distance, their inability to overcome the barriers to movement, budgetary constraints, and deficient job information. Ghetto isolation affects their ability both to receive, organize, and use labor market information from employment sources and to search out and locate jobs. As a result, the utility of other employment areas, even those in close geographic proximity, may be unknown. Even if known, lack of reinforcement about these areas and the inefficient dissemination of suitable job information by employment sources results in the failure to take these jobs. The disadvantaged require information about the job and its location which must be continually and consistently reinforced.

JOB DURATION AND WAGE RATE CHARACTERISTICS

A series of cumulative frequency curves was constructed to test the hypothesis that variations in job duration exist between inner-city groups when stratified by age, sex, education, and mode of transit available for the journey to work. The over-all findings indicate that inner-city car users are more likely than bus users to hold jobs for a greater length of time. Compari-

Table 2. *Work-Trip Differences in Miles for Low-Income Inner City Residents by Race, Sex, and Transit Mode*

	Male	
	Black	White
Bus	2.23	2.23
Car	3.32	3.04
	Female	
Bus	2.35	2.25

179

son of the distributions shows that car users are skewed toward the higher job retention periods of approximately nine months as opposed to three months for bus users. This inequality is decidedly pronounced in the 22–29 years of age category (Davies, 1970, pp. 65–72).

It was also hypothesized that the disadvantaged inner-city resident who has a car available for the journey to work, when classified by race, age, sex, and educational level, receives a higher wage rate than individuals whose mode of transit is by bus. The findings (figure 3) suggest that improved accessibility permits car users to obtain jobs which generally pay higher wages (Taylor, 1968, pp. 375–90). The mean for bus users occurs in the $1.46 – 1.65 wage-earning category as opposed to $1.86 – 2.05 for auto users.

The higher wage rates, longer job duration, and wider employment area for motorized workers are presented as evidence of the need to improve the channels of access for car-less, unemployed job seekers. Provided that transit and suitable job opportunities are available to the disadvantaged, the suburban industrial job frequently offers more lucrative opportunities for the inner-city resident to upgrade his standard of living.

DISTRIBUTION OF BLACK EMPLOYMENT

Certain explanatory variables that are often advanced as affecting the distribution of Black employment do not appear to be significant in this study.[4] For example, it cannot be contended that the job opportunities are above the skill levels and educational capabilities of the workers, since both were carefully matched. Racial discrimination presumably is not an issue, since every firm that filed with the Indianapolis Employment Security Division had to comply with the fair-employment-practices code. Differential wage rates do not appear to be a factor, as the hourly wage rate did not vary appreciably when controlled by type among the sampled workplace areas. The level of the wage rate does not appear to be a deterrent in the manufacturing and miscellaneous jobs, since the average hourly rate of $3.00 was higher than other low-skilled opportunities available in the metropolitan area.

It is the thesis of this paper that the spatially restrictive nature of the ghetto inhibits the ability of Blacks to reach employment opportunities and reduces the level of job information available to them. As a consequence, knowledge of suitable employment opportunities and the ability to reach such opportunities is severely reduced. A product of this restriction is the resultant barrier effect of the increasing distance between low-income Black residences and jobs in the suburbs. This barrier affects Black people's ability to locate and to reach the place of employment. The lack of a suitable

4. Data deficiencies precluded an assessment of disadvantaged White employment patterns.

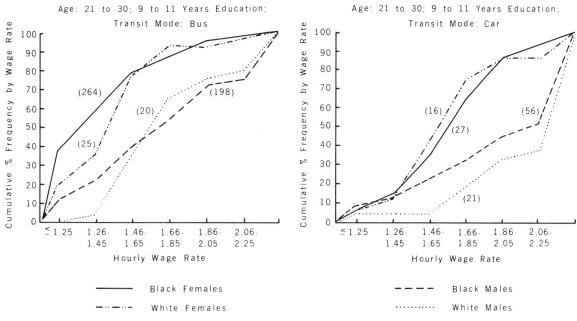

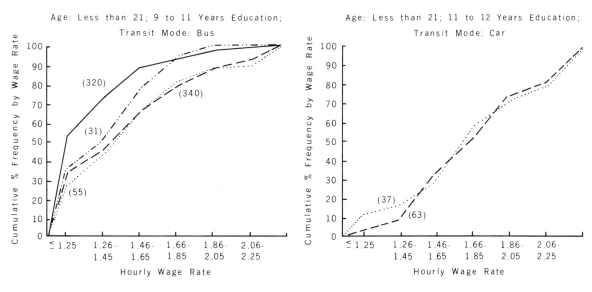

Figure 3. Wage distribution for inner-city residents of Marion County by race, sex, age, education, and transit mode, 1968. (Data furnished by the Indianapolis Employment Security Division.)

means of transit to overcome this distance, the transportation costs incurred, and the decline in the quality and quantity of labor market information available to Blacks cause them to be under-represented in distant workplaces.

Knowledge of ghetto labor markets originates, in part, from research on Black residence-to-workplace relationships (Conference on Poverty and Transportation, 1968). Unlike those previous studies in which highly aggregated data have been utilized, the present investigation incorporates data that have been differentiated with respect to the skill level and educational capabilities of the workers and the required skill level of available job opportunities. The analysis focuses on the relationship between the actual distribution of low-skilled Black employment emanating from the ghetto and the spatial distribution of low-skilled job opportunities.

Sorting of the applications of the job seekers was based upon previous employment of the male applicant in a low-skilled manufacturing or miscellaneous-type job and the female applicant in a low-skilled clerical, sales, or service job. Individuals excluded from the sample included construction workers whose workplace locations vary and high-school students seeking summer jobs or part-time work. Each application was examined to determine where the applicant had been most recently employed, and a spatial distribution of these workplace locations was constructed. A grid of squares, each 4,800 feet by 4,800 feet, was made to fit the rectangular shape of the Indianapolis SMSA and the city block structure. This reference base was superimposed over the distribution, and an enumeration was made of all male and female workplace locations in each square. For matching the skill levels of the applicants, only those job-order forms filed by employers seeking low-skilled manufacturing and miscellaneous, clerical, sales, and service labor were considered. A map was constructed to illustrate the location of these job opportunities. The reference base was placed over the map and the number of job opportunities by type, per square, was enumerated.

There were a total of 224 squares which contained the previous work locations of 1,230 Black males and 1,920 Black females. The employment opportunities located in these squares were as follows: 2,790 manufacturing and miscellaneous job opportunities and 6,565 clerical, sales, and service job openings. The proximity of each of these 224 squares to the ghetto was derived by computing the linear distance, in miles, from the ghetto centroid to the midpoint of each square. Another measure of proximity was calculated by superimposing the reference base on the isochrones of public transit time and measuring the travel time from the central business district (CBD) to each square.

ANALYSIS

A linear regression model was used separately for Black males and females in order to determine the concomitant variations of job opportunities and Black workplaces with distance from the ghetto centroid and the CBD:

$$\hat{Y}_i = a + b_1 X_{1i} + b_2 X_{2i}$$

The dependent variable is the number of jobs previously held by Blacks per workplace zone. This is a surrogate measure for total actual Black male and female employment: Y_m represents Black males and Y_f Black females. The first independent variable is the number of low-skilled job opportunities per square, differentiated as to type—a proxy variable for the general distribution of all such low-skilled jobs in these areas. In the male equation, X_1 represents manufacturing and miscellaneous and in the female equation represents clerical, sales, and service job opportunities. Since the effect of distance on transportation costs and knowledge of job opportunities may result in Blacks' being under-represented in distant workplaces, distance is represented by linear distance from the ghetto centroid and by linear distance and public transit time from the CBD. This second independent variable, X_2, represents alternatively: ghetto centroid distance, CBD distance, and public transit time from the CBD. From previous research (Kain, 1968), it is postulated that both coefficients b_1 and b_2 will be positive and negative, respectively, and differ significantly from zero.

Table 3. *Beta coefficients: Dependent Variables, Low-Skilled Black Male Workplaces* Y_m *and Black Female Workplaces* Y_f

Black Workplaces	Constant	Mfg., Misc.	Clerical, Sales, Service	Ghetto Dist.	CBD Dist.	Time	Coefficient of Determination
Y_f	1.97		0.21		*		0.57
σ			0.01				
"t"			17.04				
Y_f	9.65		0.21	*			0.57
σ			0.01				
"t"			53.67				
Y_m	6.99	0.36			−0.99		0.41
σ		0.04			0.29		
"t"		8.66			−3.33		
Y_m	8.84	0.35		−1.34			0.42
σ		0.39		0.30			
"t"		6.75		−4.49			
Y_m	20.25	0.29				−0.54	0.38
σ		0.07				0.16	
"t"		4.36				−3.36	

*Coefficient concerned does not differ significantly from zero at the 99 percent confidence level.

A difference between the male and female equations is the proportion of total variance explained (table 3). Almost 60 percent of the total variance in the dependent variable is explained in the female regressions as opposed to 40 percent in the male equations. The smaller coefficients of determination in the male regressions indicate that spatial variations in male workplaces are not so readily associated with or "explained" by variations in the more dispersed and inaccessible manufacturing and miscellaneous jobs. In the regression equations, the distance coefficients have the correct sign but are statistically significant only in the male model. The male model, which explains less about the spatial variability of male Black employment, suggests that his geographic separation from growing job centers in the suburbs reduces to some extent his employment opportunities. This spatial disparity has considerably less effect on female employment. The inner-city labor market appears to be a more probable source of low-skilled employment for female Blacks. Of the explanatory variables used, clerical, sales, and service (X_1) exhibits the highest correlation coefficient with female employment locations $(r = 0.75)$. These job opportunities have a close proximity to the ghetto, are polarized around the CBD, and are readily accessible by public transit. The coefficients of determination, although not large, indicate that the independent variables are useful in forecasting the workplaces of Blacks. This is helpful since the geographic distribution of low-skilled job demand acts as a surrogate measure for the general distribution of all commercial and industrial activity in the Indianapolis SMSA. When related to the spatial configuration of the Indianapolis Transit System, the finding that Black workplaces can be roughly predicted from the spatial distribution of low-skilled job opportunities and, to a lesser extent, distance from the CBD should allow future studies to ascertain pockets of deficient Black employment.

The lack of suitable transit to overcome the geographic separation of work and home site, transit deficiencies such as inadequate routing and excessive costs in time and money, and the poor quality and insufficient quantity of labor market information available to the disadvantaged is a more acute problem for the car-less Black male than the Black female. The residence and workplace locations of low-skilled Black labor are not presently subject to substantial change, but it is possible to change the transportation linking these locations. The short-run strategy of redistributing public transit routes and initiating innovative forms of transportation to improve the mobility of the disadvantaged offers potential benefits to the city and the unemployed by contributing to a reduction in unemployment levels. The provision of subsidies to private or public transportation systems would alleviate some unemployment, and its related social ills, at a relatively low cost (Mooney, 1968, pp. 309–11).

A SOLUTION FOR THE REVERSE COMMUTER PROBLEM: TRANSIT DESIGN

The solution for reverse commuting problems in Indianapolis can be selected from a series of short-run strategies structured to increase access to higher paying jobs in the suburbs. These policies advocate provision of subsidies to private or public transportation systems. The advantages and disadvantages of the following schemes are related to the conditions in Indianapolis in order to select the transit design most suitable for the city's individual needs.

1. Automobile Ownership

Some experts argue that automobile ownership for inner city residents is a partial solution to the accessibility problem. The evidence produced in this paper documents a lack of car ownership in the Indianapolis poverty pockets. The residents of these areas could be assisted by liberalization of credit-lending policies, delayed down payments, and advice in the strategy of purchasing automobiles. Meyers (1968) advocates such a form of liberalized financing in a program he terms "New Volks for Poor Folks."

2. Rehabilitation of Old Cars

The same author also proposes mobility assistance through the rehabilitation of old cars. A casual observation of the Indianapolis poverty pockets, particularly the Hillside-Martindale area, will attest to the excessive number of old cars in front yards, back alleys, and wasteground. Ghetto maintenance cooperatives could rebuild some of these bodies and use parts from others. This would contribute to improved mobility and provide additional employment as well as reduce junk heaps which are an eyesore in ghetto areas. The opportunity for the exposition of Black capitalism would satisfy the current demands of both militant Blacks and some White groups.

3. Car Pools

Another possible remedy for the reverse commuter problem is for the city to set up a series of car pools. This plan necessitates initial leasing of cars by the city. The car pool allows for maximum flexibility and convenience, provided the driver and equipment difficulties are eliminated. Absenteeism among members of a pool would be significantly reduced by their mutual stimulation to keep costs down. The selection of drivers would have to be based on the exacting criteria of reliability and the certainty of obtaining insurance among individuals of the hard-core unemployed. However, the city would find it difficult to justify to taxpayers such "luxury" items as car pools for the poor.

Private industry might be encouraged to assist their car-less employees in finding transportation to areas outside the service of the Indianapolis Transit System. Chevrolet, Ford, and other large manufacturing plants in Indianapolis designate employees to slot new recruits into existing car pools. These men arrange rides for their car-less work force according to the work shift and area of residence in the city. This has proved an effective means of overcoming the access problem.

An unexplored avenue of transit innovation in Indianapolis is the contribution of an employer to labor pick-up. Suburban employers could shuttle employees from centralized inner-city locations or transit terminal points to the factory. Since large industries retain their own truck and auto maintenance plants, upkeep costs would be kept to a minimum. This transit method is wide-spread in comparatively car-less Europe where employers have to provide transit facilities for their work force.

4. Car Maintenance and Driving Skills

A more realistic measure would be for central city schools to equate knowledge of auto maintenance and auto maintenance and auto driving skills with the three R's (Kraft and Domencich, 1968). The number of job seekers recorded as car-less could be taken as an indication of the number of non-license holders. This paucity of licenses may stem from revocations based on alcoholism, drugs, or lack of driving skills. In the latter case, a considerable service to society could be made through schools' instructing their older pupils in driver skills and making sure that they possess a license when they finish school.

5. Free Public Transit

Kraft and Domencich investigated free public transit for low-income residents. They found the use of the transportation system as a vehicle for the redistribution of income in kind is not as efficient as making direct income payments to the recipients. Free public transit would subsidize high-income people as well as low. Since this system would be funded from taxes, the income transfer from non-users to users would not be politically acceptable, especially by automobile owners. The case for free public transportation is further weakened since the present route system of the ITS does not provide adequate service to the peripheral areas of increasing job opportunity.[5]

6. Metro-Coach and Rail

The metro-coach and rapid rail transit designs are two of the least feasible plans for Indianapolis. Both must be eliminated at present because of extraordinarily high costs. However, the several railroad lines which converge on the central city are adaptable for rail-bus transit. The ITS would need to establish connector lines from the terminal ends of the rail lines to the main industrial parks. The metro-coach, a 24-seater bus whose capacity lies between the 12-seater minibus and a 50-seater vehicle, is useful for transit lines having low demand. The high cost of purchasing a new fleet of metro-coaches, $20,000 per unit, precludes their use.

7. Taxi Service

Taxis are adaptable for numerous origin-destination trip patterns or as feeder lines for main transit routes (Rosenbloom, 1968). It has been proposed that they be used to pick up and deliver suburban employees. Taxis, however, are unavailable at crucial morning and evening peak hours because facilities are stretched to full capacity at these times. An increase in the number of cabs is currently barred by the city of Indianapolis because of restrictive control through franchises and monopolies initiated in the 1930s. Prior to this there had been an easy entry and an easy exchange of operator licenses.

The advantages in relaxing the restrictions on the number of operator licenses and creating an open market on cab driving would be to ease the entry of ghetto entrepreneurs into the cab industry. This low-skilled employment as full-time or part-time drivers and maintenance men would satisfy the present desire for Black capitalism and allow ghetto residents to participate in alleviating their own transit problem.

8. Jitneys

Restrictive legislation against the jitney was successful nationally by 1920 (Rosenbloom, 1968). City statutes were introduced by transit companies because of the jitney's potential threat to bus usage. Their demise produced a market monopolized by the taxi. The main advantages associated with the jitney are speed and flexibility through door-to-door service in ghetto areas. This vehicle mode is best suited to low levels of employee demand and is flexible enough to adapt to any spatial changes in the demand. This service, in conjunction with such sensitivity schemes as the "buddy system," would

5. The United Fund in Indianapolis effectively allocates funds in the form of free bus tokens. This aids the poor job seeker in traveling to a job and during his first week at work. Bus fares have been found to have a barrier effect at this initial stage but have little effect once the job has been obtained.

decrease absenteeism and lateness and would improve work habits. It would increase the probability of a disadvantaged resident's retaining his position of employment.

A disadvantage of the jitney is the opposition it would generate from the taxi and transit companies. The jitney is a potential threat to both systems. It would be difficult with the strong transit union presently operative in Indianapolis to introduce a private fleet of jitneys subsidized by loans from the federal government and drawing patronage from currently served transit areas. A further disadvantage associated with the mini-jitney system is that the city would have to purchase a fleet of such vehicles.

9. Public Ownership of Mass Transit

One criticism of publicly owned transit is that risks which are not borne privately may be underestimated by government workers. Further, public demand for low pricing of government enterprise could force an overstatement of benefits and an understatement of costs. This might result in a slow replacement of equipment, obsolescence, and consequent discomforts of urban travel. Further, the progress of urban mass transportation systems is frequently hampered by rural or suburban political pressure.

Ideally, public ownership of mass transit would decrease the number of fragmentary agencies and offer the opportunity for a unified effort in solving transportation problems. For the process of decision-making, a publicly controlled agency is more likely to have at its disposal a greater array of relevant information than a private concern. Besides eliminating wasteful competition and the duplication of services, this type of ownership would primarily concern itself with the public interest. Where risks are involved, the potential disadvantages can be spread over a larger system (Fitch, 1964, pp. 16–18).

The possibilities of initiating these foregoing innovative methods of mass transit are reduced by administrative complications, restrictive costs, and statutory limitations. However, the federal government, while unable to launch a full-scale urban mass transit program, does stimulate localized experimentation to improve existing facilities.[6]

TRANSIT DESIGN FOR INDIANAPOLIS

The solution advocated for Indianapolis is a restructuring of the existing bus system by the adaptation of new transit routes to link central city poverty pockets and areas of suburban employment (figure 4). The nature of these bus lines contrasts with the radial transit

6. The federal government has approached this employer access problem in three ways: through technical study grants, transportation demonstration grants, and a jobs/employer reimbursement program. The first allows cities to determine the extent of their access problem, the second finances possible solutions, and the third is a direct approach to the employer. The Mass Transit Demonstrations grants, which encourage innovations in public transportation, are administered jointly by DOT and HUD and usually provide 90 percent of the funds. The experimental Services Development Grants Program used in this study is an offshoot of the Department of Transportation's Urban Mass Transportation Demonstration Grant Program. It is approximately three years old and is a device for initiating new transit lines which connect the car-less inner-city unemployed to previously difficult points of job access. See U.S. Department of Transportation, Urban Mass Transportation Administration, "Preliminary Supplement to Instructions for Completing UMTA Form I Application for Mass Transportation Demonstration Grant," Washington, D.C., pp. 1–16.

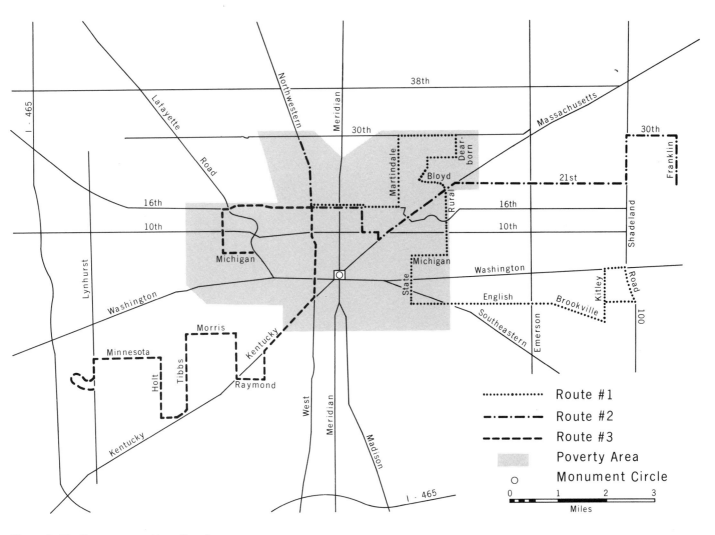

Figure 4. The three proposed transit routes.

system centered on the CBD. The routes are constructed to cross both low-income Black and White poverty areas with frequent stops for passenger loading. Once outside the poverty pockets, the buses take a direct path toward the areas of suburban manufacturing and commercial development. The Indianapolis Transit System (ITS) provides a functional operating base and experienced administrative and managerial personnel. With the aid of federal subsidies, its equipment, maintenance facilities, and work force can be adapted to the new reverse commuter transit routes. These bus lines will not directly generate new positions of employment, but they will aid in alleviating the present inner-city unemployment problem by providing the opportunity for the hard-core unemployed to seek and retain a position of employment in locations previously inaccessible or difficult to reach.

Several factors are important in deciding upon the spatial pattern of these new transit routes. (1) To offset expenses, there must be adequate population density along the routes to generate sufficient patronage. (2) The bus routes must run as near as possible to customers, oriented on a block basis. (3) The routes should be kept reasonably direct yet provide adequate coverage of the poverty pockets and areas of industrial and commercial activity. (4) The schedules must be dependable, well-maintained, and reasonably attractive to the potential rider.

The three bus lines are designed to aid inner-city residents in the following order of priority. First, those hard-core unemployed residing in the poverty neighborhoods will have an opportunity to obtain and then retain a position of employment in peripheral areas. Secondly, those who are temporarily unemployed will be able to resume a position of employment. Thirdly, carless residents already employed will have the option of choosing an alternative job location. Finally, car users who are already employed along the new routes will have an opportunity to change to bus transit for their journey to work (Haney, Crain and Moon, 1969, pp. 8–31).

The budget is based on the anticipated costs of the planned routes, that is, the expected net operating losses plus charges (Urban Mass Transportation Authority, 1969). Payments to the ITS would be based upon the actual net losses incurred through the services. These service losses would be estimated from the lower anticipated running costs of each separate route rather than the total average system's costs. The three routes register faster running times in the suburbs than in the more congested central city areas.

Potential payments to the ITS (a private company) through the grantee, the MTA (a public agency), would be based on the estimated unit costs in cents per bus mile of service for each separate route (table 4). The key item is the estimated unit cost per bus mile of service (item 13). This is based on the estimated non-driver (item 9) cost which is attributed to maintenance, utilities, transportation supervision, and taxes and is the same for all routes and on driver (item 12) cost which is composed of salary, fringe benefits, workman compensation payments, and any additional expenses involved in providing for the driver of the vehicle. The driver costs per bus mile is the quotient of the average hourly driver cost and the scheduled route speed. The combined driver and non-driver costs produce the estimated unit cost per bus mile listed as item 13. This item and the route distance are naturally covariants. Item 13 is added to items 14 and 17 to produce item 18, the total aggregate charge per bus mile of service. Item 17 is the project administration profit factor for the ITS.

The estimated revenue per bus mile over the life of the project for Route #1 is $0.235. An estimated 40 fares at $0.30 per fare for a two-way trip is $12.00. For two trips, this amounts to $24.00. The distance traveled for two trips is 102 miles. Thus, the total revenue over the life of the project (102 miles) provides item 19 (0.235), the estimated revenue per bus mile. This item, subtracted from the total charge per bus mile, item 18, produces item 20, the expected unit project charge per bus mile. Item 20 multiplied by the total bus miles of service, item 22, produces the expected contribution to the project cost of the specific route in question. The costs of the three routes are then aggregated to produce the total project budget of $69,485.

TRAVELER AND COMMUNITY BENEFITS

Rather than present a definitive justification of the new transit routes, some of the major traveler and community benefits are identified (Kalacheck, 1969). The new services offer a significant time savings in the work-trip for the residents of the transit areas. Since travel costs are a function of time consumed en route plus fares paid, then a travel-time reduction will result in decreased travel costs and thus provide a traveler benefit. Those presently using automobiles who change to bus travel will find costs savings through reduced operating costs, parking, vehicle ownership, and accident expenses. This cost reduction, however, must be balanced against the increased costs of bus travel time and the intangible cost associated with the loss of privacy (Quarmby, 1966).

The routes will encourage the central city job seeker to widen his range of job search by applying for what were previously inaccessible suburban jobs. The disadvantaged central city resident would now be able to compete with the suburbanite for outlying jobs. The

Table 4. *Estimated Budget for Projected Transit Routes*

Operational Data			
1. Route designation	#1	#2	#3
2. Route description	Southeast	Northeast	Southwest
3. Total revenue route miles per run	12.5	9.5	13.5
4. Total route miles (includes non-revenue miles per run)	25.5	27	23
5. Number of runs	4	4	4
6. Total bus–hours of service per day	6	6	6
7. Estimated number of bus miles of revenue per day	50	38	54
8. Estimated number of bus miles of total service per day (including non-revenue mileage)	102	108	98
Unit Cost Data			
9. Estimated "non-driver" cost per bus mile	$0.54	$0.54	$0.54
10. Average driver cost per hour	$7.90	$7.90	$7.90
11. Estimated schedule speed	16.5	16.5	16.5
12. Estimated driver cost per bus mile (item 10/ item 11)	$0.48	$0.48	$0.48
13. Estimated cost per bus mile (item 9 + 12)	$1.02	$1.02	$1.06
14. Other cost per bus mile	–	–	–
15. Total cost per bus mile (item 13 + item 14)	$1.02	$1.02	$1.02
16. System-wide cost per bus mile as listed in last report to regulatory body	88.30¢ 89.57¢	Year ending 31 Dec. 68 Current	
17. Required profit per bus mile (% of total cost— item 15)	$0.09	$0.09	$0.09
18. Total charge per bus mile (item 15 + item 17)	$1.11	$1.11	$1.15
Unit Revenue Data			
19. Estimated revenue per bus mile over life of project	$0.235	$0.22	$0.26
Unit Project Charge			
20. Expected total charge per bus mile (item 18 – item 19)	$0.875	$.089	$0.89
Total Cost Data			
21. Proposed days of service	260	260	260
22. Total bus miles of service (item 8 × item 21)	26,520	28,080	23,920
23. Total project charges for route in question (item 20 × item 22)	$23,205	$24,991	$21,288

improved employment opportunities generated by the transit line may reduce the normal time it takes the job seeker to find employment. Few benefits would be realized, however, if jobs attained through the routes last only a few weeks. Likewise, no resultant over-all unemployment reduction would develop if only one unemployed person merely competed with another for a scarce job. Substantial benefits would result only if these routes allowed individuals previously unemployed to obtain higher paying positions for a longer period of time.

The improvement in the labor catchment area for firms will shorten the time required for industries to fill job vacancies. The further possibility of a decrease in absenteeism and tardiness could contribute to a reduced industrial turnover rate. Employers who are presently reluctant to hire workers without means of transport for the journey to work will be able to relax this restriction. Individuals will be able to utilize the transit routes until they join car pools or have sufficient capital to purchase their own mode of transportation.

If the results of this experiment prove beneficial, the Indianapolis Transit System could bolster its declining patronage by reorienting some of its routes along the crosstown paths projected in this design. At the same time, it would provide a vital "life-line" to the hard-core unemployed residents in downtown ghetto areas. Even if the routes do not prove to be self-sufficient, it may be possible to argue that they generate enough community benefits to warrant their subsidization.

The major benefits accruing to the community upon the implementation of transit routes are a decline in unemployment and resultant relief to overburdened welfare services. The employment gains that accrue to welfare recipients will reduce their need and the public cost in welfare payments. Through decreasing inner-city unemployment and poverty, the routes bring about a reduction in the required subsidies for other social costs such as crime, health, and substandard housing. Further, it will decrease unemployment compensation paid by Indianapolis employers.

After initiating the project, a benefit-cost analysis would assess whether additional public transit linking poverty pockets to peripheral areas of low-skilled job demand significantly contributes to a reduction in the unemployment levels and related social ills in the city's low-income neighborhoods. This analysis could determine whether total benefits from the project (traveler and community benefits) are in excess of total costs. The results would suggest future courses of action. The alternatives facing the city will be to retain the service, to drop it, to subsidize it by local funding, or to initiate some new policy (Crain, 1969). The over-all analysis will determine the relationship that exists between the transit facilities available to project area residents and their levels of unemployment. The short-run strategy will be evaluated by the traveler and community benefits generated when balanced against the cost of the transit system.

CONCLUSIONS

The preceding research has documented that work-residence spatial disparities constrain the employment opportunities of inner-city residents. The primary contributing forces to this problem, restrictive residential patterns and economic decentralization, show relatively few signs of changing. The radial orientation of bus routes and the lack of crosstown connections reduces the effectiveness of the Indianapolis Transit System for the car-less disadvantaged. These "captive riders" are forced to find employment opportunities either within walking distance of their homes or along the routes of the transit system. An increase or decrease in the spatial configuration of the transit network affects the disadvantaged residents' market for low-skilled job opportunities.

The residence and workplace locations of low-skilled labor are not presently subject to substantial change, but it is possible to change the transportation linking them. The short-run strategy of redistributing transit routes offer potential benefits to the city and the unemployed central city resident. This short-term goal will alleviate the effects of the in–out transit problem until more comprehensive long-term goals are initiated.

It is not implied that deficient access to employment is the most urgent problem of residents in poverty areas. Rather, it is argued that a remedy for mobility deficiencies is an important step in a series of ameliorative policies destined to upgrade the living standard of the disadvantaged. The contention is that an investment in this essential facet of urban life will contribute to the mitigation of inner-city deprivation.

REFERENCES CITED

Community Service Council of Metropolitan Indianapolis. 1964. *Study of Relocation Problems: Indianapolis*, pp. 1–16.

_____. 1966. *Characteristics Analysis of Eleven Selected Poverty Target Areas in Indianapolis, Indiana.*

Crain, J. L. 1969. *Benefit-Cost Model Service Development Grant Program.* Appendix C. Menlo Park, Calif.: Stanford Research Institute.

Davies, C. S. 1970. "The Reverse Commuter Transit Problem in Indianapolis." Ph.D. dissertation, Indiana University.

Deskins, D. R. 1970. "Residence-Work Place Interaction Vectors for the Detroit Metropolitan Area, 1953 to 1965." *Interaction Patterns and the Spatial Form of the Ghetto.* Special Publication No. 3. Evanston, Ill.: Department of Geography, Northwestern University.

Doeringer, P. B. 1968. "Ghetto Labor Markets and Problems and Programs." (Harvard and MIT Joint Program on Regional and Urban Economics, Discussion Paper No. 35.) Harvard University.

Downs, A. 1968. "The Future of American Ghettos." *Daedalus* 82: 1331–78.

Feldman, P. A., et al. 1969. "Low Income Labor Markets and Urban Manpower Programs: A Critical Assessment." (Harvard and MIT Joint Program on Regional and Urban Economics, Discussion Paper No. 42.) Harvard University.

Fellman, G., and Rosenblatt, R. 1968. "The Social Costs of an Urban Highway." Conference on Poverty and Transportation, Brookline, Mass.

Fitch, L. C. 1964. *Urban Transportation and Public Policy*, pp. 16–18. San Francisco: Chandler Publishing Co.

Georgia Institute of Technology. 1969. *Methods of Job Development for the Hard Core Unemployed.* Atlanta, Ga.: Industrial Management Center.

Greater Indianapolis Progress Committee. 1966. "Study of Housing Conditions for Urban Renewal and of Low Income Housing." Mimeographed.

Hamilton, W. F. 1968. "Transportation Innovations and Job Accessibility." Conference on Transportation and Poverty, pp. 5–8.

Haney, D. G.; Crain, J. L.; and Moon, A. E. 1969. *Traveler and Community Benefits from the Proposed Los Angeles Rapid Transit System.* Menlo Park, Calif.: Stanford Research Institute, pp. 8–31.

Indianapolis Employment Division. 1967. "Recording Race, Color and National Origin on Local Office Records." Memorandum No. 601.

Indianapolis Employment Security Division. 1967. *Covered Employment: Marion County, September 1967.* Indianapolis: Research and Statistics Dept.

Indianapolis Manpower Coordinating Committee. 1967. "The Indianapolis Area Cooperative Manpower Plan. Fiscal Year 1968," p. 9.

Indianapolis Transportation Task Force Committee. 1969. "Indianapolis Personnel Association Survey."

Indianapolis Regional Transportation and Development Study. 1966. Transit Inventory, Job 4210.

Indianapolis Regional Transportation and Development Study (IRTADS) 1968. "A Transportation and Land Development Plan for the Indianapolis Region: A Summary Report." Chicago: Barton-Aschman Associates.

Kain, J. K. 1968. "Housing Segregation, Negro Employment and Metropolitan Decentralization." *Quarterly Journal of Economics* 82: 175–97.

Kalacheck, E. 1969. *Benefits of Improving Public Transportation between the Central City and Suburban Work Sites: Preliminary Report on a Case Study.* St. Louis: Washington Institution for Urban and Regional Studies.

Kraft, G., and Domencich, T. A. 1968. "Free Transit." Conference on Poverty and Transportation, Brookline, Mass., pp. 1–38.

Metropolitan Planning Commission of Indianapolis. 1967. "Metropolitan Indianapolis Housing Study: Summary Report," p. 26.

Metropolitan Planning Department, Marion County. 1968. "Preliminary Projection of Housing Needs, 1967–1985." Technical Work Paper No. 1. Prepared by Hammer, Greene, Siler Associates, p. 9.

Meyers, S. 1968. "Personal Transportation for the Poor." Conference on Poverty and Transportation.

Mooney, J. D. 1968. "Housing Segregation, Negro Employment and Metropolitan Decentralization: An Alternative Perspective." *Quarterly Journal of Economics* 83:299–311.

Ornati, O. A. 1969. *Transportation Needs of the Poor.* New York: Praeger Press.

Pascal, A. H. 1967. *The Economics of Housing Segregation,* pp. 30–56. Santa Monica, Calif.: Rand Corporation.

Quarmby, D. A. 1966. "Transport Planning and the Choice of Travel Mode." Summary Report to the Transport Committee of Leeds City Council.

———. 1967. "Choice of Travel Mode for the Journey to Work: Some Findings." University of Leeds: Department of Management Studies. Mimeographed.

Rosenbloom, S. 1968. "Taxis, Jitneys and Poverty." Conference on Transportation and Poverty, Brookline, Mass.

Sheppard, H., and Belitsky, H. 1965. "The Job Hunt." In P. B. Doeringer, ed. ———. Baltimore: Johns Hopkins Press.

Taylor, D. P. 1968. "Discrimination and Occupational Wage Differences in the Market for Unskilled Labor." *Industrial and Labor Relations Review* 21:375–90.

Taeuber, K. E., and Taeuber, A. F. 1965. *Negroes in Cities.* Chicago: Aldine Press. p. 30.

Thornbrough, E. L. 1963. *Since Emancipation.* Indianapolis: Indianapolis Division, American Negro Emancipation Authority.

Urban Mass Transportation Authority. 1969. "Preliminary Supplement to Instructions for Completing UMTA Form 1 Application," pp. 1–16.

U.S. Department of Commerce. 1967. *Special Report on Household Ownership and Purchases of Automobiles and Selected Household Durables, 1960 to 1967.* No. 18, p. 65.

U.S. Department of Housing and Urban Development. 1966. *A Research Project of the State of California to Determine and Test the Relationship Between a Public Transportation System and Job and Other Opportunities of Low Income Groups.* Project No. CAL–MTD–9, Contract No. H–730.

U.S. Department of Housing and Urban Development and Department of Transportation. 1968. Conference on Poverty and Transportation. Summary Conclusions and Papers Presented. American Academy of Arts and Sciences, Brookline, Mass.

U.S. Department of Labor, Manpower Administration. 1968. *Definition of the Term Disadvantaged Individual.* Washington, D.C.

9

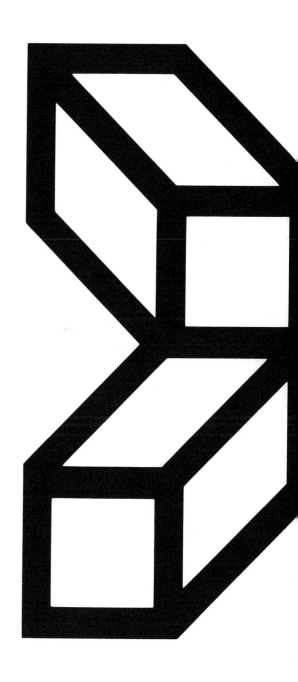

Donald R. Deskins, Jr.
University of Michigan

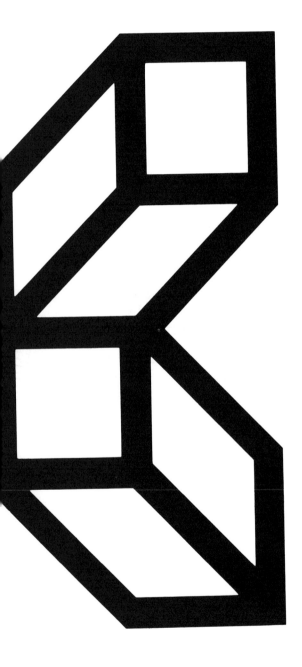

Race, Recreation, and Region in the United States

ABSTRACT

A temporal-spatial analysis of racial participation
in recreational activities was undertaken in order to
determine the extent of non-White participation in
selected summer outdoor recreational activities. The
data were drawn from two national recreational
surveys conducted by the U.S. Bureau of the Census,
providing compatible participation measures stratified
by race and region. The Friedman Two-Way Analysis
of Variance by Ranks was used to test two hypotheses:
(1) there is no regional difference in White/non-White
recreational participation by activity within a given
period, and (2) there is no regional change in the rate
of recreational participation for either racial group
over time. The results show that the White/non-White
differentials in regional recreational participation
were quite pronounced in 1960 but much smaller in
1965. Changes in rate of participation over time are
positive for both racial groups, with the non-White
group experiencing the greater change. The findings
presented here are tentative; however, they strongly
suggest that as minority income and educational levels
increase, racial differentials in regional participation
in the summer recreational activities diminish.

Although geographers have long maintained an interest in recreational patterns, the current interest is evidently less than that held in the past. For example, in the middle 1950s recreational geography was cited as one of the discipline's major branches in the introspective survey *American Geography: Inventory & Prospect*.[1] However, since 1954, American geographers have published little on this subject, although the literature by other social scientists is so voluminous that its assimilation would be a formidable task.[2]

Of the geographic literature reviewed, only one article specifically focused on the recreational patterns of non-White Americans, namely Hart's "A Rural Retreat for Northern Negroes."[3] Although Hart's study is primarily concerned with the development of a specific non-White resort area, he realized the need for further examination of the broad-scale recreational participation patterns of non-White Americans. Hart predicted that "with urbanization, larger incomes, shorter hours, and a shorter workweek, the American Negro will demand, rightfully enough, improved facilities for recreation, including resort areas."[4] Implicit in this statement is that, in the past, non-Whites have not fully enjoyed or participated in a broad range of summer outdoor recreational activities (hereafter, references to recreation are synonymous with summer outdoor recreation) in all sections of the nation.

OBJECTIVE

It is the objective of this paper to present a temporal overview of racial and regional recreational participation trends in the United States for the period 1960–1965 by examining the results of two national recreational participation surveys. An effort will be made to identify, evaluate, and interpret regional trends in recreational participation for both non-White and White racial groups within a socio-economic context. Only in this manner can the recreational participation of non-White Americans be placed in the proper national perspective.

DATA BASE

The data used in this analysis were drawn from two national surveys conducted by the U.S. Bureau of the Census, the *National Recreation Survey* (1960–1961) and its sequel "The 1965 Survey of Outdoor Recreation Activities."[5] Although the sample designs of both surveys follow that employed in current population surveys[6] and therefore are presumed to be representative of the respective populations from which they were drawn, the surveys differ from each other in temporal and spatial stratification, as well as in the list of activities studied.

1. Preston E. James and Clarence F. Jones, eds. *American Geography: Inventory and Prospect* (Syracuse: Syracuse University Press/Association of American Geographers, 1954), pp. 251–57.

2. R. I. Wolf, "Perspective on Outdoor Recreation: A Bibliographical Survey," *Geographical Review* 54 (April, 1964): 203.

3. John Frazier Hart, "A Rural Retreat for Northern Negroes," *Geographical Review* 50 (April, 1960): 147–68.

4. Hart, "A Rural Retreat for Northern Negroes," p. 149.

5. Bureau of Outdoor Recreation (hereafter referred to as BOR), "The 1965 Survey of Outdoor Recreation Activities." Mimeographed report (October, 1967); and Outdoor Recreation Resources Review Commission (hereafter referred to as ORRRC), *National Recreation Survey, No. 19* (Washington, D.C.: U.S. Government Printing Office, 1962).

6. "Concepts and Method Used in Household Statistics on Employment and Unemployment from the Current Population Survey," *Current Population Reports*, Series P–23, No. B (Washington, D.C.: U.S. Bureau of the Census, June, 1964); "Concepts and Method Used in the Current Employment and Unemployment Statistics Prepared by the Bureau of the Census," *Current Population Reports*, Series P–3, No. 5 (Washington, D.C.: U.S. Bureau of the Census, May 9, 1958); and "The Current Population Survey: A Report on Methodology," Technical paper No. 7 (Washington, D.C.: U.S. Bureau of the Census, 1963).

Recreation Survey 1960–1961

The 1960–1961 recreational survey, which provides seasonal participation information, actually consists of four surveys conducted during the period beginning with the summer of 1960 and continuing through the spring of 1961. The sample sizes — 4,409, 4,432, 4,447, and 4,464 for summer, fall, winter, and spring, respectively — represent the United States population 12 years or older at the time of the survey: 130,506,000 (summer/ 1960); 131,187,000 (fall/1960); 131,631,000 (winter/ 1960–1961); and 132,134,000 (spring/1961). All samples were drawn on a probability basis from approximately 4,360 households located in 333 primary sampling units, each of which consisted of a single county or group of counties. Six hundred and forty-one counties and independent cities in the conterminous United States, including the District of Columbia, were included.[7] Continuing this sampling design, the population was further stratified by race, region, residence (urban-rural), income, education, and occupation. Information on their recreational participation in 23 activities was elicited for each person selected in the respective sample. These activities include: attending outdoor concerts and similar events; attending outdoor sports events; bicycling; boating other than sailing or canoeing; camping; canoeing; driving for pleasure; fishing; hiking with packs on trails; ice skating; horseback riding; hunting; mountain climbing; nature walks; picnics; playing outdoor games or sports; sailing; sightseeing; sledding and tobogganing; snow skiing; swimming; walking for pleasure; and water skiing.[8]

Recreation Survey—1965

In scope and design, the 1965 survey closely follows that taken in 1960–1961. However, in 1965, only one survey was conducted, and it was taken during the summer season. The sample size was nearly double that of the earlier survey with the 7,194 households selected representing a national population of 141,252,000 12 years of age or older. The sample was drawn from households in 357 primary sampling units consisting of 701 counties and independent cities in the 50 states and the District of Columbia. Stratification by socio-economic category was identical with that used in the earlier survey. Regional stratification was further subdivided into divisions.[9] Participation data for all 23 activities used in 1960–1961 were also generated, with the addition of bird watching and wildlife–bird photography.[10]

Comparison of 1960–1961 and 1965 Survey Data

Upon examination of the summary tables in each survey, it is apparent that an analysis based on regional

7. ORRRC, *National Recreation Survey*, p. 104.

8. ORRRC, *National Recreation Survey*, pp. 105, 108–109.

9. BOR, "The 1965 Survey of Outdoor Recreation Activities," pp. 132–34, 151–52.

10. BOR, "The 1965 Survey of Outdoor Recreation Activities," pp. 132–42.

and racial stratification can be conducted. White and non-White categories were used in reporting levels of participation throughout each survey, providing racially stratified data on a census region basis for both years. Although participation rates were reported by residential location (urban-rural), income, education, and occupation, these data are not amenable to analysis since they were not stratified by race or region.

The data are further limited because only the June–August period was surveyed in both 1960–1961 and 1965. Since the analysis is restricted to summer participation rates, only those activities which have peak participation during those months were considered. Although there is information on 23 activities in the 1960–1961 survey and 25 activities in 1965, matched data are available for only the following 17 summer recreational activities: (1) attending outdoor concerts and similar events; (2) attending outdoor sports events; (3) bicycling; (4) boating other than sailing or canoeing; (5) camping; (6) driving for pleasure; (7) fishing; (8) hiking with packs on trails; (9) horseback riding; (10) hunting; (11) nature walks; (12) picnics; (13) playing outdoor games or sports; (14) sightseeing; (15) swimming; (16) walking for pleasure; and (17) water skiing. Thus, this analysis will focus only upon the regional and racial differences of participation in the seventeen summer activities as well as the changes in racial participation in these activities from summer 1960 to summer 1965.

Unfortunately, the surveys are inconsistent because the samples of each are drawn from a different size area. In 1960–1961, the sample population consisted of persons residing only in the conterminous United States, including the District of Columbia, while in 1965, Alaska and Hawaii were included.[11] For purposes of this analysis, the operational definition of the United States will be assumed the same for both periods. Therefore, all conclusions reached should be interpreted with this assumption in mind.

OPERATIONAL DEFINITIONS

The categories used throughout this inquiry follow those employed in the two census surveys. Definitions of population, race, region, recreational activities, and participation measures for the most part follow those regularly used by the U.S. Bureau of the Census and in the two National Recreation Surveys. Elaboration of these definitions which go beyond those that follow may be found in the 1960 census of population and the two recreational surveys.[12]

Population

The sample population includes those persons residing in the 50 United States, including the District of

11. ORRRC, *National Recreation Survey*, pp. 109–110.

12. BOR, "The 1965 Survey of Outdoor Recreation Activities"; ORRRC, *National Recreation Survey;* and U.S. Bureau of the Census, *U.S. Census of Population, 1960 United States Summary* (Washington, D.C.: U.S. Government Printing Office, 1962).

Table 1. *United States Population 12 Years and Over, Summer 1960–65*

	Regions				
	United States	Northeast	North Central	South	West
1960 Population					
All	130,506,400	36,674,400	37,592,000	38,243,200	17,996,800
White	116,860,800	34,276,800	34,957,600	30,547,200	17,079,200
Non-White	13,764,000	2,397,600	2,634,400	7,696,000	917,600
1960 Sample Population					
All	4,409	1,239	1,270	1,292	608
White	3,948	1,158	1,081	1,032	577
Non-White	461	81	89	260	31
1965 Population					
All	141,252,000	36,251,000	40,892,000	40,948,000	23,161,000
White	126,010,000	33,608,000	38,117,000	32,714,000	21,571,000
Non-White	15,242,000	2,643,000	2,775,000	8,234,000	1,590,000
1965 Sample Population					
All	7,194	1,846	2,083	2,085	1,180
White	6,418	1,711	1,942	1,666	1,099
Non-White	776	135	141	419	81

Source: BOR. *The 1965 Survey of Outdoor Recreation Activities,* table A, p. 154; and ORRRC, *National Recreation Survey,* table 1.02.01, p. 121.

Columbia, that were reported to be 12 years of age or older at their last birthday in the year the sample was conducted. The sample and population represented for both years are given in table 1.

Race

The racial classification, *White,* includes Caucasians and Mexican-Americans if they are not of Indian or other non-White origin. All other individuals are classed as *non-White,* a category dominated by Blacks. Black dominance of the non-White category is strong in all regions, contributing a minimum of 90 percent in every area except the West where Blacks contribute 50 percent. Nevertheless, Blacks remain the largest single non-White group found in the West.[13]

13. U.S. Bureau of the Census, *Census Population and Housing 1970, General Demographic Trends in Areas 1960 to 1970,* Final Report PHC (2)–1 (Washington, D.C.: U.S. Government Printing Office, 1971), pp. 1–23, 24.

* Alaska and Hawaii not shown, but included in this region

Figure 1. United States regions. (Source: U.S. Census of Population, 1960, United States Summary.) *Alaska and Hawaii are not shown but are included in this region.

Region

Both data sets provide information assembled by the Bureau of Census on land use and economic conditions. States are grouped according to these categories and the groups are assumed to be homogeneous. The regions derived are:

Northeast (NE)	North Central (NC)
Connecticut	Illinois
Maine	Indiana
Massachusetts	Iowa
New Hampshire	Kansas
New Jersey	Michigan
New York	Minnesota
Pennsylvania	Missouri
Rhode Island	Nebraska
Vermont	North Dakota
	Ohio
	South Dakota
	Wisconsin

South (S)	West (W)
Alabama	Alaska
Arkansas	Arizona
Delaware	California
District of Columbia	Colorado
Florida	Hawaii
Georgia	Idaho
Kentucky	Montana
Louisiana	Nevada
Maryland	New Mexico
Mississippi	Oregon
North Carolina	Utah
Oklahoma	Washington
South Carolina	Wyoming
Tennessee	
Texas	
Virginia	
West Virginia	

Recreational Activities

Seventeen outdoor recreational activities were selected from each survey. Each activity category is defined in table 2 for both periods and is accepted as being compatible, although some minor changes in definition have occurred.

Participation Rates

Participation data for the 17 selected outdoor recreational activity categories are defined in both surveys in three ways:

(1) *Percentage of population participating* was estimated by using the reported number of persons engaged in an activity as the numerator and the number of persons in the adjusted sample population as the denominator.

(2) *Activity days per person* were generated by dividing the total number of reported days of participation by the number of adjusted sample cases for the activity represented.

(3) *Activity days per participant* were generated by dividing the accumulative number of reported days of participation in the adjusted sample for the recreational activity being considered by the number of those reporting participation.

The participation measures were adjusted to the actual population represented (table 1), thus providing sufficiently standardized data to assess differences by race, region, and recreational activities over time.

ANALYTICAL PROCEDURE

To determine whether there is any difference in recreational participation rates by race and region over time, it is hypothesized ($H_0 1$) that there is no regional difference in non-White/White recreational participation by activity within the period 1960–1965 and ($H_0 2$) that there is no regional change in the rate of participation in recreational activities for either racial group over time. In order to test these hypotheses, it was necessary to employ a technique which would analyze data (participation measures) arrayed in a 2×4 matrix and yield results in a form which would allow for the acceptance or rejection of the respective hypotheses.

Since the data are summaries of disaggregated observations whose variance is not known, one possible approach is to employ a nonparametric statistical technique. Such a method may be conservative, but it is justified by the small size of the data matrix and the lack of knowledge of the variance among these data. The nonparametric approach may suppress some of the hypothesized relationships in the data; however, the alternative method, a parametric procedure, seems comparatively undesirable, since it might add spurious information.[14] The nonparametric approach appears the more judicious choice and was therefore employed in this analysis.

Friedman Two-Way Analysis of Variance by Ranks

Among the various nonparametric techniques which meet the criteria of ability to test for differences between

14. Hubert M. Blalock, *Social Statistics* (New York: McGraw-Hill, 1960), pp. 187–88; and Sidney Siegel, *Nonparametric Statistics for the Behavioral Sciences* (New York: McGraw-Hill, 1956), pp. 30–34.

Table 2. *Seventeen Outdoor Recreational Activities*

	Definitions	
Category	1960	1965
1. Attending outdoor concerts and similar events	Musical, dramatic, artistic or other non-sporting events which are conducted out-of-doors. Attending drive-in movies is excluded.	Same.
2. Attending outdoor sports events	Attendance at any outdoor sports event in which the respondent is not a participant, official, etc. The same events are included here as in playing outdoor games or sports.	Same — excludes qualifying note on relationship to playing outdoor games or sports.
3. Bicycling	Bicycle riding for pleasure. If a respondent rides a bicycle to work or to school, he is excluded.	Same.
4. Boating, other than sailing or canoeing	Recreational use of any boat other than canoes, sailboats or houseboats. This category includes the use of rowboats, outboard motorboats, rafts, floats, etc.	Same — includes houseboats.
5. Camping	Living out-of-doors, using a bed roll, sleeping bag, trailer, tent, or a hut open on one or more sides, if the person takes his bedding, cooking equipment, and food with him. Camping is often done in combination with other activities such as fishing, hunting, etc. (When such a combination is reported, all associated outdoor activities are also recorded.) Does not include formal camps for teenagers, such as Boy Scout camps, etc.	Same — excludes qualifying note on reporting this activity when done in combination with other activities.
6. Driving for pleasure	The key word in this definition is pleasure. Both riding and driving are included. If the driving was mixed, the determining factor is whether	Same — excludes racing qualification.

206

Table 2. (*continued.*)

Category	Definitions 1960	1965
	or not it was primarily for pleasure. Activities such as racing are included under sports and games.	
7. Fishing	The taking of fish for noncommercial purposes. Spearfishing while skin diving should also be included.	Same — spearfishing statement not included.
8. Hiking with packs on trails	The limitation, "with packs on trails," excludes casual walking and nature walks. A pack would normally include provisions and some sort of shelter.	Same — the "with packs on trails," limitation not stated.
9. Horseback riding	Includes only recreational riding. Riding to or from work or school or riding as part of a job such as a "cowboy" or mounted policeman is not included.	Same.
10. Hunting	Hunting is the search for or stalking of animals in order to kill them for recreational purposes. No form of commercial hunting is considered.	Same.
11. Nature walks	Nature walks for the purpose of observing either plants, birds, or animals, collecting specimens, photographing natural subjects, etc.	Same.
12. Picnics	Outdoor activity away from home, the primary purpose being the preparation or eating of a meal out-of-doors. Other activities are often associated with picnics.	Same — with qualification that includes cookouts or barbecues in neighbors' yards but not in one's own yard.
13. Playing outdoor games or sports	All team sports, such as basketball, football, outdoor basketball, etc., as well as usually non-team sports, such as tennis, golf, etc. Record	Same.

Table 2. (*continued.*)

Category	Definitions 1960	1965
	events (such as trying to set a speedboat record) are included. The name of the sport was required of the respondent. A requirement for including the activity is the aspect of competition, either against other people, the clock, a record, etc.	
14. Sightseeing	Looking at something of interest, the major limitation being that the sightseeing must be intentional. Excluded are such things as casually looking from the car window during a trip. If the person took a particular route or went out of his way to see a particular sight, it is classified as sightseeing. Excluded are activities such as window shopping wherein the emphasis is not on the out-of-doors.	Same.
15. Swimming	The ability to swim is not necessary for inclusion. "Bathing," playing in the surf, etc., are included as well as skin or scuba diving and surfboarding.	Same.
16. Walking for pleasure	Any walking not included under hiking or nature walks, from early morning "constitutionals" to long all-day walks which do not require a pack.	Same — with qualifying requirement that walks last 30 minutes or more.
17. Water skiing	Any of the various sports where the person is towed behind a boat. This includes the use of aquaplanes, water skis, or any other apparatus of this type.	Same.

Table 3. *Difference by Race and Region in Percentage of Population Driving for Pleasure in the United States, 1960*

| | | k(4) | | | |
		NE	NC	S	W
N(2)	Non-White	[3]* 41	[1] 55	[4] 38	[2] 42
	White	[3] 55	[1] 58	[4] 46	[2] 56
	R_j	6	2	8	4

$$\chi_{r^2} = \frac{12}{(2)(4)(4+1)} \, [(6)^2 + (2)^2 + (8)^2 + (4)^2] - (3)(2)(4+1) = 6.0$$

*Numbers in brackets are percentages of persons participating converted to rank.

summary data arranged in a small matrix is the Friedman Two-Way Analysis of Variance by Ranks. This technique is designed to test whether there is a difference between *two* variables under *four* conditions. Here, the *two* variables are White and non-White and the *four* conditions are the census regions: Northeast, North Central, South, and West. Friedman's equation reads:

$$\chi_{r^2} = \frac{12}{Nk \, (k+1)} \sum_{j=1}^{k} (R_j) \, 2 - 3N \, (k+1)$$

where   N = number of rows
   k = number of columns
   R_j = sum of ranks in jth column
   $\sum_{j=1}^{k}$ = the sum of the squares of the sums of the ranks over all k conditions[15]

Testing Hypothesis (H₀1)

Friedman's equation is applied to the percentage of population driving for pleasure in order to illustrate the use of the technique to test hypothesis ($H_0 1$) (table 3).

There is a significant regional difference in 1960 in both the White and non-White test groups' frequency of driving for pleasure ($H_1 1$): the χ_{r^2} value is significant at the 0.05 level. Probabilities are determined from the "Table of Probabilities Associated With Values as Large as Observed Values of χ_{r^2} in the Friedman Two-Way Analysis of Variance by Ranks."[16] Therefore, the null hypothesis ($H_0 1$) should be rejected and the alternative hypothesis ($H_1 1$) adopted.

Significant differences by race and region were identified by applying the Friedman equation to the three sets of participation data: (1) percentage of population participating, (2) activity days per person, and (3) activity days per participant for each of the 17 selected recreational activities by year. This procedure was repeated 102 times (table 4). Those activities whose racial and regional differences in recreational participation are significant are denoted by asterisks. The direction of difference, determined by comparing the levels of White and non-White participation in tables 5 through 10, is noted in table 4 by (N) if the direction favors non-White or (W) if the inverse is true. Direction is indicated only when χ_{r^2} values are so large that their probability of occurring by chance is less than 1/20 (0.05).

Testing Hypothesis (H₀2)

By slightly modifying the input data, the Friedman nonparametric procedure was repeated to determine whether there was a significant change in participation within a racial group by region over time. In this test,

15. Siegel, *Nonparametric Statistics*, pp. 166–73.

16. Siegel, *Nonparametric Statistics*, p. 281.

the two variables are the participation measures for a single racial group during the two time periods. Driving for pleasure by White participants (activity days per person) was selected as the example to illustrate the testing procedure (table 11).

The χ_{r^2} values indicate that there is a significant change from 1960 to 1965 in the number of activity days per person for Whites driving for pleasure ($H_1 2$). Therefore, ($H_0 2$) should be rejected and ($H_1 2$) accepted. Again, the resulting 102 χ_{r^2} values were referred to the probability table specifically created for the Friedman's test to determine whether the results occur by chance (table 12). The direction of change was determined by comparing the actual number of activity days per person recorded for pleasure driving in each of the two years to

Table 4. *White/Non-White Difference in Regional Outdoor Recreation Participation in the United States by Year According to Friedman's Two-Way Analysis of Variance by Ranks* (Values = χ_{r^2})

Activities	Participation					
	Percentage of Population		Activity Days Per Person		Activity Days Per Participant	
	1960	1965	1960	1965	1960	1965
1. Attending outdoor concerts, and similar events	2.7	2.7	6.0*(W)	2.4	13.8*(W)	1.8
2. Attending outdoor sports events	1.8	3.6	.6	4.2	5.7	4.2
3. Bicycling	1.5	4.2	3.0	6.0*(W)	5.7	6.0*(W)
4. Boating other than sailing or canoeing	2.4	3.6	5.4	4.2	13.8*(W)	.6
5. Camping	1.5	.1	3.6	1.5	13.8*(W)	1.8
6. Driving for pleasure	6.0*(W)	2.7	3.6	5.4	5.4	1.8
7. Fishing	5.4	2.7	5.4	5.4	7.5*(W)	1.8
8. Hiking with packs on trails	3.0	.3	3.0	1.8	13.8*(W)	1.8
9. Horseback riding	2.7	.6	5.7	5.4	13.8*(W)	4.2
10. Hunting	.9	4.5	4.2	1.5	16.5*(W)	.6
11. Nature walks	2.7	.3	.9	1.8	13.8*(W)	3.0
12. Picnics	6.0*(N)	5.4	3.6	3.0	.9	4.2
13. Playing outdoor games or sports	2.7	3.6	1.8	4.8	1.8	5.4
14. Sightseeing	4.8	2.7	4.8	5.4	7.5*(W)	3.6
15. Swimming	5.4	.9	2.4	5.4	1.5	4.2
16. Walking for pleasure	5.4	3.9	3.0	6.0*(N)	1.8	4.2
17. Water skiing	13.8*(W)	.6	13.8*(W)	6.3*(W)	13.8*(W)	3.0

*$p \leq .05$ according to χ_{r^2} distribution created specifically for Friedman's test.

Direction of difference: (N) = non-White. (W) = White.

determine if there has been an increase from summer 1960 to summer 1965. Only when the p ≤ .05 is the change recorded as a (+) or as a (−) near the appropriate χ_{r^2} marked with an asterisk in table 12.

DIFFERENCES IN REGIONAL PARTICIPATION

The summary values (table 4) derived from testing (H_01) suggest that significant racial differences in regional recreational participation exist for various activities. These differences in participation are revealed regardless of which of the three measures of participation—percentage of population, activity days per person, and activity days per participant—are considered.

Percentage of Population

In 1960, there were no racial differences in the percentage of population participating in 14 of the 17 summer recreational activities examined. Significant

Table 5. *Percentage of Population Participating in Outdoor Recreational Activities by Race and United States Regions, 1960*

	Race							
	White				Non-White			
	Regions				Regions			
	NE	NC	S	W	NE	NC	S	W
Activities	(1)	(2)	(3)	(4)	(1)	(2)	(3)	(4)
1. Attending outdoor concerts and similar events	13	11	3	11	9	5	2	6
2. Attending outdoor sports events	22	28	20	25	22	21	24	45
3. Bicycling	9	10	6	10	5	7	12	16
4. Boating other than sailing or canoeing	21	28	23	24	12	7	3	6
5. Camping	5	8	9	18	2	<1	2	10
6. Driving for pleasure	55	58	46	56	41	55	38	42
7. Fishing	21	33	34	30	20	31	30	23
8. Hiking with packs on trails	7	5	5	9	2	5	2	10
9. Horseback riding	4	5	5	10	2	4	3	19
10. Hunting	3	2	6	3	<1	3	4	6
11. Nature walks	15	16	13	16	16	10	9	23
12. Picnics	57	58	46	54	58	62	34	52
13. Playing outdoor games or sports	34	34	21	27	30	46	21	42
14. Sightseeing	40	47	37	56	23	51	27	45
15. Swimming	53	42	44	48	43	33	25	42
16. Walking for pleasure	42	27	25	35	54	51	33	26
17. Water skiing	5	6	7	10	<1	<1	<1	<1

Source: ORRRC, *National Recreation Survey*, tables 1.02.02–1.02.18, pp. 122–38.

racial variations, however, are found in the remaining categories: driving for pleasure, picnics, and water skiing. A higher percentage of Whites took part in driving for pleasure and water skiing; more non-Whites participated in picnics. A comparison for 1965 shows that none of the 17 recreational activities had significant racial differences by region.

Activity Days Per Person

The results of the analysis of activity days per person show that in 1960 there were significant differences in racial participation only in attending outdoor concerts and similar events, and in water skiing. In each of these categories the direction of difference favors White participants. Five years later, significant differences in level of participation were noted for bicycling, walking for pleasure, and water skiing, with a greater non-White participation only in the category, walking for pleasure.

Table 6. *Percentage of Population Participating in Outdoor Recreational Activities by Race and United States Regions, 1965*

	Race							
	White				Non-White			
	Regions				Regions			
Activities	NE (1)	NC (2)	S (3)	W (4)	NE (1)	NC (2)	S (3)	W (4)
1. Attending outdoor concerts and similar events	14	12	7	15	7	9	6	10
2. Attending outdoor sports events	29	36	25	32	22	32	23	20
3. Bicycling	15	21	14	16	17	22	16	9
4. Boating other than sailing or canoeing	22	31	25	27	8	12	6	5
5. Camping	4	11	9	21	2	2	1	9
6. Driving for pleasure	57	59	51	61	45	45	34	56
7. Fishing	21	34	36	32	10	17	31	17
8. Hiking with packs on trails	6	8	5	12	4	2	2	3
9. Horseback riding	5	11	8	11	*	4	3	3
10. Hunting	3	4	5	4	1	2	2	*
11. Nature walks	11	16	11	23	10	14	5	8
12. Picnics	57	64	52	63	57	60	33	53
13. Playing outdoor games or sports	40	41	30	43	48	45	29	30
14. Sightseeing	51	51	43	60	42	45	26	60
15. Swimming	57	46	46	56	34	27	22	41
16. Walking for pleasure	55	47	38	57	53	48	43	53
17. Water skiing	5	8	7	8	*	*	1	1

*Small number larger than 0.

Source: BOR, "The 1965 Survey of Outdoor Recreation Activities" (Unpublished tables).

Activity Days Per Participant

The following ten summer recreational activities recorded for 1960 exhibit significant racial differences in the frequency of participation by individuals: attending outdoor sports events, boating other than sailing and canoeing, camping, fishing, hiking with packs on trails, horseback riding, hunting, nature walks, sightseeing, and water skiing. In all ten categories, White frequency of participation was greater than that of non-Whites. In 1965, only the category bicycling showed a significant difference, and the frequency again favored Whites.

CHANGES IN PARTICIPATION OVER TIME

The data suggest that recreational participation by a

Table 7. *Activity Days Per Person Engaged in Outdoor Recreational Activities by Race and United States Regions, 1960*

	Race							
	White				Non-White			
	Regions				Regions			
	NE	NC	S	W	NE	NC	S	W
Activities	(1)	(2)	(3)	(4)	(1)	(2)	(3)	(4)
1. Attending outdoor concerts and similar events	.33	.26	.07	.23	.22	.13	.06	.10
2. Attending outdoor sports events	1.17	1.66	1.28	.91	.94	.93	1.55	3.42
3. Bicycling	1.53	1.98	1.41	1.58	.69	2.21	2.97	6.65
4. Boating other than sailing or canoeing	1.46	1.56	1.05	1.14	.26	.43	.08	.06
5. Camping	.35	.43	.46	1.07	.07	*	.05	.58
6. Driving for pleasure	7.45	8.08	5.84	5.22	4.12	7.26	4.23	4.97
7. Fishing	1.86	2.10	1.99	1.96	.32	1.44	3.02	.45
8. Hiking with packs on trails	.30	.22	.20	.51	.04	.08	.05	.16
9. Horseback riding	.30	.34	.45	.70	.09	.07	.38	4.10
10. Hunting	.23	.09	.22	.16	*	.20	.45	.06
11. Nature walks	1.18	.62	.62	.69	.51	.27	.25	.68
12. Picnics	2.90	2.36	1.40	2.09	1.60	2.08	.94	2.13
13. Playing outdoor games or sports	3.96	3.94	2.76	2.86	3.15	6.95	3.71	12.94
14. Sightseeing	2.09	2.69	1.81	2.86	.74	2.99	.78	1.48
15. Swimming	7.18	4.81	4.56	5.39	1.63	2.20	1.65	4.74
16. Walking for pleasure	6.56	3.46	2.79	3.98	5.15	6.30	4.71	2.19
17. Water skiing	.31	.23	.42	.45	*	*	*	*

*Small number larger than 0.

Source: ORRRC, *National Recreation Survey*, tables 1.02.02–1.02.18, pp. 122–38.

racial group increases over time regardless of which race is being considered or which participation measure is employed. Evidence of significant increase is found in table 12.

Percentage of Population

During the interval 1960–1965, there is only limited evidence of increases in recreational activities. Among non-Whites, the only significant changes observed are in picnicking and water skiing. Picnicking began to show a slight decrease in popularity, while water skiing began to attract the attention of non-Whites. Meanwhile the extent of White participation showed an increase in the following three categories: attending outdoor sports events, boating other than sailing and canoeing, and fishing.

Table 8. *Activity Days Per Person Engaged in Outdoor Recreational Activities by Race and United States Regions, 1965*

	Race							
	White				Non-White			
	Regions				Regions			
Activities	NE (1)	NC (2)	S (3)	W (4)	NE (1)	NC (2)	S (3)	W (4)
1. Attending outdoor concerts and similar events	.46	.35	.22	.42	.11	.22	.14	.24
2. Attending outdoor sports events	1.40	1.97	1.74	1.76	1.33	2.61	2.01	.79
3. Bicycling	2.89	4.36	3.22	2.84	2.53	4.20	3.79	.99
4. Boating other than sailing or canoeing	1.50	2.20	1.54	1.49	.13	.32	.26	.31
5. Camping	.27	.81	.53	1.43	.04	.12	.04	.24
6. Driving for pleasure	7.14	7.71	5.83	6.68	4.44	6.61	3.85	5.55
7. Fishing	1.88	2.68	2.60	1.93	.46	.88	2.61	.83
8. Hiking with packs on trails	.36	.31	.26	.64	.11	.25	.07	.03
9. Horseback riding	.36	.82	.49	.68	*	.43	.11	.04
10. Hunting	.14	.26	.29	.34	.41	.10	.05	.10
11. Nature walks	.66	.85	.68	1.42	.28	.66	.22	.44
12. Picnics	3.40	3.82	2.67	3.79	1.98	1.91	1.20	2.09
13. Playing outdoor games or sports	7.58	6.86	4.98	6.52	8.17	9.26	6.74	4.35
14. Sightseeing	3.49	3.36	2.32	4.61	2.61	3.15	1.28	3.30
15. Swimming	8.85	6.32	6.28	8.79	3.81	1.75	1.52	3.09
16. Walking for pleasure	9.35	6.58	4.99	7.72	13.83	8.55	8.07	9.29
17. Water skiing	.32	.58	.47	.55	*	*	*	.01

*Small number larger than 0.

Source: BOR, "The 1965 Survey of Outdoor Recreation Activities" (Unpublished tables).

Activity Days Per Person

Significant changes in non-White per capita days of participation occurred in fishing and water skiing, with only the latter category showing growth. White participation, however, exhibited change in the following five activities: camping, fishing, hunting, playing outdoor games or sports, and walking for pleasure. For all five categories, the change was positive, suggesting that the number of White activity days per person in 1965 was significantly higher than in 1960.

Activity Days Per Participant

Ten categories show a positive change in non-White activity days per participant. Growth is observed in attending outdoor concerts and similar events, boating

Table 9. *Activity Days Per Participant Engaged in Outdoor Recreational Activities by Race and United States Regions, 1960*

	Race							
	White				Non-White			
	Regions				Regions			
Activities	NE (1)	NC (2)	S (3)	W (4)	NE (1)	NC (2)	S (3)	W (4)
1. Attending outdoor concerts and similar events	2.50	2.40	2.30	2.10	*	*	*	*
2. Attending outdoor sports events	5.30	5.90	6.40	3.60	*	*	6.50	*
3. Bicycling	16.40	18.90	22.30	16.30	*	*	25.70	*
4. Boating other than sailing or canoeing	7.00	5.60	4.60	4.80	*	*	*	*
5. Camping	7.00	5.40	5.10	5.90	*	*	*	*
6. Driving for pleasure	13.50	13.90	12.70	9.30	10.00	13.20	11.10	*
7. Fishing	8.90	6.40	5.90	6.50	*	*	10.10	*
8. Hiking with packs on trails	4.30	4.40	4.00	5.70	*	*	*	*
9. Horseback riding	7.50	6.80	9.00	7.00	*	*	*	*
10. Hunting	7.70	*	3.70	*	*	*	*	*
11. Nature walks	7.90	3.90	4.80	4.30	*	*	*	*
12. Picnics	5.10	4.10	3.00	3.90	2.80	3.40	2.80	*
13. Playing outdoor games or sports	11.60	11.60	13.10	10.60	*	15.10	17.70	*
14. Sightseeing	5.20	5.70	4.90	5.10	*	*	2.90	*
15. Swimming	13.50	11.50	10.40	11.20	3.80	*	6.60	*
16. Walking for pleasure	15.60	12.80	11.20	11.40	9.50	12.40	14.30	*
17. Water skiing	6.20	3.80	6.00	4.50	*	*	*	*

*Small number larger than 0.

Source: ORRRC, *National Recreation Survey*, tables 1.02.02–1.02.18, pp. 122–38.

other than sailing and canoeing, camping, hiking with packs on trails, horseback riding, hunting, nature walks, sightseeing, and water skiing. Changes in White participation frequency were observed in fewer categories — bicycling, driving for pleasure, swimming, and walking for pleasure — with all but one activity, driving for pleasure, experiencing growth.

ACTIVITIES RANKED BY PARTICIPATION

Recreational activities ranked by level of participation provide some insight into group recreational preference. It may be argued, however, that the level of participation is more likely a reflection of the availability of recreational resources within the effective travel range of participants. The presence or absence of these resources greatly influences the recreational opportuni-

Table 10. *Activity Days Per Participant Engaged in Outdoor Recreational Activities by Race and United States Regions, 1965*

	Race							
	White				Non-White			
	Regions				Regions			
Activities	NE (1)	NC (2)	S (3)	W (4)	NE (1)	NC (2)	S (3)	W (4)
1. Attending outdoor concerts and similar events	3.29	2.87	3.03	2.86	1.64	2.49	2.32	2.31
2. Attending outdoor sports event	4.89	5.43	7.02	5.56	5.44	8.22	8.66	4.05
3. Bicycling	19.80	20.62	23.78	17.97	15.01	18.99	24.16	10.95
4. Boating other than sailing or canoeing	6.85	7.11	6.26	5.44	1.57	2.73	4.56	6.19
5. Camping	8.59	7.39	5.80	6.85	2.51	5.65	3.20	2.91
6. Driving for pleasure	12.62	13.08	11.42	11.02	4.84	14.78	11.30	9.99
7. Fishing	9.17	7.00	7.33	6.08	4.64	5.29	8.49	6.25
8. Hiking with packs on trails	6.09	4.17	4.85	5.53	4.20	12.32	3.17	1.00
9. Horseback riding	6.98	7.44	6.22	6.20	*	10.25	4.00	1.49
10. Hunting	5.40	6.45	6.21	7.69	50.00	4.61	2.11	*
11. Nature walks	5.91	5.42	6.47	6.33	2.75	4.79	4.25	5.26
12. Picnics	6.01	5.95	5.12	6.03	3.46	3.20	3.68	3.98
13. Playing outdoor games or sports	18.75	16.57	18.89	15.29	17.00	20.78	22.96	14.37
14. Sightseeing	6.87	6.62	5.39	7.70	6.17	6.98	4.87	5.52
15. Swimming	15.67	13.80	13.71	15.85	11.27	6.40	7.04	7.62
16. Walking for pleasure	17.12	13.93	13.09	13.63	25.98	17.91	18.96	17.68
17. Water skiing	6.30	6.85	6.65	6.67	*	*	1.00	1.00

*Small number larger than 0.

Source: BOR, "The 1965 Survey of Outdoor Recreation Activities" (Unpublished tables).

Table 11. *Changes by Region in Activity Days Per Person Driving for Pleasure for Whites in the United States, 1960–1965*

		k(4)			
		NE	NC	S	W
N(2)	White 1965	[2]* 7.14	[1] 7.71	[3] 5.83	[4] 6.68
	White 1960	[2] 7.45	[1] 8.08	[3] 5.84	[4] 5.22
	R_j	4	2	6	8

$$\chi_{r^2} = \frac{12}{(2)(4)(4+1)} \left[(4)^2 + (2)^2 + (6)^2 + (8)^2 \right] - (3)(2)(4+1) = 6.0$$

*Numbers in brackets are actual days per participant converted to ranks.

17. ORRRC, *Prospective Demand for Outdoor Recreation, No. 26* (Washington, D.C.: U.S. Government Printing Office, 1962), pp. 2–3.

18. Siegel, *Nonparametric Statistics,* pp. 206, 212.

ties for prospective participants. At this time, sufficient data are not available to clarify this distinction; therefore, this discussion will address the racial differences in the level of participation by recreational activities for each year as well as within each racial group during the time span of this analysis. This will be accomplished simply by using level of participation as a surrogate of preference which is limited by the availability of recreational opportunities (acreage, parks, developed facilities, etc.).[17] Table 13 contains a "high to low" listing by rank of yearly White and non-White participation in the summer activities for each of the three participation measures. To determine how these ranked activities match between races as well as within a single racial group over time, a Spearman rank correlation coefficient was calculated for each comparison (table 14).[18]

Rank by Percentage of Population

Activities ranked by percentage of population reveal that for Whites in 1960, picnics and driving for pleasure were the most popular recreational activities, followed in descending order by swimming; sightseeing; walking for pleasure; playing outdoor games and sports; fishing; boating other than sailing or canoeing; attending outdoor sports events; nature walks; attending outdoor concerts and similar events; bicycling; camping; water skiing; hiking with packs on trails; and horseback riding with hunting the least popular. The Spearman correlation coefficient $r = 0.95$ between the White and non-White rankings suggests that there is little difference between White and non-White recreational preferences when percentage of population participating is used as an indicator. A similar comparison of activities ranked by percentage of population participating by race for 1965 produces $r = 0.93$, again revealing that there is only a slight difference in the order of activities. The recreational preferences of each racial group remained stable over time (from 1960 to 1965) as indicated by $r = 0.98$ for Whites and $r = 0.97$ for non-Whites. It appears that throughout the entire period, picnics and driving for pleasure were the most popular activities for both races, while hunting and water skiing were the least popular. The former activities represent those characterized by easy access, whereas the latter require the investment of larger amounts of capital and of travel time.

Rank by Activity Days Per Person

When the rank of participation by activity days for both Whites and non-Whites is examined, the relationship between the order of activities was $r = 0.82$ for 1960 and $r = 0.89$ for 1965. These values suggest that there was a better match of activity days by race in 1965 than existed five years earlier. Within each racial group, the correlations are much higher for the period 1960 to 1965; 0.94 for Whites and 0.95 for non-Whites. When activity days per person are ranked by recreational activity, driving for pleasure and walking for pleasure rank first, with the categories hiking with packs on trails, camping, hunting, and water skiing least preferred.

Rank by Activity Days Per Participant

Activities ranked according to activity days per participant show the weakest correlations generated. In 1960, the correlation coefficient calculated from the ordered activities by race was 0.62; whereas in 1965, the value was 0.47, suggesting a wide racial difference in activities ordered by the intensity of participation. Although in 1965, both races preferred bicycling and play-

Table 12. *Change in Regional Outdoor Recreation Participation in the United States by Race According to Friedman's Two-Way Analysis of Variance by Ranks (Values χ_{r^2})*

	Participation					
	Percentage of Population		Activity Days Per Person		Activity Days Per Participant	
Activities	White	Non-White	White	Non-White	White	Non-White
1. Attending outdoor concerts and similar events	2.1	1.5	5.4	1.8	5.4	13.8*(+)
2. Attending outdoor sports events	6.0*(+)	.6	4.2	.6	4.2	5.7
3. Bicycling	3.9	.6	3.6	1.8	6.0*(+)	5.7
4. Boating other than sailing or canoeing	6.0*(+)	4.8	.9	3.6	4.8	13.8*(+)
5. Camping	5.4	4.2	6.0*(+)	.3	5.4	13.8*(+)
6. Driving for pleasure	5.4	2.1	1.5	5.4	6.0*(−)	5.4
7. Fishing	6.0*(+)	2.1	6.0*(+)	6.0*(−)	3.6	5.7
8. Hiking with packs on trails	3.9	4.2	6.0*(+)	3.0	3.6	13.8*(+)
9. Horseback riding	.6	2.1	4.2	1.8	3.0	13.8*(+)
10. Hunting	2.4	4.2	1.8	.9	.1	13.8*(+)
11. Nature walks	.6	3.6	.3	4.2	4.2	13.8*(+)
12. Picnics	5.4	6.0*(−)	2.4	5.4	4.2	2.7
13. Playing outdoor games or sports	1.5	4.2	6.0*(+)	1.8	2.7	1.5
14. Sightseeing	2.7	4.8	5.4	4.8	3.6	7.5*(+)
15. Swimming	1.5	5.4	5.4	2.4	6.0*(+)	.3
16. Walking for pleasure	5.4	2.7	6.0*(+)	3.0	6.0*(+)	4.2
17. Water skiing	2.7	15.9*(+)	2.4	20.7*(+)	.0	18.0*(+)

*p ≤ .05 according to χ_{r^2} distribution created specifically for Friedman's test.

Direction of difference: (+), (−) compared with values for latest year (1965).

ing outdoor games or sports first and second, walking for pleasure and swimming third and fourth, fishing sixth, and horseback riding eighth, the lack of correspondence among the remaining 11 activities accounts for the wide difference in participation preference denoted by the small correlation values.

A comparison of the change in preference from 1960 to 1965 for each race reveals a stability of preference for recreational activities during that period. For Whites, the large correlation coefficient of 0.88 indicates that the 1960 and 1965 activity preference ranks are quite similar. On the other hand, the correlation between non-White ranks is only 0.55, suggesting that preference showed significant shifts over time. These shifts probably reflect improvements in income level, educational levels, and changes in place of residence.

Table 13. *Summer Recreational Activities Ranked by Intensity of Participation by Percentage of Population — Activity Days Per Person, and Activity Days Per Participant for White and Non-White, 1960–1965* (Values Are Ranks)

| | Percentage of Population | | | | Activity Days Per Person | | | | Activity Days Per Participant | | | |
| | 1960 | | 1965 | | 1960 | | 1965 | | 1960 | | 1965 | |
Activities	W* (1)	N (2)	W (3)	N (4)	W (5)	N (6)	W (7)	N (8)	W (9)	N (10)	W (11)	N (12)
1. Attending outdoor concerts and similar events	12	13	12	11.5	15	14	16	12	17	11	17	14
2. Attending outdoor sports events	8.5	8	7.5	7	10	7	9.5	7	10	7	15	5
3. Bicycling	12	10	10	9	8	4	5.5	4	1	1	1	1
4. Boating other than sailing or canoeing	8.5	11	9	11.5	9	13	9.5	11	11	12	11	12
5. Camping	12	13	13	16	17	15	12	16	9	13	7	13
6. Driving for pleasure	1.5	2	2	3	1	3	3	3	3	4	5	15
7. Fishing	7	7	7.5	8	7	5	8	8	7	5	6	6
8. Hiking with packs on trails	15	15.5	15.5	14.5	14	16	15	15	15	14	16	9
9. Horseback riding	16	13	14	13	12	10	13	13	6	15	8	8
10. Hunting	17	15.5	17	14.5	16	12	17	14	8	16	12	5
11. Nature walks	10	9	11	10	11	11	11	10	12.5	9.5	13	10
12. Picnics	1.5	1	1	2	6	8	5.5	9	16	9.5	14	11
13. Playing outdoor games or sports	6	6	6	4.5	4	2	4	2	5	2	2	2
14. Sightseeing	4	4	4	4.5	5	9	7	6	12.5	8	10	7
15. Swimming	3	5	3	6	2	6	1	5	4	6	3.5	4
16. Walking for pleasure	5	3	5	1	3	1	2	1	2	3	3.5	3
17. Water skiing	14	17	15.5	17	13	17	14	17	14	17	9	17

*W = Whites; N = non-Whites.

Source: ORRRC, *National Recreation Survey,* tables 1.02.02–1.02.18, pp. 122–38.

INTERPRETATION

It has been strongly suggested in other studies that the level of participation in recreational activities is a function of income, cultural preference, and education.[19] Tentatively then, much of the racial variation in regional recreational participation occurring during 1960–1965 may be attributed to differences in White and non-White socio-economic characteristics. Furthermore, certain socio-economic characteristics of the participants may partially explain the change in regional recreational participation patterns over time for both Whites and non-Whites.

Income and Participation

Participation in certain recreational activities is costly and tied to income level. Investments in equipment, travel costs, and associated expenditures for lodging, etc. are necessary outlays for participation in some recreational activities.[20] According to the *National Recreation Survey* (1960–1961), the relationship between income and participation in selected recreational activities can be easily separated into three categories. The first group includes those activities in which increased participation accompanies increased income for both lower and higher than average income classes. Recreational activities comprising this group are boating other than sailing and canoeing, sightseeing, swimming, and playing outdoor games and sports (figure 2). The next group includes attending outdoor sport events, camping, driving for pleasure, and picnics. Here, participation increases with increased income for the lower than average income class and levels off or dips for the higher than average income class (figure 3). The third group includes fishing, hunting, and walking for pleasure, in which there is no clear relationship between participation and income across all income classes (figure 4).

Since a relationship exists between income and participation for selected recreational activities, a consideration of White and non-White income differentials may provide insight into racial variations in regional recreational participation patterns. An examination of the 1959 median family income reported for the United States and each of its regions shows that there are income differences by race (table 15). For the United States as a whole, the non-White median family income was only 54 percent of the median white family income. Regional variations ranged from a high of 76 percent in the West to a low of 46 percent in the South. The figures for the Northeast and North Central regions are 67 percent and 72 percent, respectively. In 1967, the regional family income variation had changed little from

Table 14. *Spearman Rank Correlation Coefficient Values Describing the Relationship Between Activities by Level of Participation for Racial Groups by Year and Within Each Racial Group Over Time*

	r_s	t
Percentage of population		
1960 by race (1, 2)	0.95	11.69*
1965 by race (3, 4)	0.93	9.63*
1960–1965 White (1, 3)	0.98	18.97*
1960–1965 Non-White (2, 4)	0.97	15.34*
Activity days per person		
1960 by race (5, 6)	0.82	5.53*
1965 by race (7, 8)	0.89	7.52*
1960–1965 White (5, 7)	0.94	10.51*
1960–1965 Non-White (7, 8)	0.95	11.63*
Activity days per participant		
1960 by race (9, 10)	0.62	3.04
1965 by race (11, 12)	0.47	2.06
1960–1965 White (9, 11)	0.88	7.10*
1960–1965 Non-White (10, 12)	0.55	2.75

*$p \leq .001$.

(1, 2) = Columns of input data found in table 13.
Spearman rank correlation coefficient:

$$r_s = 1 - \frac{6 \sum\limits_{j=1}^{N} d_{i^2}}{N^3 - N}$$

Testing the significance of r_s:

$$t = r_s \sqrt{\frac{N - 2}{1 - r_{s^2}}}$$

Source: Siegel, *Nonparametric Statistics,* pp. 206, 212.

19. ORRRC, *National Recreation Survey,* p. 6.

20. ORRRC, *National Recreation Survey,* Chap. 8, pp. 66–76.

Table 15. *White/Non-White Median Family Income in United States Regions, 1959–1970*

	US	NE	NC	S	W
1959					
White	$ 5,893	6,318	5.994	5,009	6,444
Non-White	3,161	4,371	4,320	2,322	4,937
Non-White as percentage of White	54%	67%	72%	46%	76%
1967					
White	$ 8,318	8,746	8,414	7,448	8,901
Non-White	4,939	5,764	6,540	3,992	6,501
Non-White as percentage of White	59%	66%	78%	54%	74%
1970					
White	$10,236	10,939	10,508	9,240	10,382
Non-White	6,274	7,774	7,718	5,226	8,001
Non-White as percentage of White	61%	71%	73%	57%	77%

Sources: (1) U.S. Bureau of the Census, *U.S. Census of Population: 1960, Characteristics of the Population, Part I, United States Summary* (Washington, D.C.: U.S. Government Printing Office, 1964).

(2) U.S. Bureau of the Census, BLS Report No. 394, Current Population Reports Series No. 38, *The Social and Economic Status of Negroes in the United States,* July 1971, p. 23.

(3) U.S. Bureau of the Census, BLS Report No. 347, Current Population Reports No. 347, *Recent Trends in Social and Economic Conditions of Negroes in the United States,* July 1968.

21. John B. Lansing and Gary Hendrick, *Automobile Ownership and Residential Density* (Ann Arbor, Michigan: Institute for Social Research, The University of Michigan, 1967), p. 166.

1960. The lowest percentage was still found in the South. It should be noted, however, that on the national level the gap between White and non-White family incomes was closing — notably in 1967, when non-White family income was reported to be 59 percent of that for White families, a gain of five points. A further narrowing of the White/non-White income differential occurred in 1970 when non-White income was reported to be 61 percent of that for White families. For both of these years, the regional data show similar improvement in non-White income. By 1967, the median family income of non-Whites living in the South was 54 percent of that for Whites, the same as the national White/non-White relationship in 1959; however, it was still the lowest percentage found in any region. Although the southern region's percentage is low, the increase is the highest recorded for any region. Since specific income data are not available for 1965, the 1967 data are assumed representative of 1965 trends. Therefore, with the narrowing of the racial income gap, it appears that some of the income constraints which influenced activity preferences would be minimized. It can be further speculated that as non-Whites increase their financial status, they will increase the variety of recreational participation as well as their participation rates.

As non-Whites participate in a wider range of activities, their participation pattern may be expected to change, so that the distinctions previously associated with race will become minimal. For example, in 1960, when the percentage of population participating in the 17 summer recreational activities was examined, significant regional differences in racial participation were found in the following activities: driving for pleasure, water skiing (in which a larger percentage of Whites participated), and picnics (where the non-White percentage of participation dominated). Although there are no 1960 data on the relationship between income and participation in water skiing, it can be assumed that heavier White participation is related to positive White income differentials. Similarly the extensive White participation in driving for pleasure is related to higher White automobile ownership, a function of higher White incomes.[21] A lower percentage of non-White pleasure drivers can be explained by the lower non-White income and its manifestation, lack of automobile ownership, which precludes participation. On the other hand, costs associated with picnicking are low compared with those for driving for pleasure, a fact which allows for wider participation by those on a limited budget. While a relationship between non-White picnicking and income does exist (one similar to that described for driving for pleasure), non-White picnicking can be better explained by cultural variations.

Cultural Influence on Participation

Traditionally, non-White community life (especially that of Black people) has centered on the non-White church and associated institutions which have traditionally provided this group with nearly all its meaningful social services and activities.[22] This inward dependence was first forced upon Blacks as an outgrowth of slavery, specifically as the result of a lack of social response to their needs after emancipation. Non-White intracommunity dependence provides the group with an identity as well as a sense of security. It may be argued that the American society has matured to the extent that it is responsive to the needs of all persons so that it no longer is necessary for non-Whites to look inward and continue to confine their social (recreational) interaction patterns among their racial peers. However, there is still a strong tendency, as well as a need, for non-Whites to be identified as a group and to interact among themselves. Although this need may be diminishing, it is undoubtedly manifested in the higher non-White participation in picnicking, a recreational activity which provides personal satisfaction while interacting with members of a group who share a common experience. Throughout history, non-Whites have been viewed as a distinct social group and presently, at best, there is national ambivalence about fully accepting non-White Americans into the mainstream.[23] This reluctance to fully accept minority Americans has no doubt adversely affected the scope of non-White participation in recreational activities which are transracial in nature.

Limited non-White participation resulting from segregation and culturally distinct recreational preferences is not evident in regional White/non-White differences in participation observed in 1965. In 1965, significant racial differences in regional participation rates were absent among the 17 recreational activities examined. This lack of racial difference in participation patterns may be attributed to a narrowing of the income gap between the races which occurred from 1960 to 1965. It may also be attributed to the opening of facilities and the civil rights compliance rider accompanying public recreational development grants which are vital to the development of new recreational facilities.[24] With increased recreational opportunities by 1965, the non-White participation patterns are very similar to those of Whites. Similarly, few significant racial differences are found among regions in 1965 when activity days per person and activity days per participant are examined.

When the 1960 activity days per participant for both races are compared, significant racial differences in the frequency of participation are found in ten of the 17 categories, with White participation being more intense.

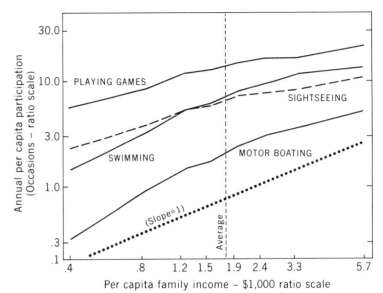

Figure 2. Relationship between income and participation in selected activities for which participation increases with income for both lower and higher than average incomes. (Source: ORRRC, *National Recreation Survey*, p. 67.)

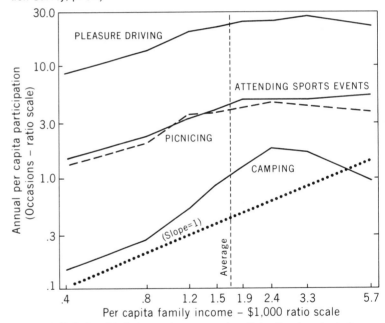

Figure 3. Relationship between income and participation in selected activities for which participation increases with income for lower than average incomes but levels off or declines for higher than average incomes. (Source: ORRRC, *National Recreation Survey*, p. 68.)

22. ORRRC, *Trend in American Living and Outdoor Recreation*, No. 22 (Washington, D.C.: U.S. Government Printing Office, 1962), p. 208.

23. Angus Campbell, *White Attitudes Toward Black People* (Ann Arbor, Michigan: Institute for Social Research, The University of Michigan, 1971), pp. 19–20.

24. *Land and Water Conservation Fund Act of 1965*, PL 88–578, September 3, 1964; and *U.S. Civil Rights Act of 1964*, Title VI, Section 601.

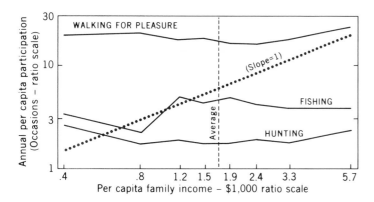

Figure 4. Relationship between income and participation in selected activities for which per capita participation is largely determined by factors other than income. (Source: ORRRC, *National Recreation Survey*, p. 70.)

By 1965, activity days per participant were significantly different only in the bicycling category, further illustrating the narrowing of White/non-White accessibility to nearly all recreational activities examined in this study (table 4). The virtual absence of significant racial difference in regional recreational participation access in all but one of the 17 recreational activities may also be attributed to desegregated facilities along with increased non-White income. In this instance, the greater White participation in bicycling may be attributed to either cultural background or change in White life style, growing out of the increased interest in the quality of the environment. Non-Whites, on the other hand, have not become caught up in the environmental movement and thus would not yet be expected to show a preference for driving for pleasure beyond that expressed by bicycling.

Educational Levels and Participation

An examination of the median school years completed as reported for both races during the 1960s reveals that each group has advanced its level of formal education. Although the White median school years completed remains higher than that of non-Whites, the White/non-White difference has narrowed (table 16). The narrowing of the White/non-White educational gap parallels similar changes in the White/non-White income differential observed during the decade. Undoubtedly, non-White educational gains have contributed to the group's increased recreational participation. A higher level of formal education has made non-Whites more aware of their social and economic circumstances, thereby stimulating this group to rightfully demand an opportunity to participate fully in all aspects of American life, including more participation in recreational activities.

Gains in non-White participation also can be attributed to informal education. It is widely known that through public advertisement, large masses can be persuaded to purchase certain commodities.[25] Utilizing this technique, the federal government has publicized its efforts to stem segregation and to protect the civil rights of its citizens, although many would contend that these efforts have not been adequate. The exposure, however, has been so extensive that few have escaped it. In this manner, non-Whites have been made aware of existing opportunities, undoubtedly triggering desires to share equally in the nation's wealth of recreational opportunities. Indirectly, this desire to participate has been further stimulated by public advertisements which often employ a recreational event or outdoor scene as background.[26]

Table 16. *Median School Years Completed in United States by Race, 1960–1970*

	1960	1970	1960–1970 Change
White	10.9	12.1	1.2
Non-White	8.2	10.2	2.0
White/Non-White difference	2.7 (W)*	1.9 (W)	.8 (N)

* Direction of difference or change: W = white, N = non-White.

Source: U.S. Bureau of the Census, *Statistical Abstract of the United States, 1971*, 92nd Edition (Washington, D.C., 1971).

25. William C. Welch, "Outdoor Recreation Motifs in Magazine Advertisement" (M.A. thesis, University of Michigan, 1966).

26. Vance Packard, *The Hidden Persuaders* (New York: David McKay, 1957).

CONCLUSIONS

The results of this investigation indicate that racial variations in regional recreational participation in the United States existed during the period studied. Specifically, these variations were more evident in 1960 than in 1965, and in nearly every case in which a difference occurred, the variation positively favored Whites. Regardless of the participation measure employed (percentage of population, activity days per person, or activity days per participant) or the specific recreational activity considered, the number of Whites participating was usually larger, as was the rate of participation. Although the level of White participation remained higher than that of non-Whites, non-White participation generally improved in all regions by 1965, greatly diminishing the White/non-White participation gap which was clearly evident in 1960. Increases in the number of non-Whites participating in recreational activities as well as the increased amount of their participation paralleled improved non-White income and education. These increases also may have occurred in response to the opening of new opportunities to a group which previously had been denied full access. It seems that White and non-White preferences for the 17 summer recreational activities matched quite closely for both years considered.

When the recreational preference structure for each racial group was examined over time, it was found that when percentage of population participating and activity days per person are used as input, there was relatively little preference change for either racial group. When activity days per participant were used as data, the preference structure for Whites remained quite stable over time; the non-White preference structure, on the other hand, changed dramatically.

FUTURE PROSPECTS

Future projections indicate that Americans will continue to turn, in increasing numbers, to recreational pursuits. It has been estimated that by the year 2000, participation in the major summer recreational activities will be between three and four times greater than that during the summer of 1960.[27] Furthermore, the fact that non-White increases in participation were slightly higher than those of Whites suggests that non-White Americans will have a greater share in this projected participation than they have had in the past.[28]

The degree of similarity between White and non-White recreational preferences and regional participation patterns, in large measure, will be determined by how fast the White majority is willing to accept non-Whites as full citizens. Discrimination along racial lines

27. BOR, *Outdoor Recreation Trends* (Washington, D.C.: U.S. Government Printing Office, 1967), pp. 5–6; Charles J. Cicchetti, Joseph J. Seneca, and Paul Davidson, *The Demand and Supply of Outdoor Recreation: An Econometric Analysis* (New Brunswick, New Jersey: Bureau of Economic Research, Rutgers University, 1969), p. 207; and ORRRC, *Outdoor Recreation for America* (Washington, D.C.: U.S. Government Printing Office, 1962), p. 47.

28. Cicchetti et al., *The Demand and Supply of Outdoor Recreation*, pp. 202–203.

appears to be the only barrier to full non-White participation in recreational activities. Once eliminated, there would be no significant racial difference in participation.

A full understanding of the role that discrimination has played in determining non-White participation is essential for recreational planners, if their goal is to provide adequate recreational opportunities for *all* American citizens. Too often, American recreational planners and those who make the decisions lack an understanding of the goals of non-White Americans, sharing only the cultural perspective of the White middle-class.[29] This insensitivity leads toward a too rigid posture, based on inadequate information—an attitude which takes either one of two forms. Both of these positions are dangerous if blindly adopted; neither will result in meeting the recreational needs of all American citizens. First, there is the position that non-White Americans possess a separate culture and that recreational programs for non-Whites should be developed outside of the general design. The second position is held by those who think they know how to meet the needs of non-White Americans because they understand "those people." Adherents to this position are those prone to stereotype non-Whites by type and behavior, feeling that they can easily resolve non-White recreational problems. For example, it is possible that one who shares this view assumes that non-Whites do not like to participate in swimming, horseback riding, etc., and prefer to participate in games and other recreational activities which conform to the non-White stereotype. On the contrary, evidence found in the social science literature suggests that non-Whites seem to enjoy a full range of recreational activities once they have the opportunity to engage in these activities.[30]

All evidence suggests that recreational planners need to be fully knowledgeable of non-White preferences and aspirations and of how closely these desires match those of the larger community. Only then can recreational planners design programs and facilities which meet non-White recreational needs. Unfortunately, this goal of achieving racial similarity in regional recreational participation can be reached only when all racial barriers are eliminated.

29. William R. Burch, Jr., "Recreation Preferences as Culturally Determined Phenomena," in B. L. Driver, ed., *Elements of Outdoor Recreation Planning* (Ann Arbor, Michigan: University Microfilms, 1970), p. 62.

30. E. Franklin Frazier, *Black Bourgeoisie* (New York: The Free Press of Glencoe, 1957).

10

**FUNCTIONAL AND SPATIAL
INNOVATION IN THE
DELIVERY OF
GOVERNMENTAL
SOCIAL SERVICES**

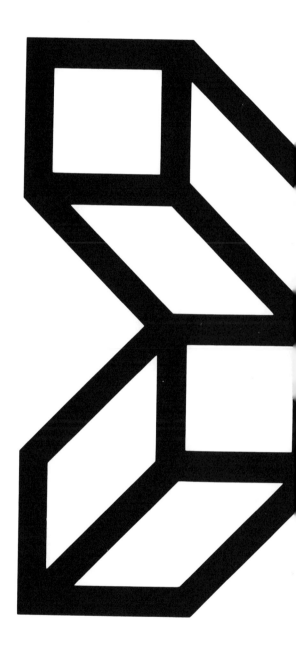

Paul D. Marr
State University of New York, Albany

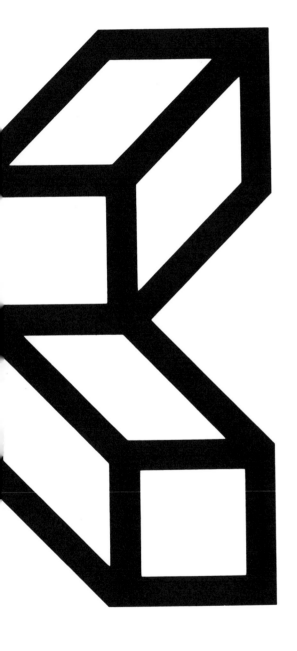

Functional and Spatial Innovation in the Delivery of Governmental Social Services

ABSTRACT

Governmental social services have been a major
means of improving the living conditions of the impov-
erished in the United States. Since the establishment
of social services in the latter part of the nineteenth
century, these services have inadvertently become more
specialized and remote from the clientele they were
intended to assist. The seriously deteriorating condition
of the urban ghettos in the last fifteen years has necessi-
tated a re-examination of welfare services, resulting
in the functional reorganization and spatial reorientation
of these services. However, one of the principal new
forms of delivering social services has countered the
trend to even greater specialization. This is the multi-
service center which provides a variety of assistance
at one location. It has become apparent that many of
the poor require more than one form of aid for themselves or their families and are not sufficiently mobile
to make use of widely scattered welfare facilities.
Consequently, it is considered essential to relocate the
multi-service centers in the areas of greatest need.
In addition to the spatial redistribution of such offices,
it is also considered necessary to increase the density
of assistance in ghetto service areas. One of the principal agencies to reflect these changes is the State of
California Service Center Program. From its original
six facilities, the experience of the San Francisco
service center provides the most illuminating example
of efforts to implement new methods of spatially
distributing social services to an ethnically diverse
population.

Social services,[1] with their broad spectrum of related activities, have been the traditional means of ameliorating the condition of the destitute and the incapacitated. However, the worsening condition of America's urban areas and the social upheavals of the middle and late 1960s cast serious doubt on the effectiveness of this means of assistance. Angry reactions of Blacks and, later, other minorities, to their social and economic environments required that previously accepted methods of delivering social assistance be critically analysed and reformulated into more effective systems. In the course of this process of analysis and reformulation, important changes were also made in the basic assumption that our culture is a "melting pot." This assumption had led to the belief that effective programs could be devised to serve all those in need, irrespective of possibly diverse patterns of culture and life styles. Reactions to the need for new forms of social service resulted in modifying the operational structure and function of welfare agencies. These changes which, in part, included the relocation of public facilities and the regional intensification of services provide a valuable example of the context in which public welfare and the spatial dimension of governmental services intermix. The ghetto conditions that required new approaches for providing social services set off a series of governmental endeavors, seeking to accommodate the particular social needs of inner-city ethnic and poverty groups. The changes in the spatial structure of public services made the location of governmental facilities significantly more interesting by injecting new cultural and social elements into the calculus of spatial decisions and spatial operations.

It is the purpose of this paper to examine how these changes in function, geographic location, and intensity of service occurred. Although a number of organizations were established to deal with this crisis in the provision of social services, attention will be directed to the multi-service center concept and, more specifically, to the experience of the State of California Service Center Program.[2]

DEVELOPMENT AND FRAGMENTATION OF WELFARE SERVICES

The organization of welfare services in the United States originated with the work of Jane Addams who founded Hull House in Chicago in 1889. In a neighborhood of recently arrived immigrants, she provided an array of social services which were directly related to the social requirements of the district. This settlement house was the principal forerunner of contemporary social services which, during the intervening years, expanded and fragmented among a variety of public and private agencies. A seemingly unconscious drift oc-

1. The term "social services" used here includes, but is not limited to, social welfare, employment services, vocational rehabilitation, public health, the emergency provision of subsistence, and referral services.

2. The initial research was performed while the author was associated with the Department of Geography and the Institute of Governmental Affairs of the University of California at Davis. Funding was originally provided by the State of California Service Center Program and the Institute of Governmental Affairs.

curred toward increasingly professionalized and specialized social services which did not always benefit the client as much as the operational efficiency of particular agencies. As a result, family members in need of aid were seldom able to obtain assistance at one facility and might have to visit several offices in their neighborhood, a centralized administrative office, or scattered offices often located with a greater concern for cost minimization than for client accessibility.

The specialization and consequent fragmentation of social services situated in a civic center or in widely distributed offices resulted in a loss of sensitivity to the needs of specific districts and the establishment of a physical barrier of distance between social service offices and clients. Together, these two factors reduced the effective distribution of assistance. Minority people often became hesitant to seek aid if a number of trips to various offices were required, if the affairs of the offices were conducted in a strange or unsympathetic manner, if the offices were situated in culturally unfamiliar neighborhoods, or if the offices were incapable of providing the needed range of assistance. The difficulties of matching assistance to the needs of clients were further aggravated by problems of co-ordination between private and public agencies—whether local, county, or state. The combination of problems in delivering welfare services by agencies and in obtaining welfare services by clients generated an alienation on the part of ghetto dwellers who felt that the agencies were indifferent to their needs. As a consequence, many potential clients did not try to obtain assistance. They became resigned, if not embittered, about their poverty and psychologically turned inward to their neighborhoods.

CHANGES IN THE DELIVERY OF SOCIAL SERVICES

Beginning in the late 1950s and continuing throughout the decade of the 1960s, changes were made which reflected an awareness of serious urban, social, and economic problems which required new solutions. As examples, the Youth Offenses Control Act and the Economic Opportunity Act were passed in 1961 and 1964, respectively. Both sought to provide services directly to the areas of need through offices situated in poverty neighborhoods. The latter program was particularly radical at the time it was established because it provided for the funding of programs administered, in part, by the poor in their own districts. However, it did not significantly resolve the problem of fragmented assistance. Although it did reflect a need to design programs more responsive to the particular ethnic, social, and economic needs of clients, many offices provided only a few services. As a consequence, individuals and family units were still denied ready and comprehensive assistance.

This persistent problem was resolved, however, by experimental multi-service facilities which combined a range of social services in single facilities situated in the areas of greatest need. Thus, in the mid-1960s there again occurred the development of welfare facilities designed to meet the particular needs of neighborhoods by providing a comprehensive array of services similar to those that Jane Addams had endeavored to provide in Chicago over seventy years before. In addition, there was an attempt to combine the talents of a variety of specialized welfare workers into a single operating unit and thereby further to benefit from many of the technical advances that had been made in welfare services during the intervening period.

Multi-service centers were established at local, state, and federal levels of government. The most ambitious was inaugurated by the federal government, but it was subsequently decentralized into quasi-independent units in thirteen cities.[3] The most extensive of the state programs was the State of California Service Center Program which initially operated six offices in the most tense urban ghettos of the state.[4] This program operated from 1966 to 1969 when it was absorbed into the newly formed State of California Department of Human Resources Development. The three-year experience of the California Service Center Program provides a valuable opportunity to observe the spatial aspects of policy changes in the delivery of social services. With this particular program, the State of California sought to accomplish two specific tasks relating to the spatial dimension of public welfare: (1) location of comprehensive welfare facilities in areas of greatest need, and (2) greater intensification of services within ghetto areas through aggressive out-reach and follow-up procedures and through special staffing from poverty neighborhoods.

THE CALIFORNIA SERVICE CENTER PROGRAM

The California Service Center Program was an outgrowth of the 1965 Watts riot in Los Angeles. Immediately following this disaster, the state established employment offices and vocational rehabilitation offices in Watts and in the nearby Mexican-American district of East Los Angeles. Early in the following year it was decided to augment these offices with other state services. However, it became apparent that it was necessary to co-ordinate the activity of the several state agencies by means of common client-processing sections and small supervisory staffs.[5] The combination of formerly independent units of state agencies with the reception and administrative sections became the nucleus of the California Service Center Program. In effect a new service to clients was created, not through the implementa-

3. For a discussion of the federal multi-service centers, see Beck, Pilnick, and Strauss (1967); Burch and Newman (1968), March (1968, 1969); and O'Donnell (1968).

4. For a discussion of the California multi-service centers, see Marr, (1969); and Weschler, Marr, and Hackett (1968).

5. The agencies contributing the largest number of staff to the Service Center Program were employment and vocational rehabilitation. Lesser staff contributions were made by agencies providing services such as social welfare, public health, mental hygiene, parole, youth guidance, fair employment enforcement, and a program for apprenticeship opportunities.

tion of a preconceived idea of social service reform, but because of the necessity of finding a means for increasing the exposure of specialized agencies in a desperate effort to reduce community tension. During 1966, personnel were selected and trained for this new service, and by late in the following year, six offices were operating with staffs ranging in size from approximately fifty to two hundred persons in the larger facilities in Los Angeles. The offices were located in those major urban poverty areas of the state which were considered to have the greatest potential for future riots; viz., Richmond, San Francisco, Los Angeles (Venice and Watts districts), East Los Angeles, and San Diego. Oakland was not included because of plans to establish a federal service center in that city.

The operating philosophy of the California Service Center Program during the formative years of 1966 and 1967 reflected the policies of various state agencies whose units became a part of the program and, to a lesser extent, also reflected the policies of newly developing federal, state, and local multi-service units emerging elsewhere in the country. As the client-oriented concept of the program became clear to its organizers, it was expanded to include, wherever feasible, representatives of local and private agencies in the various field offices to further broaden the range of assistance available to clients. The "supermarket" approach to providing welfare aid in its various forms in the areas of need was considered too passive without further efforts to locate potential clients. As a result, out-reach and follow-up programs were initiated to intensify the delivery of assistance. The programs included the use of staff as community representatives who were to distribute information concerning the program and to seek out persons in need of aid. The follow-up activities were intended to check on the effectiveness of assistance to clients and provide a means of eliciting changes to improve the efficiency of the program. The California Service Center Program, from the viewpoint of pre-existing welfare services, was a major step toward decentralization; but from the viewpoint of the client, it was a new centralized service offering a comprehensive array of assistance in a single facility.

Although the combining of social services in a single facility was a major advance in the provision of welfare, the spatial innovations were equally significant. The enlargement of urban areas and the characteristic location of many governmental services at either governmental centers or least-cost sites often created hardships for persons and families in need of aid. Consequently, the problem of effectively distributing assistance to clients was complicated by social distance between the increasingly professionalized welfare worker and the client as well as by geographic distance. To the newly arrived person or family seeking assistance and to the ghetto dweller unfamiliar with areas beyond his immediate neighborhood, wide-ranging trips to seek aid become in many instances an effective barrier to the delivery of social services. To counteract these situations, the California Service Center facilities were located in poverty areas, thereby changing the mode of coverage from a city-wide orientation of many different facilities to the district orientation of a multiple-service facility. The major criterion for the location of service centers was convenience for its clients, which meant a site as close as possible to the core of the area to be served, taking into account proximity to public transportation (State of California, 1966, Section 260). The most effective site, therefore, was the commercial district of the ghetto where neighborhood traffic patterns customarily converged. A valuable off-shoot of these poverty-oriented locations was the rebuilding of confidence of the local population in governmental services through the presence of service centers conspicuously and conveniently providing local assistance.

The second spatial problem facing the Service Center Program was the necessity for rapid distribution and intensification of assistance within the immediate service areas of the newly established facilities. It was considered an essential part of the new program to disseminate information about the program, to seek out the hesitant who required aid, and to assure an adequate quality of service by providing a feedback mechanism for modifying the program. This aggressive aspect of the program was the result of experience indicating that many persons and families in need of aid were not requesting it because they lacked information on available programs or because they were disenchanted and cynical about welfare programs that they had previously contacted but which appeared to be inadequate. Consequently, the Service Center Program decided to forego the traditional passive provision of welfare services and to use a special staff recruited directly from the immediate district to assist its operational integration into the service areas designated for each of the centers. These staff personnel were usually non-civil-service trainees who performed an array of tasks seldom undertaken by professional social workers but which were considered necessary to assure a more complete delivery of services. Their work included liaison with individuals and groups to disseminate information about the program and to provide the program with valuable information about community feelings and conditions. Their external activities in disseminating information and obtaining clients were termed "out-reach" activities. These were matched by "follow-up" field work concerned with ascertaining whether the assistance prescribed by the center staff was satisfactory to the clients; how long it took to obtain services; and what the apparent reasons were for perceived inadequacies of the program (State of California, 1966, Section 124.2). These activities by non-professionals were innovative at the time they were implemented. They increased the effectiveness of professional case workers and employment specialists and greatly helped to intensify the service of the respective centers in the areas in which they were assigned. The workers bridged the gap between the middle-class oriented professional and clients from the immediate poverty areas. Even Black, Mexican-American, Oriental, and Caucasian professional workers were often in need of "translators" to communicate effectively with the clients of their own ethnic stock.

THE SAN FRANCISCO SERVICE CENTER—
AN EXAMPLE OF FUNCTIONAL CHANGE,
RELOCATION, AND INTENSIFIED SERVICE

Of the six original centers in the program, it is most illuminating to examine the San Francisco service center because it was originally intended to serve a number of ethnically diverse poverty neighborhoods. This center opened in November 1966 with a staff of 45 persons. The staff grew to approximately one hundred within a year and a half and included representatives of eight state agencies concerned with personal welfare and the most frequent problems of the ghetto areas. In time, additional local public and private agencies participated in the activities of the center. Although several agencies had only token representation, their combined services were available at one site and thereby provided the clients with ready access to assistance from one or several agencies. This alleviated the necessity of making time-consuming referral trips to different offices scattered throughout various sections of the city. The integrated approach to providing assistance was a new welfare function of great convenience to the client. It also provided the staff with better insight into how their formerly fragmented assistance could be applied as a single comprehensive prescription of aid for families and individuals. This was a rare opportunity for the staff to experiment and innovate in new formats for providing assistance, and they began their work with great hope of making a major breakthrough in welfare service.

Limited allocations for Service Center Program staff and offices in 1966 and in subsequent years resulted in a single facility being allocated to San Francisco. This office was located strategically in the principal business district of the city's Western Addition—Fillmore District, the city's largest Black neighborhood and poverty district (figure 1). At this site, the Service Center Program was readily accessible to the most critical area of need within the city. A combination of easy accessibil-

Figure 1. Service areas of the San Francisco Service Center.

ity from within the district as well as the special staff of Black aides working in this area assured the center a larger proportionate share of clients from the Fillmore district than from any of the other five poverty districts in San Francisco (tables 1 and 2). The 1967 data indicate that from 39 to 59 percent of the clientele originated from within the immediate Western Addition—Fillmore District. In 1968, the months for which data are available show that the volume of clients from this district ranged between 34 and 48 percent, despite persistent efforts to obtain a greater number of clients from other districts. By comparing the criterion used in the final column of table 2, providing an approximation of the relative distribution of poverty in San Francisco and of the average distribution of new clients, it can be seen that the Western Addition—Fillmore center serves its immediate neighborhood most effectively and that poor populations at greater distances from the center are not always served in direct proportion to their needs.

The other five poverty areas of San Francisco which were to be served by the center in the Western Addition—Fillmore District are, in increasing order of distance from the Service Center, midtown Tenderloin, the racially mixed South-of-Market area, the predominantly Spanish-speaking section of the Mission District, Chinatown and the contiguous Italian North Beach area, and the Black Hunter's Point area. The relatively high percentage of service to residents in the Tenderloin and the South-of-Market areas may be the result of assistance

Table 1. *Distribution of San Francisco Service Center Clients, January 1967 to September 1968**

Service and Non-Service Areas	1967						1968					Total		Families— $3,000 or Less Income Per Year— 1960	
	Jan.	Mar.	May	Jul.	Sep.	Nov.	Jan.	Mar.	May	Jul.	Sep.	No.	%	No.	%
Mission	4	7	9	12	17	5	10	7	18	10	6	105	6	2080	9
South of Market	3	3	4	6	0	8	8	3	1	3	4	43	2	505	2
Hunter's Point	2	4	13	5	8	12	9	9	12	9	5	88	5	1514	6
Tenderloin	1	1	5	8	4	5	7	8	6	4	2	51	3	808	1
Chinatown—North Beach	0	6	9	6	0	4	9	3	4	2	2	45	3	1592	6
Western Addition— Fillmore	49	53	56	69	92	86	110	65	57	77	65	779	44	3646	15
Other San Francisco	24	29	50	67	72	56	80	74	69	64	63	648	37	14866	61
TOTAL	83	103	146	173	193	176	233	169	167	169	147	1759	100	24511	100

*50 percent sample of new San Francisco cases.

Sources: California Service Center Form SC–2A and Bureau of the Census, *Census of Population and Housing:* 1960, Final Report PHC (1)–137, Table P–1.

provided to low-income single persons residing in these two areas. Data on low-income single persons were not included with the family income data because of the lack of suitable stratified income data for single residents in the 1960 census reports. Of equal interest is the increase in clientele from outside the poverty target areas in the city, which reached a high of 44 percent in March 1968. The substantial number of low-income families, approximately 61 percent, who did not reside in any of the six poverty areas indicates that the incidence of poverty is widely distributed in San Francisco. Although the service areas include the most apparent minority-poverty areas, they do not encompass significant numbers of poor persons in the less troubled and less blighted neighborhoods.

The relatively low patronage from the three most distant service areas, Chinatown — North Beach, the Mission District, and Hunter's Point, is apparently a function of the greater distance to the service center and the hesitation of persons from one ethnic district to travel to what is perceived as the service center of another ethnic district. A definite distance decay factor is evident in the low percentage of Blacks from the most distant Hunter's Point area who use the Western Addition — Fillmore center. A trip from Hunter's Point to the Fillmore area using public transportation requires several transfers and an elapsed time of an hour or more. Time, distance, and inconvenience of public transportation evidently also account for the low percentage of

Table 2. *Percentage Distribution of Service Center Clients, January 1967 to September 1968*

Service and Non-Service Areas	1967						1968					Average Percent	Percentage of Families—$3,000 or Less Income Per Year—1960
	Jan.	Mar.	May	Jul.	Sep.	Nov.	Jan.	Mar.	May	Jul.	Sep.		
Mission	5	7	6	7	9	3	4	4	11	6	4	6	9
South of Market	4	3	3	4	0	4	3	2	1	2	3	3	2
Hunter's Point	2	4	9	3	4	7	4	5	7	5	4	5	6
Tenderloin	1	1	3	5	2	3	3	5	4	2	1	3	1
Chinatown–North Beach	0	6	6	4	0	2	4	2	2	1	1	2	6
Western Addition–Fillmore	59	51	39	39	48	49	48	38	34	46	44	45	15
Other San Francisco	29	28	34	38	37	32	34	44	41	38	43	36	61
TOTAL	100	100	100	100	100	100	100	100	100	100	100	100	100

Sources: California Service Center Form SC–2A and Bureau of the Census, *Census of Population and Housing:* 1960, Final Report PHC (1)–137, Table P–1.

clients from Chinatown, North Beach, and the Mission District, but ethnic differences and the lack of equally intense out-reach activities are undoubtedly even more important factors in the low use of the center by persons from these areas. Persistent out-reach efforts by aides of Chinese extraction in Chinatown were particularly discouraging. Efforts to interest persons from this district—the poorest of all San Francisco poverty districts—in visiting the Service Center office, even made by Chinese-American field representatives, met with such small long-term success that such efforts were finally curtailed after a year and a half. The number of clients from the Mission District increased, but it was still proportionately underrepresented. Once Spanish-speaking aides began to work in this area, however, the number of clients from this district began to increase. Antagonism between Black and Brown and the apparent feeling that the Fillmore center is a Black rather than a city-wide center tended to limit the use of the center by Mission District residents.

The foregoing description of the operation of the San Francisco Service Center confirms a basic program assumption that a facility offering a comprehensive array of social services, located in the neighborhood of need and integrated into the community, would attract a greater number of clients from the immediate vicinity of the center than from the city as a whole. Unfortunately, it could not be tested whether a single centrally located facility in a diverse and yet compact city, such as San Francisco, might not actually accommodate a greater number of clients from the entire city. The experience of this center demonstrates that not only is physical distance a barrier to the movement of clients but that ethnic differences and social distance are also barriers to a free flow of clients to welfare offices. The experience of the staff does suggest that the negative effects of ethnic diversity and distance on patronage can be overcome with an aggressive out-reach program. The data are certainly suggestive of the importance of the out-reach program in obtaining a considerable patronage from the Mission District, despite some degree of interracial tension. In the case of Chinatown, however, a persistent effort could not overcome the reluctance of persons of Chinese ancestry to go to the Black neighborhood for assistance, even when services were badly needed by Chinese-Americans. In this instance, the experience of the center indicates that poverty is not always a sufficiently strong binding force to overcome strong ethnic consciousness of diverse populations in a city such as San Francisco. The experience of the San Francisco Service Center also indicates that effective delivery of social services in an ethnically diverse city can only be accomplished by a set of branch facilities ethnically staffed wherever appropriate and operationally integrated with their respective neighborhoods.

OPERATING REALITIES

The service center programs that were developed in the mid-1960s were the product of social crises which stimulated innovations in more effective methods of delivering welfare services to clients. Although many of these programs have persisted, they did not bring about a widespread re-organization of welfare delivery systems. Rather than continuing as the forerunners of major changes in welfare systems, they became viewed as experiments with the implication that they were to be evaluated and not necessarily allowed to develop in the immediate future (State of California Legislature, 1967, pp. 858–73). This was legitimate for a radically new program, but it also led to underfulfillment of the service center programs through a leveling-off of support considered essential to meet the ever-increasing load of clients.

The limitation imposed upon the California Service Center Program is demonstrated in the low number of clients it served in most of its San Francisco service areas late in 1968 (tables 1 and 2). The spatial patterns of patronage supported the opening of new centers or branch facilities, but in 1969 only one branch was being seriously discussed. This was, if authorized by the State administration and legislature, to be situated in the Mission District. During the second year of operation, the San Francisco service center continued to receive new clients but was not able to increase its staff sufficiently to work effectively with its new case load. The center, because of its location and the array of services offered, found itself in an ironic situation. As a state agency it could not exclude clients. Also, as an agency hoping to become more than an experiment, it wished to justify its operation as a regularly functioning welfare program. Consequently, because of its optimal location with regard to clients, it was continually visited by new persons seeking assistance. These individuals were admitted to the program much more rapidly than they or earlier clients could be successfully assisted. In time, the ever-increasing case load became a burden and began to strangle the operational effectiveness of the program. Despite these very difficult problems, various centers continued to experiment with ways of handling clients which would increase the quality and speed of service.

Late in 1969 the comparatively small California Service Center Program was merged into the newly established State of California Department of Human Resources Development, an agency dominated by the former State of California Department of Employment.

237

Although the Service Center Program has officially ended, its six offices have been maintained and its original aggressive, client-oriented philosophy has been specifically written into the legislation establishing the new department. This change offers the opportunity to infuse the original spirit of the Service Center Program into a larger bureaucracy which will have a far greater potential for resolving many of the serious social problems of cities in California.

REFERENCES CITED

Beck, Bertram M., Pilnick, Saul, and Strauss, Helen May. 1967. "Neighborhood Service Centers: A Study and Recommendations." *Examination of the War on Poverty, Staff and Consultants Reports.* Subcommittee on Employment, Manpower and Poverty of the Committee on Labor and Public Welfare, U.S., Congress, Senate, 90th Congress, 1st Session, 3:739–84.

Burch, Hobart A., and Newman, Edward. 1968. "A Federal Program for Neighborhood Services." Paper presented at the National Conference on Social Welfare, San Francisco, California.

March, Michael S. 1968. "The Neighborhood Center Concept." *Public Welfare* 26:97–111.

————. 1969. "Neighborhood Service Centers: Recent Federal Experience." Unpublished manuscript.

Marr, Paul D. 1969. "Staffing Structure of the Service Center Program." Institute of Governmental Affairs, Research Report No. 6. Davis, California: Institute of Governmental Affairs, University of California.

O'Donnell, Edward J. 1968. "A Place to Go and A Place to be From: The Neighborhood Service Center." *Welfare in Review* 6:11–21.

State of California, Legislature. 1967. "Analysis of the Budget Bill of the State of California for the Fiscal Year 1 July 1967 to 30 June 1968." *Report of the Legislative Analyst to the Joint Legislative Budget Committee,* Sacramento, pp. 858–73.

State of California Service Center Program Handbook. 1966. Sacramento, California: State Office of Printing.

Weschler, Louis F.; Marr, Paul D.; and Hackett, Bruce M. 1968. "California Service Center Program: Neighborhood Anti-Poverty Centers." Davis, California: Institute of Governmental Affairs, University of California.

11

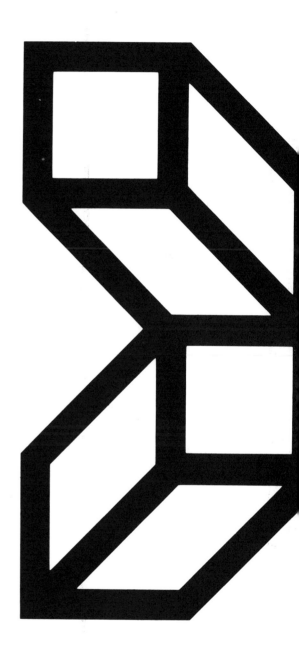

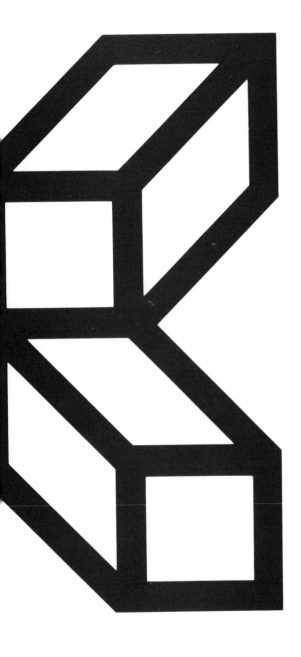

Curtis C. Roseman
Charles M. Christian
Henry W. Bullamore
University of Illinois

Factorial Ecologies of Urban Black Communities

ABSTRACT

Factorial ecologies of the Black residential areas of Los Angeles, Chicago and Milwaukee reveal that five basic dimensions describe much of the variation in socio-economic characteristics of Blacks in these three cities. Four of these factors, economic status, family status, segregation, and in-migration, closely parallel the major dimensions that have been derived in similar studies for *entire* cities. The spatial patterns of the dimensions show striking similarity in the three study areas but do not correspond with the generalized patterns of similar factors derived for cities as a whole. Hence, the aggregate spatial differentiation of Blacks in urban areas has a different spatial character from that of the total urban population.[1]

1. This paper represents the results of but one aspect of a research project supported by the Research Board of the Graduate College, University of Illinois.

In spite of considerable research dealing with Black populations of North American cities, little is known about the spatial patterns of the socio-economic attributes of these populations. Although it is generally agreed that there are significant variations in socio-economic characteristics of urban Blacks (Downs, 1968; Taeuber and Taeuber, 1965, p. 184; Duncan and Duncan, 1957, pp. 297–98), the spatial manifestations of these variations are described in only fragmentary form and thus are not easily understood. As examples, Frueh and Lewis (1971) described the spatial variation of economic and family status factors derived from a factorial ecology of the Detroit Black residential area; Sanders and Adams (1971) analyzed spatial patterns of age structure within the Cleveland Black area; Edwards (1970) described patterns of income and family characteristics in the Milwaukee Black community; and Duncan and Duncan (1957, p. 291) related numerous qualities in the Black community of Chicago to distance from the Central Business District. In terms of obtaining a workable understanding of the spatial patterns of the socio-economic attributes of Black communities, these studies provide sound yet incomplete information.

The purpose of this paper is to synthesize and extend the knowledge in this area by analyzing the factorial ecologies of the Black populations of Chicago, Milwaukee, and Los Angeles in 1960. The results of similar studies for *entire* cities are well known (Salins, 1971). Three factors—economic status, family status, and ethnic status—consistently explain a sizeable proportion of the variance in sets of socio-economic variables, and each factor displays a distinct spatial pattern. The degree to which the Black population differentiates itself along similar dimensions, and the spatial patterns of differentiation, are the major questions underlying this analysis. The role of this paper is viewed as largely descriptive. It is argued that the types of descriptions that are contained herein are both prerequisites for, and supplementary to, the understanding of spatial and social processes operating in the urban area.

STUDY AREAS AND DATA

Socio-economic data were obtained for the non-White populations of the three cities at the census tract level (Bureau of the Census, 1962). In the cases of Chicago and Milwaukee, those tracts within the central cities which contained a minimum of 400 non-White residents and 100 non-White heads of households (a criterion used by the Bureau of the Census for separate enumeration of data on non-Whites by census tract) were used in the analysis. An additional criterion of contiguity was used to delineate the study area in the Los Angeles analysis, thus eliminating some dispersed

Table 1. *Study Areas*

	Number of Tracts in Study Area	Total Non-White Population in Study Area	Study Area Non-White Population as a Percentage of Total Non-Whites in SMSA	Percentage of Non-White Population in Study Areas Identified as Negro
Chicago	229	811,787	88.3	97.3
Milwaukee	29	58,856	89.3	94.7
Los Angeles	164	419,331	71.0	90.9

tracts within the city and including some contiguous tracts in municipalities adjacent to Los Angeles. Elimination of these peripheral tracts significantly reduced the number of non-Whites classified as other than Negro. As noted in table 1, the three study areas contain large proportions of Negro non-Whites and hence, for purposes of the analysis, are considered as Black residential areas. In essence, then, with the exception of a few peripheral non-contiguous tracts in Chicago and one in Milwaukee, the three study areas are each conterminous Black residential areas.

Twenty-one variables were chosen for analysis. They represent a spectrum of income, education, family, occupation, mobility, and segregation attributes of the Black populations within the study areas and provide a comparison with results of factorial ecologies of entire cities and a meaningful profile of the Black populations.

THE ANALYSIS

The variables for each study area were subjected to a principal components analysis.[2] Varimax rotation was employed for those factors whose eigenvalues were larger than 1.0. The results, summarized in table 2, reveal that five factors account for 69.1, 76.3, and 80.1 percent of the variation among the variables in Chicago, Milwaukee, and Los Angeles, respectively. Communalities (table 2), indicating the degree to which the five rotated factors statistically explain each variable, are high for most of the variables in each study area. A notable exception was variable 15, percentage of males unemployed, which is poorly explained in all three cities.

The similarity among the three factor structures is striking. Factors I and II clearly represent aspects of economic status and family status, respectively, for all three cities. Median family income (variable 2), percentage of households headed by married couples (variable 7), percentage of families with income over $8,000 (variable 17), and percentage of families with income under $1,999 (variable 1) consistently display high loadings on factor I. Percentage of the population under 18

2. The factor analysis computer program used in the analyses is described in Dixon (1968, pp. 169–84).

Table 2. *Rotated Factor Matrix**

Variables	Economic Status FACTOR I			Family Status FACTOR II			Segregation FACTOR III		
	Chicago	Milwaukee	Los Angeles	Chicago	Milwaukee	Los Angeles	Chicago	Milwaukee	Los Angeles
1. Families with income under $1,999 (%)	−.728	−.813	.843						
2. Median family income	.927	.911	.919						
3. Dwellings with 1.01 or more persons per room (%)				.780	.694	.832			
4. Dwellings owner-occupied (%)	.786	.859	−.708						
5. Median school years completed	.707		−.738						
6. Population per household				.883	.917	.940			
7. Households headed by married couples (%)	.855	.786	−.711			.561			
8. Total non-white population							−.682	−.802	.885
9. Population under 18 years (%)				.924	.757	.931			
10. Population over 65 years (%)		.593		−.607	−.567	−.634			
11. Labor force employed as professionals and managers (%)			−.759						
12. Labor force employed as craftsmen and opera- tives (%)		.547				.596			
13. Labor force employed as laborers (%)						.525			
14. Labor force employed as private household workers (%)			.583				−.574	−.725	
15. Male labor force unem- ployed (%)	−.569		.725						
16. Females in the labor force (%)		.743		−.586		−.669			
17. Families with income over $8,000 (%)	.837	.835	−.871						
18. Population over five years of age who lived outside the SMSA in 1955 (%)	.471								
19. Population over five years of age who lived in a dif- ferent house within the SMSA in 1955 (%)									
20. Sound dwellings (%)	.557								
21. Non-Whites in tracts (%)							−.831	−.856	.857
Eigenvalue	6.41	7.38	7.38	3.64	3.30	4.74	1.86	2.35	2.12
Percentage of total variance	30.5	35.1	35.1	17.3	15.7	22.6	8.9	11.2	10.1
Cumulative percentage of total variance	30.5	35.1	35.1	47.8	50.8	57.7	56.7	62.0	67.8

*Only factor loadings whose absolute values are larger than 0.5 are presented in this table.

In-Migration FACTOR IV			FACTOR V			Communalities		
Chicago	Milwaukee	Los Angeles	Chicago	Milwaukee	Los Angeles	Chicago	Milwaukee	Los Angeles
						.613	.745	.765
						.902	.905	.902
						.880	.884	.936
						.692	.874	.865
						.802	.692	.860
						.860	.928	.907
						.869	.695	.890
						.670	.762	.830
						.892	.859	.897
−.598		.510				.812	.832	.808
				.613		.444	.657	.771
			.704			.639	.518	.607
				−.882		.484	.900	.728
		.517				.521	.765	.770
						.352	.286	.548
						.675	.759	.724
						.810	.846	.841
					.684	.474	.749	.804
.783	−.826	−.858				.697	.758	.801
			−.554	.577	.602	.679	.675	.684
						.750	.934	.880
1.40	1.65	1.51	1.21	1.35	1.07			
6.7	8.0	7.2	5.7	6.3	5.1			
63.4	70.0	75.0	69.1	76.3	80.1			

years of age (variable 9), percentage of dwelling units with 1.01 or more persons per room (variable 3), and population per household (variable 6) have high loadings on factor II. The emergence of these two factors in Black residential areas is consistent with the findings of Frueh and Lewis (1971) for Detroit and Meyer (1971, p. 337) for Detroit and Memphis. Factor III is essentially a product of the inclusion of two variables which reflect the degree of segregation of tracts—total non-White population (variable 8) and percentage of total tract population which is non-White (variable 21). The appearance of this dimension in all three cities initially suggests that variation in density of the Black population is independent of basic variations in socio-economic structure of the Black population. Percentage of the non-White population over five years of age who moved into the tract from outside of the Standard Metropolitan Statistical Area (variable 18) has the highest loading on the fourth factor in all three study areas. This indicates that settlement patterns of in-migrants tend toward independence from other basic socio-economic dimensions and also from density of the Black population. The fifth factor is not directly comparable among the study areas, except for common loadings of only moderate strength on variable 20, percentage of dwellings classified as sound.

The first four factors parallel those usually derived for entire cities, indicating that there are indeed similarities between the ways that Blacks differentiate themselves in urban space and that of the entire urban population. The factors derived and their spatial patterns are discussed in detail in the following sections.

Factor I—Economic Status

Factor I is the designated economic status and accounts for at least 30 percent of the variation in the variables for each study area. Its composition is similar to comparable dimensions derived for entire cities but may be aligned somewhat closer to income rather than education, partly due to the inclusion of only one measure of education as opposed to three measures of income in this analysis. Nevertheless, there appears to be a weaker relationship between income and education in Black areas than in larger, more heterogeneous populations. The simple correlation between median school years completed and median income is 0.73 for Los Angeles, 0.69 for Chicago, and 0.38 for Milwaukee.

The spatial patterns of factor scores on the economic status dimension are depicted in figures 1–3. In each case there is an increase in economic status with distance from the CBD. In Chicago, the entire range of economic status is spanned as distance increases southward from the CBD, and a range from low to

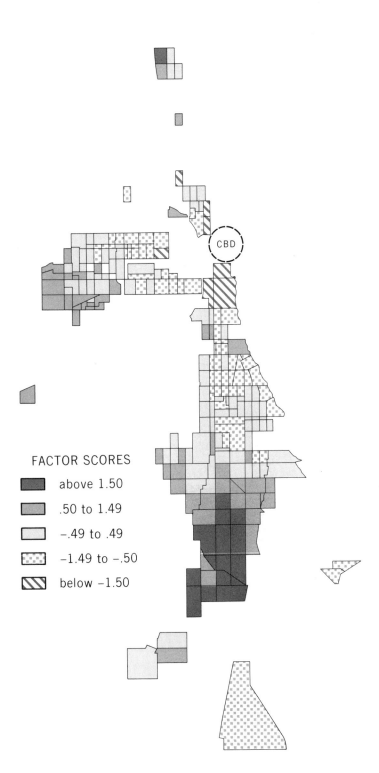

CBD

FACTOR SCORES

- ▉ above 1.50
- ▨ .50 to 1.49
- ☐ −.49 to .49
- ▨ −1.49 to −.50
- ◪ below −1.50

Figure 1. Chicago: Factor 1, economic status. Above 1.50 indicates high economic status.

moderately high status occurs with distance westward from the CBD in the West Side Black area (figure 1). Exceptions to this over-all pattern arise in two non-contiguous areas to the southeast and far south. No significant departures from the general pattern of increase in economic status with distance from the CBD is found in either Milwaukee (figure 2) or Los Angeles (figure 3).

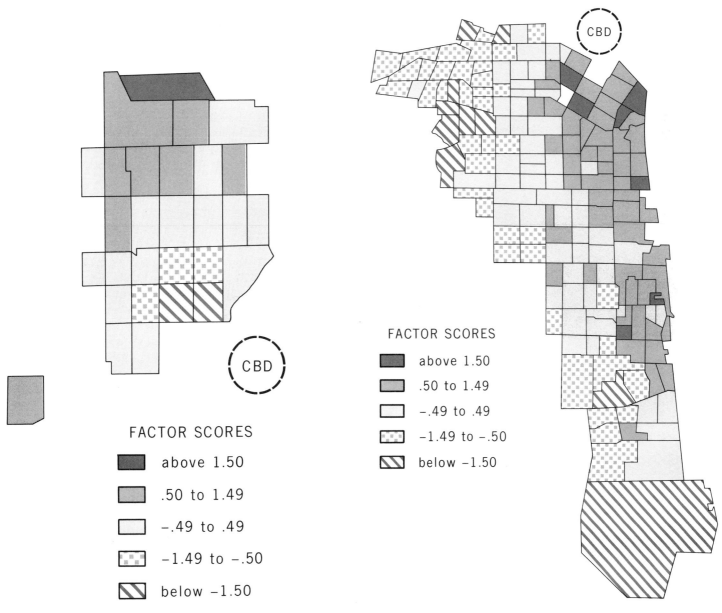

FACTOR SCORES

■ above 1.50

▨ .50 to 1.49

□ −.49 to .49

▥ −1.49 to −.50

▨ below −1.50

Figure 2. Milwaukee: economic status. Above 1.50 indicates high economic status.

FACTOR SCORES

■ above 1.50

▨ .50 to 1.49

□ −.49 to .49

▥ −1.49 to −.50

▨ below −1.50

Figure 3. Los Angeles: economic status. Below −1.50 indicates high economic status.

This degree of consistency of spatial pattern is not surprising—as early as 1937, Frazier identified such a pattern for the Black population of Chicago. More recently, Frueh and Lewis (1971), Meyer (1970, p. 112), and Duncan and Duncan (1957, p. 291) found distinct increases in variables related to economic status with distance from the CBD. Although the pattern seen here is concentric with respect to the city as a whole, the spatial pattern of economic status for entire cities is generally more sectorial in nature. However, no contradiction is argued since it has been recognized that within a single economic sector of a city, there is usually a gradient outward from the center of the city (Johnston, 1971).

Factor II–Family Status

Factor II, designated as family status, accounts for 17.3, 15.7 and 22.6 percent of the variance for Chicago, Milwaukee and Los Angeles, respectively. This dimension is similar to the family status factors derived for entire urban populations and is clearly oriented toward family size and composition attributes, but only moderately related to the percentage of females in the labor force (table 2). Hence, for each of the three cities, tracts maintaining a high loading on this factor are identified as having a large population per household (variable 6), large numbers of children (variable 9), few elderly persons (variable 10), and/or a large number of persons per room (variable 3).

With regard to the spatial expression of this factor for Chicago, there is no clearly discernible pattern and no evident relationship with distance from the CBD, as is normally characteristic of family status dimensions derived for entire cities. Tracts with factor scores larger than 0.5 are found in virtually every distance range from the CBD, as are tracts whose scores are smaller than −0.5. One phenomenon which serves to explain this pattern is the location of public housing. Most tracts with high scores and thus large families and greater numbers of persons per room contained housing projects in 1960. As a result, any conclusions regarding the manner in which Blacks are differentiated spatially with respect to family status must give strong consideration to the location of public housing projects. In Milwaukee there is a concentration of tracts with low scores near the CBD, but high scoring tracts are more dispersed.

The pattern in Los Angeles is somewhat more clearcut. Here, areas immediately to the southwest of the CBD display low scores, and the areas directly south of the CBD, including the Watts district, have a majority of high scores. As in the case of Chicago, the location of public housing may have had a major influence upon this pattern.

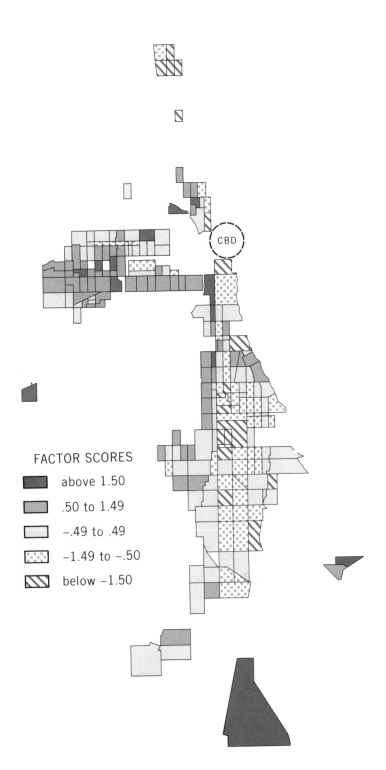

FACTOR SCORES

■ above 1.50

▨ .50 to 1.49

□ −.49 to .49

▨ −1.49 to −.50

▧ below −1.50

Figure 4. Chicago: Factor 2, family status. Above 1.50 indicates large families, young population.

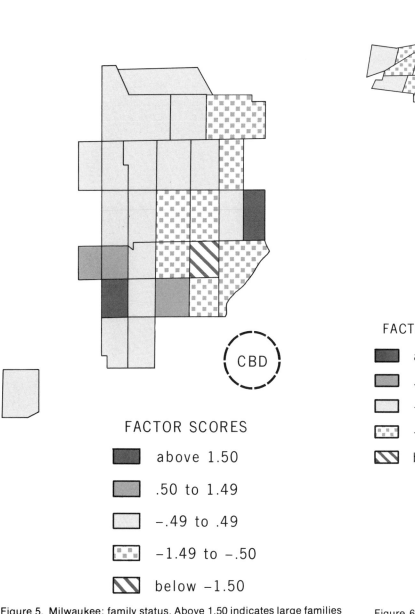

FACTOR SCORES

■ above 1.50

▨ .50 to 1.49

□ −.49 to .49

▦ −1.49 to −.50

▧ below −1.50

Figure 5. Milwaukee: family status. Above 1.50 indicates large families and a young population.

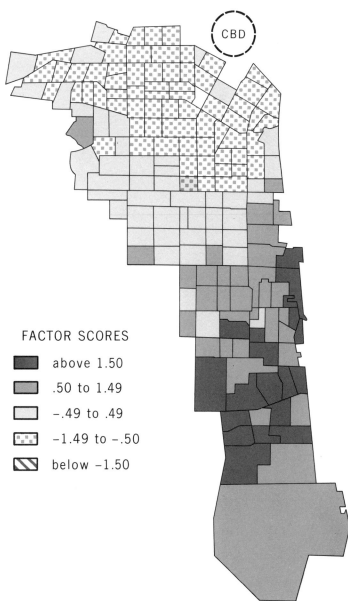

FACTOR SCORES

■ above 1.50

▨ .50 to 1.49

□ −.49 to .49

▦ −1.49 to −.50

▧ below −1.50

Figure 6. Los Angeles: family status. Above 1.50 indicates large families and a young population.

Factor III–Segregation

The third factor accounts for at least 8.9 percent of the variation for each city (table 2). This factor is designated as a dimension of "segregation" because of its consistent relationship with the percentage of total tract population that is non-White (variable 21) and total non-White population (variable 8). In essence, this dimension differentiates tracts with large numbers (and

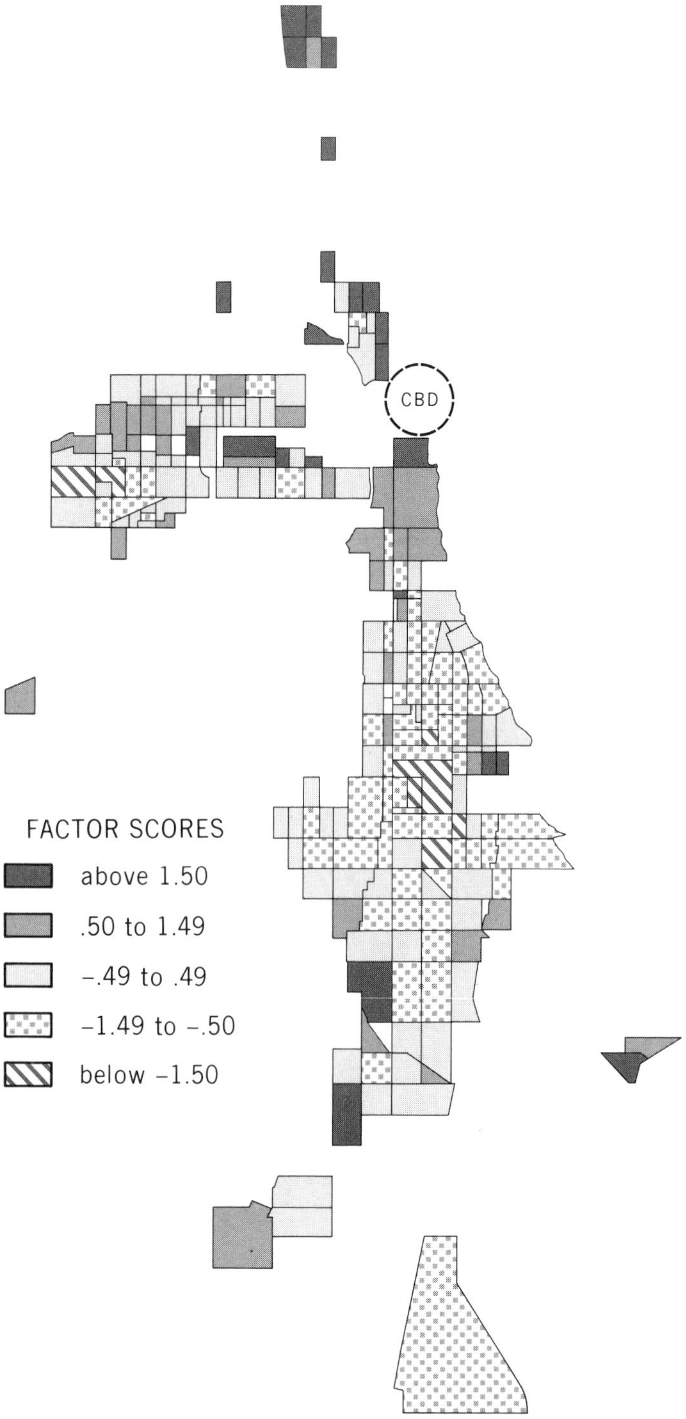

FACTOR SCORES

- above 1.50
- .50 to 1.49
- −.49 to .49
- −1.49 to −.50
- below −1.50

Figure 7. Chicago: Factor 3, segregation. Below −1.50 indicates high segregation.

FACTOR SCORES

- above 1.50
- .50 to 1.49
- −.49 to .49
- −1.49 to −.50
- below −1.50

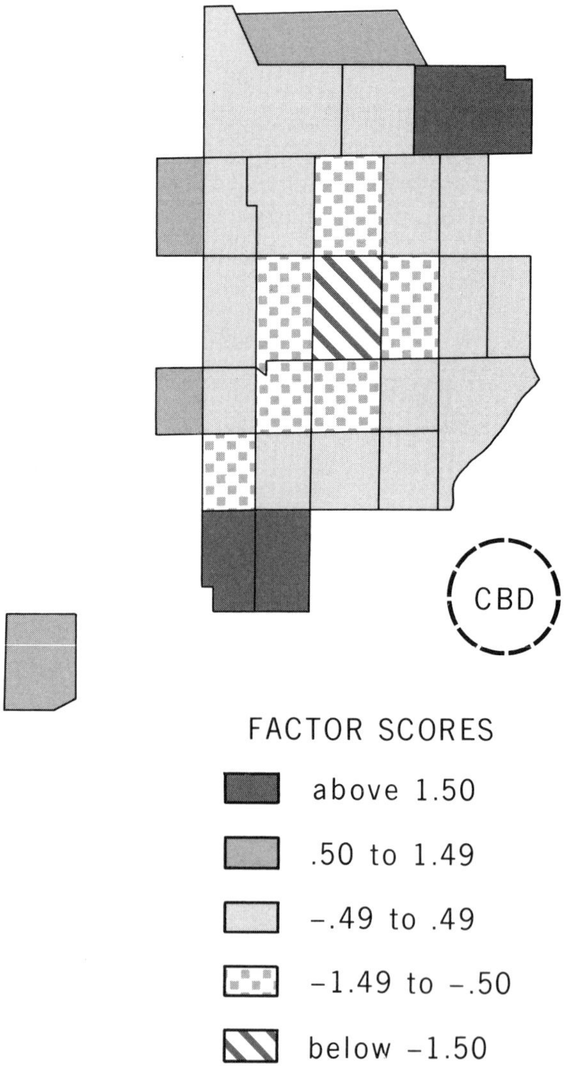

Figure 8. Milwaukee: segregation. Below −1.50 indicates high segregation.

high percentages) of Blacks from tracts which are racially mixed and contain fewer Blacks.

Figures 7–9 reveal a consistent core-periphery pattern in all three cities. Highly segregated tracts tend to cluster near the centers of the cities, whereas racially mixed tracts are generally the most recently entered tracts and occur largely on the edges of the study areas. The spatial patterns of this factor, then, reflect the patterns of Black residential expansion.

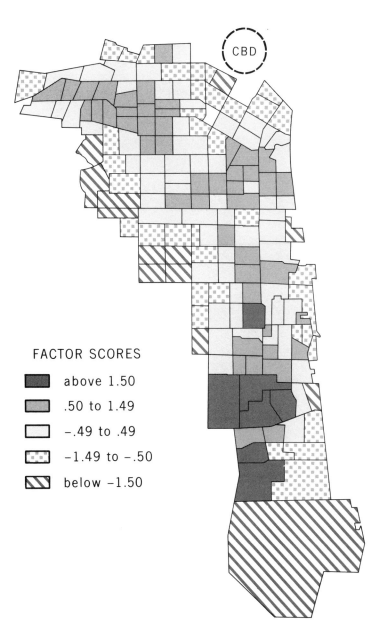

FACTOR SCORES

above 1.50

.50 to 1.49

−.49 to .49

−1.49 to −.50

below −1.50

Figure 9. Los Angeles: segregation. Above 1.50 indicates high segregation.

Factor IV–In-migration

Factor IV is defined by consistent relationships with the percentage of persons over five years of age who lived outside the SMSA in 1955 (variable 19) (table 2). Although a "mobility" dimension is commonly found in factorial ecology studies of entire cities (Berry and Horton, 1970, p. 347; Rees, 1971, p. 230), it usually reflects migration from within, as well as from outside

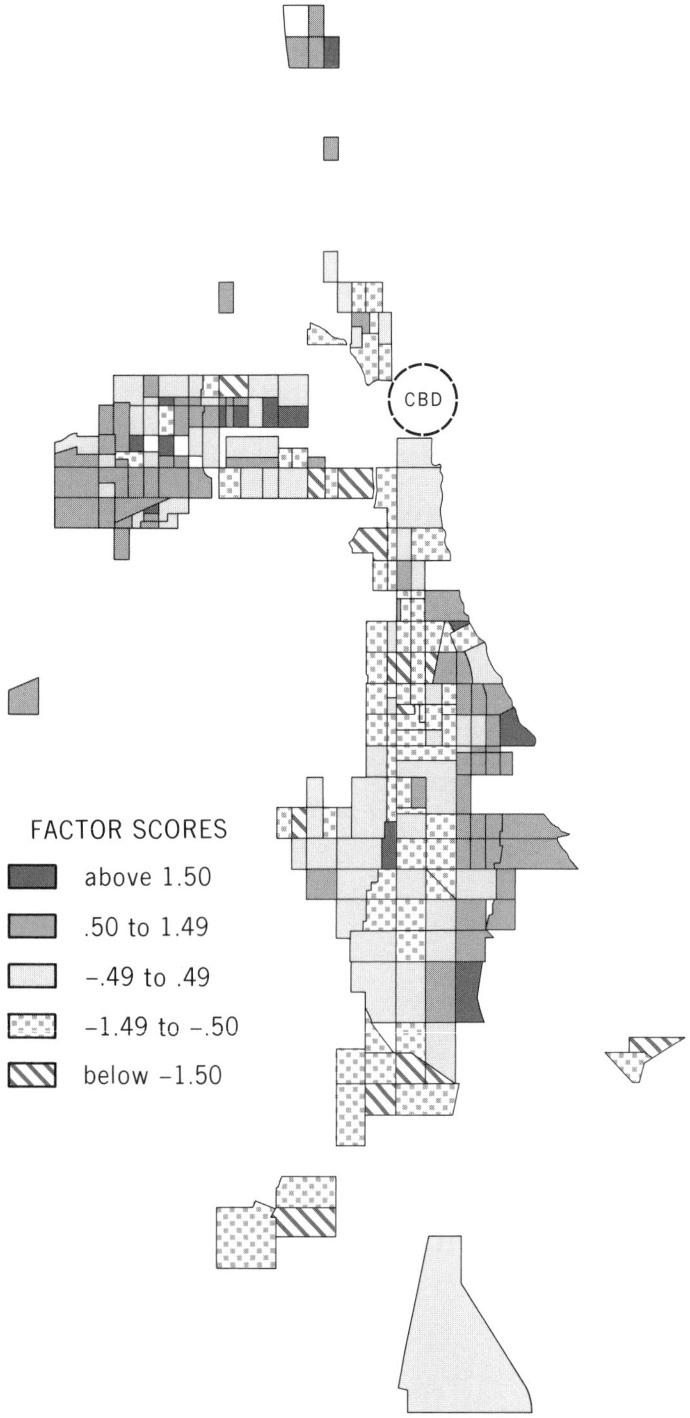

FACTOR SCORES

above 1.50

.50 to 1.49

−.49 to .49

−1.49 to −.50

below −1.50

Figure 10. Chicago: Factor 4, in-migration. Above 1.50 indicates high in-migration.

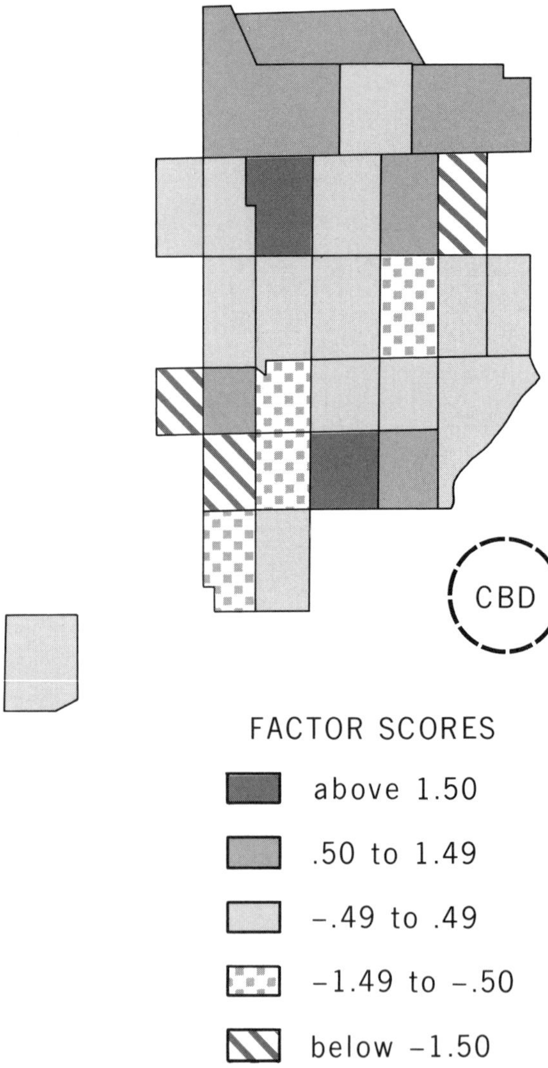

FACTOR SCORES

above 1.50

.50 to 1.49

−.49 to .49

−1.49 to −.50

below −1.50

Figure 11. Milwaukee: in-migration. Below −1.50 indicates high mobility.

the SMSA. Here, identification has been made of a single-variable dimension, which reflects a settlement pattern of in-migrants which is independent of other major socio-economic and density attributes of Black areas. This is witnessed by the consistently low correlations in table 3. Low correlations with migration from within the SMSA are also evident.

Explanation of this relative independence from in-migration lies perhaps in the concept of a "migrant

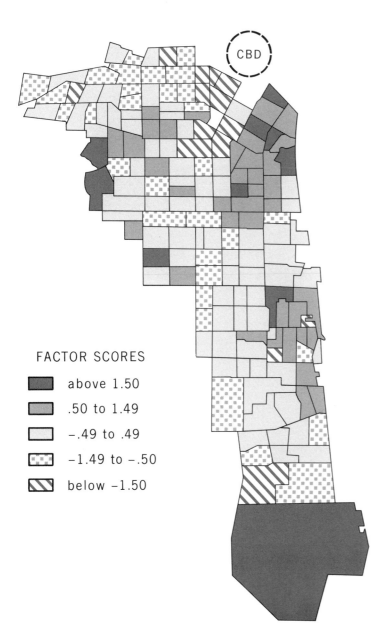

FACTOR SCORES

above 1.50

.50 to 1.49

−.49 to .49

−1.49 to −.50

below −1.50

Figure 12. Los Angeles: in-migration. Below −1.50 indicates high mobility.

Table 3. *Simple Correlations Relating In-migration to Selected Variables*

	Percentage of Tract Population Over Five Years of Age Who Lived Outside the SMSA in 1955		
	Chicago	Milwaukee	Los Angeles
Median family income	−.08	.07	−.02
Population per household	−.05	.24	−.15
Percentage of population non-White	−.14	−.12	−.36
Percentage of tract population over five years of age who lived in another house within the SMSA in 1955	.05	−.28	.06

zone'' (Freedman, 1950, p. 110), an area which receives a disproportionately large number of in-migrants. Although the existence of an intense migrant zone has been questioned (Taeuber and Taeuber, 1965, p. 150), the percentage of in-migrants ranges from near zero to over 23 percent in different tracts within the three study areas, indicating that certain zones play a much greater role in attracting in-migrants than others. The factor score patterns of this dimension (figures 10, 11, and 12) reveal some clustering of tracts with high in-migrant percentages, supporting to some degree the migrant zone concept. In Chicago, major clusters of in-migrants are found on the far West side and south of the CBD near Lake Michigan (figure 10). In Milwaukee, five tracts on the southwest side of the study area have high in-migrant characteristics, and in Los Angeles, a cluster is found immediately to the southwest of the CBD. Other tracts receiving high proportions of in-migrants are rather widely scattered throughout the study areas.

Factor V

In each study area a fifth factor emerges above the 1.0 eigenvalue cut-off (table 2). It is related to occupational categories — craftsmen and operatives (variable 12) in the Chicago analysis, and laborers (variable 13) in the Milwaukee analysis. In Los Angeles, it is related to migration from within the SMSA (variable 18). Factor V is also related, to a lesser degree, to the percentage of dwellings classified as sound (variable 20). Maps of this factor reveal no discernible (nor explainable) pattern.

SUMMARY AND PROSPECT

These analyses have revealed that five basic dimensions describe much of the variation in socio-economic characteristics of Blacks in three metropolitan study areas. Four of these dimensions are essentially identical, both in composition and degree of importance, for all three cities. In addition, they closely parallel the major dimensions that have been derived in similar studies for entire cities. The spatial patterns of these dimensions show considerable similarity in the three study areas but do not correspond with the generalized patterns of parallel factors derived for cities as a whole.

Explanation of these patterns lies in the investigation of the various processes underlying the residential location decisions of urban Blacks and is therefore beyond the scope of this study. However, the results cited above suggest that the same basic processes exist but that the locational patterns resulting from these processes are quite different, due to the nature of constraints and choices confronting Blacks. In the case of economic status, spatial differentiation among Blacks is much the same as that among total urban populations; however, it is expressed in a spatial pattern that is concentric with respect to the center of the city. Variations in the nature of the housing market at differing distances from the CBD and the outward expansion of Black residential areas have influenced this pattern. The spatial distribution of family status for the Black population is strongly influenced by the location of public housing and thus disguises any "natural" spatial differentiation. The spatial pattern of the segregation dimension is a distinct reflection of the process of expansion of Black urban space, and the spatial pattern of the in-migration dimension suggests the existence of clusters of neighborhoods that act as "reception areas" for Blacks entering from outside of the SMSA.

REFERENCES CITED

Berry, Brian J. L., and Frank E. Horton 1970. *Geographic Perspectives on Urban Systems.* Englewood Cliffs, New Jersey: Prentice-Hall.

Dixon, W. J. ed. 1968. *BMD Computer Programs Manual.* Los Angeles: UCLA Press.

Downs, Anthony 1968. "Alternative Futures for the American Ghetto." *Daedalus* 97: 1331–78.

Duncan, Otis Dudley, and Beverly Duncan 1957. *The Negro Population of Chicago.* Chicago: University of Chicago Press.

Edwards, Ozzie 1970. "Patterns of Residential Segregation Within a Metropolitan Ghetto." *Demography* 7: 185–92.

Frueh, Linda K., and Lawrence T. Lewis 1971. "A Factorial Analysis of the Black Community of Detroit." Paper read at the Association of American Geographers, West Lakes Division, annual meeting. Iowa City, Iowa.

Johnston, R. J. 1970. "On Spatial Patterns in the Residential Structure of Cities." *Canadian Geographer* 4: 361–67.

Meyer, David R. 1970. *Spatial Variation of Black Urban Households.* Research Paper No. 129 University of Chicago, Department of Geography.

———. 1971. "Factor Analysis Versus Correlation Analysis: Are Substantive Interpretations Congruent?" *Economic Geography* 47 (Supplement): 336–43.

Rees, Philip H. 1971. "Factorial Ecology: An Extended Definition, Survey, and Critique of the Field." *Economic Geography* 47 (Supplement): 220–33.

Salins, Peter D. 1971. "Household Location Patterns in American Metropolitan Areas." *Economic Geography* 47 (Supplement): 234–48.

Sanders, Ralph A., and John S. Adams. 1971. "Age Structure in Expanding Ghetto-Space, Cleveland, Ohio, 1940–1965." *Southeastern Geographer* 11: no. 2: 121–32.

Taeuber, Karl E., and Alma F. Taeuber. 1965. *Negroes in Cities.* Chicago: Aldine Publishing Company.

U.S. Bureau of the Census, 1967. *U.S. Census of Population and Housing: 1960 Census Tracts.* Washington, D.C.: U.S. Government Printing Office.

12

SOME COMPARATIVE ASPECTS
OF THE WEST AFRICAN
ZONGO AND THE BLACK
AMERICAN GHETTO

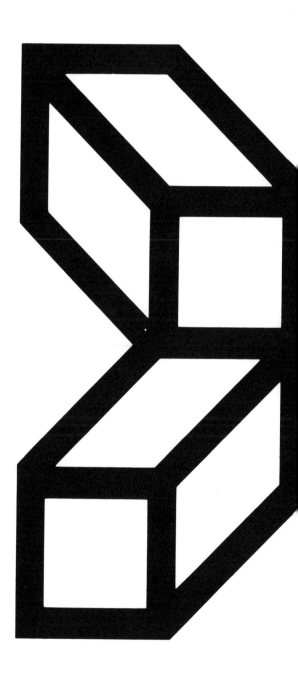

Barfour Adjei-Barwuah
Indiana University

Harold M. Rose
University of Wisconsin

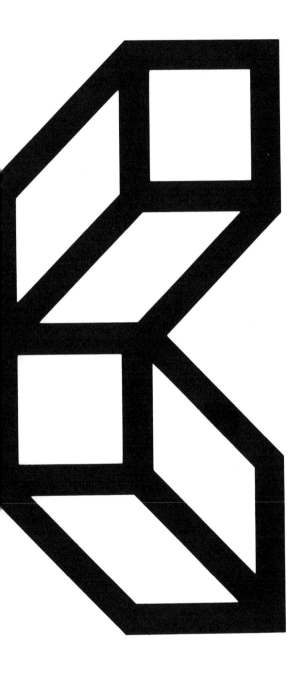

Some Comparative Aspects of the West African Zongo and the Black American Ghetto

ABSTRACT

The zongo is a residential enclave within selected West African cities which serves as the place of residence for recent migrants to the city. While the zongo is not the exclusive preserve of the Hausa, it is members of their ethnic group who dominate the economic life of this segment of urban space. In many ways the zongo is similar to the Black ghetto which is a commonplace racial residential enclave in large American cities. This paper attempts to point out both conceptual and concrete similarities between these urban residential configurations by citing examples from Ghanaian and Nigerian cities and comparing them with American ghettos in general and the Louisville, Kentucky ghetto as a specific case. Observations made here reflect the importance of both culture and race on the evaluation and maintenance of ethnic specific territories.

The evolution of urban residential enclaves occupied by persons of common social class and ethnic and/or racial origin is common in many areas of the world. Such group affinity expressed via the mechanism of spatial clustering fosters the evolution of patterns which are highly pervasive in their impact on the fabric of urban life. In this instance an attempt will be made to compare a set of identifiable residential enclaves occurring in West African and American cities. The principal purpose of investigation is to determine what forces are responsible for the evolution of highly segregated, territorially based Black communities in American cities vis-à-vis ethnic communities of similar form in West African cities. A review of the forces which operate to promote the evolution of the residential enclaves, identified as the zongo and the ghetto, should shed light on the role of race and ethnic characteristics in the formation of territorial entities inhabited by Black Africans and Black Americans under quite different economic and political structures.

To date the spatial structure of the West African[1] zongo has received only limited attention. However, this is simply a result of the meager knowledge of the internal structure of West African cities in general, excluding Mabogunje's detailed analysis of Ibadan. Mabogunje has attributed the inability to describe precisely the structure of small areas in Nigeria to the large size of the data-collecting unit employed—from 10,000–60,000 persons (Mabogunje, 1968). The American ghetto has only recently become the frequent object of investigation by researchers representing a territorial perspective. Nevertheless, work completed since the early 1960s has led to a sound understanding of the spatial structure of the ghetto. Thus, one of the purposes of this investigation is to determine the congruency between these phenomena at a time when there exists a heightened desire on the part of Black Americans and Black Africans to understand their individual plights and to strengthen their linkages.

THE ORIGIN OF THE ZONGO

Barbour and Prothero (1961) contend that in every Ghanaian town of any size there exists a zongo where African strangers live. While this statement might be questioned by some and thought by others to be an exaggeration, it does point out the ubiquity of this urban residential configuration in Ghana and in Nigeria.[2] Although it is generally true that the zongo is a residential area set aside for African strangers, it should also be pointed out that zongos are more specifically identified with the Hausa people than with any other group. Acquah (1958), for instance, identified the zongo in Accra as essentially a Hausa stronghold with Hausas

1. The term "West Africa," as employed in this paper, refers only to Ghana and Nigeria. It is only in the major cities of these countries that the zongo is a readily identifiable segment of internal urban structure.

2. In Nigeria the term "Sabon Gari" (New Town) is used instead of "Sabon Zongo." In this paper the Ghanaian term "zongo" is used interchangeably with the term "Sabon Gari" or Sabo.

constituting about 44 percent of the total population. Cohen (1967) also observed that of all the "native" strangers in Ibadan, the Hausa stand out as the most exclusive, sharply delineated ethnic group with the majority of them clustered in one sector of the zongo, even though the Hausa were among the first of the migrant "strangers" to settle in Ibadan.

The Role of the Hausa in Zongo Development

A number of factors can be employed to explain this ethnic exclusiveness which serves as the basis for the existence of the zongo. The first of these is the external pressure applied by the indigenous society. It must be remembered that the population of the zongo is made up predominantly of migrant laborers who are alien to the towns in which they are located. The growth of the zongo, then, can be fostered or hindered by the attitudes and actions of the indigenous people. In the case of Ibadan, Yoruba chiefs in 1907 demanded that the Hausas be required to live in a special settlement allotted to them. The British colonial administration, yielding to Yoruba pressure and also in furtherance of its policy of indirect rule through local authorities, acquiesced in this plan. The settlement of the present Hausa quarter thus began in 1916.

In Accra, the Hausas were originally located in such areas as James Town, Tudu, and Ussher Town. These were areas principally occupied by the indigenous Ga population. They were the older, settled parts of the city, which were already congested, and thereby offered little possibility for Hausa territorial dominance as long as the population replacement process was inoperative. However, in order to ease the congestion in these areas, the Hausas were encouraged to move out and settle in the zongo (see figure 2).

This official encouragement of Hausa exclusiveness should not be construed to mean the enforcement of strict ethnic segregation. Even in Ibadan where a policy of segregation was in existence, it was never strictly enforced. Since the 1930s, individual Hausas have managed to live in other parts of the city if they so desired, and non-Hausas have never been actively prevented from living in the zongo. The same applies to Accra and Kumasi. The New Zongo area of Kumasi, for instance, is anything but a Hausa stronghold (see figure 1).

The second and most important reason for the ethnic character of the zongo is the residents' feeling that their sojourn in the cities will be temporary and the resultant desire on their part to "cling together" as a means of preventing their assimilation into the culture of the indigenous peoples. The Hausa, especially, usually regard themselves as temporary residents, and thus it is only natural that they should maintain some measure of

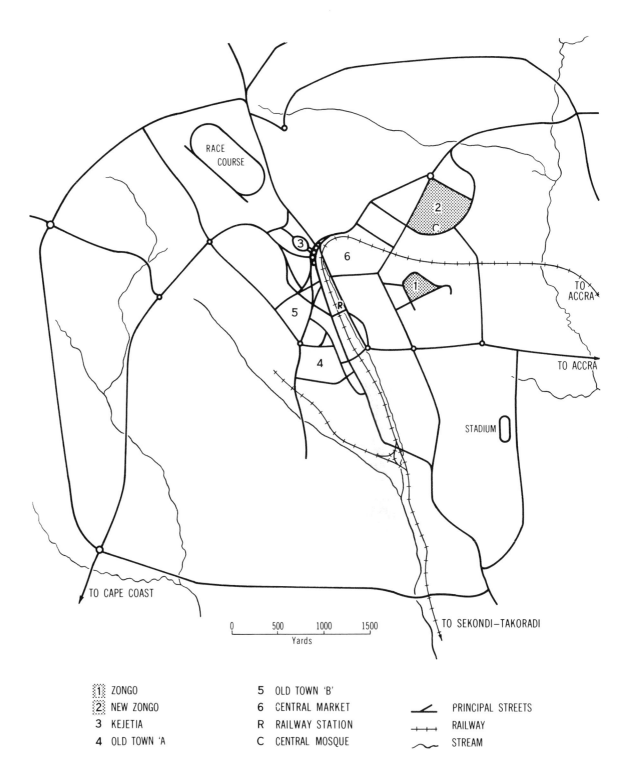

1   ZONGO
2   NEW ZONGO
3   KEJETIA
4   OLD TOWN 'A
5   OLD TOWN 'B'
6   CENTRAL MARKET
R   RAILWAY STATION
C   CENTRAL MOSQUE

PRINCIPAL STREETS
RAILWAY
STREAM

Figure 1. Central Kumasi—location of the zongo.

cohesion in order to preserve those things that are culturally meaningful to them. Hence in Ibadan, for instance, during the 1930s and 1940s, the Hausas petitioned the city to compel the Hausa population which had dispersed itself throughout the city to return to the zongo, although the zongo was already congested.

This tendency toward voluntary separation may be better understood if it is realized that most of the residents of the zongo are Muslim by religion, whereas most of the cities in the southern areas of West Africa (where the zongo has become a *fait accompli*) are essentially populated by persons of non-Islamic faith. The one major exception is Ibadan which in 1952 was approximately 60 percent Muslim (Mabogunje, 1968, p. 219). Thus, clustering is employed as a very effective mechanism to organize and preserve religion. It should also be pointed out that the Hausa of Ibadan have strengthened their ethnic exclusiveness as a result of threats to abolish the Sabo by joining the Tidjaniyya order of the Islamic faith. This order is a highly ritualized segment of the Islam religion (Cohen, 1969, p. 125).

It should also be recognized that in clinging to an exclusive segment of the urban space, the migrants gain some political recognition and rights. For instance, in Kumasi, the zongo has representation on the city council; and on enskinment, the Zerikin Zongo (the official head of the zongo community), swears allegiance to the Asantehene; an act which might be interpreted to mean that the Zerikin Zongo is a recognized divisional chief in the traditional organization of the city.

Hausa enterprise could also be considered one of the important factors underlying the persistence of the zongo. Many Hausas serve as middlemen, hotel keepers for transient populations, and, often, one-man employment agencies. The mutuality of economic interest goes a long way to foster ethnic separatism. Thus, a combination of forces revolving around Hausa ethnicity and their role in the urban economic structure of selected West African cities abets the development and maintenance of the zongo long after it has fulfilled its role of providing temporary housing for migrants representing the nonregional dominant tribal zones.

The zongo, then, is a phenomenon which has emerged as an outgrowth of the flow of migratory labor from North to South in West Africa. Though its initial establishment might have been promoted by official and semi- or unofficial policies and attitudes, it is true that its growth and endurance have been the result of the voluntary desire of the residents to remain distinct —in dress, diet, religion, language, and culture in general—and at the same time to maintain economic power and advantage and, in some cases, also to reap political benefits.

THE ZONGO AND THE GHETTO: CONGRUENT OR NON-CONGRUENT SPATIAL ENTITIES?

In attempting to compare the ghetto with the zongo, it is advisable to distinguish between the original ideas of the ghetto as it existed in Europe and the Black ghetto as it presently exists in American cities. According to Wirth (1928), the ghetto concept originated as a European urban institution aimed at separating the Jewish population from other segments of the European population by confining them to the walled sectors of the cities. If the original definition is adhered to, the ghetto in America was best exemplified in the South following the abolition of slavery when, in most places, legal and extra-legal sanctions were used to effect specific ethnic patterns of residential location. A street or railroad track usually served as the physical barrier employed to separate the races.

It is the type B ghetto, the typical Black residential enclave in cities of the American South (Rose, 1969, p. 327), rather than its northern counterpart, which most closely resembles the zongo. The type B ghetto is similar to the zongo in a number of ways, but the most important fact is that the zongo is not a zone of population replacement. Similarly, the housing in the older settled areas is often of vernacular form. The one basic difference is the larger proportion of Black Americans found in the total population of southern cities than that of the Hausa populations in West African cities, despite the migration of Hausas from the northern regions of both Ghana and Nigeria to southern cities. Like the zongo, the ghetto is a territorial manifestation of the unwillingness of culturally dissimilar groups to share a common residential space. However, although the zongo is both by definition and character an area of strangers, it is very doubtful that this definition may be validly applied to the ghetto, since the term *strangers* in this instance frequently refers to persons of alien background or of foreign national identification.

The development and persistence of Black ghettos in American cities is buttressed by the explicit recognition of Blacks, by Whites, as persons possessing life styles which the Whites hold in very low esteem. It is this White belief and the attitudes which thus emerge which foster behavior that leads to White abandonment of residential areas after Black entry surpasses a minimum critical level. The ghetto-forming process can be recognized simply as a system whereby the Black populations serve as a replacement population for "fleeing" White populations in contiguous residential space; a condition which during the past decade has also been observed in cities in the American South. Thus, the type B American ghetto is beginning to converge with the type A configuration common to cities of the American North.

As a phenomenon directly resulting from discriminatory realty practices, the ghetto may be seen as the consequence primarily of the individual and collective attitudes of White Americans. However, it should be recognized that the persistence of the ghetto is more a function of the operation of the housing market than that of any other single economic or social subsystem. The difficulty with which Blacks obtain mortgage loans, the often inflated prices at which property is sold to Blacks (the so-called color tax), and the phenomenon of block-busting have all contributed to the relative immobility of the Black population within the larger urban community and have thereby insured the endurance and growth of the ghetto.

It is interesting to note that the growth of the ghetto, like that of the zongo, is strongly influenced by migratory behavior. There is little doubt that the rapid rise of the Black ghetto in northern cities in the United States is directly linked to an increase in the general mobility of the American population as a whole and the increased propensity of Black Americans to enter migration streams. It is pertinent to observe that, like their counterparts in West Africa, Black Americans who enter migration streams are largely motivated by economic considerations. But seldom do the Black migrants view their decision to uproot themselves from the cultural hearth simply as a temporary measure designed to permit them to acquire wealth, eventually hoping to return to the area of origin to live out their lives. This is a major distinction between migrating Black Americans from southern rural areas and migrating West Africans from northern rural areas. Both the zongo and the ghetto are the products of migration and are ethnically specific areas of the urban territory. The mechanisms that produce both phenomena are associated with social, economic, and, sometimes, political variables which individually and jointly create the necessary climate for their growth and endurance.

Both the zongo and the ghetto may be regarded as manifestations of social pluralism, if by social pluralism one means the involuntary operation of a set of forces designed to minimize social interaction between groups possessing differences in ascribed status. However, in the case of the zongo, these forces are generated *by* the residents, who, regarding themselves as alien, adopt a strategy of ethnic exclusiveness designed to support the economic and political objectives of the Hausa territorial community. In the case of the ghetto, the historical strategy has been one designed to foster assimilation rather than separation. However, the unwillingness of the larger society to accept the Black minority as equals led to the development of territories where members of the group were permitted to interact socially only with one another. At this stage in the development of the

265

zongo it appears that a situation which might have originally represented a condition of social pluralism has now emerged into a state of cultural pluralism. The culture of the zongo is native to the residents of the area and alien to the remainder of the urban population. But, as Cohen (1969, p. 50) has previously indicated, the culture of Sabo (zongo) Hausa is distinct from the culture prevailing in the area of migrant origin. The Sabo (zongo) culture has evolved essentially as an adaptive mechanism which has permitted Hausa tribesmen to survive successfully in an alien environment.

Ghetto culture, while possessing many unique attributes, is more often viewed as a cultural variant which might be more properly described as an American subculture. The extent to which aspects of the subculture dominate the life style of the group's members is inextricably linked to social class status. In this regard ghetto Blacks have pursued a strategy more similar to that employed by the Ibo in western Nigerian cities than to that of the Hausa. Nevertheless, the culture traits, which are in some measure group specific, have evolved out of a condition of social isolation. As is true with Sabo (zongo) Hausa, an American ghetto culture has evolved which can in many ways be distinguished from the culture prevailing in the rural south, the zone of early migrant origin.

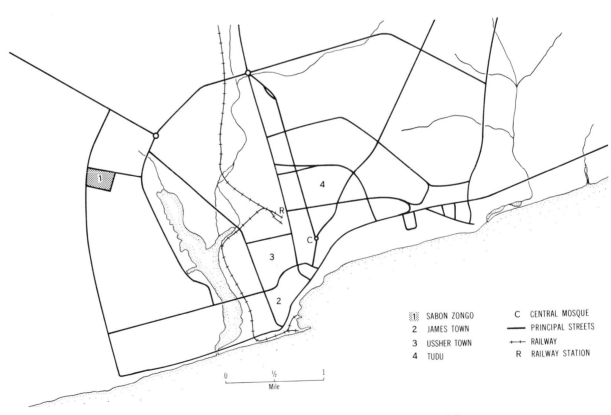

1	SABON ZONGO	C	CENTRAL MOSQUE
2	JAMES TOWN	—	PRINCIPAL STREETS
3	USSHER TOWN	+—+	RAILWAY
4	TUDU	R	RAILWAY STATION

Figure 2. Central Accra—location of the zongo.

Locational Characteristics and Physical Character of Residential Accommodations

The zone of Black concentration in American cities varies in its spatial pattern as a function of region of origin and topographic characteristics of place. The ghetto is often situated in older central city locations from which it tends to expand. In a number of major American cities, the ghetto is characterized by many polynucleated settlements of varying size, although one or two major settlements represent the modal class. The spread of the ghetto in any given direction is conditioned by the presence of a hostile population in contiguous space; the presence of luxury housing in the wake of ghetto expansion; and/or the presence of physical barriers. Initially, the centralized location of the ghetto was advantageous because it placed a low-income population in close proximity to sources of employment, although these ghetto locations were frequently characterized by blight and slum conditions. These initial locational advantages are steadily weakening, as employment sources join the flight to suburbia. Among southern cities there are still some examples of isolated Black communities located near the periphery of the built-up area. These areas are similar in character to ethnic communities located along the margins of West African cities.

As in the case of the ghetto, the zongo is also characterized by a variable locational pattern. However, the zongo is most often situated in the "newer" sections of town. It is generally found on the "outskirts of town" as in Ibadan and Accra (see figures 2 and 3). In this case, "the town" refers to the older settled parts of the city. Some writers contend that cities in developing areas have a characteristic tendency for immigrant slum areas to evolve on the outskirts of the city. However, it must be remembered that "outskirts," as used in connection with the zongo, differs from the idea of "being on the fringes of the metropolitan area." It may also be recognized that in both Accra and Ibadan the location of the zongo has been the result of deliberate policy; an attempt to ease congestion in the former and the response to political pressure in the latter. The location of the central mosques in both cities, in relation to the peripheral location of the zongos, illustrates the illogical, although necessary, location of the zongo.

The Kumasi zongo offers a departure from this general pattern. Instead of being in one of the old towns (see figure 1), it is located in a comparatively new section of the older part of the city. However, the location of this zongo is basically related to the location of the central market and the Kejetia (central truck park). Many of the residents of the zongo are wholesale merchants dealing in such commodities as smoked meat, fish, and kola nuts; some own businesses in the market

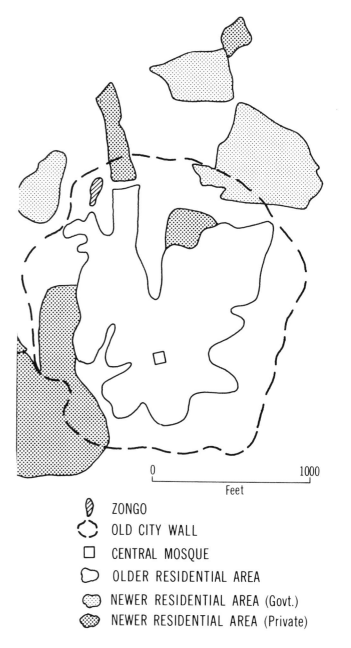

ZONGO

OLD CITY WALL

CENTRAL MOSQUE

OLDER RESIDENTIAL AREA

NEWER RESIDENTIAL AREA (Govt.)

NEWER RESIDENTIAL AREA (Private)

Figure 3. Ibadan—location of the zongo. (After map 6 in Lloyd et al.)

and a large proportion work as kaya kaya (common carriers) in both the market and the Kejetia. Thus the zongo in Kumasi, in terms of location, resembles the American ghetto more than the zongos in Accra and Ibadan.

What is common to the zongo and the ghetto, especially in their core areas, are poor housing and generally unkempt conditions. In the case of the ghetto, the substandard quality of housing is usually related to the fact that the ghetto population is a replacement population, occupying buildings that were already beginning to decline prior to Black entry. If they are older, type B ghetto communities, the housing was intended to have a short life expectancy. The maintenance of property is usually poor, either because of the lack of necessary financial resources on the part of homeowners or because of the indifferent attitudes of some non-resident owners of rental property, sometimes described as "slum lords."

The quality of housing in the zongo, though affected by age, is usually the result of poor construction and indifferent architecture. This is understandable if one takes into account that a population which considers itself alien and temporary is unlikely to invest in permanent and architecturally pleasing housing units. It is also relevant to note that most people in the zongo tend to emphasize savings and therefore would be disinclined to invest a large part of their earnings in housing. After all, the average migrant laborer is expected to return home with evidence of relative prosperity—this

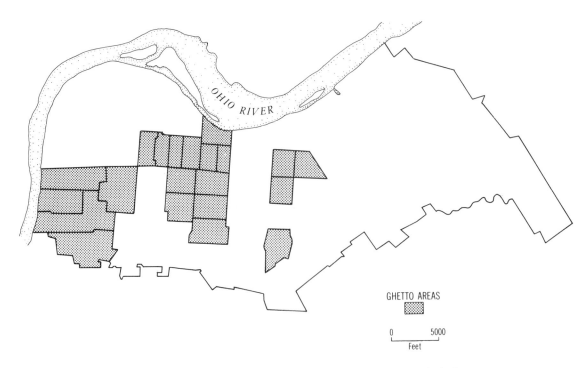

Figure 4. Central Louisville—location of ghetto areas.

is usually expressed in the acquisition of material items such as bicycles, motorcycles, etc., or hard cash which is to be used in fulfilling certain social and non-social obligations. Stated differently, the poor conditions in the zongo can be largely blamed on the exploitative attitude of the migrant population with respect to the local economy; the conditions of the ghetto on the social and economic subjugation and exploitation of the Black population by a highly impersonal economic system in which Blacks make only minimal input. In both instances the underlying forces responsible for the nature of the physical characteristics of these residential enclaves are related to the nature and functioning of very dissimilar economic systems and the differing roles played by members of the respective groups in these systems.

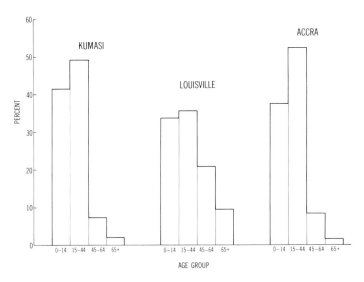

Figure 5. Distribution of population into age groups.

SELECTED DEMOGRAPHIC CHARACTERISTICS OF THE ZONGO AND THE GHETTO

The age structure of the population is frequently an important key to its demographic history. Spatial variations in fertility levels and migratory behavior are readily observable in graphic illustrations of the age structure of individual places. The prevalence of high birth rates and the continued attraction of migrating populations to both the zongo and the ghetto insure the predominance of a youthful population. However, it is likely that aging Afro-American ghetto populations will increase relative to those in the zongos of West African cities as a result of the sharp decline in birth rates in recent years. The extent to which migration is likely to influence the age structure is difficult to establish at this time. The propensity to migrate is generally higher among younger people and particularly among African males. These, in addition to the previously stated fact that both the ghetto and the zongo are to some extent products of the migratory behavior of a segment of the population, suggest that the population of the two areas will continue for some time to show signs of youthfulness and will be characterized by flux or transiency, as well as a persistent sex imbalance (for a discussion of this point, see below).

In 1960, 90.8 percent of the population of the Kumasi zongo were in the 0–44 age category. The proportion in this age range in Accra was 90.1 percent, while in the Black ghetto of Louisville, Kentucky, only 69.6 percent were concentrated in this age range[3] (see figure 5). These figures obviously testify to the youthfulness of the population of these areas,[4] but likewise indicate that a larger percentage of the ghetto population is beyond the prime working ages, at least in a single type B ghetto. The comparative youthfulness of the population of the zongos may be explained by the relative youthfulness of the population of Ghana (or West Africa)

3. These figures are based on the 1960 census of Ghana and the United States, respectively. In the case of Louisville, Kentucky, the ghetto is defined as the group of census tracts in which Black people constituted at least 30 percent of the total population. The zongo was formally defined by the Ghana Census Bureau. The decision to employ data describing the Louisville, Kentucky, ghetto is related to the fact that the senior author conducted field work there in connection with his doctoral dissertation which is being completed at Indiana University (1972).

4. The proportions of the total population found in the age group 0–14 in each of the respective residential enclaves in 1960 were 41.6 percent, 37.7 percent, and 33.9 percent. The smaller proportion in the Louisville ghetto suggests a lower fertility level there than in either of the stranger zones of Kumasi or Accra.

as a whole. Also, since migration in West Africa entails in some cases the crossing of international boundaries, it is likely that the "rigor" of international travel tends to restrict migration to the youngest elements within the migrant age group. If one considers the arduous nature of the journey and the modal transport form, then the age selectivity of the migrant population is even better understood.

Unlike age composition, the expectation of a pre-dominance of males in the population was not borne out in all three areas. In 1960, females constituted 46.3 percent of the population of the Kumasi zongo, 43.8 percent of the Accra zongo, and 55.9 percent of the Louisville ghetto. This difference may be explained as follows. African males are traditionally more mobile than African females and thus dominate the migration streams. In the United States, Black males are apparently not significantly more migratory than Black females. It might even be generally shown that Black females have a greater propensity to migrate, although the differences in migration rates as a function of sex are probably minor. Nevertheless, the predominance of females in the ghetto population is an almost universal phenome-non. This latter condition recently prompted Jackson (1971, pp. 36–39) to facetiously assess the feasibility of polygynous marriages among Blacks as a means of adjusting to the problem of a surplus female population in those states containing the largest ghetto popula-tions. It is possible that Louisville is a migrant staging area and thus itself a source of migration as well as a destination. Comparatively, this explanation may even hold true in accounting for the higher female element in the Kumasi zongo than in Accra's.

The mobility data shown in figure 6 are not based on a common set of questions. The question employed to determine the level of mobility for the zongo popula-tion was *where is your place of birth,* whereas the ques-tion employed to determine ghetto mobility was *where did you live five years ago.* The manner in which the mobility question was structured in the Ghanaian and United States Census makes comparison of results difficult at best. Nevertheless, it is generally recognized that migration continues to play a significant role in the development of culturally unique territorial communities on both sides of the Atlantic. Among the various zongo populations, Kumasi shows a relatively low percentage (16.4) of people born in other African countries and a high percentage of locally born people. Although this suggests a condition of low population mobility, there is still evidence of the prevalence of high rates of migra-tion, considering the fact that the locally born group is most likely dominated by persons under 15.

The prevailing mobility rate in Accra with its relatively high proportion of foreign-born persons (33.9 percent)

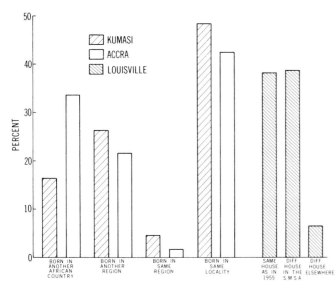

Figure 6. Mobility and transiency.

is greatly in excess of that in Kumasi. The large proportion of foreign-born persons in Accra tends to help maintain the zongo. During the colonial period migrants apparently made no effort to fit in with the local population since they were protected by the colonial power (Peil, 1971, pp. 207–208). The Kumasi mobility status partly reflects the fact that it is a staging area for migrants on their way to such places as Accra. Thus, Kumasi's role in the migration process is somewhat similar to that of Louisville's. However, when the number of foreign-born and those born in other regions of the country are taken into account, both zongos seem to be areas of excessive population mobility.

The Louisville ghetto also exhibits a high rate of population mobility, but much of this mobility is associated with intraurban movement. In 1960 only approximately 7 percent of the increase in the Louisville ghetto population could be attributed to net in-migration. The Louisville ghetto, like many of those falling in the type B category, was not the destination of large numbers of Black migrants. Louisville, located in a border state with a relatively small Black population, did not have direct access to a large Black migration source region. Although the results of the 1970 Census would indicate that Louisville is becoming even less important as a location of Black in-migration, it does possess modest attractiveness for a small number of migrants.

Aside from the similarities mentioned thus far, it is perhaps the low levels of educational attainment and low levels of economic achievement that the zongo and the ghetto have most in common. As shown in figure 7, unemployment is high—8.8 percent in Kumasi and 10.7 percent in Accra in 1960. In the Kumasi zongo, 40.3 percent of the people fifteen years or older were engaged in commerce in 1960. Of this number (4,522), 83.5 percent were involved in petty trading. In Accra the comparable figures were 38.6 and 79.4 percent, respectively. The zongos appear dominated by individuals engaged in either menial jobs or commercial undertakings characterized by low returns. In Nigeria the role played by zongo residents in the economy of the city is influenced strongly by their culture. Education of zongo (Sabo) residents is dictated by their Arabic tradition. "Their [Hausa traders'] pattern of trade, however, is traditional, and no matter how long they stay in modern cities like Accra and Lagos, they remain conservative with regard to education, religion, and politics, and remain aloof from modern bureaucratic and industrial occupations" (Melson and Wolpe, 1971, p. 198). It is true that poverty is more widespread in the zongo than in other parts of the city, but as in the ghetto, poverty, however defined, is characterized by a great deal of internal spatial variation. The recent expulsion of foreign residents from Ghana was carried out in the

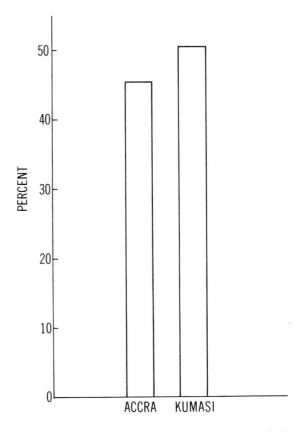

Figure 7. Education characteristics—proportion of the population 15 years of age and over with no education.

hope of reducing the general level of poverty by removing economic competition for jobs previously held by aliens. It was demonstrated that alien Hausas dominated jobs in certain occupational categories, such as butchers and truck park operators. Nigerian aliens were also active as petty traders in Ghanaian cities. After the expulsion of aliens, approximately 4,000 market stalls were abandoned in Ghanaian cities. These stalls were immediately claimed by Ghanaian women.

SUMMARY AND CONCLUSIONS

In attempting to compare the ghetto with the zongo, one is confronted by the full range of problems inherent in cross-cultural analysis. Cultural and social values differ; so do levels of economic development and potential. Historical sequences and their effects are also dissimilar. All of these factors converge to make comparisons difficult. Another problem is that of data availability. Whereas much information is available to facilitate geographic analysis of the ghetto, only limited information is available which would lead to sound understanding of the zongo. Many interpretations may be mere inferences which reflect the personal opinions or convictions of a researcher who has conducted an in-depth analysis at a single site.

The identification of ghetto space, as well as the employment of the official census definition of the zongo, can have a pervasive outcome on research efforts of this type. In this paper, for example, the use of the 30 percent threshold for demarcating the ghetto is subjective, although not arbitrary.[5] Likewise, adherence to the census definition of zongos in Ghana might be challenged. However, one is forced to make use of the best current information available when attempting to shed light on a little understood phenomenon. In no way should the places which have been singled out for description be considered as typical of all such configurations. Their choice was influenced by convenience.

The purpose of this paper was to point out some of the similarities and dissimilarities of a set of residential enclaves occupied by peoples of African origin in two major world regions. One enclave is the result of voluntary isolation on the part of a largely alien population which has essentially been unchallenged by authority. The other is the result of discrimination against an indigenous minority by an indigenous majority. The recent expulsion of aliens from Ghana is an oblique testimony to the economic "importance" of the zongo. The tension and violence in American cities testify to the fact that the ghetto is a social and economic powder keg. Whether the zongo and the ghetto exist as indictments on the societies in which they occur is not the issue here. Rather, the basic issue is conceptual and is related to

5. Rose, in his previous work, has used the 50 percent threshold as the lower limit for defining ghetto space but has agreed that the 30 percent zone constitutes an area of transition. Thus, in this instance, because of the limited area of transition associated with type B ghettos found in Louisville, the larger area was defined as the ghetto.

how a similar configuration in a very different setting might enable an identifiable minority group to effectively deal with the situation in which they find themselves. Cohen (1969, pp. 190–92) has described the strategy employed by the Hausa of Nigeria as a case of political ethnicity which deviates sharply from the practices associated with Hausaland.

There is reason to believe that a similar strategy has been chosen by segments of the ghetto population, in which the positive aspects of Blackness are emphasized. However, the success of such a strategy and its associated cultural practices may fail to satisfy group goals because of the strong orientation away from the ghetto by a large segment of the ghetto population. In the final analysis the success of such adaptive mechanisms as the zongo and the ghetto may be heightened through a more thorough understanding of cross-cultural concepts as they apply to what appear superficially to represent common problems. The solutions will of necessity have to vary, given the real differences which prevail in the two settings, but answers might be more easily arrived at if African and American scholars can establish common research linkages.

REFERENCES CITED

Acquah, I. 1958. *Accra Survey*. London: University of London Press.

Barbour, K. M., and Prothero, R. M. 1961. *Essays on African Population*. Routledge and Kegan Paul.

Cohen, A. 1967. "The Hausa." In P. C. Lloyd; A. L. Mabogunje; and B. Awe, eds. *City of Ibadan*. New York: Cambridge University Press.

Cohen, Abner. 1969. *Customs and Politics in Urban Africa*. Berkeley: University of California Press.

Jackson, Jacquelyne J. 1971. "But Where are the Men?" *Black Scholar* 3:30–41.

Mabogunje, Akin L. 1968. *Urbanization in Nigeria*. London: University of London Press.

_____. 1968. "Research in Urban Geography in Nigeria." *Nigerian Geographical Journal* 2:101–114.

Melson, Robert, and Wolpe, Howard. 1971. *Nigeria: Modernization and Politics of Communalism*. East Lansing, Michigan: Michigan State University Press.

Peil, Margaret. 1971. "The Expulsion of West African Aliens." *The Journal of Modern African Studies* 9:205–229.

Rose, Harold M. 1969. "The Origin and Pattern of Development of Urban Black Social Areas." *The Journal of Geography* 68:326–32.

Wirth, Louis. 1928. *The Ghetto*. Chicago: The University of Chicago Press.

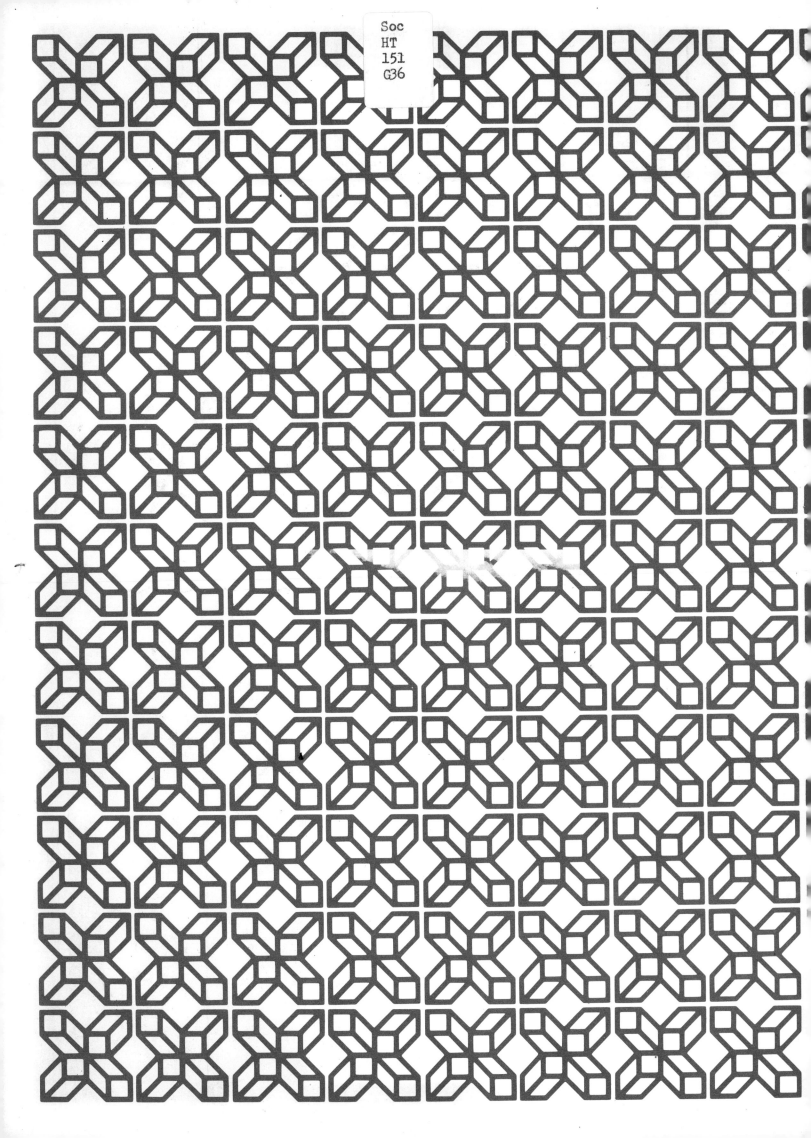